# Everyday Discourse and Common Sense

## The Theory of Social Representations

Wolfgang Wagner and
Nicky Hayes

palgrave
macmillan

Publication of this book was supported by the Austrian Federal Ministry for Education, Science and Culture

First published 2005 by
PALGRAVE MACMILLAN
Houndmills, Basingstoke, Hampshire RG21 6XS and
175 Fifth Avenue, New York, N.Y. 10010
Companies and representatives throughout the world

PALGRAVE MACMILLAN is the global academic imprint of the Palgrave Macmillan division of St. Martin's Press, LLC and of Palgrave Macmillan Ltd. Macmillan® is a registered trademark in the United States, United Kingdom and other countries. Palgrave is a registered trademark in the European Union and other countries.

ISBN-13: 978–1–4039–3304–1
ISBN-10: 1–4039–3304–9 paperback

This book is printed on paper suitable for recycling and made from fully managed and sustained forest sources.

A catalogue record for this book is available from the British Library.

A catalog record for this book is available from the Library of Congress.

10   9   8   7   6   5   4   3   2   1
14   13   12   11   10   09   08   07   06   05

Printed in China

# Contents

# Figures and Tables

## Figures

## Tables

# Foreword

The everyday man in the street has become the involuntary hero of all theoretical machinations incited in the human sciences. He has inconspicuously dislodged the man of the masses by adopting a role in which he is liberated from his predecessor's demonic impulses (in the Goethean sense) and appears modest and peaceful. Shakespeare's theatre, with its stormy passions, dark forces and trying myths, is abandoned in favour of Beckett's theatre with its superficial ruminations, minimal dialogue and metaphysical clichés. The man in the street, like the man of the masses, plays that role (albeit in different forms) which befits the anonymous individual in society, in the anonymity of everyday life, in everyday thought, in the intangible realm of existence. Therefore, everything which appears familiar, routine and commonplace has occupied a superior position amongst things which demand meticulous understanding. Interest has shifted from large-scale industry to the cottage industry of social facts, which is no easy task because it is for the very reason that they are so familiar that those varied, anonymous phenomena elude our usual means of investigation. Thus the shift of attention towards everything regarded as everyday life and thought entailed a change in most human sciences; a change which took place here and there, hesitantly and inconspicuously, in the 1960s; which has now almost become the orthodoxy; and which will soon appear to be an obstacle. This book, however, portrays everyday life and common sense using a critical sense and a constant effort to be clear and discrete, in my opinion, whilst not insignificantly displaying talent as well.

It is important to stress at this juncture that although all human sciences and even philosophy show an interest in this concept and in this field of human reality, they have a rather profoundly different way of looking at it. It is true that we remain, strictly speaking, in the science of human understanding when we talk about those popular sciences that are customary in everyday life, such as popular psychology, political economy, popular physics and so on.

But we are able to talk about them and make use of them, describe intimate people and things, discuss and anticipate the behaviour of other people, self-assuredly interpret their beliefs and intentions, and spend a considerable amount of our time reconstructing the world accordingly.

To what extent are these popular sciences valid? To what extent may we develop them and make use of them? These questions often set philosophers, anthropologists and social psychologists off against each other. The origin and value of this knowledge are often disputed, since, despite being absolutely necessary, they can easily mislead us. Whatever the case may be, a considerable part of research in social psychology has been sensitive towards everything that appears routine and stereotypical in human understanding. There have been efforts, using a theory of social stereotypes (since, as Sperber points out, schema, scripts and prototypes belong to the family of stereotypes) to demonstrate the way in which the man in the street processes and uses information under everyday circumstances. This kind of analysis reveals that certain features of the human mind appear biased and defective when it comes to judging its own capacity, its possibilities of grasping reality, and explaining private or public events.

How could they be any different when they are stereotypical and, it might be said, naive? The awkward issue of how we should free ourselves from the categories and judgements of common sense has remained for three centuries a matter for science and philosophy, which are concerned with destroying our spontaneous faith in the language that we speak and the world in which we grew up. One cannot deny the fact that the prevailing Western world-view of the superiority of science is dependent on whatever is defined as unscientific, whether it be tradition, or the traditional knowledge of so-called primitive peoples. This superiority appears all the more plausible when we consider the unscientific with regard to its aspect of conventionality, stereotype and tendency to deceive, that is, the aspect which gives rise to doubt in ordinary people's rationality of human understanding in their daily business and in their rough understanding of the social and physical world in which they live. We cannot dispute the 'cognitive miser' research findings which have so often demonstrated his shortcomings. All the same, we do not accept them without that caution expressed by the American philosopher, Daniel Dennet, in his work *The Intentional Stance*:

How rational are we? Recent research in social and cognitive psychology . . . suggests, we are only minimally rational, appallingly ready to leap to conclusions or be swayed by logically irrelevant features of situations; but this jaundiced view is an illusion created by the fact that these psychologists are deliberately trying to produce situations that provoke irrational responses – inducing pathology in a system by putting strain on it – and succeeding, being good psychologists. No one would hire a psychologist to prove that people will choose a paid vacation in preference to a week in jail if offered an informed choice. At least not in the better psychology department.

Although perhaps somewhat unjust, the irony of this comment reminds us of a certain truth which we should always bear in mind. At least Wolfgang Wagner and Nicky Hayes appear to have borne it in mind when they mention the theories of everyday social thinking and the empirical findings which we have just as little right to ignore as the things that they teach us about common sense (i.e., about ourselves). From their angle they do it in a measured and skilful way. We see that everyday judgements and explanations form a normative interrelation which determines our thoughts and experiences in everyday life.

But what makes this book original is undoubtedly its elaboration of the theme which links everyday life and thought with social representations. From the start the theory of social representations has aimed in whatever way to defend the rights of ordinary people and traditional knowledge against the attacks and slander to which they have been subjected. I shall begin by listing the thematic positions which, I believe, can be discussed in this regard.

The first of these central themes relates to the simple fact that most of our perceptions – what we see and hear – our beliefs and our information about people and things, are not directly factual. We acquire them from other people, via conversations, mass media and handing down, so that their origin is interpersonal or social.

The second theme relates to the quality of knowledge obtained in this way. Even though this knowledge may be partially uncertain, hazy or even incoherent, that cannot be the whole picture, for, otherwise, we would not be capable of speaking to one another, understanding ourselves, or leading a satisfactory life. We acquire it early and fast at the same time as its application in everyday business and in our relations with parents, neighbours and friends who make up our 'miniature world'. If we contemplate the weaknesses of this shared knowledge, we notice how often we are unable to describe our feelings or assuring ourselves that we can understand ordinary physical phenomena or foresee the consequences of our dealings as parents, teachers or consumers. But if we look into its strengths, we discover broad realms in which traditional knowledge is strikingly accurate. For example, studies by English social psychologists have shown that the lay public, as it were, is just as able as psychologists when it comes to describing personality traits and deciding whether somebody is an extrovert or an introvert.

Furthermore, this knowledge seems to embrace 'theories' of remarkable effectiveness and scope. Every time we take on a new task or meet people in an unfamiliar situation we can quickly and effortlessly judge what to do, how to interpret the situation and adapt ourselves. We can discuss our judgement and consider the different arguments in order to find out what is correct and acceptable. Philosophers have often been surprised by this human ability and Bertrand Russell wondered: 'How comes it that human beings, whose contacts with the world are brief and personal and limited, are able to know as much as they do?' Surely part of the reason is that people obtain their knowledge from other people, friends, neighbours and teachers to a far greater extent than from their immediate consciousness, and because they acquire this knowledge from an early age via their mother tongue and culture.

The third central theme relates to the fact that our everyday knowledge consists of a specific network of concepts, images and beliefs which are commonly shared and belong to particular human groups (i.e., social representations which we all produce and reproduce). Psychology and anthropology are interested in this network for different reasons. The main reason, however, is that they occur in all cultures and, just as with language, they depict basic phenomena. They enable people of one group or society to understand their world clearly and distinctly, to interpret fortunate or unfortunate events, and to predict and judge the behaviour of others. In this process representations are acquired publicly and collectively, sometimes standardised in myths, religions, art works, mass media and the like. All of this lends representations a special status as a research subject of social psychology.

The fourth theme is an attempt to clarify what distinguishes the theory of social representations from the other ways of dealing with everyday life and thought. It has often been viewed as innate (a viewpoint nowadays represented by Chomsky and Fodor), as

well as an unhistoric, stagnating repertoire of illusions and super-
stitions that has not changed in millennia. This interpretation has
been changing for about twenty years and this book explains in a
subtle way why this is the case. Anyhow, our theory radically insists
on the social origin of human understanding and everyday thought,
as well as the fact that they develop to a large extent from daily
conversations and collective actions. Furthermore, they are constantly being changed. Their contents, that is, the images and language categories, change in the bosom of culture. It is especially in
our culture that there is a mutual interchange between art and
science and everyday thought. On the one hand, 'protoscientific'
knowledge, perceptions and beliefs become science, as many
researchers have noted. On the other hand, scientific theories, concepts and images are spread amongst broad strata of society to the
effect that they become protoscientific, as is the case with the
theory of 'natural selection', probability theory or psychoanalysis,
to mention just a few well-known examples. One could even maintain that every academic science produces a 'Doppelgänger' of traditional knowledge; with economics producing popular economics,
nuclear physics a form of popular nuclear physics, psychoanalysis
a psychoanalysis of the masses, and many more. If the former
contain explicit and more or less objective theories, the latter will
be formed on the basis of social representations, that is, legitimised
by an implicit consensus.

In brief, although the prevailing point of view may deem it paradoxical, everyday knowledge and human understanding are historical creations which run parallel with scientific creations or those
of the arts; just as styles of furniture, clothing, advertising and
urban planning run parallel with styles of painting, architecture or
pottery. It is, however, a plausible fact – perhaps too plausible to
judge conclusively – that social representations contribute to the
spread of scientific knowledge and artistic style in our everyday life.
This may seem an exaggeration, and may indeed be one, but it
deserves some highly innovative research to demonstrate to what
extent it is exaggeration.

The fifth central theme relates to our endeavours to treat the
layperson and the scientist, the amateur and the expert, as worthy
of the same respect. In this regard we have categorically refused to
make the expert the model for the amateur, briefly elevating his
way of knowing and thinking to universal criteria which must be
valid for everybody; in the way, for example, that Western logic

was previously seen as the rationality criterium for all logics that existed in the world. Without considering the ideological aspects, it is clear that this widely held attitude infects the social and psychological processes with an error. A large amount of research over the past twenty years has shown that an expert solves a range of problems better than an amateur who makes various mistakes and is biased. But if we compare whatever task this person or that has accomplished, we cannot demonstrate the way in which each of the two do it; and if we were able to, what use would it be to us? Should we correct the amateur's mistakes and make him an expert? If an individual were to train to become a specialist in all areas of his everyday life, that would result in a cognitive strain.

We are equally of the opinion that it is impossible for scientific thought to replace everyday thought and deal in a detached way with beliefs, desires and ideas which are deeply linked with the life of the person or the community. Thus, the layperson, the man in the street, will continue to exist, and it will be his popular sciences, and not the expert, which will continue to govern dealings in everyday life.

It is true that the more sophisticated and scientific our technological surroundings become, the more we use them like technological idiots. It takes more knowledge to prepare tasty roast beef than to use a magical computer! Thus, all these comparisons between the qualities of the expert and the defects of the amateur can only result in our obscuring our understanding of their respective talents. The English philosopher Paul Grice writes:

> Part of the trouble may arise from an improperly conceived proposition in the minds of some self-appointed experts between 'we' and 'they'; between that is, the privileged and enlightened, on the one hand, and the rabble on the other. But that is by no means the only possible stance which the learned might adopt towards the vulgar; they might think of themselves as qualified by extended application and education to pursue further and to handle better just those interests which they derive for themselves in their salad days; after all, most professionals begin as amateurs. Or they might think of themselves as advancing in one region, on behalf of the human race, the achievements and culture of that race which other members of it perhaps enhance in other directions and which many members of it, unfortunately for them perhaps, are not equipped to advance at all. In any case,

to recognise the rights of the majority to direct the efforts of the
minority which forms the cultured elite is quite distinct from
treating the majority as themselves constituting a cultural elite
*(Studies in the Way of Words*, p. 378)

It is exactly because of this that criteria and models are foisted upon
them that are not their own.

Most of these themes are considered in this book with great care
along with the intention of enriching them with contributions from
philosophy and anthropology. This is done with an unerring intellectual energy which expounds the theory in a stimulating way as
well as the numerous studies supporting it. Thus I must confess that
reading this book has taught me a great deal and impressed me with
a number of original approaches not thought of before. The
authors very lucidly deal with difficult issues and illustrate complex
ideas in concrete terms, a feat for which every reader will be
grateful.

The concept of 'social representations' may have a long history
behind it, even a successful history, to the extent that it ought to
be at least as widely recognised as the concept of charisma, ideology or 'Weltanschauung'. However, since its introduction it has
come up against confused opposition which has not yet been overcome. One can certainly put it down to the fact that there was a
lack, until recently, of a specific theory about the internal organisation and the processes of social representations. This on its own,
however, is not enough to explain the nature of this opposition. I
have often asked myself the question why it is so difficult to accept
the concept despite the fruitfulness it has demonstrated in the
human sciences since Durkheim outlined the first model. Understandably, it gives me a cause for concern inasmuch as I have dedicated a great part of my life to constructing this theory and it seems
to me to form the coherent basis of a social psychology. Without
striving for any authority in this field, I believe that there are two
causes underlying this opposition:

*(a)* One cause is that the theory and the concept of social representations lend rationality to collective belief and thinking,
be they religious, myths or traditional knowledge. For they are
dealt with directly as cohesive systems of concepts and images
akin to a practice or ritual, which as a consequence may result
in their existing in an independent way and in their own right.

These systems, however, are not only cohesive; they are also abstract systems in the sense that the concepts have the same character of generality and idealisation as a philosophical or scientific concept and that their relations can be deduced just as with those of energy conservation or the comparability of time and space. We may not be dealing with abstractions which can be compared with those of physics and mathematics, but they seem naturally comparable with those occurring in ethnology or geography. This conflicts with most opinions (whether scientific or not) which refuse to grant this rationality and abstractness to collective beliefs and opinions, and which cannot accept that popular science or social myths and classifications can be dealt with from the same viewpoint as the more secure forms of knowledge. They consider it impossible to deal with them from the same viewpoint because rationality – the possibility of making a considered and calculated choice – is rated as exclusively attributable to the individual, yet in no way to the collective.

(b)    This gives rise to another source of opposition in which we consider that we not only share, but also jointly produce our common beliefs, images or expertise. This would be a particularly radical version of what is described as a representation and of how we describe and explain events in our collective life – a version which not even those who harbour the greatest sympathy for a social perspective are prepared to support. It is easier and probably more directly comprehensible to think that it is the individuals who in a social environment imagine, describe and explain things rather than to view these individuals as members of a group which jointly carries out these tasks. I must confess that my own idea of the theory has sometimes been receptive to this radical interpretation, whilst I regard the dichotomy between social and individual as somewhat outdated. It is nevertheless impossible to insist on this image of an individual in a social environment because, throughout centuries, ongoing generations have been creating a whole range of phenomena such as myths, religions, languages and expertise, which can neither be viewed as the work of individuals nor can their psychology provide an explanation. Most of us have hesitated hitherto to accept the alternative idea of a collective psychology, even though it would appear imperative in the mind of a Wundt or Freud. To be sure, we possess one model of this psychology which is, of course, everyday life and everyday knowledge. That is reason enough to research the meaning of collective phenomena as far as possible. Nevertheless, the concept may appear 'abstruse' or 'extreme', thereby inciting a backlash in a culture which thinks and feels so many things from the individual's standpoint.

This is an awkward issue. I felt the need, however, to talk about these 'uneasy' aspects of the theory of social representations and of the opposition which it has encountered. But this is also what makes it worthwhile and appealing as it allows us immediately to grasp and understand in their entirety phenomena in which assorted human sciences are only partly interested. This is doubtless due to its ability to create a certain lucidity from a wide range of facts, and the fact that it has won the approval of so many researchers in many countries whilst official social psychology, at worst, does not take it into account. If this is not the case, it would be impossible to understand why, over the past 30 years, numerous researchers have come back to the theory, contributed to it in a gainful manner, and advanced it to the position which it now holds. As a matter of fact, this means that this theory is exerting an influence in culture just as it is in science, and we cannot close our minds to this state of affairs. Wolfgang Wagner and Nicky Hayes are aware of this state of affairs and this book goes far beyond the boundaries of our discipline and our method. It deals directly with contemporary social problems in an acute and precise way. We can only be grateful for the authors' effort, and thank them for the result achieved; a result which will be of service to many over the coming years.

Serge Moscovici

# Preface

This book is about the everyday knowledge and discourse which pervades every group's space and time, and which is at the same time both individual and social in nature. Given the pervasiveness of everyday thinking, knowledge and talking in social life, it is surprising to find only one or two handful of theories which deal explicitly with this field. Of these we consider the theory of social representations the most useful.

The theory of social representations has been in the marketplace of social sciences for a few decades, but has gained acknowledgement in the non-French-speaking world only in the last ten to fifteen years. In this period there appeared a few key books on this approach, notably Denise Jodelet's *Madness and Social Representations* (1991) and Serge Moscovici's *Social Representations-Explorations in Social Psychology* (2000), which involves some of his original texts translated and edited by Gerard Duveen. Apart from a few other books which have applied the theory to particular issues or which collect papers from various authors, the theory has never been presented in its entirety in a book-size publication. We thought this to be a deplorable situation, and got to work on the present text.

This book builds upon and extends a German book by the first author. Although it preserves some elements of the original structure, the present book has little in common with its forebear. It presents the majority of existing theoretical work in the field and emphasizes processes on the collective level, as well as giving due attention to representational issues on the individual level of analysis. We refer to a great number of French, German, Spanish and other language publications, which are too often inaccessable to English-speaking scholars. In doing so we attempt to convey due respect to the many researchers who did remarkable work in their own language without being widely recognised due to the language barrier. We do not, however, hesitate to admit that every such enterprise bears the risk of overlooking some piece of work that has escaped our attention.

Being intended as a text for students on advanced level social sciences and psychology courses, we have also thought of it as a reference book for scholars working directly in the field or in neighbouring disciplines.

Wolfgang Wagner and Nicky Hayes

# Acknowledgements

The contents of a book often grow imperceptibly and without design: as a condensation of personal experiences, as a by-product of daily research work, from making sense of thoughts in conversations and discussions with colleagues and friends. Without wanting to burden them with responsibility for our way of treating the theory, the first author would like to thank a range of people whose knowledge, thought and feeling provided a mirror to reflect and shape our understanding of social psychology, everyday knowledge and social representations.

These people include present and former colleagues at the University of Linz, Eduard Brandstätter, Erich Kirchler, Hermann Brandstätter, Nicole Kronberger and Volker von Gadenne. Numerous, and sometimes emotional, debates with Serge Moscovici, Denise Jodelet, Gerard Duveen, Sandra Jovchelovitch, George Gaskell, Fran Elejabarrieta, Helene Joffe, as well as with Agnes Allansdottir, Alain Giami, Angela Arruda, Anna-Maija Pirttilä-Backman, Annamaria de Rosa, Christian Guimelli, Emda Orr, Geneviève Coudin, Gina Philogène, Ivana Markovà, Janos Laszlo, José Valencia, Marie-Claude Gervais, Mary-Jane Spink, Robert Farr, Uwe Flick and Willem Doise who all contributed to fleshing out our present understanding of the theory. Antonia Paredes, Celso Pereira de Sá, Clelia Nascimento Schulze, Fátima Palacios, Jyoti Verma, Lucia Duarte, Maria-Auxiliadora Banchs, Martin Bauer, Michel-Louis Rouquette, Oya Paker, Paula Castro, Rosário Carvalho, Saadi Lahlou and many others suggested new angles under which the theory can be seen. My brother Günter P. Wagner provided a healthy corrective against social science 'fundamentalism'.

Mark Lawrence prepared a great translation of a difficult text. Helene Joffe kindly agreed to offer one of her paintings for the book's cover art. Andrew Mcaleer, Magenta Lampson and Penny Simmons were most helpful in all editorial issues.

We gratefully acknowledge financial support from the Austrian Federal Ministry for Education, Science and Culture, the government of the state of Oberösterreich, the City of Linz and the Linzer Hochschulfonds.

# Chapter 1
# Introduction

## 1.1 History, memory and psychology

### 1.1.1 Mentalities

In his *Memorias del fuego* (The Memory of Fire) Eduardo Galeano tells the story of six natives who were burned at the stake in La Concepción in 1496. They had been found guilty of sacrilege because they had buried images of Christ and the Virgin Mary in the earth. This blatant and heretical crime was considered adequate reason for the Spanish governor to commit the men to the fire. However, no one had asked them why they had buried the images. In actual fact, they had hoped that the new Christian gods might bless their seed, bringing growth to their maize, yucca, batata and bean crops (Galeano, 1985, p. 60f.)

This story illustrates a clash of two different worlds. The world of the natives and that of the Spanish conquerors did not differ particularly in their structural characteristics – both the society of the natives and the European society of the Spaniards had known wars of conquest and feudalism as well as cruelty and capital punishment. What distinguished them was the shared representations of their imaginary worlds. Although the American natives worshipped the gods in a metaphorical way, as did the Europeans, their way was associated with the reproductive activities of their everyday existence in a much more practical manner than the European Catholic mentality of this time. There was no place in Catholic dogma for blessing and fertilising life-essential agricultural land by burying holy symbols in the soil.

Such an act was a sin because – apart from a few exceptions – earth was viewed as 'impure' in the European imagination. Purity and impurity are not defined as absolutes, but always in relation to things brought into contact with each other (Douglas, 1966). Shoes with soil on them in the bedroom are regarded as dirty, while the same shoes on the consecrated stone floor of a church may be seen as an expression of the faith of the wearer, who did not have the time to change them beforehand. And the wearer of those same shoes would be a malicious sinner against the sacredness of an Islamic mosque if he did not take them off before entering. The Spanish Inquisition in the example above may have felt the same repugnance at the dirtying of holy statues with soil when they interpreted the natives' ritualistic act as sacrilege.

Ideas of purity, dirtiness and taboo are part of a comprehensive cultural system of social imagination, shared by the representations of a culture, society or a social group. This mental macro-system forms the framework within which emotional, motivational and cognitive processes of cultural representations develop. It defines the boundaries of what is conceivable as well as the boundaries of conceivable meanings, and also those of many elements in psychological processes. We do not need memorable examples such as Galeano's story to learn the meaning of this mental macro-system. Cultural contact, and the problems in understanding arising from it, can be demonstrated within any society: whether it be the antithesis between intellectuals and the so-called 'man in the street'; the lack of understanding of members of other social classes; or the sometimes frightening inability of contemporary tourists to understand – or at least accept – the intentions behind the actions of their hosts, and their belief and knowledge systems.

It is predominately cultural anthropology, and to a varying extent sociology, which traditionally deal with these mental macro-systems. A relatively short time ago representatives of other sciences also began to fathom the significance of collective systems of belief for their subject areas and to integrate those methods and theories into their own science. In the science of history, this includes the school of the 'Annales d'histoire économique et sociale' from the interwar period onwards, which has begun to deal with the history of mentalities and the historical phenomena associated with them. In Social Psychology, it was Moscovici's 1961 publication *La psychoanalyse: son image et son publique* which began systematic work on this problem and others. Earlier individual efforts within Social Psychology – such as, for example, Wundt's *Völkerpsychologie* ('Psychology of the People/Cultures', 1900–20) or Thomas' and Znaniecki's *The Polish Peasant in Europe and America* (1918–20) – did not meet with sufficient response to establish a research tradition in Social Psychology (Jaspars and Fraser, 1984).

Individuals and masses throughout Western Christendom have been zealously participating in the great adventure of the Crusades since the year 1095. Population growth and incipient overpopulation, the material greed of the Italian cities, a papal policy aimed at constructing unity out of a fragmented Christianity in the face of unbelief – none of these reasons explain the whole picture and they might miss the essential part altogether. It requires the appeal of a terrestrial version of the heavenly Jerusalem and the power of its image to mobilize the souls. What are the Crusades without a certain religious mentality?

(Le Goff, 1989, p. 18)

With this example, Le Goff questions the responses of a classical science of history, which does not include human motives or the reconstruction of the collective protagonists' actual motivations in its inventory of explanation, other than the descriptive and structural parameters of historical events. Traditional political history's explanation of historical events limited itself to correlations between the intentions of the powers-that-be, the socioeconomic structural characteristics of the historical epoch, and the event to be explained. This approach ignores the force that moved the masses embroiled in the events of the day.

The 'New History' of the 'Annales' group, by contrast, designated new objects of study, 'which have hitherto generally been the exclusive realm of anthropology (e.g. diet, body, gestures, metaphors, accounts, myth, gender)' (Le Goff, 1990, p. 38). It is concerned with the underlying cognitive, ethical and affective dispositional substratum – in other words the mentality - of the historical protagonists (Raulff, 1989). Its perspective concentrates on processes of 'longue durée'. Mentalities are at any one time the most sluggish components of historical change. They lag behind historical change in the areas of technology, social structure and economics; and establish contradictions and rogue complications in historical development. In this way, they become the driving force behind new change. How else can we understand the changes in values and behavioural norms since the sixteenth century? This was the development which led to new methods of production and the capitalist movement of goods, giving rise to Max Weber's 'Protestant work ethic' with its hitherto unknown and novel orientation towards work and money (Le Goff, 1989).

Historical research also complemented its newly discovered interest in mentalities by turning its attention to the 'ordinary' private lives of different peoples (Aries and Duby, 1987). Yet, barring a few exceptions, everyday life had up to that point been a mystery to history, and not considered worth investigating since hardly any historically formative forces were attributed to the living conditions of the common people. The personal human sphere only attracted attention when it became necessary to explore the formative conditions of historical mentalities; so that the 'secrets de l'histoire' became 'histoire du secret'[1] (Vincent, 1987, p. 157). Private mysteries accompany official cultural, scientific and technological history, 'according to an a-historical and anachronistic rhythm: the fear of death, the difficult relationship with one's body, sexual dissatisfaction, the obsession with money, the immense zones of stability with an air of tragedy and loss, the difficulty of living, just interrupted by some moments of joy that were rarely euphoric' (Vincent, 1987, p. 158). They are the objects of a science of historical psychology, which has yet to be invented other than within the school of history.

Our present-day thinking is based on a succession of historically evolved mentalities; on mental edifices which previous generations have constructed, pulled down, renovated and extended. Past events are compressed in images and metaphors which determine our present thinking even if we are not always aware of them. Common sense is the thickly viscous form of the past, the reflex of history which, like the story about a puppet and a chess-playing machine, always triumphs. The puppet – clad in Turkish garb and with a hookah in its mouth – was sitting in front of a chessboard on a large table. A cunning arrangement of mirrors created the impression of being able to see underneath the table. In actual fact, there was a dwarf sitting underneath who was a chess master, and controlled the puppet (Benjamin, 1974, p. 693). We can imagine the continuous effect of historical experience acting like an ugly, unloved and happily forgotten dwarf, moving the pieces in the chess game of our everyday life.

Its few lines catch a babble of voices, a social product. The unknown and nameless speak here: a collective voice. But the ensemble of these anonymous, contradictory utterances combines to gain a new quality: stories turn into history.... For the masses, history is and remains a collection of stories. It is what is memorable and suitable for being told again: their version retold. In this process, tradition is quite happy to indulge in legend, triviality or error as long as it latches on to an idea of past struggles. Hence the notorious powerlessness of science when confronted by illustrated broadsheets and cheap sensationalism. 'Here I am and there's nothing I can do' – 'and the earth moves anyway'... The Paris Commune and the Storming of the Winter Palace, Danton on the guillotine and Trotsky in Mexico: collective imagination makes a greater contribution to these images than any science. For us the [Maoist] Long March is ultimately what we have been told about the Long March. History is an invention for which reality provides material. Yet it is not an arbitrary invention. The interest it arouses is based on the interests of those who tell it; and it permits those who belong to it... to define their interests more precisely. We owe much to scientific enquiry which thinks without bias; yet it remains a fictional character. The true subject of history casts a shadow. It casts it forward as collective fiction.

(Enzensberger, 1972, p. 12f)

The voices of the past exist in the guise of our common sense. Who could say offhand 'who was here and had no other choice'? It is not the historical truth of ideas that make them so particularly useful in collective discourse, but their 'symbolic truth' in dealing with everyday disputes, past and present. This truth lends importance to the banal propositions of common sense in pragmatic and everyday life.

New material is constantly being added to the numerous strata of contemporary mentality. Much of it is short-lived and leaves no trace. Yet some survives the frantic change of modern myths, including the fragments of scientific knowledge which almost compulsively need to form part of every modern discourse if it is to be taken seriously (Barthes, 1964). It is surprising enough that something approaching a consistent form, which we call common knowledge, can develop from this 'misrepresentation'. There can, of course, be differences in opinion as to consistency, but even so such knowledge demonstrates itself in the (admittedly subjective) opinions of protagonists in everyday experiments repeated billions of times in daily practice.

Taking common sense as an object of scientific research gives rise to simultaneous agreement and rejection. We find agreement within the ranks of those who wish to bring science, above all social science, and here particularly social psychology, closer to the people. This implies constantly tracing the object of contemporary social psychology back to its substance in real life, and examining it afresh – can it actually be the real individual sitting opposite me in the pub? Or is the object of social psychology nothing more than a homunculus that was constructed in laboratories and whose form is reminiscent of the golem (the clay man whom everyone feared) of Jewish legend? Is this object Robert Musil's 'Man without Qualities' who even lacks the essential quality of existing somewhere? Or is man nothing more than a generic being – a construct which elevates universality to the highest value at the expense of the sociality of mankind?

Bringing social psychology closer to the people does not mean taking science on to the streets like a market trader selling his produce; or like G. Miller (1969), calling for more publicity for the results of psychological research; or the way that popular science television programmes peddle science to their audience. This type of undertaking has already been assessed by the editors of such programmes, who only occasionally feel the desire to present and popularise the findings of social psychology. Is this simply because of the editors' ignorant lack of interest in the realities of contemporary social psychology? Or is the failure of social psychology to achieve the Olympus of media recognition already predetermined by its subject matter? Why has Freudian psychoanalysis so penetrated the public mind that in the middle of the twentieth century it was even possible to carry out investigations into its collective image (Moscovici, 1961)? Its object may not resemble the real individual in the pub, but it is useful as a guide and prescription for interpreting collective imagination, in the 'chess game' of our everyday lives. Admittedly, Sigmund Freud's findings must be censured for being if not fraudulent, then at least misguided and manipulated; closer analysis has exposed some of his stories of healing as being little more than just stories (Degen, 1991). Yet this is irrelevant, because psychoanalysis draws its truth from the directly comprehensible symbolism of its images, and not from scientific verification of its findings.

Making ordinary people the subject of social psychology is met with cautious rejection by those who view the aseptic purity of physical and psychological experiment as the most important approach for producing scientific facts. Such purity prevails when meaning is clearly isolated from psychological process. In this way, the murky depths of meaning can be avoided, and the sunlit peaks of process-oriented theories climbed.

The debate over the past 20–40 years about the so-called 'Crisis of Social Psychology' has meanwhile resulted in boredom, now finding only rather weak resonance in a few journals. Even if there was no easy answer, the debate had consequences for the tolerance of the research community towards such 'soft' subject matters as ordinary people. Editors of journals are increasingly accepting works that are not exclusively bound to the methodological inventory of experimental social psychology, and which venture into the still uncharted territory of everyday problems and phenomena. In this sense, the views expressed in this book should not be interpreted as a criticism of social psychology, but as a tentative attempt to tap its object - to find substance in reality and map out the territory of everyday social life.

## 1.1.2 Social psychology and social sciences

Authors of social psychology textbooks hardly ever make reference to the interrelationship existing between social sciences, like sociology, economics and cultural anthropology, which transcends the relatively superficial demarcation of social psychology from these sciences. The demarcation is largely based on a purely quantitative distinction of the units of investigation, or of methodological differences. This demarcation process, or perhaps 'demarcation ritual', endures by negating any common ground. 'The boundaries between the social sciences can be understood in terms of the different levels of analysis that serve as the focus of activity within each field of study' (Tedeschi and Lindskold, 1976, p. 5). This statement is cited as an archetypal example of the standard demarcation from advanced textbooks. Other social psychology texts differ only in their understanding of the nuances of the relationship between the social sciences.

It is not our aim here to doubt the legitimacy of these demarcations. The problem of self-definition arises as part of the historical development of every science. The basic need to separate one's own subject matter from the object of research of rival and adjoining disciplines exists alongside positive self-definition. Both self-definitions, the positive and the negative, presuppose each other; forming the necessary elements defining any science.

Yet later phases of the development of an original discipline can be hindered by things that were initially beneficial and indispensable to the evolution of autonomous scientific research paradigms. Negative definition and demarcation blur the common ground shared by objects of research. This is particularly true when dealing with virtually the same subject matter as that investigated by the social sciences: humans as a social species and their activities. Some writers (e.g. Moscovici, 1972) regard the lack of a 'view across boundaries' as part of the crisis of contemporary social psychology.

It may be necessary to explain the structure and processes within every social science by keeping exclusively within the conceptual framework prescribed by its respective scientific methodology, but it is still possible to identify many non-trivial problems which seem to underline a need to expand the scope of explanation. There are phenomena for which adequate conceptual terminology can only be created by breaching the classical boundaries of the individual social sciences.

This actually happens very often. Many theories of social psychology contain explanatory concepts whose origins in sociology or cultural anthropology cannot be denied. A cursory glance at the indexes of relevant textbooks brings to light such terms as 'cultural norm', 'behavioural role', 'ideology', 'gender', and so on. These often assume a blatantly explanatory function in psychological theories. Alternatively, they are sometimes held responsible, as 'residual variables', for effects which cannot be resolved by directly manipulating variables in psychological experiments. The inevitable relationship between social science terminology and theories of diverse origin is therefore very clear. It is also highlighted by social psychologists: 'The solution to the substantive problem of interdisciplinary relationships . . . is seen in defining the bearings of one's discipline relative to others, of knowing when and who is needed, and in interchange directed toward borrowing from others what is needed for one's own discipline' (Sherif and Sherif, 1969, p. 15).

Such a step must, of course, be taken when reflecting on the possible relationships between the subject matter of the social sciences and the terms and theories which define them. It is nowhere nearly as straightforward for social psychology theory to draw on a sociological concept, for example, as is suggested by the superficial plausibility and intuitive 'fit' of the terms. As Sherif and Sherif (1969) suggested, borrowing terms from other social sciences requires an initial translation, however problematic, to explicate the extensive and intensive alterations to which the term is subjected when it is applied to different levels of aggregation.

When dealing with our subject matter – the relationship between everyday life and social conditions – recourse to other sciences cannot be avoided, even (or all the more so) when it concerns a social and psychological viewpoint. The demand is raised by the subject matter itself, owing to the different levels of analysis within which the subject is revealed. If we are to avoid neglecting any of the aspects involved, then we need to take views into account which can only be mastered through the methical approaches of other social sciences. The danger, in so doing, of overlooking inconsistencies in interdisciplinary terminology is a risk which can only be justified by the even greater danger of psychological myopia.

Lyotard (1986; 1987) believes that we are at the end of an era of grand narrations - a hallmark of the modern age. The postmodern era has humbled the ideal of rational understanding having exclusive rights to the title of 'knowledge'. But that should not mean, under any circumstances, that systems of knowledge should be irrationally discharged of their obligation to validate and present empirical evidence. Rather, the reflection of other potential sources and systems of knowledge which appear rational within their own cosmology should be understood and subtly accepted. Everyday thought and life cannot be measured by the same yardstick that befits science:

Knowledge in general cannot be reduced to science, not even to cognition. Cognition would be exclusively the set of merely that evidence which denotes or describes subject matters and is capable of being declared true or false. Science would be a subset of cognition. To the extent that it may give denotative evidence as well, it imposes two additional conditions on its acceptability. These are first of all that the objects to which they relate be accessible as a recourse, i.e. be subject to the explicit conditions of observation; furthermore that one should be able to decide whether any of this evidence belongs to the language which is viewed as proper by the experts. But far from there being solely one set of denotative evidence meant by the term 'knowledge', the ideas of being able to act, live, hear etc. are part of this as well. It is therefore an area of competence that exceeds the definition and application of one's own criterion of truth, extending to those criteria of efficiency (technical qualification), justice and/or happiness (ethical wisdom), tonal and chromatic beauty (auditory and visual sensitivity) etc. . . . It does not consist in an area of competence covering just one particular type of evidence, for example cognitive evidence, at the exclusion of others. . . . It coincides with a comprehensive formation of competencies.

(Lyotard, 1986, p. 63 onwards)

It is the agreement which allows us to distinguish competence from incompetence in cognition that determines the culture of a people (p. 72). Ultimately, it is consensus which legitimises the truth of knowledge (p. 78).[2] The great amount of minor everyday discourse reveals one or the other of those aspects comprised by this extensive knowledge.

Perhaps we need a dose of the term 'postmodern' and its associated reflection across boundaries of scientific and technical knowledge to propel the subject matter of everyday life into the consciousness and subject canon of social psychology. Although this may not be necessary if we consider that psychology also used to be in a position to show ordinary people a mirror reflecting their everyday shortcomings in rational thought, recollection and decision making. But it is exactly here that we find the difference between a psychology married to bias, and the attempt to recognise people's 'ability to act', 'ability to live' and 'ability to hear' as their original qualities.

Seen like this it becomes a scrutiny of a social psychology which interprets, or misinterprets, the freedom of its theories from context and content as implying their universal validity. If individuals are stripped of their social identities, human beings in general remain representatives of the genus. The use of this device by social psychology led to not a few successes, as explained in textbooks. However, we would require lengthier justification for a different orientation and different viewpoint also to be regarded as having its own legitimacy or indispensability. The following chapters discuss some of the reasons which prompt us to seek the non-individual, the social and the *a priori* cultural explicitly in the individual.

Modern social psychology can be described as having four basic characteristics (K. Gergen, 1988): (1) the acceptance of a basic, identifiable subject of scientific research; (2) a requirement for universal validity of interrelations once found; (3) the experimental method as a vehicle of causal research; and (4) research understood as a progressive and cumulative undertaking. Each of these characteristics has been challenged (cf. also Ibañez, 1991; Michael, 1991).

For example: (1) the material strength and tangibility of the subject dissolves in the realisation of scientific theory that subjects, particularly in the social sciences, are dependent on discourse, language and method; (2) the search for contexts of validity, whether dependent on population or situation, erodes the claim to universality; (3) the use of strict method, with experimentation first and foremost, has lost its previous status of 'via regia'; and (4) the big oil painting of knowledge and its accumulation has retreated before the water-colours of many smaller theoretical narrations, which owe their chances of asserting themselves not to their inherent, objective truth, but to the way that they fit with local intelligibility, persuasiveness and usefulness (cf. Bevan, 1991).

The postmodern tendency in science in general, and in social psychology in particular, has also significantly effected a reflexive modernisation (Beck, 1992). Proponents of science are beginning to consider more clearly how their conduct can be accommodated than they did even 20 years ago. One implication of this is the natural incorporation of science into the sociopolitical network, with its associated debate about ethical responsibility – for example, in the way that it accompanies contemporary ecological and feminist discourse. It is no longer an immaterial question whether the results of an experiment are backed up by method and theory (i.e., are 'true'), or whether they have been simultaneously attributed the sociopolitical inflections of scientists, who impose limitations on largely arbitrary interpretations made by decision makers and spin doctors. Too often, 'objective' data have appeared to support two contrary political courses of action simultaneously (depending on the capriciousness of the non-scientific interpretation). It is regrettable that proponents of science should have to rack their brains over this as well. Yet heightened moral alertness is certainly not harmful to academic life; especially as the point must be made that pure data does not imply value judgements.

The second point, which we consider to be at least as important, is the way science relates to itself: to its unvoiced assumptions and those political, cultural and social prejudices which pre-empt problem phraseology and theorisation. It matters, of course, whether one uses the humanities and social sciences to formulate and prove by experiment causal theories based on a reactively mechanistic impression of the humen being; or whether one uses them to formulate descriptive theories which are subject to an impression of humans being proactive, thinking beings and shaping their environment. It is acutely necessary to consider the underlying 'Menschenbilder' (images of man and woman), especially in the social sciences. Indeed, this problem has been under discussion at least since the advent of the 'humanist psychology' movement.

There is, arguably, a discrepancy between the moral reasons for the pursuit of either the natural sciences or psychology (Mixon, 1990). If it is the promise of the natural sciences to enable better understanding – and therefore better mastery – of nature, then it would seem to be a plausible assumption that such an undertaking could be of potential benefit to everyone. Pursuing natural sciences is therefore a good thing. On the other hand, if a psychology researching cause and effect promises better understanding of behaviour – and better control of it as a consequence – then it would seem to be a plausible assumption that such an undertaking might not benefit everyone (and certainly not those being controlled). This is strategic knowledge, which cannot be justified by referring to its general utility. Although it would appear analogously and morally justifiable in natural science, it can barely be justified, at least in a democratic society (Mixon, 1990, p. 105).

As far as the social sciences are concerned, in the majority of cases scientists are simultaneously members of the same society as the 'objects' they observe. The validity of evidence therefore becomes applicable to us, and implies the need for us to define our own place within the research field (K. Gergen, 1991). Yet such a reflexive approach harbours dangers which we have at best only a limited chance of avoiding. For example, multilateral cultural comparison may be a step towards the mutually applicable validation of psychological theories (W. Wagner, 1990).

Scientific discourse is no more free from rhetorical trends and semantic ambiguities than the language of everyday life. Lopes (1991) carried out a detailed analysis of the so-called 'cognitive bias' literature to demonstrate how sales rhetoric is transforming fields of research. The language of theories, which placed the cognitive process in the context of logically experimental criteria, was originally non-judgemental (like the language of perception theories when they deal with delusions). However, the character of the language has undergone transformation due to spread and popularisation, as well as application to real decision-making procedures. It has become increasingly judgemental, to the extent that in the place of process description, ordinary people have begun to be portrayed as irrational, with their cognitive shortcomings seeming to warrant such descriptive terms as 'illusion', 'misconception', 'insensitivity' and 'bias' (p. 76). The term 'cognitive heuristics' (which on its own has only positive connotations) has become transformed to 'cognitive inability'. This occurs even though close analysis of the relevant experiments reveals that use of heuristics produces correct judgements in the majority of cases – even the decision-making problems employed by Tversky, Kahneman and others – as long as the variation range of independent variables has been exhausted (p. 72 onwards). The result is that scientific rhetoric not only reduces the scope of problems of concern to researchers, it also reduces the attention of the public. The extent to which such cases may be awash with deliberate and profit-driven conceptual deception is a matter which everyone can judge for themselves.

Scientific reflexivity requires that theories be taken seriously. It reminds researchers of their own conduct, which would have its methodological rules validated in the research process; and of its products (scientific explanations and theories) whose validity has relevance even for academia. It is not only when dealing with experimental 'subjects' that theories have to be taken seriously. The cultural background of those people is also largely shared by us, and its related processes will also have their effect in the experimenter.

It would be tempting to consider and elaborate these points more thoroughly, and with regard to their consequences within scientific theory and scientific history. We will return to such problems at suitable points in the text, albeit in a subject- and problem-specific form. The entire text is, after all, a critical analysis of the problematic nature of meaning: of the claim to universality and the possibly inadequate standardization of criteria for psychological results.

## 1.2 Layout of the book

The thoughts which are presented and discussed in this book revolve, above all, around two fundamental concepts. The basis and starting point is the search for the theoretical treatment of the everyday in contemporary social psychology. We start from the premiss that the everyday life experienced by individuals continuously and stubbornly refers to the social conditions in which they live. This has as a consequence that the investigation of everyday people by social psychology cannot be closed to the social *a priori* if it wishes to be relevant. There is at least implicitly a place for society in individuals' forms of thinking and experiencing and their reproduction of cultural and social conditions. The theory of social representations attempts to establish precisely this link between society and individual mentality. Its presentation and discussion form the main part of this book.

On the whole, the presentation refers to the phenomena and is not orientated on the disciplines of social sciences. This means that we take the freedom to refer to any social science whenever a concept or phenomenon such as 'everyday thought' is discussed. In particular these social sciences include social and cross-cultural psychology, social and cultural anthropology as well as sociology. It seems to us that an orientation based on disciplines instead of phenomena, as, for example, Denise Jodelet (1985, 1989a) does in some of her works, is not very helpful for the present purpose. If the concept of social representations makes sense in actual fact, then it is because it allows us to describe a transdisciplinary phenomenon. Splitting up our treatment of the theory into its respective disciplinary parts would jeopardise the phenomenon.

Chapters 2 and 3 mark out the global framework of a social psychology interested in the everyday man. Chapter 2 seeks to define the concept 'everyday', and confronts related concepts such as 'common sense'. Discussion about the content of everyday thought takes us to the issue of the dependence versus independence of content and process features in cognitive processes and the theories that they describe. Closer analysis reveals both to be tightly linked with each other. If, for example, cognition is abstracted from the content of thought and is reduced to pure structure and process, then it is unnecessary to consider the social environment in which we think. A content-free social-psychological theory is necessarily also an asocial theory.

Subsequently we deal with the rational aspects of everyday thought. Far from attempting a comprehensive discussion of the philosophical problems of rationality, the presentation confronts relevant social-psychological, anthropological and sociological approaches, with regard to the difference between 'wild' and 'domesticated' thought (or scientific thought, if we prefer). Wild thought is not just located in the discourse of peoples with traditional ways of living, but is a fundamental feature of everyday thought in general, independent of the technological level of development. There follows a discussion of the problems raised by the criteria which social psychology applies to the cognitive performance of its test subjects.

Chapter 3 begins with a portrayal of the preconditions of everyday life, the safeguarding of social survival and the pragmatic efficiency of spontaneous action. This is followed by describing three characteristics: concreteness, similarity and the 'need' of explanation, which lay out the functional domain of everyday thought. This is followed by an analysis of the content of collective discourse – what we call the field of content-rationality – and the sources of its evidence, in connection with some logical features of common sense.

The next chapters are given to the theory of social representations. It proved problematic, however, to choose the order in which to portray the diverse aspects of the theory, since here, just as in other sciences, the theory follows a logic of justification that runs counter to the logic of discovery. Following the logic of justification would imply beginning with social and collective aspects before 'descending' to the individual, in the hierarchy of levels of analysis. This order was not chosen here for both pragmatic and didactic reasons. The order of the chapters 'individual representations', 'collective discourse' and 'epistemological status', follows the logic of discovery which, in our opinion, guides social-psychological debate. The form of expression of social representation at the individual level as a distributive property is followed by a discussion of how representations acquire their social character.

Chapter 4, 'Introducing Social Representations', describes the theory's general features and its connections with other concepts of psychology, together with attempts to circumscribe the concept.

Chapter 5, 'The Topography of Modern Mentality', illustrates the content areas of contemporary mentality using exemplary research. We distinguish between three areas: popularised science, representations of and in the area of social and political processes and, finally, cultural objects with a long history.

In Chapter 6, 'The Organisation and Structure of Social Representations', we discuss how representations can be modelled as mental entities with a metaphorical and iconic form. The structural concepts of central core and periphery are subsequently discussed, and relevant research is examined.

'The Dynamics of Social Representations', Chapter 7, deals with processes to do with representations serving as cognitive metasystems, structuring thinking and perception. From this we go on to investigate the social determinants of categorisation and anchoring, and how everyday knowledge becomes objectified in thinking.

Chapter 8, 'Discourse, Transmission and the Shared Universe', leads up to the social conditions in which representations arise and are elaborated. First we discuss some features of dialogue and collective discourse, as well as the issue of situatedness and the related issue of sharedness. The next section is devoted to culture change and the phenomenon of cognitive polyphasia. Finally, we present the function of the mass media in an epidemiology of social representations.

The reality-creating consequence of co-ordinated interaction is addressed in Chapter 9, 'Action, Objectification and Social Reality'. This has to do with the action-related aspects of social representations; and how novel phenomena are socially constructed to result in 'domesticated' objects populating local worlds. From there we consider Bourdieu's theory of habitus, and contrast it with Moscovici's approach in social psychology. The chapter concludes with some thoughts about the role of public discourse and knowledge of other groups' representations in concerted interaction.

Chapter 10 attempts to pin down some epistemological aspects of the concept of social representations. We touch on the topics of explaining rational behaviour in social psychology; the difficulty of articulating levels of analysis in research involving the problem of reduction versus macro-reduction; and the potential problem of circularity of social representation theory. We conclude with a theoretical note on the relationship between people as representatives of the species 'homo sapiens' and people as representing particular sociocultural groups.

Chapter 11 presents some methodological aspects of research in the field. In the foregoing chapters, when presenting important research, we have provided a short description of the methodology used. The chapter reflects recent changes in methodology as well as addressing the challenges of conducting real-world research, and issues to do with triangulation and validity. We conclude by noting the need for multi-level exploration of social issues, preferably extended across time, or at least dealing explicitly with the temporal dimension.

In covering the topic of social representation theory and research we emphasise the presentation of classical research in the field, and integrated research, that was published in French language. The reason is that these respective sources are often difficult to access although they play an important role in the contemporary development of the approach. In the end, we are aware of the fact that there are lacunae in our presentation that would have deserved to be covered. Nevertheless we hope this book will serve as a useful working manual for researchers and as a study guide to students who are interested in an approach that attempts to articulate the social with the individual.

Readers who are short of time, have special interests or who are not particularly interested in the elaboration and discussion of a psychology of everyday life and vernacular thinking may skip Chapters 2 and 3 without disadvantage.

# Chapter 2
# Everyday Life, Knowledge and Rationality

## 2.1 The concept of 'everyday'

### 2.1.1 'Everyday' as a category in social psychology

As Descartes remarked, 'nothing in the world is so fairly shared out as common sense'. Everybody claims it for themselves and seems to feel offended by any implication that they might lack it. Is there anyone who can admit to possessing too little common sense? Such a confession would be tantamount to a declaration of mental bankruptcy which would effectively deprive us of our practical right to exist.

Common sense is our spontaneously available background knowledge. It is largely used without thinking, and is subject to our everyday practice. Our background knowledge encompasses a heterogeneous variety of areas which play a role in everyday life. It brings in our knowledge of natural events: 'a roof tile always comes down'; our opinions about social relations: 'teasing is a sign of affection'; and our moral values: 'crime doesn't pay'. There is hardly any area of everyday life where some appropriate truism would not occur to us straight away.

### Textbooks

The concepts 'everyday life' and 'everyday knowledge' play a very minor role in contemporary social psychology. This may be because experimental and (here especially) cognitive social psychology do not generally make a distinction between everyday knowledge and other knowledge.

As result, they take the view that a difference in ideas does not automatically mean a difference in the characteristics of cognitive processes. The objects, things, persons and events and so on with which a cognitive act has to deal seem irrelevant for the functioning of cognition. Someone standing at the bus stop and envisaging the ingredients for his next meal so as to complete his shopping, can in principle be equated to the thought processes of executive managers of great firms, and to the decision processes of aircraft pilots and scientists. If differences can be found, then they are usually put down to accompanying emotional circumstances such as stress, motivational influences, and cognitive capacity and complexity.

A cursory look at the contents pages of social psychology textbooks, however, creates the impression of a pronounced distinction between cognitive processes relating to different subject matters. Under the heading 'social cognition' we find chapters such as person perception, self-perception, causal attribution, prejudice, social identity and attitude change. These chapters obviously deal with cognitive processes relating to those subject matters: other people, the self, the causes of behaviour, outside groups, one's own group, attitudes and the like, analysing them, processing them and committing them to memory. This subject subdivision gives the impression that it is dealing with fields with subject-specific process characteristics – in other words, their own cognitive logics. Therefore, those cognitive processes which relate to groups are differentiated from the processes which relate to the self or other individuals. But this is not the case. Fields differentiated by subject may be grouped together by comparable cognitive process, such as the logic of attribution processes, the logic of remembering and forgetting, the logic of consistency and so on. The underlying assumption is that of a procedural unity with diversity regarding content.

However, a different picture contradicting the assumption of procedural unity is shown by the fact that it appears necessary in social-psychological textbooks to distinguish the field of social cognition from the study of non-social cognition in general psychology. This creates an impression of a difference in principle between research fields relating to psychology in general and those relating to social psychology. We wish to return to this contradictory aspect later in this chapter.

It is largely up to the personal feeling of the researchers whether they consider it necessary to integrate explicitly the 'everyday' into their work, as a category that is relevant and lends itself to research. However, seeing the Everyday as unlike the Unusual or the Scientific can open our eyes to whole areas of life which are left out of mainstream social-psychological research. It is as if topics only become established in psychological research if the personal involvement of the researcher is in inverse proportion to its probability of occurrence.[1] This effect only appears to contradict the dictum that researchers prefer to research into topics with which they associate personal problems, since dealing with the everyday does not usually pose us any problems. On the contrary, it is an area of our life which appears to work without glitches. The better something works, the less analysis there is of everyday practice, with the result that it appears less worthy of research.

It is either in this way, or through an implicit assumption that those phenomena which have been analysed theoretically are about everyday phenomena anyhow, that we can explain why the concept 'everyday' does not even appear in current textbooks of social psychology. In fact, if we take an (admittedly arbitrary) sample of twelve social psychology textbooks (Beauvois, 1984; Brandstätter, 1983; Doise, Deschamps and Mugny, 1980; K. Gergen and Gergen, 1986; Herkner, 1981; Moscovici and Hewstone, 1986; Munné, 1980; Perlman and Cozby, 1983; Rexilius and Grubitzsch, 1986; Tajfel and Fraser, 1978; Tedeschi and Lindskold, 1976; Witte, 1989), we find that the concept is relatively rare. We find the entry 'everyday' and 'everyday knowledge' mentioned twice: in relation to environmental psychology, definition of the field, and methodology (Rexilius and Grubitzsch, 1986) and in relation to the epistemology of 'common sense' (Paicheler in Moscovici and Hewstone, 1986). It is also mentioned once in a title (Beauvois, 1984). Apart from Moscovici and Hewstone's book (1986), which is an exception in many ways, there are only three books which make implicit reference to the topic: one occasionally referring to everyday experience and everyday feeling (Brandstätter, 1983), one which refers to the test subject as an everyday person and citizen (Doise, Deschamps and Mugny, 1980), and one that makes observations of the social construction of the (everyday) world (K. Gergen and Gergen, 1986).

## Naive psychologies

Heider (1977) was one of the few who referred explicitly to everyday thought and common sense in conceptual studies of the psychology of interpersonal relations. In the introduction to his book he remarks that he uses as his main starting point 'non- or half-formulated knowledge about interpersonal relations: how it is expressed in our everyday language and everyday experiences' (p. 13). This book is a systematisation of everyday knowledge about psychological facts. The basis of everyday knowledge remains explicit, even though the author does not simply aim to describe this knowledge faithfully but also to use this knowledge as a step towards understanding what lies behind it.[2] Heider's criticism of his contemporaries – that all psychologists use ideas of common sense in their scientific thought, this, however, largely without analysing them or making them explicit (p. 15) – is still justifiable today. It is no coincidence that his book is quoted as regularly as it is: it testifies to the importance of psychological ideas of naivety in human behaviour. However, only a few works (e.g. Laucken, 1974) have been devoted to his principal approach: that of ascertaining the naive ideas of behaviour and psychological process both conceptually and in an explicitly everyday-related manner.

## Ecological psychology

Ecological psychology approaches everyday life from a completely different angle. It takes as its starting point the socially formed material environment of modern man, examining architectonic urban design, places of work, homes, streets and the like along with other related factors. In that context, it is interested in their effect on the well-being, experience, actions and identity of the people living there. As a result, it captures people in the centre of their everyday lives – the 'spaces of everyday life' (e.g. Graumann, 1978; Kaminski, 1986; Kruse, Graumann and Lantermann, 1990; Mehrabian, 1976).

A large part of psychological research of ecology, however, is geared towards a 'Stimulus – (X) – Reaction model'. The objectively defined environment is presented as the stimulus whose effects on psychological experience and behaviour are being studied. The meaning of the variable X, the psychological and cultural provision of people in society, acts merely as an intervening construct – for example, through cognitive scripts (Kruse, 1986). Everyday hypotheses which give objects in the environment their significance and symbolic meaning are only occasionally (e.g. Boesch, 1971, 1991) of interest in ecological psychology.

If we look at them from the perspective of a socioculturally orientated psychology of everyday knowledge, we find that many studies of environmental psychology adopt a strikingly 'mistrustful' view of their subjects. When Barker (1968) and colleagues developed his theory of behaviour settings by observing for almost 20 years the behaviour of people at different locations in a small town (e.g. at the church, in shops, restaurants, etc.) in order to identify the stable behaviour patterns typical of these locations, the outcome was exactly the same as one he could have deduced – at far less expense – from talking to or questioning a few inhabitants of the town.[3] Instead of recognising the competence of the inhabitants' knowledge of their environment (i.e., the representation of this environment in their system of knowledge), and taking seriously the togetherness and interdependency of the living environment and those living in it, the Stimulus – (X) – Reaction model demands an objectivist definition of the environment and a mechanistic description of behaviour, as if it were independent of the participants involved in it. Are not the forms of engagement between people and their environment represented in the social and cultural world as well as in the actors? This determines the form of encounters between protagonists and their environment. The stimuli of the normal environment would not exist without the collective activity of the protagonists (without their architectural endeavours, for example). They anticipate the image of the environment in order to be able to create it.

### Researching real life

Some researchers approach the subjective side of everyday experience using time-sampling diary methods. This approach gets subjects to spend a considerable amount of time filling in a standard diary page at particular times, classifying the entries later. It allows a relatively direct recording of the subjects' subjective view of their environment, their activities and psychological action. Studies using this method show the close overlapping of subjective situation definitions with emotional, motivational and cognitive experiences, in a wide variety of environments (Brandstätter, 1990; Brandstätter and Wagner, 1989; Kette, 1991; Kirchler, 1989b).

For Hofstätter (1966), the task of social psychology lies in viewing everyday routine matters as an expression of the homogeneity of a social group, and making it the object of analysis (p. 58 onwards). The everyday life of the people researched will ultimately be the basic litmus test of all psychological theories and concepts – a very firm test at that, and one where, as we know, countless theories have already come a cropper. The following section aims to develop a definition of everyday life and vernacular knowledge. For this purpose it seems useful to take the approaches of some authors of sociology as a starting point, and extend them to the individual analysis level of social psychology.

## 2.1.2 Defining 'everyday life'

### Macro views

The concept of everyday life plays a prominent role in the traditions of sociology.[4] Everyday life in a sociology partially inspired by Marxism revolves around the processes of production and reproduction, understood both economically and in the sense of social perpetuation. The work and reproductive activities of people under given social conditions create and form not just the products but also the body and needs of man (Lefebvre, 1977, p. 103 onwards). At the same time, everyday life is also the 'sphere where needs and goods meet'. If we exclude the specialised and structured higher activities of society, everyday life represents that totality which is 'in fundamental relation to all activities' and encompasses it 'with its differences and conflicts'. The complex of everyday activities indicates 'absolute continuity', as is contained in the expression 'everyday' (Heller, 1981, p. 28ff.). This continuity forms the basis of 'people's way of life'. According to Heller, the routine of everyday life, its continuity, is where the 'unity of personality' is realised for people. For them, 'everyday life is "real life"', and through it they acquire 'all the basic abilities and basic feelings and forms of behaviour' with which they can transcend their immediate surroundings and relate to the wider world. In this sense, the theory of everyday life is partly a theory of needs, anchored in its genesis on the one hand, and in its fulfilment in everyday life on the other. It is also partly a theory of the community's reproduction of social and cultural identity (Remy, Voye and Servais, 1991).

From these approaches up to Schütz (1981) and ethnomethodology we can identify a process of declining abstractness in the definition of everyday life. The focus increasingly shifts from the sphere of relations of production structuring man as a social species, to the individual activities and cognitive acts which structure social relations. This process retains the concept of production and reproduction, which even in ethnomethodology remains the determining quantity of everyday life. 'The material basis to the "timetable" of day-to-day occurrences is crystallised in the necessity to do work for society, which is linked with an inevitable continuous loss of time for living and of personal energy' (Matthes and Schütze, 1981, p. 23). The timetable encompasses the ordinary and extraordinary life occurrences experienced by members of society and characterising different life stages, as 'the day-to-day sequence of events to which the member of society is subjected here and now, in view of obligations to do with career, family, free time, and others' (p. 22).

Everyday knowledge as a tool to deal with everyday occurrences therefore consists 'less of considered elements of knowledge, than of various layers of unconscious and unconsidered routine knowledge' (p. 22). It makes day-to-day events appear natural and in 'effortless order'. The effortlessly organised everyday timetable is, on the one hand, a precondition and, on the other, a consequence of the 'natural attitude' of the individual which leads to accepting the world as it is and without question (Schütz and Luckmann, 1979, p. 25ff.) and which is equally expected from the Others (p. 87ff.).[5]

Matthes and Schütze (1981 p.47ff.) summarise the most significant aspects of the relation between everyday knowledge and social reality in three propositions, which can also provide a useful template for social-psychological research:

1. 'The formal pragmatic structure of everyday knowledge is largely identical to the interactively logical structure of action . . .'

2. 'With its sociohistorical or specific forms and as a symbolising idea system, everyday knowledge breaks away from current

actions, its conditions and consequences. But at this level, even if it contradicts the reality of the action, everyday knowledge is extraordinarily action relevant, and to this extent forms an essential element of social reality. Its specific contents make everyday knowledge a necessary orientation and interpretation basis for action processes.'

3.  'Whilst expectation types, situation definitions and interpretations (especially the latter two) are constantly transforming so that the discrepancies of the current action performance can be reviewed, "theories" can be maintained even in the long term against contradictory action performances . . . At the most elementary level (i.e., leaving aside all power-stabilising legitimations, calculated "theory productions" of special occupational groups etc.) theories have the function of stabilising social units (such as identity of the self, identity of groups, etc.) . . .'

These theses form a marginal comment, as it were, aiming to outline a view of everyday knowledge whose social-psychological aspects for the time being cannot be explained. This view will influence social-psychological discussion in the following chapters in connection, with the reality-creating consequences of social representations.

At the same time, the micro- and meso-theories of ethnomethodology complete the process that began with the sociological macro-views. Their contribution leads directly to the topic of interest here. We must first attempt a definition of the term 'everyday' which enables us to get our social-psychological bearings.

## Semantic clarification

In the context here we are dealing not so much with everyday views and opinions about the functioning of psychological processes which was, for example, Heider's interest, but with a more general view on everyday life. Elias (1978a p. 26) examines this concept by comparing a selection of applications of the term 'everyday':

1.  Everyday contrasted with special days.
2.  Everyday as a routine contrasted with extraordinary spheres of society.

3.  Everyday as working days contrasted with bourgeois areas of life.
4.  Everyday understood as the life of the majority of people contrasted with the life of the privileged and powerful.
5.  Everyday as domain of events of daily life contrasted with 'great' events, major and national events.
6.  Everyday as private life contrasted with public and professional life.
7.  Everyday as a sphere of natural, spontaneous, unconsidered, true experience and thought contrasted with the sphere of considered, artificial, non-spontaneous, and in particular also scientific experience and thought.
8.  Everyday or everyday consciousness as the quintessence of ideological, naïve, unconsidered and false experience and thought contrasted with correct, genuine and true consciousness.

The author rightly points out the fact that it is not enough just to talk about what we understand by the 'everyday'. There must be more extensive explanation of its opposite, against which the research field of everyday life should stand out. The points listed above identify the main usage of the term 'everyday' in the social sciences, but seem only partly suitable for the purposes of social psychology.

## Definition

The subject matter of this chapter is everyday knowledge. If we leave aside comparison (8) in Elias's list, which is only the inverse evaluation of (7), then we have here a thoroughly useful definition for our purposes. It is the sphere of natural, spontaneous, more or less unconsidered experience and thought which is to be understood by a 'social psychology of everyday life' in the current context. This experience and thought concerns the domain of events of daily life, and forms the cognitive and affective basis of everyday routines. The opposite of research into this subject matter would therefore be concerned with considered, artificial, non-spontaneous, and in particular scientific experience and thought – the type of thought which is not realised in the everyday domains of the majority of people, but in exclusive domains such as in science, at managerial levels of economic entities or at high political committee levels. Although the people active in these domains of life may well make them routine, this is not the everyday routine of the mass of people.

Almost everybody, however, whether cobbler or scientist, cook or manager, participates in both spheres (cf. Born, 1983, 1991). Which way of thinking prevails depends on the times and places at which somebody is active. Both professional and skilled trades are to a great extent based on knowledge that has been reflected on and is open to further reflection. Everyday life outside of the office usually functions more spontaneously than professional work.

This definition should not make an artificial distinction between the everyday and the special day. Extraordinary events, celebrations, rituals and connected ways of acting and thinking are just as much a part of the concept of everyday life as, for example, housework routines or the daily journey to work. Even regular and irregularly occurring festivities are ingrained in spontaneous knowledge, are to a large extent routine in their proceedings, and invoke judgements that appear spontaneous. The emphasis of the concept is more in the nature of the knowledge and thought than in the occasions where it is realised.

As later chapters will show, the comparison[6] between spontaneous and considered knowledge which we are making here is rejected by methodological orientation and theoretical construction in central parts of social psychology. Instead, many theoretical models attempt normatively to predetermine the rules of scientific reflection for everyday thought, that is, overvaluing one pole at the expense of the other. This reduces everyday practice to an incomplete and degenerate imitation of scientific action.

## Specialised knowledge and lay knowledge

Modern society's hierarchical processes of stratification have institutionalised the split of social knowledge into general and specialised (although it is not just modern society which does this, as the classes of philosophers and priests in pre-industrial societies show). Both sorts of knowledge differ not only according to the places, roles, institutions and organisations in which they are thought and applied, but above all according to the nature of knowledge transfer. Lay knowledge includes those elements of the social supply of knowledge which 'are transmitted to everybody normally and as a matter of routine' (Sprondel, 1979, p. 148). This knowledge is in principle accessible to everyone, even if the elements differ in content in diverse societies according to classes and subcultures. Possessing this knowledge defines lay status.

The acquisition of special knowledge is linked to social preconditions: the occupation of particular roles and their expert nature. Even if in democratic societies everybody has free physical access to the literature of university libraries, that knowledge in reality remains closed to most, since it does not depend so much on the information that one would like to acquire, as on the possession of the methodological thought patterns and capacities necessary for its acquisition, which are imparted at special institutions.

Those representing this exclusive specialised knowledge, the experts, therefore have one foot in each domain of life: both the exclusive and the everyday domain of their families and more intimate private surroundings. The consequence of this is that their thought and knowledge about 'reality' may arise from these two relatively closed domains (Born, 1983).

## Common sense

So what distinguishes a person who can be claimed to possess that 'natural, spontaneous, unconsidered and true experience and thought', which we refer to using the abbreviation 'common sense'? Do people possess common sense who will not touch a naked flame and also tell this to their children? Or do people possess it who will not leave home without an umbrella when there are thunder clouds looming? Or is it that common sense is not possessed by people who will still walk over a level crossing although the headlights of the oncoming train are already visible, with the effect that other people nearby think they 'have taken leave of their senses', and 'have got no sense and must be blind'?

Does it take a chemist who knows the oxidation processes of tissues at certain temperatures, a meteorologist who knows the dynamics and distribution of energy in thunder clouds, or a railway operative who knows that the approaching train will first make a stop before the crossing? If we knew that the people mentioned above base their actions purely on their professional knowledge, then we could neither acknowledge their common sense nor suppose a lack of it. That must be proved by first placing them in situations where they have no expertise and then seeing whether they are spontaneously able to act correctly and not just on the basis of their professional knowledge. Common sense defines itself generally as the opposite of an ordered and conscious knowledge complex, rather than as considered knowledge. Common sense is perceived as given from immediate experience, directly forced on us by facts. Common sense refers to the world as it is and not as it seems to be.

Admittedly, this definition is itself a component of common sense, and probably a requirement for common sense to function at all. If common sense admitted doubt of everyday impressions, or if this doubt were necessary, then we could think of hardly any situation in which a direct and unambiguous way of behaviour would be possible (Jones and Gerard, 1967). This self-definition is not imported to this area of knowledge from outside: it is an ideological element of function, which is part of self-justification.

Scientific analysis of the system of common sense requires a different image: 'If we say that someone has common sense, that is not only supposed to mean that they use their eyes and ears, but that they keep them open, as it were, and use them meaningfully, intelligently, and in a way conducive to forming opinion and reflection, or at least attempt it, and that they are in a position to deal with everyday problems in an everyday manner with a degree of efficiency' (Geertz, 1983, p. 264). The distinction 'between perception of pure factuality . . . and the simple everyday knowledge, judgements and assessments of this factuality', which is not available in common sense's conception of itself, must be reintroduced in order to allow us to analyse common sense as an ordered complex of comprehensive knowledge and as a cultural system (Geertz, 1983, p. 263ff.). What follows, after a few preliminaries, will investigate the content structure, cognitive preconditions and reasons of everyday knowledge, and show this to be preliminary work to the theory of social representations.

The way everyday knowledge is treated is very closely connected to the distinction between psychological processes and its social and cultural meanings. We therefore wish the following to show that we can only speak meaningfully of process if it is to do with a psychological lawfulness to which the human species is entitled. Closer observation reveals findings that are valid only in smaller populations to be elements of content rather than process.

## 2.2 Excursus: content and process in theory and cognition

'What one thinks about has some influence on how one thinks' (Shweder, 1980, p. 270). The question of the changing relationship between form and content, or process and content in mental activities has been answered differently over the course of time. The answer depends on the traditions followed by the researchers concerned. It is not really an easy problem to settle, since views which argue that the two are independent are directly incompatible with those which argue dependence. It seems obvious that the decision one way or another needs to be resolved empirically. In principle we would only need to establish whether we can find experimental examples to prove that thought processes differ in their dependence on content.

On the other hand, we can also look at theoretical and research-oriented reasons for or against the separation of content and process. For example, the research-practicality argument suggests that combining content and process would mean that the scientific analysis of cognition would become unmanageably complex. Applying the spirit of Ockham's Razor, we want to avoid enlarging the theoretical complexity following from such a view. But we would still want to be sure that this methodically and theoretically simpler premiss involved in separating process from content will produce results which are as valid as the more complex assumption. The next section outlines and discusses in formal terms the arguments and empirical evidence for or against the dependence of content and process.

### 2.2.1 Formal defining elements

#### Statements

The concepts 'content' and 'process' will be defined in psychological and in particular social cognitive theories as the start of a broader discussion. By a theoretical statement of psychology, we wish to interpret a proposition of the form:

$$(p \rightarrow_s q)$$

in which $p$ is an event which temporally precedes event $q$ and $\rightarrow_s$, an implication for which it is true that

$$(p \rightarrow_s q) AND \; NOT \; (NOTp \rightarrow_s q)$$

and where $\rightarrow_s$ is an empirical relationship. This means: 'if $p$, then $q$, but not if $NOTp$ then $q$' (von Kutschera, 1982, p. 101ff.).[7] A psychological expression of this form can therefore be expressed as a triple:

$$\{A, B, \rightarrow_s\},$$

whose term $A$ contains a set of events, situations and conditions, which in the framework of the statement imply a set of behaviour patterns $B$. In psychological theories, $A$ contains the sum of all conditions in which a specific behaviour pattern from set $B$ can be observed as a consequence.

Let us take as an example the classic experiments on dissonance theory. The usual view in this theory is: 'If a test subject is brought into a state of cognitive dissonance, their subsequent behaviour will act to reduce their dissonance experience' (Festinger and Carlsmith, 1959). Set $A$ in this statement contains all those conditions in which cognitive dissonance can be expected: such as situations of forced compliance or after decisions (Brehm and Cohen, 1959),[8] and including all other conceivable operationalisations. Set $B$ contains all those behaviour patterns, (i.e., measures) which can be regarded as indicators of dissonance reduction. For example, it includes the subsequent revaluation of a task that is burdensome but completed, or the devaluation of alternatives that were not chosen when a decision was made.

## Process

By processes, such as the process touched on by dissonance theory, we mean the transformation of the initial circumstances into the final circumstances – that is, the entire relation which is expressed by:

$$(a \rightarrow_s b)$$

in which *a* is an arbitrary element of *A* and *b* is an element theoretically compatible with *B*.

## Content

We understand the content of the statement to refer to its possible realisations – that is, those situations, in which the process of dissonance reduction can be observed. The elements *a* and *b* are related to each other – that is, they must be compatible with each other, because not every situation from *A* is compatible with every behaviour pattern of set *B*. Taking this into account, the content can be expressed by the set:

$$\{(a,b),P\}$$

The pair (*a,b*) portrays the interrelated situations and behaviour patterns whose characteristics are specified in the theory. Even more fundamental is the subset *P*, which is the set of all populations for which the statement is true.

Although the kind of sample and population with which a phenomenon is observed is usually described in empirical reports, there is rarely any mention of it in the results and discussion sections of relevant articles. This is all the more surprising considering that test subjects (as all long-suffering people carrying out experiments can attest) are not passive 'reactors'. Rather, they bring their ingrained ideas, attitudes and cultural impressions into the test situation and its operationalisation, establishing a background in which the laboratory conditions themselves also become an influencing factor. Making a situation out of a set of facts and a psychologically effective stimulus out of a physical condition requires both: the changing relationship between the laboratory environment created by the person carrying out the experiment, and the spontaneous interpretations of the situation made by the test subject. The population of an empirical study realised by the sample or its pre-experimental attitudes must therefore be understood as an integral component of the content.

## Independence

The content and process of psychological theories should be independent of one another, according to this model, if the set {(*a,b*),*P*} does not contain any elements which do not satisfy the process relation $(a \rightarrow_s b)$ – that is, if it does not contain either pairs $(a,b)$, or populations as elements of $P$. Using the example of dissonance theory, we could argue for independence if, first, we were unable to find any forms of reward which evoked the same amount of dissonance reduction (or less) with under-reward as with over-reward and, second, if we are unable to find any population which does not show the expected effect. If there is independence, a process statement can be viewed as generally valid, so that the population term $P$ covers the entire species of *homo sapiens*. Postulating independence in a broader sense would therefore require successful intercultural replication. However, there is also independence in a narrower sense, and this is probably what is tacitly assumed to be the normal case in social psychology. It can be expressed as the situation if no attention is paid to the population term $P$ in set $\{(a,b),P\}$.

## Interdependence

Interdependence between process and content can be identified if the theory contains a superordinate statement of the form:

$EXISTS\ c_k, c_l\ IN\ C{:}(c_k \rightarrow_s (a_i \rightarrow_s b_i)p)$
$AND\ (c_l \rightarrow_s\ NOT\ (a_i \rightarrow_s b_i)p),$

$a_i\ IN\ A, b_i\ IN\ B, p\ IN\ P, c_k \neq c_l$

or alternatively:

$EXISTS\ p_m, p_n\ IN\ P{:}(c \rightarrow_s (a_i \rightarrow_s b_i)p_m)$
$AND\ (c \rightarrow_s\ NOT\ (a_i \rightarrow_s b_i)p_n),$

$a_i\ IN\ A, b_i\ IN\ B, c\ IN\ C, p_m \neq p_n$

The superordinate conditions $C$ and $P$ define subsets in the content set $\{(a,b),P\}$ which restrict the validity of the statement $(a \rightarrow_s b)$ within the given domain. Such a statement corresponds to the quadruple:

$\{C, P, (a \rightarrow_s b), \rightarrow_s\}.$

This means that there are either well-defined pairs $(a,b)_i$ from stimuli $a$ and behaviour patterns $b$ or elements $p_i$, that is, partial populations, to which the relationship $(a_i \rightarrow_s b_i)$ applies; and simultaneously different pairs $(a,b)_j \neq (a,b)_i$ or elements $p_j \neq p_i$ to which a different relationship $(a_j \rightarrow_s b_j)$ applies. In this way, each of the two original partial process statements $(a \rightarrow_s b)$ becomes the content of the superordinate statement, namely part of the content triple:

$$\{(c,(a \rightarrow_s b)), P\}$$

Similar to a statistical interaction, the superordinate condition:

$$(c \rightarrow_s (a \rightarrow_s b))$$

of a theory formulates an interaction between content and process within the given domain.

## 2.2.2 The relativity of process and content

The above model of psychological processes stresses the need to establish that there are no populations or situation conditions to be found which relativise the process statement. Ultimately such statements only describe processes which concern the psychological provision of the genus 'man' and are consequently universal. If, for example, a process statement is only valid in a specific population which differs from other populations in its social or cultural attributes, then one must necessarily assume that it is precisely these attributes which cause the phenomenon of the psychological process. Since, however, such superordinate ideological, social or cultural conditions themselves can be spoken of rather more as contents than as process elements, these apparent process statements likewise concern phenomena that can be defined regarding content, and require ideological, social or cultural description and explanation. Figure 2.1 depicts this context schematically.

The figure shows that our understanding of what appears as process or what appears as content depends on the degree of generality of the population being studied. The diagram depicts three partly overlapping areas of aggregation and phenomena from the most general and universal to the most particular and idiosyn-

Arrow indicates the direction from
the general and shared to
the particular and idiosyncratic

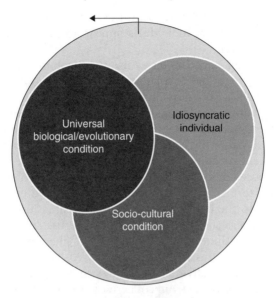

FIGURE 2.1 The relative relationship between content and process in psychological theories depending on aggregation level
NOTES: The darker and more overlapping an area, the more it appears to be a process with regard to the content of the lighter areas. The lighter an area, the more it appears as content for the processes described in the darker areas.

cratic.[9] The weight of the shading and the degree of overlap demarcate the different areas of psychological interest and is chosen in such a way that the area or aggregation level with a darker shading appears as a process with regard to the area or level with a lighter shading. Thus, in the opposite direction, the area with a lighter shading represents a content in process theories located at the higher level with a darker shading.

Ideally, we speak of a process in a narrow sense if there is a psychological conformity which applies to all members of an ultimately biologically defined human race. Psychological processes as such are only identified in the biologically defined individuals who make up the human race if they are independent of the subjective or idiosycratic contents of experience and thought, and independent of the contents of the sociocultural conditions under which an individual lives. There, individuals appear arbitrarily interchangeable and equivalent.

For illustration purposes let us use the attribution bias towards internal or situational explanations of behaviour (Ross and Anderson, 1980). If individuals *within* a culture consistently showed attribution tendencies that differed in different situations, then these situationally dependent attributions are the content to be explained either by sociocultural processes assigning significantly different meaning to the situations or by universal psychological processes that explain the differences between situations in evolutionary terms, as, for example, situations involving one's kin or strangers. In the latter case the finding of situation dependence of attribution bias should hold, of course, across cultures.

Let us now assume that a psychological phenomenon such as attribution bias is consistently different *across* cultures, such that subjects from more individualist cultures show a tendency towards more internal, and those from collectivist cultures show a tendency towards more situational attribution (Nisbett and Ross, 1980; Shweder and Bourne, 1984). In this case the fact of different attribution biases in different cultures are *descriptions* of *characteristics* or *traits* of particular cultures that are the content to be *explained* by cognitive processes at the universal level. If we pointed out that attribution tendencies correlated with other cultural traits such as individualism versus collectivism this would just constitute a description of the functional system characterising these cultures and be a dispositional explanation at best. Stating that individualisticaly organised societies motivate internal and that collectivistically organised societies motivate situational attributions is logically equal to stating that glass breaks when hit by a stone, but does not break when hit by a soft-ball. Both observations are consequences of the glass's, the stone's and the soft-ball's dispositions of brittleness versus elasticity. A hard explanation of consistent attribution differences across cultures can only be given by universal cognitive processes at the superordinate level which allow for cultures to be adaptive to local conditions and by a cognitive aparatus that enables attribution behaviour at all (for more details on this argument, see W. Wagner and Yamori, 1999).

The search for well-founded evidence differentiating the sphere of validity of social-psychological theories by and large corresponds to McGuire's (1983) demand for contextualism. Discussing logical empiricism, he remarks that

> a theory (like knowledge on any other level) is an oversimplified and distorted representation of any situation. It can be a brilliant cost-effective representation in certain contexts and dangerously misleading for others. Because all hypotheses are true, all are false. A hypothesis or its contradictory is each adequately true in a few appropriate contexts and each is dangerously false in many others. Contextualism's second disagreement with logical empiricism is its regarding empirical confrontation not as a test to determine whether the hypothesis is true or not, but rather as a continuing discovery process to disclose the hypothesis's full meaning by revealing its hidden assumptions and so specifying in which contexts its misrepresentations are tolerable and in which seriously misleading.
>
> (McGuire, 1983, p. 7ff.)

The validity of research depends on using a suitable research programme to check whether a theory is correct in varied contexts and, one must add, with varied populations. Empirical work with experiments should therefore not be understood chiefly as a testing of hypotheses, but as a heuristic programme to discover the peripheral reaches of a theory and the variants of phenomena.

If we assume independence between content and process in psychological phenomena, that psychological processes do not depend on what is being processed, then we must also ask why we would need to divide the psychology's subject matter into different realms of social-psychological and general psychological inquiry. Indeed, there are reasons to expect the biological bases of human psychology and cognition to differ across content domains. The natural habitat imposes problems that are sufficiently different from problems arising from group life and reproduction to expect domain specificity (cf. Barkow, Cosmides and Tooby, 1992; Hayes, 1999; W. Wagner and G. Wagner, 2003).

There are also reasons to suspect that content domains within culture modify the functioning of cognitive processes. In the following we will present some empirical evidence for this.

## Memory

A study on short- and long-term memory in Yucatan found that high-level mnemonic strategies lag more than a few years behind the expected level of development (D. Wagner, 1974, p. 395). Moreover, if school education is lacking, mnemonic strategies often do not become developed at all. At the same time the author touches on the close connection between educational content and the ability to think. If the content is missing, then processes do not become developed either. He showed, on the one hand, that variation of the memory, measured as recall, depended on years of schooling and not on age;[10] and, on the other hand, that the time elapsed between stimulus presentation and the test correlated with the number of items recalled only for those test subjects who could show at least five years of schooling. Samples from Morocco show comparable results (D. Wagner, 1978). Since schooling and age are hopelessly interconnected in developed countries, that is, educational effects inevitably vary according to effects of age, it is chiefly studies undertaken in less developed countries which can answer such questions. Do the 'higher memory functions', referred to by the author, therefore appear to be a content feature or a process feature? Can one speak of processes imparted at school, or are they rather contents (Cole and Scribner, 1975)?[11]

Comparable findings have been obtained in research on folk-mathematics in Brazil and multi-ethnic schools in Britain (de Abreu, 1995; de Abreu and Cline, 1998). A close relationship exists between the things that are being calculated, the content, and how the calculations are being carried out. This has to do with the societal valorization of different realms of life and the cultural identity of children.

## Attribution

Just as with the previous findings, there are many others which show that human inference can be both encouraged and hindered by the content as well as the context of a problem (Evans, 1991). A further example suggests itself in the 'fundamental attribution error' (Ross and Anderson, 1980), to which we referred earlier in this section. This describes the well-known tendency to explain the behavioural acts of others in terms of their dispositions, whilst supposing the causes of or reasons for one's own behaviour to be to do more with one's situation. Numerous experiments prove that this effect is at least partially influenced by perceptual factors, such as visual perspective (e.g. Storms, 1973).

A similar problem about distinguishing content and process was raised by Kruglanski (1979) in his experiments on the 'internal-external' distinction in causal statements within the context of attribution theory (Kruglanski, Hamel, Maides and Schwartz, 1978):

*Method.* A group of test subjects was presented with the task of deciding whether it was worth buying tickets for a film X. The other group had to decide whether John should be invited to a party on Saturday evening. The joint assumption by both groups was that John had already bought tickets for film X in order to see it on Saturday evening. The test subjects could choose from two sets of information: one set concerned the 'internal–external' distinction in causal judgements, i.e., the question of whether John wanted to see the film purely for his own personal interest (internal), or because film X is good (external). The second set of information concerned the 'endogenous versus exogenous' distinction of whether John wanted to go to the cinema because he absolutely wanted to see the film (endogenous), or due to the fact that he was bored (exogenous).

Although it seems as though the external causal dimension of the endogenous end – means distinction as well as the internal causal attribution of the exogenous one are equivalent and could be reformulated accordingly, their functionality actually differs for the two types of task of the two groups of test subjects. The causal dimension is useful for the first task of buying tickets, and allows the person to decide whether to see the film. The ends–means distinction is relevant for the second task of inviting John to the party. If John only wants to go to the cinema to fight his boredom, then he is likely to become enthusiastic about the party easily. In the other case this is not so. The results of the study confirm these expectations.

It is the teleological functionality of the information in relation to the task at hand which determines the attribution dimensions. The nature of the task determines the manner of the search for information, as well as the model of deduction which can be used to make a decision either for or against. Capturing but a small detail of life, the experiment shows that attribution processes and attributional dimensions, regardless of their type, are not universally and meaningfully applicable to all contents (or cover stories). They become an aspect of content when a superordinate theory about teleological functionality limits the scope of their validity. The psychological process depends on the concrete contents which are supposed to illustrate it.

## Cultural comparison

A social psychology concerned with solving process phenomena must start by establishing that specific behaviour patterns within a social group are theoretically and justifiably representative as a cultural phenomenon, and therefore an aspect of content. The Laboratory of Comparative Human Cognition (1979, p. 168) therefore demands theoretically justified observations inside cultural groups in order to identify culture-specific behaviour patterns which can be regarded as representative of the culture. These measures help us to carry out culturally comparative experiments, which permit us to define cross-cultural hypotheses, in the form of a statistical interaction of variables without resorting to main effects. This interaction of variables can then be compared across cultures (p. 154). The phenomenon to be replicated in the experiment is therefore the (statistical) interaction, and not the main effect of variables. Theories about such interactions are, according to the authors, independent of concrete contents.

One can deduce from this that social-psychological process theories and relations between situations and behaviour describe processes independent of content only if their hypotheses can be structurally replicated in clearly distinguishable social groups. If this cannot be proven, the theoretically relevant variables cannot be identified either as process or as content related. As a result, processes and the contents[12] cannot be distinguished other than arbitrarily or as an *a priori* assumption.

The above examples of attribution theory illustrate both the relationship between the operationalisation of content (set *(a,b)* in the formulae stated above), and between population contents (set {*P*}) and the postulated psychological processes. The first case, the studies on internal attribution bias, shows the influence of the type of definition brought forward to the situation by the subjects, which makes the same setting appear as two different situations. This makes the attribution process dependent on the population and its perspective. The second experiment on teleological functionality in attribution shows that if superordinate contexts are taken into account, process statements can become operationalised as contents.

## 2.2.3 Explanations for the interdependence of process and content

The relationship between content and process in cognition cannot be discussed independently of theoretical contexts of research orientation (the set of peripheral conditions *C* designated in the aforementioned formal model). Here there are three basic orientations which can be distinguished in the field of cognitive research: evolutionary-biological theories, theories relating to individual experience and learning, and socio-cultural theories. The Wason Selection Task (Wason, 1983) is frequently chosen for this kind of cognitive test.[13]

### Evolutionary explanation

The results from Cosmides (1989) provide us with a prototype example for an evolutionary explanation of context effects in the Wason test. She proposes an evolutionary perspective to explain the domain specifics of cognitive processes, according to which 'natural selection has shaped how humans reason by creating specialised, domain-specific cognitive mechanisms "designed" to solve discrete adaptive problems, by activating reasoning procedures appropriate to the domain encountered' (p. 190). Evidence in favour of this idea would be that the processes of deduction do not only differ according to the 'considered' content, but also take on a form in a predictable adaptive biological direction.

A biologically relevant domain, according to Cosmides, would be the logic of social exchange which has become genetically set in the course of human evolution. This would have given *homo*, who came on to the scene at least 3 million years ago, sufficient time for its evolution during his social existence as a hunter and gatherer, taking a generation to be around 20 years. A cognitive theory of social exchange demands the following two characteristics, according to the author (p. 196):

1. The human mind must possess algorithms which are in a position to estimate the cost–gain ratios in exchange relations.
2. The human mind must possess procedures of deduction which make it possible for it to recognise deception in social relations.

This means that individuals must be capable of recognising deception, so that they do not themselves have to pay 'fitness' costs without any compensatory yield. There is also a game theoretical claim according to which reciprocity in social exchange can only be established if the subjects in this exchange can recognise deception (cf. Axelrod, 1984; D. Buss, 1991).

In contrast to Cosmides, other researchers have postulated alternative interpretations of content-specific cognition in the Wason task. The main one is availability theory (Griggs and Cox, 1982; Johnson-Laird, 1983; etc.), but there is also the theory of pragmatic schemata (Cheng and Holyoak, 1985; Cheng, Holyoak, Nisbett and Oliver, 1986). Availability theory views the extent of experience in a particular area of life as a cause of domain-specific deduction processes. Accordingly, the logical inference made by test subjects in the Wason test is determined above all by the strength of the associated link between '*if p*' and '*then q*' contents.

In a sequence of experiments with the Wason test Cosmides (1989) was able to show that the predictions of availability theory, by contrast with the hypotheses of her social contract theory, were not supported:

*Method.* For this purpose, situations with the relevant dimensions within availability theories, namely the familiarity versus unfamiliarity of the content of a logical statement, were crossed with the dimension formal-abstract condition versus social-contract condition. This gave rise to four situations: (i) unfamiliar standard social contract; (ii) unfamiliar descriptive problem; (iii) abstract problem; and (iii) familiar descriptive problem.

The results show that the effects are mainly dominated by the hypotheses of social contract theory: in accordance with this model, most test subjects gave correct (*P AND NOT Q*) or (*NOT P AND Q*) answers in the standard social contract situation (i), even though it contained a relatively unusual example from a foreign culture. None of the other experimental situations achieved comparably high values.

## Individually acquired schemata

Cheng's and Holyoak's (1985) 'pragmatic schemata' theory asserts that people draw conclusions about true-to-life contents chiefly by means of preformed, relatively general and abstract production rules or schemata. According to the authors, these schemata are supposed to be formed via induction processes across aim-specific domains. Not just 'obligation schemata' and 'causal schemata', exist in our society. There are others such as 'permission schemata', which mean that one can draw conclusions economically in a pragmatically correct way when dealing with authorities and bans. Such a permission schema might consist of the following four production rules (p. 397):

| | |
|---|---|
| Rule 1 | If the act is to be done, then the precondition has to be fulfilled. |
| Rule 2 | If the act is not to be done, then the precondition does not have to be fulfilled. |
| Rule 3 | If the precondition is fulfilled, then the act can be done. |
| Rule 4 | If the precondition is not fulfilled, then the act must not be done. |

Many domain-specific reactions in the Wason test fit the criteria of pragmatic schemata postulated by Cheng and Holyoak (1985).

Above all, situations of social exchange can be subsumed under this approach since the basic rules of the permission schema mentioned above describe conditional statements which relate to social contents. Situations of social exchange are actually a partial set of all permission situations.

In three experiments, Cheng and Holyoak showed that people use schematic knowledge structures for drawing conclusions which can be distinguished both from knowledge about specific experiences and also from content-free syntactical rules of inference. If one can see a reason behind content-free tasks, for example in the form of permission schema, one solves the tasks more correctly than one would without this additional information. In like manner, concrete tasks which at least syntactically correspond to one of the postulated pragmatic schema are solved even by children (Girotto, Light and Colbourn, 1988) rather more correctly than arbitrary tasks.

## Sociocultural explanation

D'Anrade (1989) discusses the experimental results from Wason (1968) and Johnson-Laird (1983) in an interpretation similar to Cosmides's theory, but within a cultural frame. If the Wason deduction tasks, especially tasks of the 'modus tollens' form[14], are couched in contexts that are culturally coherent and of a content that is familiar to the test subjects, then it can be seen that those people are in a position to solve the tasks absolutely correctly. If the coherence is capriciously illustrated with arbitrary contexts, the tasks become much more of a burden to the test subjects and the solutions become markedly less correct.

The following examples show culturally coherent contexts of the Wason task for an American sample:

'If this stone is garnet, then it is a semiprecious stone.'
'If Tom was born in San Diego, then he is a Californian.'
'If Bill cut his finger, he would bleed.' etc.

Arbitrary contexts which were hard for the test subjects to solve in a logically correct way were the following:

'If James were a guard, then he would like sweets.'
'If Howard is in France, then George is in Italy.'

'If Janet went into town, then she brought some bread home.' etc.

Both the coherent and the arbitrary examples refer to potentially real situations of American everyday life. The difference lies in the content of the cultural background knowledge of the two groups of examples. Whilst the coherent examples describe contexts for which the average test person possesses cognitive schemata or scripts (W. Brewer and Nakamura, 1984; Rumelhart, 1984), this is not the case for the arbitrary examples. There is better performance only if the representation of the problem permits the test subjects to recall past experiences of the same content (Cox and Griggs, 1982, p. 497).

D'Anrade admittedly points out the fact that it is uncertain whether good performance in relation to garnets and semiprecious stones, for example, is actually to do with real personal experience, or whether it is actually cultural schemata and collective knowledge which enable the solution to be achieved (D'Anrade, 1989, p. 140).

> The reason for the differential performance has nothing to do with the context affecting someone, but simply relates to the fact that somebody has a certain well-formed schema made up of certain content which allows a kind of processing that the same person cannot do with a formally identical but less well formed schema made up of other content. Or, to put it another way, content is not something which lies 'outside' (the context) of the representation of the problem. This just seems to be the case when one assumes that the problem is something made out of a particular logical form, rather than something made out of specific content.
>
> (D'Anrade, 1989, p. 141)

The ability to draw logical conclusions is closely linked to the inventory of culturally available schemata. With regard to living together socially, it is these collectively shared images or 'cultural models' (D'Anrade, 1981) which enable logically correct conclusions to be drawn, since the logical structure is conveyed in and by the contents. This does not reduce the importance of relatively idiosyncratic schemata which are based on personal experiences. But even these were gained in a largely socially preformed environment, which granted space for the one type of experience but not the other.

In light of the arguments for a cultural interpretation of experiments using the Wason task, Cosmides's (1989) evolutionary discussion does not necessarily remain valid. From a long-term view it is of course the evolutionary processes which have helped man as a species to a social existence, thereby indirectly participating in the formation of social schemata. However, it is the cultural development stages of society that are relevant historically, and in terms of micro-genesis, which produce the psychological background of the phenomena recorded in experiments: 'Cultural schemata are crystallizations of past individual solutions to problems of human adaptation and adjustment which are socially shared and transmitted' (D'Anrade, 1989, p. 142). They are thus an immediate premiss of findings on the relative dependency of thought content and thought process.

### 2.2.4 Reasons for assuming independence

#### Arguments from logic

There is a reason for concentrating on the process whilst simultaneously abstracting the content, contexts and populations, and it is to be sought in the formal roots of scientific work. Formal logic and its understanding of form and content in propositions is primarily useful as a model for cognitive research.

In cognitive research, as in formal logic, the rules of logically correct conclusion should be independent of the logical proposition's content: 'Logic investigates the general characteristics of statements . . . which are not dependent on which form the terms have . . . and on which linguistic means are used to express . . . the logical operators' (Sinowjew and Wessel, 1975, p. 19). Therefore logical linguistic rules can in principle be applied to all existing languages, if one succeeds in translating the logical operators. Although terms and logical statements are always components of definite and real languages, logic itself is independent of the characteristics of these languages:

It investigates only such characteristics of terms, statements and logical statements contained in them as are independent of whatever is the language in which they are used. As far as logic is concerned, all languages are in a certain sense just components of a single (summary) language. Because of its own objectives, logic does not impose any rules which are suitable for one national language and not another, or which are applicable to the language of one science and not other sciences.

(Sinowjew and Wessel, 1975, p. 19)

If the science of logic has been successful in condensing a coherent system of universally valid logical language rules out of the varied repertoire of natural languages, then it seems obvious to look upon these language rules as a foundation of human thought – as a basis of the cognitive apparatus. Formal logic will then become the teacher of correct thought (Schmidt, 1969, p. 367ff.): 'Logic is therefore concerned . . . *with the most general structure of correct thought* [italics in original]. It discovers the rules behind the forming of concepts, statements and conclusions' (Klaus, 1973, p. 8). Presupposing formal logic as a model of correct thought, it follows that an empirical psychology of cognitive processes should attempt to reproduce precisely these rules in the thought and decision-making processes of its test subjects.

### An *a priori* decision

In addition to formal logical reasoning, the assumption of independence between content and form is (if we may use a casual expression) also required for pragmatic or other reasons (Zajonc, 1989). This happens partly for reasons of definition, for example if cognitive social psychology is to be defined as a 'pure' science implicating cognitive processes with social contents. Using the trick of keeping cognitive processes investigated by social psychology independent of concrete content, it becomes possible to generalise about research findings which were gained from narrow and specific sections of population. This would quash objections about the validity of research findings on account of a limited sample spectrum with regard to culture and age-objections about, for example, the almost exclusive use of university students in US experiments (Sears, 1986), or about the extremely limited, mostly written-verbal stimulus material in typical experimental settings of cognitive social psychology.

Tedeschi (1988) poses intercultural social psychology with the provocative question of whether it is essential to its progress to study the idiosyncratic psychological peculiarities of other cultures in order to apply the contemporary theoretical framework to them as well. He refers to them as 'platypus' cultures, arguing that a side–development of biological evolution as extraordinary as the duck-billed platypus is one which bears no relevance for biology in general, implying that the exceptions of idiosyncratic psychological processes and contents of isolated tribal cultures do not require generalising into existing mainstream theories. This is a legitimate concern as far as the pragmatism of social-psychological research is concerned, since its test bed is of course the population of the modern world. The cultural and social background determining the thought contents of test subjects is therefore considered secondary, whilst the process as the target of research is of primary importance.

This point deserves closer scrutiny. If social psychology defines its subject matter as the psychological processes and behaviour patterns which concern a special class of contents, namely social, then at the same time it makes a statement about the nature of the processes as well as about the connection between content and process. If this were not the case, then it could not justify itself as its own science with its own instruments and theoretical arsenal. Both types of psychological events would then legitimately be the subject matter of general psychology. Cognitive processes are an example which only count as part of the subject matter of general psychology if they deal with cabbages, and become part of the subject matter of social psychology if these processes concern kings (cf. Lingle, Altom and Medin, 1984).

### Natural and social stimuli

Ultimately, we are only legitimately entitled to distinguish between cognitive processes about 'natural objects' and ones about 'social objects' and make them a definition of two different sciences if we assume that these two classes of process also differ structurally. It only makes sense to distinguish social cognition from 'natural' cognition if the cognitive processes involved are different. This issue can be summarised by the simple statement that process and content are not independent of each other in the self-demarcation made by social psychology at the very start, but that the content, that is, the social, determines the nature of the cognitive process. Similar considerations can also be applied to general or the social psychology of motivation and emotion. Here we stumble upon a glaring contradiction between a relatively central internal decree of social psychology and its self-definition and demarcation from general psychology.

One of the most frequent arguments against the demand for ecological validity on the part of some social psychologists, is that the majority of the conditions which one meets in the field do not cause any fundamental difference in the processes investigated. These arguments serve to validate theories only through evidence obtained in the laboratory but not necessarily through investigations in the field. So it would suffice to study such processes under the artificial and reduced circumstances of the laboratory, and to generalise the findings to everyday situations. If this argument is correct, it raises the problematical question of why it should make any difference for psychological processes whether they are investigated using 'artificial' stimuli of 'natural' objects, or using ecologically validated 'natural' stimuli of 'social' objects. If the answer to the second question is 'yes, it makes a difference if psychological processes refer to natural or social stimuli', then the answer to the first question cannot simply be 'no' without provoking a contradiction.

One way to avoid the problem of ecological validity is to see experiments not as a simulation of the social reality, but as a realisation of a certain theoretical statement (Griséz, 1975). Accordingly, the laboratory is not in the business of creating a miniaturie replication of the exact circumstances under which real situations develop. Instead, the laboratory would be about constructing and implementing the essential parameters of a theory in certain conditions, and interpreting the results in theoretical contexts (e.g. Farr, 1976). The experiment would therefore represent not reality, but a theory. This view bypasses the problem of ecological validity by not taking the problem of process and content as its theme.

In our opinion the main reason that social psychology defines its subject matter as content-free is an attempt to 'measure up' to general psychology in the generality of its ultimately biological statements and laws, and not to be perceived as 'inferior' (Harré, 1989). This emphasis on generality derives ultimately from a perception of physical sciences as the template for all exact sciences.

As we shall see, the way that social psychology accepts the contradiction mentioned above as part of its scientific understanding raises questions about its being a discipline independent of general psychology. On the one hand it sees social-psychological processes as independent of the content of culture, while on the other hand it assumes that its existence as an autonomous science is necessary and justified, since the psychological phenomena that occur in everyday life and refer to social contents represent their own well-defined and distinguishable class of processes. These points, in our opinion, underline the need not to solve the issue of the mutual interdependence of process, form and content 'ex cathedra', but to accept it as an empirical issue (Evans, 1991; Goodnow, 1989).

## 2.3   One or two forms of thinking?

### 2.3.1   Belief and knowledge

There are no such things as souls or demons, and such mental constructs as Jehova are as fictitious as those of Superman or Santa Claus. Neither ghosts nor gods exert the slightest influence on men and their behavior. But men can and do influence the behavior of one another, and the ideas they hold can have a serious bearing on how they behave. The Crusades, the Inquisition, and Hitler's 'holocaust' illustrate, not strictly the power of ideas but the influence that can be exerted by men who hold particular ideas.

      (Murdock, 1980, p. 54, cited in Shweder, 1986, p. 168)

Probably the great majority of the population of the Western world would agree that souls and demons (especially with the latter being in the plural) do not really exist. The 'everyday man' in public often accepts, even if he does so with a cautious shaking of the head, the rationality of scientific evidence by contrast with superstition, divining-rod effects and other mental constructs that cannot be so easily categorised in the world-view of the natural sciences.[15] But since public evidence and private life are two different things, there are also some publicly rational people who are wary of black cats passing from left to right and will not risk seven years' bad luck by breaking a mirror.

## Knowledge and evaluation

Obviously, rationality in everyday routine only very unsatisfactorily agrees with scientific rationality. Although belief systems and the contents of everyday knowledge may be gained from the popularised views of Western science to a not insignificant degree, the basic structure of the logic associated with it and the criteria of scientific rationality are simply not valid. This is because the overburdened 'man on the street' lacks access to the methodological inventory, both materially in the form of laboratories, computers and equipment, and immaterially in the form of, for example, mathematics and formal logic.

Quite apart from the external difficulties of the validity of scientific criteria in everyday life, the interests and needs of everyday practice also differ from scientific practice. From the most congenial aspects of daily routine, to entertainment, conversation, making contacts, gossiping about neighbours and work colleagues, right up to dealing with one's own body, the many and diverse spheres of everyday life have to be dealt with, and in this the criteria of rational organisation and cognition are only peripheral. The criteria of what is good or bad and of well-being are, however, central. Scientific rationality cannot contribute anything to this end, according to its conception.

Evaluation and well-being, viewed superficially, may be idiosyncratic and subjective concepts which seem to have validity only for particular people. If, however, they had no collective root and the central ideas of them were not shared within entire cultures and societies, then there would, for example, be no annual tourist invasions of southern Europe. It expresses the collective yearning of the people to experience the same kind of enjoyment and well-being on the beaches of the Mediterranean.

The domain of values, well-being, desires and interests is usually dealt with in motivational and emotional psychology. If these values, the notions of well-being, desires and interests are, however, collective phenomena – a part of everyday consciousness and an integral component of everyday knowledge - then they also have influence on thinking processes in their wider sense.

There are numerous research findings on the interaction between motivational situations and cognitive processes. For example, explicit and cognitively monitored causal attribution processes only begin when an event contradicts an expectation in daily routine (Wong and Weiner, 1981). The nature of the attribution, such as whether an event is ascribed to the person or the situation, also depends on the scale of the expectation (Lalljee, Watson and White, 1982). If a possible causal explanation of a social event threatens the test subject's own identity, then this explanation is avoided and attributed differently (Snyder and Wicklund, 1981). The extent of positive or negative well-being and mood influences both the perception and the cognitive processing of stimuli (e.g. Clark and Isen, 1982; Clark and Waddell, 1983; Matlin and Stang, 1978; Wright and Mischel, 1982). Needs (e.g. Levine, Chain and Murphy, 1942) and threats (e.g. Bruner and Postman, 1947) control the organisation of perception.

## Belief

The distinction between 'belief' and 'knowledge systems' is closely linked to the issue of rationality and reason. In spontaneous usage 'knowledge' denotes what we personally take to be true, whilst 'belief' denotes those opinions of other people that are different from our own. Knowledge has connotations of being verifiable, factual. Belief expresses uncertainty and ambiguity. Knowledge always rises above a belief. The evidence is always on the side of knowledge.[16]

'You believe the world is round but we know it is flat' (Black, 1973, p. 511). What can induce a speaker to make this statement? Is it the saying of a philosopher who pre-dated the Greeks and still had no knowledge of the spherical form of the earth, or is it a provocation by science sceptics? The verb 'know' in this example does not give so much information about the quality of the statement as about the state of the speaker. A statement can only be described as knowledge if the speaker acknowledges its content as being sufficiently proven by evidence. The speaker is certain of the evidence of the content of the statement, whether his criteria be substantiated by way of scientific experiment or collectively. Both give grounds for trust and certainty. Social comparison theory (Festinger, 1954) investigates precisely this process of validation of either knowledge or the transition from 'believe' and 'think' to 'know'. In this way, the everyday distinction between belief and knowledge, ascribing to one's own opinion the status of knowledge and to the contrary opinion of Others the quality of belief, becomes relative and mostly ego- or ethnocentric.

## Ideology

The broad field of ideologies is even more complex and varied than the field of belief. These too, as far as their apologists are concerned, take on the character of 'knowledge' – which simultaneously assumes the thoughts of others to be metaphysical 'belief'. Discussion of this concept in the various social sciences, but above all in sociology, has reached a magnitude which refrains us from dealing with it unless we wish to risk an unjustified reduction of subject matter. Billig (1982) has outlined a comprehensive treatment of the concept for social psychology (see also Aebischer, Deconchy and Lipiansky, 1991; Augoustinos, 1998; Deconchy, 1989b; van Dijk, 1998). Furthermore, it appears that one can subsume the essential features and functions of ideologies for social-psychological purposes under the concept of 'social representations', which is discussed in detail later (cf. Jodelet, 1991a).

Scientific language often makes a distinction between microsystems and macro-systems of knowledge or belief (Black, 1973). At the same time, knowledge denotes the pragmatic-technological background of cultural systems, as is demonstrated in numerous studies of ethno-science, ethno-botany, ethno-zoology and so on. This field includes first and foremost the knowledge relating to natural objects used in the technological, medical and economic systems which safeguard life in a given society. The use of the term 'belief' preferentially applies to collective macro-domains which, for example, have to be attributed to religion, social philosophy and systems of morality[17] – that is, which correspond to the areas which Durkheim (1967) called 'collective ideas'.

## Two traditions

The remit of everyday knowledge falls between the two poles of belief and knowledge. Although there are sufficient reasons to suspect that spontaneous everyday cognition thoroughly differs from the reasoned attempt to solve 'hard-fact' problems, opinon is divided. Correspondingly, there is divergence between the theoretical approaches which are concerned with the relationship of everyday and scientific cognition.

Typically, the dividing line runs between views which see everyday epistemology as a special case of formal scientific methodology, and opinions which see everyday cognition as structurally different from scientific cognition. There are other divergent views within social psychology, for example in whether the consistency and validity of the opinions of everyday people – that is, of the overwhelming majority of all inhabitants of this planet – may be subjected to the criteria of scientific truth. Using formal logic as a reference is only appropriate when there is no reason to accept a structural difference in principle between the reference sphere (scientific methodology) and the object being compared to the reference (performance of ordinary people). If there is even the least doubt of basic common features, then the comparison with scientific reference would be out of place. Approaches which presuppose the uniformity of both cognitive fields are referred to as theories about the 'unified mind'. They derive almost exclusively from experimental social psychology and are illustrated by attribution theories standardised by Kruglanski (1980).

The opinions of other researchers contrast with this by at least admitting the possibility of a difference in principle. It is hardly surprising that they involve social sciences which are not directly connected with experimental social psychology. In spite of their fundamentally different methodology, theories about the 'divided mind' will be briefly presented here, using the example of cultural anthropology.

## 2.3.2 The 'unified' mind

### Traps of knowledge

Even if we only look at knowledge that is analogous to science, and disregard the complications of its interaction with values, motivations and emotions, we still encounter traps, errors and impasses which challenge the validity of the product of 'knowledge'. McGuire (1983) calls problems inherent to knowledge production the 'tragedy of knowledge'. According to him, knowledge production can be described in nine steps or phases in which each of the steps yields specific results and implies specific dangers: the first step, attention, for example, can go wrong due to arbitary focusing; categorisation can go wrong due to overestimating or underestimating differences; and using knowledge can go wrong due to improper simplification and biases. According to McGuire, the traps are not just an expression of the imperfectness of our minds; they are also inherent to the subject matter and circumstances of our world.

Errors may increase cumulatively from step to step, meaning that, should we ever arrive at a valid theory, we can count ourselves lucky if it really works when applied in the real world. Admittedly, this pessimistic diagnosis is countered by our experience with technical-natural scientific development. Pragmatically applicable knowledge is obviously possible in certain areas. But it seems debatable, to say the least, to assume that this optimism is also appropriate in the wider field of everyday knowledge.

## Attribution models as everyday epistemology

Attribution models have to do with explaining events in everyday life. In this respect they represent epistemological ideas which social psychologists attribute to everyday subjects. Most attributional models, being somewhat contradictory, create the impression of a disorganised epistemological pluralism proposing a specific attribution process for each everyday subject and situation. The idea of 'lay epistemology' reduces most of these approaches to their basics and standardises them (Kruglanski, 1980; Kruglanski and Ajzen, 1983; Kruglanski and Klar, 1987). In this approach, the phenomena being considered and their subjective perception/ evaluation are the basic components of knowledge.

Knowledge is generated through an epistemological sequence which generates cognition and which also validates the knowledge gained. Cognition-generation includes the processes which form hypotheses. 'Generally speaking, this process is related to the stream of consciousness (James, 1890) depending as it may on attentional shifts, the salience of ambient stimuli (Taylor and Fiske, 1975, 1978; McArthur, 1981; Rumelhart and Ortony, 1977), and the mental availability of various ideas and beliefs (Tversky and Kahneman, 1974)' (Kruglanski and Ajzen, 1983, p. 15). Although we may know something about 'why hypotheses are generated', the process of 'how hypotheses are generated' is still largely unknown.

Cognition is validated by applying a deductive logic which the authors see as special case of induction, and deduction by analogy (ibid., p. 13). A hypothesis is checked for its possible truth by deductively associating it with knowledge about facts which already exists and is considered valid. If inconsistency appears within the context of derivation, this brings doubt of either the new hypothesis or (probably less common) of the knowledge that already exists. The doubt may be quashed by searching for additional information, from existing knowledge resources or from observation. But the authors do not argue that subjective logic must necessarily correspond to the epistemological validation of recognised formal logic. They see individuals as 'subjectively logical', following a pattern of reasoning which specifically refers to their lives.[18]

The epistemological sequence of generation and validation in itself does not contain any criteria which freeze the process, since every hypothesis can in principle be subjected to constant doubt and unending attempts at validation. Individuals are led to freeze, but also to restart, or unfreeze, the epistemological process, by cognitive capacity limits and by epistemological motivational situations.

The motivation to search for knowledge and validation arises from a need for structure, or also for ambiguity. If there is no knowledge at all about a relevant field, then even a minimum of any newly gained structure that enables orientation is helpful. Mostly, however, individuals will demand that the newly gained structure makes allowances for their current needs. Such needs may be to do with maintaining or increasing self-esteem, such as the desire to draw functional conclusions which may make past actions appear correct, or make actions planned for the future appear in a favourable light. For exactly the same reasons, it may sometimes also be desirable to arrive at ambiguity and ambiguous conclusions in order to generate freedom of action.[19]

In a study of the collective convictions of Israelis and Palestinians, Bar-Tal (1990) was able to demonstrate conclusively how the epistemological motivations of the two peoples influenced their reception of information. He starts from the needs of both groups for existence and security. These needs produce selective reception of information on both sides, which serves to maintain a specific structure for the problem. The immediate reality of the needs implies that existing knowledge remains 'frozen' and does not acknowledge new information or the discovery of the other group's parallel needs. So any unfreezing of their attitude systems and epistemological activity is prevented, for as long as new knowledge seems to threaten the satisfaction of current needs. Attribution theories can be subordinated to this epistemological model as exceptions which appear suitable for certain contents and situations. Kelley's (1972) co-variation theory, in which circumstances such as place, time, situation or person are seen as causal for the phenomenon with which they co-vary, illustrates all situations which permit causal explanations, but not teleological or functional reasons. Jones and Davis's (1965) theory of correspondant inferences can be inferred from the protagonists' motives depending on situational limits. Weiner's (1985) theory of achievement motivations and reactive emotions is just as limited in its application. All these theories address certain content, which covers only a small part of all possible epistemological interests. Moreover, each of these theories loses its validity as soon as it oversteps its boundaries. The subject of everyday cognition has the freedom of epistemological pluralism: it uses its principles differently, according to the nature of the task and the motivation.

Lay epistemology emphasises epistemological plurality and the relativity of validity criteria in subjects' judgements in psychological research. At the same time it does not ascribe common-sense cognition any principle difference from scientific cognition, so the theory can be considered a model of a unified mind. It provides a continuity between the cognitive processes of everyday life and those of science, as formulated by McGuire (1983). The alternative would be to speak of two forms of thinking.

### 2.3.3 The 'bifurcated' mind

According to some authors everyday knowledge, or the general knowledge of peoples who do not possess written records, does not follow the process characteristics outlined in the previous section.[20] Rather, one can speak of two forms of thinking which characterise the 'bifurcated mind' (Moscovici and Hewstone, 1983, p. 101). One form corresponds to scientific standards such as 'critical', 'logical', 'domesticated', 'abstract' and 'formal-logical' thinking. The other is routinised or 'automatic' (Moscovici, 1982); 'prelogical' (Lévy-Brühl, 1921); 'savage' and 'concrete' (Lévi-Strauss, 1968); or everyday thought following a 'natural logic' (Grize,

1989; Schiele, 1984; Windisch, 1990). Although the opposition between the two forms of thinking are not defined and described to the same extent by each of these authors, they represent the same facts of the matter. The question is whether the two forms of thinking represent conflicts and complements, or whether one can ultimately see them as identical, simply relating to different areas. The following discussion will explore this question using the approach by Lévi-Strauss[21] and observations on so-called natural logic. Moscovici's ideas are dealt with in later chapters.

## Savage thinking

> I found it strange at first to live among the Azande and listen to naive explanation of misfortunes which, to our minds, have apparent causes, but after a while I learnt the idiom of their thought and applied notions of witchcraft as spontaneously as [they] themselves in situations where the concept was relevant. A boy knocked his foot against a small stump of wood in the center of a bush path, a frequent happening in Africa, and suf-fered pain and inconvenience in consequence. Owing to its posi-tion on his toe it was impossible to keep the cut free from dirt and it began to fester. He declared that witchcraft had made him knock his foot against the stump . . . I told the boy that he had knocked his foot against the stump of wood because he had been careless, and that witchcraft had not placed it in the path, for it had grown there naturally. He agreed that witchcraft had nothing to do with the stump of wood being in his path but added that he had kept his eyes open for stumps, . . . and that if he had not been bewitched he would have seen the stump. As a conclusive argument for his view he remarked that all cuts do not take days to heal . . . Why, then, had his sore festered and remained open if there were no witchcraft behind it?
> (Evans-Pritchard, 1976, p. 19 onwards)

'Well, quite!' is the reply that we feel tempted to give, especially if we can foresee the difficulties we would have if we wanted to famil-iarise the young Azande with our (everyday) medical knowledge. Perhaps it might still be possible to convey the idea of microbes which delay the healing of wounds. But if the other person were then to ask why and how these microbes have an influence on the healing process, most people educated in popular medicine would either have to give up or take flight into some sort of poisoning processes which cannot be more closely defined and whose bio-chemical details are unknown to them. The magical European word 'poisoning' can therefore ultimately be considered as shorthand for limits of knowledge; and has the same character as the term 'witch-craft' for the Azande.

The magical thinking expressed in this episode contains a theory of causes in which magic is only one element. Of course, a stump of wood on which one stumbles has come about in a natural way, just like a branch which falls from a tree and kills a man. Yet the fact that one neglects to pay attention at precisely the same moment that one goes over it, or that the branch falls down at precisely the same moment a man is sitting underneath, is something which requires an additional explanation which does justice to this anomaly – the conflict with the course of events that one normally expects (Geertz, 1983, p. 268 onwards). It is this explanation which conveys the idea of magic as 'a gigantic variation on the topic of the causality principle' (Hubert and Mauss, 1974).

Although there is also recognition of those causes designated as 'natural' by us, they have no meaning on the level of social relations. The link to the Social must necessarily be created in a world which is populated by personal forces and which reproduces the structure of the society (Lévi-Strauss, 1972, p. 58). Savage think-ing is a form of thought which takes into account the social con-texts and social implications of events. Things and events earn their significance in connection with the structure of society, for example in totemism.

But wild thinking is not just functional thinking, deriving zoo-logical or botanical classification exclusively from the economic sig-nificance of animals and plants for the tribe, as Malinowski (1975) assumed. Ethnographies and field reports show that indigenous peoples in their dealings with natural life forms develop an inter-est which far exceeds the latter's immediate practical usefulness. One could conclude that 'animal and plant species are not only known to the extent that they are useful: they are considered to be useful or interesting because they are known' (Lévi-Strauss, 1968, p. 20).

Wild thinking implies exhaustive observation and continuous stocktaking, thereby creating order in the world. Each event, each object is considered in the ritual act and allocated its place. The relations and contexts discovered in this way also lead to scientif-ically reproduceable prognoses. This is the case, for example, with the Blackfoot Indians who predicted the coming of spring by the level of development of the foetuses which they found in the wombs of the female buffalo that they hunted. But this knowledge is always most closely linked with the complete set of postulated magical contexts which impose a comprehensive determinism on the world of phenomena. Sheer coincidence, that magical concept of modern science, has no place in this world (Lévi-Strauss, 1968, p. 22).

Systematic observation must also have stood at the cradle of the earliest human discoveries. Without it one could hardly understand the 'neolithic paradox'; namely the fact that the most essential cultural technologies, without which even our contemporary civilisation would be unable to cope, date from the neolithic period: agriculture, weaving and pottery. School essay topics which present such achievements as imaginative attempts, explained by trial and error – or even more fantastically by the sheer coincidence of a willow wickerwork coated in damp clay falling into the camp fire, burning the wood and hardening the clay, thus creating the first piece of pottery in world history – are exactly what they say they are: the imagination of a society which only credits itself with creativity. This coincidence would have to be repeated several times before the eyes of the same observer in order to be recognised as a principle. On the contrary, each of these technologies requires 'centuries of active and methodical observations, daring and controlled hypotheses, which are either overturned or verified by means of exhaustively repeated experiments' (Lévi-Strauss, 1968, p. 26), doing great credit to the 'Einsteins' of early history and tribal cultures (Goody, 1977, p. 19ff.).

Wild thinking also founded a scientific tradition from which we still benefit today. This is not primitive style, but rather the first type of science as opposed to the second, modern style. The two sciences do not correspond to two developmental stages of the human mind. Instead, they represent two strategic levels 'for the understanding of nature through scientific cognition, in which the one level, broadly speaking, would have suited the sphere of perception and imagination, and the other would be detached from it' (Lévi-Strauss, 1968, p. 27).

According the Lévi-Strauss, magical thinking should not be seen as a preliminary step towards modern systematic and theoretical thought, as an incomplete, theoretically blind and contradictory replication, as it were. It corresponds to the 'shadow which reveals the body' (p. 25) and represents in its totality just as ordered, coherent and articulated a system as that of contemporary science. Wild thinking and science do not conflict with each other as opposites or as stages of development. They are two types of cognition which yield different practical results, although the mental processes which lead to these results are basically the same. It is not the cognitive processes which mark the two forms of thinking as different, but the phenomena to which they refer and the methods they use.

The first type of science might be best described as handicraft (bricolage) (p. 29ff.). It is concerned with concrete reality, accessible to direct exploration. Like a craftsman, it uses the means it has to hand – incomplete collections of tools and the remains of earlier crafts – to create new and practical objects and items. This also allows the old remains to take on new meanings and functions which their previous use could not have anticipated. In the same way that the framework of modern crafts is set by concrete demand and the availability of securities, speculative mythical thinking can yield unexpected results from old images. In their unorderly and unsystematic appearance, events and experience form the raw material for speculation: 'The peculiarity of mythical thought consists, as that of handicraft, on a practical level, in working on structured wholes, not directly with the help of other structured wholes, but by using the left-overs of events' (p. 35).

Wild thinking is generalising and systematic, in the best sense. It uses categories, comparisons and familiar analogies of the form 'the same begets the same, the part stands for the whole, the conflicting affects the conflicting' (Hubert and Mauss, 1974, p. 130ff.); even though its horizon of experience may be narrowed by the definite. It satisfies intellectual claims, since it is interest led and not just led by the obligation for physical survival. Above all, it is causal and guided by a comprehensive deterministic approach. Viewed this way, the magical contents of belief appear as 'forms of expressing a belief in a future science' (Lévi-Strauss, 1968, p. 23).

What distinguishes scientific thought from wild thought are: first of all, the objective methodical structures which modern thinking creates, and which are only made possible through writing and the logical control of consistency. Without writing there can be no formulated logic, without written lists there can be no retrospective control over what has passed. The real illiteracy of contemporary and past peoples without writing, as well as the 'illiteracy of the mind' in the everyday thought of modern people, represents one of the most fundamental arguments for the comparability of wild thinking with the 'wild' type of thought in everyday life. On the other hand, it is also one of the reasons why these two types of thought are the way that they are. The absence of writing limits this first form of science to objects in the here and now, to the daily stream of events providing the raw material for our intellectual 'handicraft', and to the possible contents of memory in a particular situation, given the present strivings and needs of the individual.

## Natural logic

Although the concept of natural logic is regularly used in connection with the theory of social representations, it actually highlights a point of view which distinguishes it from the theory being dealt with here. The term 'logique naturelle' is aimed at a dichotomy between scientific and everyday thought, the 'epistemological divide' (Schiele, 1984) between two worlds.

If two people speak with one another, then they require not only a common language of the same vocabulary and grammar, but also largely comparable worlds of experience as implicit knowledge. Grize (1989, p. 154) identifies communicative acts as a 'schématisation'[22] which comprises the following elements:

1. 'Schématisation' is the bringing into conversation of;
2. the opinion of the speaker;
3. which he or she holds about a certain reality sphere;
4. which is shared by one or several of the people in the conversation;
5. in a specific situation or context.

Conversational remarks may not mention the explicit opinions of the speaker, but more significantly they mention the underlying cultural constructs and semantic implications. At the same time, such remarks also contain the position of the speaker himself, *vis à vis* social intercourse in general, as well as in relation to the people he talks to in conversation.

The most fundamental feature of natural logic, however, is expressed in the relation between object and language. Grize

(1989) illustrates this using the example of a paragraph from La Mettrie in 'L'Homme machine': 'Together fall asleep Body and Mind. As the blood motion gets quieter a sweet feeling of peace and tranquillity gains ground in the whole Machine, the Mind experiences a growing drowsiness, so do the brain fibers; by this little by little it becomes paralytic, so do all the Body's muscles'[23] (Grize, 1989, p. 156).

Even though it is a written text, it shows clearly how the object of comment is constructed as the text progresses. At the beginning is the indistinct quantity of the body, whose figure only becomes clear as the argument shifts from the 'body' via 'the movement of the blood' to 'the Machine' (capitalised in the original), thereby condensing into a clear image. Natural logic – in contrast to formal or scientific logic – is therefore more than just a more or less formal apparatus of permissible steps of thought. At the same time, it is a logic of content (*logique des contenus*) which constructs the object being addressed, by naming it and rhetorically circumscribing it using metaphors. This, of course, has consequences for an empirical methodology attempting to reach out to natural thought. Analysing the argumentative structure of discourses is not sufficient, while qualitative studies do not take into account the cultural images and metaphors which bear the object constructed in the discourse, like a scaffold of supporting beams (Grize, 1989, p. 159).

The following operations of natural thought can be identified: unlike formal thought, natural thought does not draw inferences to support the coherence of its statements with the totality, or at least with essential parts, of what is already known; rather than deriving its statements according to deductive rules, it proves their accuracy by referring to images, and the weight of directly perceptible reality and their indubitable authority.

Natural logic uses at least two types of analogy. The first is the immediate everyday world experienced in housekeeping, which supports images of natural reasoning. Everyday practice: 'the manners of eating, the manners of sleeping, the forms of gardening, the professional activities constitute the practices among the people of the popular classes, which represent the potential place to integrate their way of thinking and the unique concrete frame of reference for their own knowledge' (Schiele, 1984, p. 65).

The second type of common analogy makes straightforward comparisons with the artefacts of technological civilisation: the camera as an image of the eye, the machine as a metaphor for the body, and the computer as a model of the brain. A reflexive change turns technical objects, whose beginnings go back at least partially to the imitation of human and animal body parts and the ways that they function, into the metaphor of their origin. The thought of humans is a product of their practice.

Natural thought, unlike formal thought, is not purely about describing things and facts. It also fulfils the more important role of showing social belonging whenever it is required. Relevant contents and social codes are set as an example of belonging, indicating conformity and thereby replacing extensive reasoning with the convincing argument of subordination. This is associated with natural argumentation's value-laden state, with its prescriptions which are always felt. Demands of morality normally replace the explanatory argument of good reasons. Although rules of conduct may be logically explicable from a viewpoint outside of a certain group or social unit and appear causally necessary; within group discourse such rules and norms appear as imposed on practice and are only in rare cases seen as negotiable by argument.

One of the consequences is that the common ways of thinking of various social groups are not only different but also only partly commensurable. Although representatives with different social allegiances may use the same words in the same context, they may refer to different things. So for example, if a xenophobic person speaks with a non-xenophobe or a feminist with a 'male chauvinist', the entities that each mentions (foreigners or women) are very different things (Windisch, 1990, p. 4).

Natural thought ultimately overgeneralises the scope of its validity. It is not the details of the circumstances which are important, but the whole picture into which relevant facts have to fit. In this way it satisfies the need for stability and certainty. 'The details, bare of all necessity, appear as accessories. They only serve for masking the substance through their deceptive and illusionary diversity.' (Schiele, 1984, p. 67)

The view here presents natural logic as a different form of thinking which does not compare easily with the scientific way of thinking. Each has its own areas of validity with specific needs, within which they are able to fulfil their functions. Outside the scope of validity, formal logic will fail the conditions of everyday life just as much as the logic of natural thought fails to produce scientific subject matter. This view proves to be an extension of the structural-anthropological approach by Lévi-Strauss into the fields of the modern world.[24] But the findings by anthropologists refer to times and places in which wild thought did not have to compete with the contemporary scientific apparatus, with its thought factories and laboratories from which the 'filth' and confusions of everyday life are excluded. In that context, this thinking was able to accomplish the technological achievements that were its own, in periods of time which are no longer available to contemporary everyday thought. In technical and natural cognition, the division of labour between everyday practice and science has settled the dichotomy of the world as a dichotomy of thought within one and the same person. It is different with social development and political innovation, which remain indisputable domains of wild thought with all its contradictions, temptations and dangers.

## 2.4  Excursus: using the rational model

As the previous explanations have tried to show, peoples' everyday deductive, attributional and thought processes only follow the rules of formal logic in exceptional cases. Both Kruglanski (1980, 1989) and the protagonists of natural logic mentioned earlier share this opinion. The consequences to be drawn from this, however, differ according to the scientific tradition, so that in the attribution and social cognition literature we still find the idea that the everyday person can in principle reason just like a scientist, who resolves scientific problems with the aid of statistical methods, in particular the model of analysis of variance.[25]

Lay people, for example, systematically neglect the base rate of statistical phenomena, using the prototypicality of cases rather than their actual logical weight in their inferences (McArthur, 1972). And in any case, cognitive categories cannot be as clearly demarcated as intensional logic requires. Rather, they are polythetical – that is, their elements show a 'family relationship', and are therefore inevitably blurred (Needham, 1975).[26] The question is whether the rules of formal logic and mathematical statistics represent suitable criteria for the thought processes of people in everyday life, or whether scientists model their subjects according to their own supposed way of scientific thinking; using an unauthorised general metaphor, an image of the human which attempts to portray their test subjects as miniature scientists (Gigerenzer, 1987, 1988; Gigerenzer and Murray, 1987).

Wygotski (1971) pointed this out with reference to works by Piaget. Normal adults try to acquire empirical knowledge about their environment, about the causes and consequences of phenomena and about contingent contexts. But neither knowledge of the canon of inductive logic nor the cultural 'deification of man as a scientist' of the West is a necessary precondition for this (Shweder, 1977, p. 648). In everyday practice, the acquisition of knowledge for the sake of discovering the truth occurs only in exceptional cases: 'All adaption to reality is induced by needs' (Wygotski, 1971, p. 46).

### 2.4.1 The bookkeeper model and the script metaphor

Gigerenzer (1988) demonstrates how scientists tend towards, 'taking the familiar action of the researcher as a metaphor for that unknown thing going on in the head of the person being researched' (Gigerenzer, 1988, p. 93) during the historical process of establishing different statistical models in psychological research. Statistical accounting as the normative model of thought processes means that any deviations from the prediction of the model in the test subjects' deductive and thought processes are seen as examples of bias and error. At the same time it depends on which statistical theory underpins the research. The efforts of the test subjects appear in a different light depending on the statistical theory used, whether it is Fisherian, Thurstonian, Bayesian and so on. As soon as the metaphor leading the research has been formulated, the methodology adapts to it and determines the behaviour 'observed' as a result (K. Gergen, 1986, p. 145ff.).

### The checklist metaphor

Another metaphor arising from the image of the 'intuitive statistician' is one which we will refer to as a 'list metaphor'. Statisticians, like bookkeepers, keep lists and records about the consequences of events. A statistician is obviously a person who in the simplest case has a paper in front of her and ticks checklists relating to the appearance of defined events. These checklists form the basis for subsequent countings. A precondition for statistics is therefore the existence of a form of writing which can permanently record the results of counting. In the same vein the counting logic applied to the checklist for statistical calculation presupposes the availability of writing.

The metaphor of the intuitive statistician implies the following experimental procedure:

1. The test subject is offered a series of stimuli;
2. a list of stimulus phenomena is created simultaneously or defined previously;
3. the test subject is examined about the preceding series of stimuli; and
4. the reproductions of the test subject are compared with the written list of phenomena; and finally
5. deviations of reactions from the list are interpreted as errors.

The most notable consequence of this (as we wish to call it) 'writ' or 'checklist metaphor' is the interpretation of any deviations of the cognitive apparatus from the incorruptible list as error. The list of stimuli offered in the experiment forms the reference for judging the performance of the test subjects. In this way, a link to the past – that is, to the preceding sequence of stimuli – is created, which largely excludes the present. However, the precondition for social survival as far as the everyday person is concerned is the need to concentrate on the present, the workings of the 'here and now'. It is much less concerned with the correctness of memory as analogous to a checklist.

The implicit use of checklist metaphors in methodological and theoretical research, manifest in the idea of the test subject as statistician, makes it seem obvious that processes comparable to checklists and writing should determine the cognitive operation of individuals. The 'cognitive homunculus' of the test subject is, however, (unlike the statistician) ignorant of writing and illiterate; and in any case, neuropsychology teaches that the old idea of the 'engram' as a list analogy is erroneous (cf. Coulter, 1983). But only the comparison of lists, that is, point (4) of the experiment, can justify the terminology 'bias' and 'error' by making the implicit structural analogy between the statistician and the 'statistics homunculus', as well as by reference to the past to judge perfor-mance in the present.

## Oral traditions

Goody (1977) refers to a similar problem in anthropology. He criticises the unreflected use of lexical lists by researchers, in an analysis of the consequences of literacy for the cognitive organisation of the people of early cultures: 'The table that anthropologists and others employ to study the "primitive classifications", the symbolic systems, the modes of thought of oral cultures is, then, a graphic method of analysing concepts and categories, the use of which raises major theoretical issues' (Goody, 1977, p. 74ff.).

Written records permit a conscious synoptic perception of the past and present 'whilst simultaneously allowing contradictions to be registered, from which reflection starts to form' (Bourdieu, 1976, p. 462). Spontaneous, everyday thought related to the current situation is therefore generally felt to be free of contradiction with regard to the past, because there is a lack of cognitive checklists similar to writing which would make a rigorous scrutiny possible. Checklists of historic events, such as the records of experiments, exclude the points of reference which determine the actual experience of individuals at the point of remembering. As a result, the errors of remembering and the cognitive biases that are found reflect a process which is irrelevant to the individuals themselves and their social living. An individual defined like this, as an object of cognitive research, constitutes a methodological artefact.

Written records are of course indispensable to research both in anthropology and psychology. No science can do without literacy – indeed, it only became possible because of writing. The real problem begins where the written record becomes the model or criterion for non-literal processes – as, for example, with oral cultures or cognitions which will always be 'illiterate', even in a literate society like ours.

The amazement of social psychologists about the 'recall errors' so stubbornly produced by their test subjects resembles to some extent the astonishment of the British colonial administration in Western Africa when they realised that their written records of the number of principalities in a west African kingdom no longer agreed with the oral tradition of the people. It turned out that one of the princely lineages had ended during the period of British occupation, and the existing but reduced number of princes had rapidly become justified and embedded in the people's mythology of origin. Since these myths were handed down orally, spread by professional storytellers, later generations could only go by them, so they always saw the number of current principalities as the justified and correct quantity (Goody, 1977). Did this make the myths false or distorted? Is it the job of myths to be correct at all? Were the British written records really valid criteria for judging the myths, or did they have another purpose? The administrative checklists had the task of ensuring colonial exploitation with as little friction as possible – a task which was probably foreign to the myths of the indigenous people. Whatever functional tasks may be read into the myths, whether reasons of 'state', stability of community or anything else, the administrative checklist is not suitable as a standard for the oral tradition, and the myths are not suitable as a standard for the execution of colonial tasks.

This example shows how the attempt to validate oral traditions by means of literate techniques is erroneous. Illiterate societies use different memory aids than literate ones. One example of a mnemonic trick of illiterate cultures is the use of geographical locations in which elements of myths and current and historical events are cognitively 'filed' (Harwood, 1976).[27] But locality establishes a synchronous frame of reference, and its diachronicity is robbed when historical processes are being recollected. As a result, orally traded knowledge in such cultures constitutes a virtually timeless condensate, of value only in limited circumstances and of use only for current information. Historical exactness is only sought if what has passed has had a concrete effect on the present; and even then the historical character of the event is not localised in a real-time continuum. For the most part, it becomes antedated to an ahistorical 'time of origin' which symbolises the beginning of the particular culture.

## Contextualisation

The pragmatic and functional demands that everyday life makes on the cognitive functioning of individuals, and the need to protect one's self-image even when recalling and reconstructing one's personal life story (Greenwald, 1980) are orientated (as are those of peoples without writing) towards the present. For example, experiences are very rarely coded verbally at the exact moment of the event. Reference is usually made to what has happened only during later questioning or in a spontaneous conversation. Only then is the experience verbally encoded:

> Talking is a creative process by which an underlying knowledge, to a large extent analogic in nature, is crystallized into propositional and linguistic structures. It is true that some, perhaps a great deal, of this crystallization will have taken place when the knowledge was first acquired. But much of it will not. And in order to explain things that we find in the use of language – such as inconsistency and hesitation in subchunking, propositionalizing, and categorizing, and even such a basic thing as the use of modifiers – it is necessary to recognize this as-yet-uncrystallized state of much of our knowledge.
>
> (Chafe, 1977, p. 245)

Previously acquired knowledge may not be instantly available in verbal form, but at the moment of verbalisation it becomes subject to the affective and cognitive conditions of the current context, just like oral *vis-à-vis* written language (Greenfield, 1972). Measuring the correctness of memory and cognitive processes to a diachronic standard such as written checklists would seem to be an inappropriate criterion. By contrast with structural features of the cognitive process, variations in the cognitive checking process like encoding, mnemonics and categorisation, appear to be consequences of schooling and cultural education (D. Wagner, 1978).

## Conventions

Forgetting and remembering are not abstractly cognitive processes and memory functions do not only depend on capacity and proficiency parameters – that is, the functional features of the cognitive apparatus. They also depend on social demands, which make forgetting and remembering into a social act (Shotter, 1990). 'Forgetting is not simply an issue of not remembering, nor simply of not remembering but once having known, seen, and so on, but is rather tied inextricably . . . to social conventions governing "the operation of memory" in practical affairs. Just as memory is tied to what is memorable according to standards of reasonableness available in culture, so also is forgetting tied to what is forgettable (for some occasion, situation, interactional context of disclosure)' (Coulter, 1985, p. 133).

Forgetting is subject to situation-dependent norms within social practice. It is also subject to different motivations. To open up, give away something, or conceal it, whether it is desired or not; whether it is open to scrutiny or not, depends on the issue at stake (Coulter, 1985, p. 137). To interpret forgetting or apparently false remembering as a defect may seem appropriate in a purely rational-normative point of view, but not in a social context.

Of course, analogies between illiteracy and the mastering of writing in cultures, and the view of the mind as illiterate as opposed to the experimental psychologist using writing, are not easy ones to draw. First, the literacy of a culture or of individual groups within a culture influences the type of social organisation, the possession of power by those who know writing, and the kind of possibilities for social control. Second, the use of written systems of recording changes some aspects of the way that the cognitive apparatus of individuals function (Goody, 1977; Goody, Cole and Scribner, 1977; Scribner and Cole, 1978; Wygotski, 1971). Although the vast majority of test subjects recorded in psychological experiments doubtless know how to write, there remains a remnant of illiteracy in the functioning of cognitive processes which must be taken into account in scientific interpretation. If the test subjects do not have recording instruments at their disposal, paper and pencil in the simplest case, then they are thrown back to relying on memory techniques corresponding to those used by members of oral cultures. Therefore, the consequences of non-written remembering can on a number of points be compared with the schemata valid in such cultures. These are the embedding of diachronic contents into synchronic ways of representation; the consideration of current pragmatic needs (i.e., the contextualisation of contents); and also the regulation of the processes of remembering and forgetting by social norms.

## 2.4.2 Criteria of validity

### Criterion validity

The preferred criteria for evaluating human cognition used by experimental social psychology derives from the application of normative models as well as the judgement of the researcher (Kruglanski and Ajzen, 1983). All criteria based on statistical and logical methods of science derive from normative models. Methods such as Bayes's statistics, Fisher's inference statistics and propositional logic are used to measure the reactions of the test subjects. These methods were developed to ensure the best possible functional presentation of real facts, as demonstrated by physical objects, for example, in agriculture and physics. But these types of veridicality are only rarely required for everyday life. If we accept those criteria, then the sole option for helping people reach correct opinions would consist of tutoring them in the canon of scientific thought and empirical work (Ross and Lepper, 1980). Whether this 'ideal' can be reconciled with the demands of everyday life is a different question.

Many facts can also be verified by direct observation. If, for example, we wish to know which numbers came up in the last rounds of a game of roulette, we can create a list by observation and check the sequence at any time. This, admittedly, only on the banal condition that we have at our disposal a piece of paper and a writing implement in order to satisfy the list criteria.

For some problems involving test subjects in experimental situations, it is the judgement and knowledge of the experimenter which forms the sole criterion for correctness. The person in charge of the experiment is the only person who knows all the details of the experimental situation and what they are all about. The well-known experiment by Ross, Amabile and Steinmetz (1977) is an example. In this, the experimenters first define the situation in front of all the test subjects by randomly selecting two people: one to take on the role of quiz master, and the other to answer. The quiz master is encouraged to pose questions, derived from his or her personal field of interest, to the other person. The other person is barely able to answer, normally, since they do not happen to possess the same expertise. It comes as no surprise that the test subjects observing the experiment ultimately judge the quiz master to be more intelligent and knowledgeable than the person answering.[28] Of course, such situations occur very seldom in ordinary life, or if they do, then they always arise from certain combinations of motives, such as the person wishing to increase their self-confidence by provocatively demonstrating their expertise. If we are aware of this background, then we can minimise the likelihood of making a precipitous judgement about intelligence and knowledge, even though cheaters will still often succeed. The bare situation is hard to assess when background information about motivations is lacking. It is only the experimenter who knows that – in this case – direct observation is the key to verification.

If one sees – as in social psychology – the goal of cognitive processes in their technical functionality – that is, in cognition's ability to reproduce a field of causalities and object relations and apply formal logic to produce correct conclusions – then statistics is indeed the suitable model for distinguishing between faulty and correct thought processes. If, however, the critieria of social psychological inquiry have to do with coming to terms with everyday life, with its blurred conditions and concepts, then only that same everyday practice can be an acceptable criterion. In order to be able to formulate this criterion, it is ultimately necessary to measure the conditions of everyday practice and the demands made on its protagonists, that is, its pragmatic functionality. If this is not done, the model of the everyday person as a scientist, statistician and bookkeeper very quickly becomes the Procrustean bed of social understanding in everyday life.

For example, Lave (1988), in her research into the everyday use of arithmetical ways of thinking (e.g. simple calculation operations when shopping), found deviations from the formal-mathematical model of rational decision making. These deviations did not come about due to calculation errors, but arose from consideration of multi-layered and highly complex peripheral conditions – the result of the idiosyncratic conditions of people's lives. In the case of a choice between a small bag of sugar and a bag twice the size which was somewhat cheaper, the decision in favour of the cheaper bag was not made 'automatically'. The choice was decisively modified by taking into account such fuzzy peripheral conditions as storage room at home, the next shopping trip, consumption of sugar in the family and so on – that is, parameters which are in no way directly connected with the immediate decision to purchase. For this reason the decision made, or whatever other decision might have been made, might not have been less rational, but at least differently rational than the one prescribed by a normative model.[29] 'Problem-solving operations that occur in everyday life follow different rules of practice than those typically discovered in the laboratory and on which much of our understanding of cognitive processes has been founded' (Sampson, 1991, p. 283).

## Criterion relativity

We have criticised some of the criteria which are regularly applied to everyday cognition since they are only rarely reconcilable with practical dealings. Another point of criticism is raised by the theory of lay epistemology, (cf. Weimer, 1976), which is based on a 'non-justificationist' theory of science. This points out that a necessary premiss of criteria is that they represent normative and therefore true knowledge within the bounds of what is possible, and thereby do justice to their own claim. Users of these particular criteria must therefore distinguish between facts (the findings gained by lay people when using their own criteria) and hypotheses (their assumptions). Only if the assumptions of the test subjects do not correspond to their own facts, can they be false or be subject to bias.

Other theories of science, however, relativise the distinction between hard facts and mere assumptions (Kuhn, 1970; Lakatos, 1974; Manicas and Secord, 1983; Popper, 1972). According to this, all knowledge – including established scientific fact – only constitutes relative truth which must be viewed both in historical perspective and in relation to current situations. This viewpoint may appear to be banal, and a repetition of philosophical knowledge which is almost taken for granted. But it is not banal if social psychologists do not take into account this relativity in their interpretations.

This is not meant to say that the veridicality of various statements cannot differ. It may be that 'anything goes' in the field of knowledge (Feyerabend, 1978), but not 'everything'. With normative models we can never say how well the theoretical construct actually maps 'reality' (Kruglanski and Ajzen, 1983, p. 17 onwards). This is true both of models that are formulated in natural languages and of those in formal languages. It is only inductive knowledge whose truth cannot, in principle, be precisely established. Even if we are successful in using technical knowledge to create masterpieces of technical development, alternative methods and alternative knowledge might have been just as useful, and that possibility can never be ruled out. Above all, it cannot be established whether knowledge gained with scientific methods is actually more correct than knowledge using alternative methods – for example, knowledge gained using everyday thought about everyday problems.

The same goes for validation by means of direct observation. A fact gained from observation is just as much a conceptual construct as any other hypotheses – as consistently demonstrated by the psychology of perception. The views of the experimenter are equally inadequate as valid criteria, even though he or she may have conceived the experiment. Differing perceptions of test subjects about events in the laboratory may allow just as valid hypotheses as are normally only ascribed to the experimenter.

## Perspectives

Metaphorically speaking, the individual in everyday life takes on the role of the experimenter if he exercises at least partial control over the setting in familiar situations. In so doing, he possesses more background information regarding such natural surroundings than for the artificial ones of the laboratory (Funder, 1987; McArthur and Baron, 1983). The local correctness of the naive subject (Swann, 1984) making judgements is very hard to simulate under laboratory conditions.

Vallone, Ross and Lepper (1985) asked two groups of test subjects to assess the media coverage of events during the so-called 'Beirut massacre' of 1982. Unsurprisingly, pro-Arab test subjects judged both the course of events and the background to them completely differently from pro-Israeli test subjects, even though they had the same information sources at their disposal. Similarly, and perhaps also understandably, the perceptions of those who took part in a violent riot in a city in England differed very considerably from the perceptions of observers of these events who did not take part (Reicher and Potter, 1985). Although the second example also involved differences in perspective for the respondents, subjects in the first example generated different perceptions from the same visual, though not social, perspective (cf. also the results of aggression research in Mummendey, 1984).

This raises the question of which contents accompany the perception and assessment of social events, and determine the 'correctness' or 'incorrectness' of the responses (Kruglanski, 1989). While the psychologist, who wishes to ascertain the correctness of test subjects' rendering of the course of events, refers to their physical representation, this is only half the truth for subjects with a symbolic investment. Perception in real contexts refers only peripherally to the physical situation. A video film of the events therefore does not constitute a criterion on its own, since it first requires an observer. Social perception takes into account the previous conflicts between social groups, includes the actual motivations of the various parties involved, the aspects of the groups' self-perception, the dynamics inherent to the event, as well as the assessment of their ideological backgrounds and the resulting damage. These elements implied by the situation develop from similar experiences and the knowledge derived from contact with others taking part. Consequently, the people involved in social events lose some of their anonymity for the respondent, and thus violence loses some of its destructiveness (Reicher and Potter, 1985). The fact that experimenters mostly miss the shared experiences of all the groups of test subjects involved in the experiment makes experimenters themselves singular cases, with perceptions that diverge from the judgement of real test subjects at least as much as the test groups themselves differ from each other.

Since social judgements are always judgements about the actions of other people, any measuring the correctness or incorrectness of social cognising must take into account:

(a)  the subjective criteria of the individuals, their point of view of what is the case (criterion judgement);
(b)  their version of how the target person or target group perceives or understands the facts of the matter (target judgement); and
(c)  their perception of the correspondence between the two (Kruglanski, 1989).

The many factors involved in social judgment implies that we need to be cautious when dealing with the categorisation of errors, and distortions of judgement on the basis of established criteria. It is doubtless necessary, by the nature of many experimental tasks, to qualify the performance of test subjects. But the standard which is used to qualify performance must always be orientated towards the demands of the situation as they are perceived by the persons being assessed. In a way this is a circular demand, as it were, since knowledge about the performances to be measured is also a prerequisite for designing the measurement procedure and criteria. A comparison of these performances with the epistemic possibilities of science (as the said criteria suggest) ultimately only shows that science looks at things differently from the individuals whom it pretends to judge. And it would hardly occur to anybody to want to measure the effectiveness of science according to the criteria and pragmatic needs of everyday life. We fear very much that if someone were to do it, then the canon of scientific methods will fail this task.

# Chapter 3

# Universes of Everyday Knowledge

## 3.1 The pragmatic imperative

The two metaphors, of the everyday human as a naive scientist and of the literate mind, involve criteria for human cognition based on normative efficiency. But, as we have seen, these are not necessarily valid. We need to seek out different criteria, looking first at the practical tasks and needs for which the cognitive apparatus is used, and thereby setting the criteria in terms of their optimal functioning in everyday life. Cognitive processes have to be adequate for this optimality, in order to satisfy the practical interests which, at any one time, are the centre of the cognitive apparatus's attention (White, 1984, p. 334). That leads us on to consider the forms of pragmatic logic and heuristics on which these criteria are based and it becomes apparent that they involve strategies which, in the scientific sense, are largely suboptimal – it is not about satisfying criteria based on scientific truth, but it is about safeguarding social survival.

Social survival has little to do with physical survival. If physical survival were to depend on the correctness of the decisions which direct our behaviour, there would be no trying; a wrong action ends the life of the living being, and prevents fresh attempts to put it right. The survival reactions of all organisms are actually based on experiences which have formed the gene pool of each species over the course of several million years. But this is very different from actions which are meant to safeguard social survival. In the overwhelming majority of cases, social actions are repeatable, changeable – even retractable (by apology, for example). Most of the time, too, there is more than one set of actions which can safeguard social survival. The fuzziness of social situations and the complexity of their contexts means that action sequences can achieve their aim more or less successfully in a variety of ways, ranging from adapting to social conditions, to actively forming them. Furthermore, each society offers many kinds of 'ecological niches' which allow its members to change their immediate social environment according to their ability and needs.

## Being affected

The cognitive requirements of people in everyday life are fundamentally different from those of the scientist because of real life day-to-day demands and the need to solve immediate problems as they arise. Scientists approach their problems as outside observers, not as people directly affected by them. Neutrality and distance vis-à-vis subject matter are preconditions for scientific problem solving. Many techniques have been developed to ensure this distance, thereby enabling science to be pursued with some degree of objectivity.

Another fundamental difference between scientific and everyday actions becomes apparent if an action fails. If a scientific experiment fails, or if a theory turns out to be false, this does not affect researchers directly (leaving aside the fact that they are part of an institutional academia which demands results). Everyday people, on the other hand, depend in a very different way on events in their environment and their reactions to them. The consequences of acting in the wrong way may be relative to the situation, but they can affect people's social lives – very unlike scientists pursuing the abstract truth of an idea or hypothesis. This direct relevance of their dealings means that cognition relevant to everyday life involves a fundamentally different perspective for everyday people, who need efficiency, economy and speed (Hansen, 1985). Perception and thought are not treated as independent in everyday life. They are used for taking action and, in a wider sense, adapting to circumstances (Zebrowitz, 1990, p. 178). It is not about the survival of a theory or a hypothesis, but the identity and social survival of the people themselves. Shotter (1978) describes this relevance of everyday actions incisively as a 'standpoint in action'; with the implicit cognitive activity being 'thought and language in use' (Windisch, 1990).

## Action imperative

In everyday life, people see themselves constantly confronted by the necessity of taking action – from having to concern themselves with objects, such as sawing off a branch in the garden or connecting up a recently bought stereo system, to initiating an encounter with people around them, such as submitting a request to an official or breaking news to their partner. We already have strongly automised programmes of behaviour, which require no further reflection, at our disposal, which we use for frequently occurring actions. But when no well-learned behavioural pattern exists for an action or set of actions, it is necessary to activate our own experience about the required knowledge, the object and our interaction partner, and then plan the action accordingly. This knowledge, along with attitudes and opinions about it, are an immediate prerequisite for action. They must be known, or at least believed with appropriate certainty, if effective action is to be possible, since behaviour based on clear and secure knowledge is more likely to be effective than hesitation triggered by uncertainty and half-hearted opinions and attitudes. Both everyday action (at least to the extent that it is not routine) and affectedness require an 'unequivocal behaviour orientation' (Jones and Gerard, 1967).

Ambivalence or an admitted lack of knowledge paralyses the ability to act. It is probably better, pragmatically speaking, to act on the basis of faulty and potentially incomplete knowledge than not at all. Each action changes the field of action and cognition and potentially opens up new perspectives, so that one can approach the goal of the action iteratively rather than by fruitless contemplation. This muddling through, as it were, can be observed in everyday decisions of a private nature as well as organisational decisions; and also whilst actions take place (Kirchler, 1989a, p. 237ff.; Lindblom, 1979; March and Olson, 1986).

One cognitive effect of the action imperative is the tendency for people to hold extreme attitudes and to increase the certainty associated with them whenever a directly related action is to be dealt with (W. Wagner and Gerard, 1983a).

*Method.* Eighty-six test participants were divided into 2 × 2 × 2 groups, according to the immediacy of an action to be dealt with (now, later), the time to consider the action (2 minutes, none) and the predetermined topic (2 topics). Each participant was used as an experimental participant for the one topic and as a control or monitoring participant for the other topic. They were instructed to have a discussion with others about one of the topics, and to prepare appropriate arguments. The other topic was not earmarked for discussion. In addition they were to give their views on the topic being discussed, as well as the certainty of their views. The extremity of the views on the control topic was deducted from the extremity of the views for the action-relevant topic, so as to control for arousal effects. Both topics showed moderate extremities of views on average in the population.

The results show that views become more extreme and stronger, depending on how immediate the 'threat' – in the form of behaviour related to the opinions in the discussion to be undertaken – is to the test participant (see also Gerard and Wagner, 1981; W. Wagner and Gerard, 1982).

But if this behaviour is, for example, a discussion about the topic of attitudes, then another cognitive possibility is open to the test participants. If they are given time to think before they respond to their experimental tests, and in anticipation of the discussion, they tend to moderate their views enormously. This is probably in order to secure diplomatic flexibility in conversation (Wagner and Gerard, 1983a).

This moderation can be quickly reversed, though, if an anticipated action is cancelled (Cialdini, Herman, Levy, Kozlowski and Petty, 1976; Cialdini and Petty, 1981). These experimental findings illustrate only a small fraction of the cognitive effects which can be elicited as a result of action or behaviour. The subsequent cognitive orientation is anything but strictly rational; and this holds true for many of those effects. Neither overestimationg the certainty of one's own views when there are extremes, nor moderating one's own extremity of opinion are based on any rationality substantiated by new 'data' or 'discoveries'.

Actions always pose a potential threat to one's self, or one's self-image. Will I sail through or fail in a performance situation? Will I be able to present my viewpoint appropriately in a conversation or discussion? Will I embarrass myself in an encounter with a respected person, or will I stand up for myself and be able to confirm my self-image? The self-reference of actions implies constant, fundamental judgements and affect – judgements of the situation, of one's partner in the interaction, and of one's self. Diary studies gathered by the individual over a period of time prove this judgement tendency. It is mainly seen in situations with high motivational pressure and high social implications (Brandstätter, 1981).

## Tasks and situations

It is almost impossible, but also actually superfluous, to list everyday tasks in their entirety. All readers possess their own trove of experiences, which is certainly more complete than could be portrayed here. For this reason, only a few studies dealing with the everyday life of individuals or couples are outlined here (Brandstätter, Barthel and Fünfgelt, 1984; Brandstätter and Wagner, 1989; Kirchler, 1984).

*Method.* Test participants kept a standardised diary in the form of a short questionnaire in which they entered, amongst other things, how they felt at the moment, where they were, what they were doing, who was with them right then, what they attributed their condition to, and how free or unfree they felt in their activity at that moment. This questionnaire was filled in at randomly predetermined times on average four times a day over a whole month (for the method cf. Brandstätter, 1981). The fact that the questionnaires were answered over a relatively extended timespan made it possible to ascertain a certain representivity in the recorded situations.

Table 3.1 gives an example of the kinds of activities, the variety of locations and interaction partners in everyday life.

TABLE 3.1 Relative frequency of activities, locations and interaction partners in the everyday life of housewives, compared with men and women working away from home

**Everyday activities**

| Housewives | | People working away from home | |
|---|---|---|---|
| Cooking | 0.117 | Work | 0.24 |
| Washing dishes | 0.039 | Job-seeking | 0.00 |
| Tidying home | 0.112 | Private matters | 0.04 |
| Washing | 0.024 | | |
| Ironing | 0.018 | | |
| Shopping | 0.037 | | |
| Sewing | 0.015 | | |
| Repairing | 0.005 | | |
| Appointments with officials | 0.002 | | |
| Visiting the doctor | 0.004 | | |
| Other work activity | 0.046 | | |
| Looking after children | 0.044 | | |
| Miscellaneous activity | 0.031 | | |
| *Free time:* | | *Free time:* | |
| Eating | 0.086 | Further education/ training | 0.03 |
| Watching television | 0.089 | | |
| Social get-togethers | 0.076 | Pastime | 0.02 |
| Relaxing, doing nothing | 0.073 | Sport | 0.01 |
| Reading | 0.053 | Conversation | 0.28 |
| Other leisure activity | 0.043 | Going for walk | 0.01 |
| Sport | 0.021 | Eating/drinking | 0.15 |
| Walking in the town | 0.021 | Sex | 0.03 |
| Pastime | 0.018 | Going to the toilet | 0.03 |
| Games | 0.016 | Doing nothing | 0.10 |
| Further education/training | 0.007 | Other | 0.05 |
| Sex | 0.004 | | |

TABLE 3.1 continued

## Everyday locations

| Housewives | | People working away from home | |
|---|---|---|---|
| Living room | 0.299 | At home | 0.48 |
| Kitchen | 0.279 | With friends | 0.04 |
| Bedroom | 0.063 | Company | 0.21 |
| Children's room | 0.024 | Shop | 0.05 |
| Bathroom | 0.039 | Venues | 0.01 |
| Other homes | 0.049 | Entertainment venues | 0.09 |
| Restaurants | 0.016 | Sport places | 0.03 |
| Hotels | 0.015 | Countryside | 0.01 |
| Cinema/theatre/concert hall | 0.007 | Town | 0.07 |
| | | Other places | 0.01 |
| Sports field | 0.015 | | |
| Authorities | 0.007 | | |
| Shops | 0.035 | | |
| Countryside | 0.016 | | |
| Streets | 0.020 | | |
| Public transport | 0.008 | | |
| Own car | 0.027 | | |
| Hairdressers | 0.001 | | |
| Doctor's practice | 0.007 | | |

## People present

| Housewives | | People working away from home | |
|---|---|---|---|
| Partner | 0.412 | Nobody | 0.17 |
| Alone | 0.246 | Partner | 0.19 |
| Own children | 0.185 | Children | 0.02 |
| Strangers | 0.037 | Parents/brothers and sisters | 0.06 |
| Acquaintances | 0.030 | | |
| Parents | 0.025 | Friends | 0.17 |
| Friends | 0.020 | Relatives | 0.02 |
| Relatives | 0.019 | Acquaintances | 0.25 |
| Other children | 0.016 | People in authority | 0.04 |
| Officials | 0.005 | Strangers | 0.09 |
| Neighbours | 0.004 | | |

NOTE: A relative frequency of 0.001 corresponds to approx. one minute. The working men and women were unemployed shortly beforehand (in H. Brandstätter, Barthel and Fünfgelt, 1984; Kirchler, 1984).

The large number of social situations and tasks mentioned in the studies ranges from housekeeping, securing daily income and financial 'survival', and conversations in communication and contact with others which comprises self-representation, influencing other people, or simply the pleasure which can arise from a contact.

Everyday thought develops in the tension of the situation. That tension is specified by the location, time (time of day, year and lifetime), the people present, and not least by the activity or task confronting the person: 'Everyday thinking unfolds within time and organises and transforms its objects according to a particular task and in function of a certain aim' (Caron, 1983, p. 13). Given the repetitive organisation of everyday life, thought contents, objects and judgements take the form of either 'repisodic' (Neisser, 1981) or prototypical cognitive structures, in order to satisfy constantly recurring demands. If the continuity of the repetition falls apart, it reveals the limit of common-sense's scope of validity, as shown by the somewhat provocative experiments of ethnomethodologists, for example (e.g. Garfinkel, 1967).

The kind of actions with which an individual in a certain situation responds, or takes as a reaction to events, depends just as much on the objective characteristics of circumstances as on the expectations, needs and tasks which the person brings to it. This interplay produces the 'demand characteristics' of situations which are stressed by ecological approaches in perceptual psychology (e.g. Gibson, 1979). 'A woman affords loving by some perceivers but not others. The affordance concept thus facilitates the integration of perceiver and target effects on social perceptions' (Zebrowitz, 1990, p. 178).

Testing out the multitude of possible combinations of locations, activities and people present explicitly on each of their demand characteristics would completely overwhelm the capacity of any empirical investigation. But there are efforts to try to find empirically useful situation classifications by reducing complexity through limiting conditions (see Argyle, Furnham and Graham, 1981). The variability and variety of everyday conditions, which as a rule one cannot choose oneself, demands of the participant an immediate and spontaneous readiness to act. Personal constraint and direct dependence on the results of taking action imply a high degree of affectedness, which is expressed in value judgements.

## 3.2 Pragmatic orientations

Everyday-life problems require orientations from everyday people that are different from those people working in scientific or other highly specialised jobs.[1] The previous discussion on the forms of thought and the pragmatic demands of everyday practice implies that these heuristic orientations should be investigated in three aspects: (a) reference to the concrete; (b) the power of similarity; and (c) the need to substantiate and explain. The three orientations or dimensions represent a condensation of differing social-psychological, and also anthropological, findings which characterise everyday epistemology.

### 3.2.1 Reference to the concrete

Concern with practicalities leads to an orientation toward concrete, particular, and everyday information, and toward processes most directly interactive with practicalities, such as behavioural skills. Judgmental and inferential processes are designed, therefore, for information of a concrete nature. Although this does not preclude the use of abstract and statistical information, the development of abstract, general beliefs, or a desire to make correct, accurate inferences. These tendencies are limited in extent and are invariably subservient to practical concerns as the preferred direction of inference for the layperson is from concrete to abstract.

(White, 1984, p. 334)

Generalisations from everyday cognitions are not independent of their context. Their meaning is conveyed through interaction between the action, the situation, and 'what ought to be done'. Entry into the everyday world, with its norms, recommendations and taboos, confronts us immediately with a widely differing range of conventional, legal and moral codes, and their implicit judgements. Most concepts contain evaluative components as well as descriptive aspects, and social categories in everyday life have more to do with consensus, tradition and morality than with the search for universally valid statements (Shweder, 1980, p. 265). The term 'wife', for example, is not only defined by lexical defining elements, but also (and not least) by prescriptive elements such as 'one should not deceive her', 'one must love and respect her' and so on.

Also, those prescriptive elements depend on the person who is thinking the concept, for example, whether it is the husband, his friend or his grandmother. The judging and prescriptive elements of concepts and everyday statements follow directly from the fact that people are affected by their actions. They have repercussions because they are based on actions, and actions influence the environment.

Everyday ideas and social categories are not about action; they are ideas for taking action. To put it another way, they are not models of reality, but models for reality (Geertz, 1973, p. 93). The consequence of this is that thinking in concrete ways has to take precedence over abstract thought in social living. In order to understand socially correct behaviour, it is necessary to get involved in the great variety of context-dependent knowledge. Fundamental differences in social living do not come from massive world-shaking differences, but from the small differences of the situation (Taylor and Fiske, 1975), the people involved, the time, location and gender (O'Leary and Hansen, 1984), and also from sensitivity to these differences and the ability to respond to them (Shweder, 1980, p. 267; cf. also Cronbach, 1975).

The tendency towards the concrete is illustrated by findings from 'salience' research. Salient stimuli – that is, stimuli which stand out either optically or acoustically, or because of their vividness (Taylor and Thompson, 1982) are used significantly more frequently as reference points for interpreting a phenomenon or situation than similarly available, but less salient stimuli (Taylor and Fiske, 1978). Recall of images far surpasses the ability to remember something spoken or written (Gehring, Toglia and Kimble, 1976; Shepard, 1967) and the recall of concrete words far surpasses memory for abstract words (Paivio, 1971).

Similarly, negative information – for example, about the non-occurrence of phenomena or a lack of cases – represents a degree of abstractness which is impossible for many test participants to integrate into their inferences correctly (Evans, 1983; Wason, 1980). It is well known that natural numbers – which are justifiably designated Natural – do not contain a zero or negative number. Coming from natural numbers, the introduction of zero or negative numbers represents a difficult step of abstraction, which only became possible with written records. Counting with notches on wood cannot produce a zero. A piece of wood without notches cannot do so, because it is just a simple stick (cf. Klix, 1980).

The tendency towards the concrete is one of the most important of the heuristics described by Tversky and Kahneman (1973). According to availability heuristic research, test participants use their memories of cases known to them to judge the frequency of that type of event. The more examples that occur to them from the bounds of their own experience, the higher their estimation of frequency turns out to be.[2] It is a logical consequence that this type of memory process proceeds in a situation-specific manner – that is, that chains of association and remembering are influenced by the particular situation. For example, more and different examples of relationship will probably occur to people when they are in a nightclub than at a railway station. Similarly, the availability, and with it the estimation of frequency, is influenced by ease of recall. If, owing to a lack of experiences such as accidents or other extraordinary events, a person possesses limited memory contents, which in addition might not be closely 'interlinked', the frequency of that type of event will be estimated as considerably less than in the opposite case (Slovic, Fischhoff and Lichtenstein, 1976).

Various studies in attribution theory have attempted to link the abstract assumptions of Kelley's ANOVA model, for example, into ecologically valid contexts. They show that test participants only rarely apply their causal attributions to general conditions in the way that the ANOVA model assumes. Instead, everyday causal attributions start at the other end – that is to say, with attributions to specific and local factors – and they do not always achieve the same level of abstraction as postulated by the ANOVA model (Jaspars, 1983, p. 43).

According to Jaspars, the reason for this is not to be found in a faulty understanding of the available information, but in the fact that events which elicit judgement in everyday life are concrete and life related. The explanations which a mother must give when her child fails at school are not to do with why many children fail in the same situation, or why only a few children (including her own) fail in many different situations. She does not, therefore, have to explain a general phenomenon on necessarily abstract levels, but just the behaviour of her individual child in this one situation. Given this necessity, studies show that the predictive validity of local explanations can be just as high as the validity of an explanation based on a linear combination of general factors (p. 43). So reference to the concrete becomes a direct consequence of the premise of goal-directed action under the pragmatic imperative.

## 3.2.2 The power of similarity

In his speech on being awarded the Nobel prize, Lorenz (1973b) stressed the importance of drawing analogies from similarity in bio-logical research. As we know, the idea that two entities, such as the eye of a mollusc and the eye of a mammal, may be related to each other because of their symptomatic similarities, instead of a homo-logical relationship, is not a proper form of scientific conclusion. In homology there are causal or evolutionary connections, but not necessarily symptom similarities between things: 'A homologous motor pattern may retain its original physiological causation as well as its external forms, yet undergo an entire change of function' (Lorenz, 1973b, p. 192).

However, in the everyday world, causal and historical contexts are not generally accessible when dealing with fellow people and social phenomena. Their superficial symptoms are accessible, though, so taking action in everyday life is primarily served by the availability of those superficial symptoms as a quick and simple aid to orientation. This precondition makes similarity a significant basis of pragmatic thought processes and subject to some cognitive effects.

Representivity heuristics are based on the power of similarity (Tversky and Kahnemann, 1982). The similarity which a person, a situation or some other object to be judged has to the remembered prototype is used to calculate probabilities. A well-known illu-stration of this, which also happens to be the classic stimulus used in representivity experiments, is the following problem: 'If stimulus person A was randomly drawn from a set of 70 technicians and 30 lawyers, and person A has the characteristics, interests and hobbies x, y and z, is A more likely to be a technician or a lawyer?' If the test participants' lawyers imply that qualities x, y and z would be stereotypical for lawyers, they will (sensibly) give a high probability to 'lawyer', even though the base rate information (70 technicians to 30 lawyers) contradicts this judgement.

Representivity heuristics also provide cognitive explanations for illusionary correlations. If test participants are presented with pairs of stimuli, some of which have semanitic connections or similari-ties while others are independent, they tend to overestimate the frequency with which the semantically linked and similar pairings appear (Chapman, 1967; Chapman and Chapman, 1967;

Hamilton and Gifford, 1976; Lilli and Rehm, 1983, 1984). The psychology of perception implies that one should actually be more likely to overestimate the frequency of recent and surprising events (combinations of incompatible stimuli) since those stimuli attract more of our attention than more familiar ones (Berlyne, 1960). The fact that this is not the case implies that semantic, symbolic and similarity connections between objects and phenomena exert a fundamental influence on the processes of social perception. Relations between phenomena may consist of superordinate or subordinate positions in a hierarchy, part-whole relationships, causal correlations, family relations in the sense of stereotypical or polythetical classifications, or culturally preconditioned expectations (Hastie, 1983). The effect can be found in many cultures and can be interpreted as a form of magical everyday thought (Shweder, 1977).

## 'Magical' logic

The deduction processes shown by test participants, and thereby also by ordinary people, follow a 'magical' logic of the concrete and analogous – of a confusion of statements about the world with statements about language (Shweder, 1977, p. 647) to which contingency and statistical correlations are foreign (Moscovici, 1992b).[3] When we are recalling concrete events from our own life history, similarities with stereotypes are adequate for most everyday estimations of probability, where such estimations seem necessary; and it may be doubted whether we find ourselves in the position of having to judge such probabilities very often in everyday life. Following stereotypes is always sufficient if what we need is to be able to give a suddenly necessary judgement about a fellow person effectively and swiftly, and pigeon-hole him at least provisionally into the world of one's own life. Wishing to give a judgement about a person only after a detailed study of possible sample ranges and other base rates would unduly hinder the flow of everyday actions – always assuming that such information were accessible at all – and would in all likelihood produce a not inconsiderable degree of astonishment amongst one's fellows. But the trump card held by the man and woman in the street is the ability to correct swiftly any possibly precipitous assumptions. In the simplest case, this can be achieved by using the question as a possible confirmatory strategy.

If a direct question is not possible, perhaps for reasons of politeness, other strategies within the bounds of interpersonal interaction are open:

> The defining characteristic of a confirmatory strategy for testing hypotheses in social interaction is the preferential soliciting of behavioral evidence whose presence would tend to confirm the hypothesis under scrutiny. That is, to test the hypothesis that another person was friendly and sociable by means of a confirmatory strategy, an individual would devote . . . most of his conversation to probing for instances of the presence of sociable and outgoing behaviors.
>
> (Snyder, 1981a, p. 278)

Test participants confirm their expectations both actively by seeking information and purposefully selecting new information (Snyder and Campbell, 1980; Snyder and Swann, 1978), and using memory processes and biased recalling of previously acquired information (Darley and Gross, 1983).

The fact that confirmatory strategies for checking opinions may contradict the rationality criteria of science, but are thoroughly meaningful in the social world, is related to the fact that our interaction partner is directly affected and able to react, as well as to the social construction of environments. Social knowledge is social for the very reason that it stems from the process of constructing relationships in interactions (Snyder, 1981a, p. 300 onwards). The way that one person encounters another to a large extent determines the nature of the latter's reaction (Snyder, 1984). If one wanted to apply the principles of Popper's fallibility (also largely disregarded in science) to falsify a suspicion, it would probably succeed in all cases, leaving no way of orienting towards that person. The only remaining optimistic and pragmatically representable interaction strategy, then, is an attempt to look for as many confirmations as possible for one's own suspicions.

The tendency to generalise from individual cases is a further example of pragmatically reduced thought based on similarity. One single example from experience is often enough for test participants to infer the relevant features of other events by expansion on that example, insofar as they appear similar. The more complicated the class of event, the more it suffices for test participants to take an example as a basis for generalisation (Read, 1983). Some experiences are used as a model, in accordance with which new situations and new information are judged. These so-called 'simulation heuristics' were investigated experimentally by Kahnemann and Tversky (1982).

### 3.2.3 The need for explanation

In everyday life – in politics, in the family or at the work place – one constantly encounters the implicit assumption that any social or psychological phenomenon must have a meaning or significance that explains it: there must be some sense or some perspective in which it is beneficial for someone or something – and these benefits also explain the presence of the phenomenon. This way of thinking is wholly foreign to the idea that there could be such a thing as sound and fury in social life, unintended and accidental events that have no meaning whatsoever. It takes for given that although the tale may appear to be told by an idiot, there always exists a code that, if found, would enable us to decipher it.

(Elster, 1983, p. 101)

Although the results of many actions are unintended and random, to the extent that the events surprise us the all-encompassing tendency exists to interpret them, ascribe meaning to them, and find an explanation for them (Wong and Weiner, 1981). Apparently random events thus become events which appear random.

### Terms of explanation

The term 'explanation' in everyday language usage has many meanings which are only partly to do with the scientific concept of 'explanation'. Stegmüller (1974) distinguishes among others the following pre-scientific uses of the term 'explanation':

1. Causal explanation, as an answer to the question of 'Why is this event happening?'. This is a very frequently found use of the term and it is directly approximate to the use of the term in scientific language. If there is a car accident, then the question as to its cause can be explained by its careering off the road, by an icy spot, by speeding, or by the drunken state of the driver, all depending on whether the person asked presup-

poses more the incorrect conduct of the driver or the situative conditions of the accident. A naive understanding of causality would designate all answers of this form as causal explanations.

2. If somebody falsely understands the symptoms of a fact and another person explains the real fact of the matter as a result, then we are dealing with a corrective reinterpretation. This simultaneously examines the different categorisation for those who misunderstand, and possibly,

3. resolves any discrepancy between what someone believes and what he or she perceives. If a visitor to the Scottish moorlands expects to be able to see grouse in November, then the local gamekeeper will explain to the visitor that this bird is only active in the spring and summer months before a drastic reduction of their numbers at the hands of his well-armed friends during a few days in August. An explanation also removes any uncertainty or misunderstanding here, as under point (2).

4. A child who has smashed a pane of glass with a stone will most likely be asked why he did this. The child's reply will be an explanation of his behaviour in the sense of a moral (or possibly immoral) justification.

5. Asked why she is studying late into the night, a student will explain her behaviour as being aimed towards passing the final exam. The reason for her behaviour is defined as a future event, her behaviour teleologically explained.

(Stegmüller, 1974, p. 74)

With these numerous possibilities for using the term 'explanation', it is difficult to find common features which would permit one to view 'explaining' as an intensionally definable unified concept. Rather it might be a 'family of concepts' in Wittgenstein's sense, which cannot be pinned down to a unified dimension, but shows only partially overlapping similarities. The five examples in Stegmüller's listing are all possible as far as social psychology is concerned.

Antaki and Fielding (1981) distinguish only three kinds of explanation which can be applied to social phenomena in everyday life: Descriptive explanations, explanations of the reason or cause, and moral explanations. Descriptive explanations answer the question of 'What is happening?' and essentially consist of an account of the facts of the matter. The second kind refers to questions about unexpected events such as 'Why is this happening?'. But even when things run their usual course, social individuals will mostly acquire and process a sort of understanding for what is going on around them, with the effect that one can speak of 'unconscious' or automatised explanations (p. 36).

Moral explanations either ascribe protagonists responsibility or excuse them. These explanations do not just satisfy curiosity, but represent judgements and possibly even condemnations, with all the consequences that moral devaluation of a person may have for dealing with it (Fincham and Jaspars, 1980; Scott and Lyman, 1968).

Professional and private life involves, at many levels, a balancing act between morally correct behaviour, the smallest possible expense to achieve goals, and safeguarding the optimal financial or other return. W. Wagner and Ardelt (1990) and Ardelt, W. Wagner and Wieser (1991) used a sample of higher-level employees and employers, as well as 'lower-class' criminals, to show that the discourse they used to justify immoral acts in private and business life mainly served to restore their own moral integrity, even though the test participants often saw no chance of ditching the moral burden of virtually inescapable wrongdoings in the future. They therefore applied their cognitive faculties tactically to create a discourse of justification, used equally to convince both others and themselves.

This interpersonal function of explanation and justification is lost in an attribution model wedded to an explanation model of causality. Although explanations make orientations possible in a more or less determinist environment, they also have the possibly more important function of justifying and qualifying one's own or other people's behaviour (Semin and Manstead, 1983). This ensures that experiences are embedded, not primarily in the causal structure of the everyday world, but in the moral order. At the same time, behavioural justification acts to secure self-image, the integrity of which depends not only on one's own acceptable placing in the moral order, but also on the moral position of others relative to oneself (Shotter, 1984). Therefore the structure of everyday explanations follows less the demand for veridicality, as required by scientific explanations, than the need to convince (Antaki, 1985; Semin and Manstead, 1983). The rhetorical function of justifications places them directly in an interpersonal context which must be taken on board before their often complex form can be interpreted.

Explanations are always rooted in the existing knowledge which people possess about a particular situation. This knowledge determines whether the explanation for unexpected events is sought in the protagonist or the external conditions in which the act takes place. So as a rule, the protagonist acting unexpectedly tends to be ascribed responsibility for the situation if the person judging knows that situation. Test participants reach the opposite conclusion when they do not know the situation (Lalljee, Watson and White, 1982). The predictability of the conditions determines the attribution of responsibility – people are not theory-neutral judges (White, 1984, p. 340). This means that the covariation dimension of the ANOVA attribution model only holds true with test participants in domains about which no knowledge exists whatsoever (Jennings, Amabile and Ross, 1982). An attribution model aiming to describe the explanatory behaviour of everyday people should include the points that have just been made. One must take into consideration:

(a) that the first spontaneous deduction proceeds from those concrete experiences of people which occur to them in the current situation;
(b) that confirmatory strategies are used to validate expectations;
(c) and that underlying attributional mechanisms and causal schemata appear tenable when examined from a pragmatically economical point of view.

(Hansen, 1985)

## Control and rationalization

Explanations, whether they are self-constructed or offered by others, reduce uncertainty and fear. They give individuals at least apparent control over the 'explained' phenomenon. If, for example, an unhappy event has happened in the past, a later explanation supposedly helps people to prevent its recurrence, especially if they themselves feel responsible (Bulman and Wortman, 1977; Wortman, 1976). Janoff-Bulman (1979) was able to detect such explanation processes with rape victims.

It is the same for current threats. If test participants are expecting a painful stimulus, then information about the stimulus they expect increases their ability to confront the event (Staub and Kellet, 1972). If patients about to go through surgery are furnished with information about the operation, it increases their readiness to confront it (J. Johnson, 1975). The same is true of cancer patients (Taylor, 1979).

Whilst the possession of information and explanations offers the apparent possibility of control in dealings with the world, another, second strategy can be identified which appears to give the possibility of control via one's own adaption to events.

The apparent possession of information and explanations facilitates matters by offering possibilities of control in dealings with the world. But it also offers a second strategy, which appears to give the possibility of control via one's own adaption to events. Rothbaum, Weisz and Snyder (1982) refer to this type of reasoning tendency as secondary control. They talk of it as a way of making contact with events that are difficult to control, which can take different forms. One important form is 'interpretive secondary control'. By this they mean ascribing at least interpretive sense to an otherwise inexplicable event, even if no immediate explanations in the narrow sense can be found for it. If the cancer patients in the study by Taylor (1979) were able to find meaning in their suffering, for example – even though it might be a painful one – they managed more easily with the illness and learned to cope with it more effectively than would have been the case without that interpretation.[4]

Interpretive secondary control represents a kind of rationalisation of external events. Similarly, people mainly give reasons for their own behaviour when there appears to be no sufficient reason in the conditions of their environment. This tendency towards self-justification is backed up by the large number of well-known studies on dissonance theory (Festinger, 1957). The greater the involvement and affectedness of test participants in their own fields of action, and the smaller the externally visible gain, the more they tend to seek the reason for their involvement in its intrinsic values (Festinger and Carlsmith, 1959). Cognitive dissonance, in the form of the apparent contrast between the exertion of the action and the reward, is perceived by dissonance theory to be unpleasant and annoying, therefore initiating cognitive re-evaluations to reproduce consonance (Aronson, 1980b).

In the majority of cases, though, it seems questionable whether justification strategies for one's own behaviour actually need to be motivated by dissonance. Often, the common need for explanation and to know 'Why am I doing this at all?' in everyday life is enough to produce rationalisations for one's own behavioural tendencies (Beauvois and Joule, 1981). The intrinsic value of actions is not just a compensation for unsatisfactory material gains, as market exchange principles might suggest; but also obtained through locating the motivation behind the action in higher social and cultural aims, as implied by ideologies. Rationalisation, which is able to appeal to collective needs in satisfying a crisis of explanation always appears to be more morally justified in everyday life than personal gain.

## 3.2.4 Everyday rationality and sensibleness

### Concrete prototypicality

We have identified three principles which characterise the essential features of everyday thought as a requirement of everyday knowledge: the reference to the concrete, the power of similarity, and the need to explain.

Reference to the concrete limits the 'data material' normally available in everyday life. The data used in everyday thought are preferentially true to life, vivid and tangible. Such data are the material from which everyday experiences are formed. Naturally, there are some situations experienced, some people encountered, and some events that acompany us in our way through life, which we do not automatically store as episodic memory data. Some events are condensed to 'repisodic' prototypes of events (Neisser, 1981); impressions of people are reduced to stereotypes (Cantor and Mischel, 1979); situations are generalised and classified in schemata (W. Brewer and Nakamura, 1984); one's own behavioural tendencies form a global self-schema (Greenwald and Pratkanis, 1984); and models of taking action become prototypical scripts (Hastie, Park and Weber, 1984; Kruse, 1986) and mental causal models (Jaspars, 1983, p. 42; Johnson-Laird, 1983). Once such prototypical schemata are constructed and cognitively located, they will strongly resist attempts at alteration, and will form a foundation which directs our recognition of similar stimuli. In one experiment with faces as stimuli, for example, the stimuli which had really been presented were 'recognised', but so were erroneously new but similar faces (Solso and McCarthy, 1981).

Information 'molecules' lose their individual character at the level of prototypical abstraction, but they still remain comparable, in phenomenal terms, to actual events in the real world, with the result that similarity judgements remain possible. This is one way that everyday abstractions differ from scientific generalisations. While scientific generalisations are analytical, breaking down phenomena into their defining dimensions, prototypical abstractions are synthetised and vivid. It seems obvious to attribute this difference to the need by academia to have all the options made possible by writing and written records at its disposal. As Chapter 2 showed, the mind is an illiterate entity, to which the drawing up of lists is foreign.

The heuristics of similarity arise directly from the nature of the available data material. They are a necessity, in view of memory structure defined by fuzziness; are effective if one takes into account the possibility of subsequent correction of 'hypotheses'; and are also swift in being able to follow the action imperatives of everyday life.

The comprehensive tendency to explain, in a world which demands action, makes targeted orientation of behaviour possible. Without assumptions about connections, individuals would have no option but to cast dice to find out whether their next behavioural act would be likely to be the most sensible. From a pragmatic standpoint it is less important whether assumptions about causal and other connections are true in the scientific sense. What matters is whether explanation implies a certain action which is useful for achieving an aim or avoiding failure. In a world of known coincidences and accidents, taking effective action would be simply impossible.

## Everyday rationality

It is apparent that none of the three principles outlined – concreteness, analogy and need to explain – satisfy the criteria of strict rationality. As we have tried to show, the prerequisites of successful everyday action, the affectedness, action imperative and the field of situations and tasks demand other criteria as the basis for either logic.

A scientific knowledge system can be regarded as rational if it is consistent according to certain criteria (Elster, 1983). However, logic in everyday life is obviously different, since it arises from the pragmatic demands of social existence. Scientific findings show us that the method of thought applied in practical discourse is useful for confronting different tasks. Contrasting with strict rationality, we can call this 'everyday rationality' in the sense of being sensible.[5] A systematic account of everyday life is to be considered 'everyday rational', in these terms, when its derivative:

(a) comes from the fund of concrete data in everyday life, follows at least the heuristics of similarities, serves the tendency to substantiate and explain; and also, at the very least:
(b) is locally consistent.

## Local consistency

A set of doctrines is strictly consistent when there is a possible world in which all clauses are true, that is, no contradictions can be derived from them (Elster, 1983, p. 4 onwards), and when they are believed, as Hintikka (1961) adds. The emphasis lies on the internal freedom from contradiction, which in ideal cases can be proved in a Boolean manner. Freedom from contradiction means in elementary logic that $p$ and its complement $NOTp$ may not be true simultaneously and in the same context:

NOT (p & NOTp)

The truth of the logical statements is based only on the accepted meaning of operators '&' and 'NOT'. Should one find cultures, as Lévy-Brühl (1921) says, which have statements where $p$ and its complement $NOTp$ are simultaneously correct, then this points more to a problem of translation then to a pre-logical condition of the cultural mentality (Quine, in Stegmüller, 1987a, p. 250).

Every reader will think of examples which show how statement systems or theories of everyday life which contradict one another are able to coexist in everyday life. Think, for example, of the widespread ideas or 'truisms' about healthy living, and ideas of suitable self-representation; contrasting them with those which often imply unhealthy ways of behaviour, such as smoking or alcohol consumption. These global logical inconsistencies and judgement contradictions are not normally any reason to consider either of the two knowledge subsystems to be false. Contradictions are largely accepted and not felt to be disruptive as long as the two knowledge contents are not simultaneously evoked by situative demands or raised in deliberations. It is only in those situations that inconsistencies are considered, and then resolved in dialogue (cf. Billig, Condor, Edwards, Gane, Middleton and Radley, 1988; Markovà, 2003).

This synchretism, in the form of tolerated global inconsistency, together with the tendency to eliminate currently occurring contradictions, we will refer to as the 'local consistency' of everyday knowledge systems. Locally consistent means that it is sufficient for knowledge systems of everyday life to be consistent and be viewed as everyday rational as long as their pieces are not considered simultaneously. A soft formulation of the consistency criteria is a necessary consequence of the epistemological requirements formulated in point (a), which state that we can only expect statement that are fuzzy and can only be locally substantiated. Pragmatic cognition in everyday life only requires that practical opinions be consistent with other practical opinions in closely related content – that is, with those opinions which in a certain context become simultaneously relevant and which may provide evidence for the original opinion (Sperber, 1982, p. 172).

The secondary establishment of consistency in statement systems is shown by the so-called 'Socratic effect'. If one obtains test participants' opinions on a topic, and subsequently asks them targeted questions about the contexts of their statements, they often show improved logical consistency in a subsequent exploration of the opinion structure (McGuire, 1960). Simultaneous awareness of different statements obviously leads to a reorganisation of the cognitive elements in statement systems.

Festinger's dissonance theory (1957) deals with another aspect of the process of establishing consistency. Admittedly, cognitive dissonance does not primarily describe the problem of logical inconsistency. Whilst logical consistency is derived from the demand to reject a third possibility besides $p$ and $NOTp$, psychological consonance refers principally to the relationships between value judgements. Dissonance theory is aimed at the psychological process of resolving evaluative statements, such as attitudes.

The criteria outlined constitute the minimum requirements for regarding a statement system as everyday rational and pragmatically substantiated. If these conditions are not fulfilled, statements are likely to be viewed as false, unless they are substantiated by other sources of evidence. This formal definition of the everyday rational or 'Sensible' is the basis for the following examination of the content features of everyday knowledge.

## 3.3   Content rationality, irrationality and evidence

### 3.3.1   Collective discourse and rational content

#### Cultural models and cosmologies

Common sense encompasses more than the generally accepted rational rules of correct deduction which permit orientation in real-life situations, even when these are relatively unfamiliar. In addition to the requirements for acquiring and cognitively processing individual knowledge dealt with at the end of the last section, everyday knowledge also, and most significantly, encompasses cultural maxims and collectively shared opinions and knowledge and beliefs, the core of which can be found condensed in all cultures, often in proverbs (Fletcher, 1984, p. 206).

The collection of phenomena that are salient in a culture or society are also an object of everyday knowledge. These phenomena would not exist culturally if they were not a component of a possible world whose constituent features are the rule-governed patterns of intercourse among people, both with one another and also in respect to things and the collectively shared everyday knowledge underlying those models of interaction. The emphasis here lies on 'collectively shared'. While an individual can disclose whatever idiosyncratic knowledge or opinions they like to other individuals without having to run the risk of being marginalised as mad as long as they heed pragmatic sensibleness; the domain of collective everyday knowledge being discussed here delineates which real or imagined phenomena can be the subject matter of the social discourse.

This field of knowledge has been approached by many researchers under many names, each coming from a moderately different angle. Researchers speak of folk models (D'Andrade, 1986); cultural models or cultural schemata (Keesing, 1987; Quinn and Holland, 1987; Rice, 1980); or social representations to describe the denotative and instrumental knowledge which a social group possesses about the nature and functioning of cultural objects like roles, gender, morals and social interactions. These models may be formulated relatively explicitly as in ideas about the development of disease, or implicitly as in the knowledge of speech acts contained in the lexicons of all languages. They are simultaneously cultural and public models, which are always present for the individual (Varenne, 1984). Such models refer to identifiable real objects and phenomena, at which the representatives of each culture can point the finger whenever they appear.[6]

The 'cosmology' concept from Douglas (1982a) is a somewhat more global model. It comprises interpretation and explanatory systems of a metaphysical character, which cover large areas of cultural phenomena. The concept stipulates that such areas are 'worldviews' – that is, views about nature and its contrast to culture and society, and views about time, human nature and social behaviour. Research in the area of indigenous psychologies (Heelas and Lock, 1981) specially refers to the cultural self-image of collectives. And we can also include cosmologies of cultural themes (Opler, 1946). Cultural themes can assert themselves as widely different concrete cosmologies or cultural models. They reflect macro-social processes in their dynamic character, of the appearance of theme and counter-theme in the same or different cultures. This concept is closer to the structural analysis of myths as carried out by Lévi-Strauss and others, who aimed to reveal the organisational ideas that can be found in all societies as an abstract mathematical model (Leach, 1966, p. 2; Oppitz, 1975).

## Content-rationality

Cultural models, social representations and cosmologies, everyday knowledge and common sense have to do with an understanding of reason's content (unlike formal calculation). We will call this particular domain 'content rational', in order to distinguish it from everyday rationality and strict rationality. In this sense, content rationality refers to the content designated by a statement, while everyday rationality refers to process elements playing a role in elaborating the content.

Referring to Central European 'standard culture' for example, statement (a) 'The countries of Austria and Hungary unite into an empire or they do not' constitutes a formal, logically true, content rational statement of the form:

$$(p \ OR \ NOTp)$$

It is sensible (regardless of whether $p$ or $NOTp$ is correct in an individual case), acceptable and above all understandable.

It is different with statement (b) 'Sylvia is the seventh reincarnation of the sacred dog, or she is not'. In spite of the formally equivalent form of the two statements (a) and (b), (b) appears to us stupid, unacceptable and hard to understand. It may be logically correct, but statement (b) is not part of the Central European content-rational system which the local world describes. This fact logically turns out to be the external negation:

$$NOT(p \; OR \; NOTp)$$

If we are confronted with the choice of whether $b$ or $NOTb$ is correct, while

$$b = (p \; OR \; NOTp)$$

it is not difficult for us to decide on $NOTb$, we reject the entire statement. Moreover, the concrete truth content of whether $p$ or $NOTp$ are actually correct does not play any role other than to say something about our lack of ability to say anything about $p$ or $NOTp$. That which is indistinguishable within a content-rational system, and falls victim to external negation, is what we would call 'irrational'.

Sperber (1982) makes a useful distinction between factual and representational beliefs. A factual opinion encompasses opinions which form part of the total representations about the world, stored in encyclopaedic memory; together with all the representations deriving from this store of knowledge. Representational opinions are those which also include the credibility of a factual opinion, for example convictions and attitudes which allocate a truth value – for example as in fuzzy logic – to a factual statement. A representation $R$ becomes a representational opinion if the individual simultaneously confirms that $R$ is positively the case – that is, if he can say: 'the proper interpretation of $R$ is true' (Sperber, 1982, p. 172 onwards). The reasons why a representation can become an opinion with a claim to truth lie in the available evidence. In this conception, the scope of the content-rational knowledge described above comprises all statements about representations which can be (a) properly interpreted by the member of a culture and (b) considered to be true.

## Irrationality

When someone is drawn to stupidity, this generally occurs because he or she contradicts local content rationality rather than because the formal or pragmatic rules of rationality or formal logic have been infringed. Everyday judgements on reason versus stupidity are therefore based on the content, and not the formal rules, of the thought leading the discourse. This is also the case for judging the clinically mentally ill, whose illness is expressed more in content confusion than in formal faultiness of thought. Let us imagine a hypothetical mentally ill person who is conspicuous because he walks exceedingly cautiously and is panickingly intent on not bumping into anything. Asked why he is so careful not to touch the doorframe, for example, he replies that he is afraid of being smashed as everybody knows that glass is fragile; and after all, he is of course made out of glass (in Foucault, 1969). The logic of our mentally ill person is utterly correct and ultimately comprehensible, even if we do not really know what it feels like to be made out of glass. But the content-rational basis, of consensus about possible and impossible statements, is infringed.

It seems appropriate to point out that this definition of the Irrational is more stringent, in my opinion, than the alternative view in Shweder (1986), for example. This author, like many other psychologists, understands by irrational a loss of the faculties which make strict rationality possible. In our culture this includes, for example, losing the control of one's will, the inability to distinguish oneself from others, or differentiate between past, present and future (p. 180). These phenomena, strictly speaking, exclude individual pathological processes from sensible discourse just like false statements. They are understood as being in contrast to everyday-rational statements, or to metaphorical comparisons such as the lovers' 'We feel as one'. But, as is yet to be demonstrated, metaphors play a central part in systems of everyday knowledge (Chapter 6).

## 3.3.2 Evidence

We have defined content-rational systems as organised sets of statements about entities, independent of whether those entities are of a real or imagined nature. But what justifies these statement systems as sensible? First of all, surely, because of their pragmatic rational basis, as explained above; since they satisfy the epistemological prerequisites of everyday life. Second, content-rational systems surely do not win their acceptance from their correspondence with the things of the world, in the sense of a correspondence theory of truth. If that were required, then it would be hard to imagine how different cultures and religions could have arisen as collectively shared models of experiences. It would also be impossible to ascertain the correspondence of doctrines about imagined things with precisely these objects. This demand is obviously too strict. Along with Elster (1983), we want to see the basic rationality of belief systems and opinions in their evidence: 'The (substantive) rationality of beliefs concerns the relation between the belief and the available evidence, not the relation between the belief and the world' (p. 16).

As far as individuals are concerned, the credibility and sensibleness of content-rational systems comes from the evidence accessible to them. However, this is not fed exclusively by the criteria of pragmatic rationality already discussed, in the way that individual everyday knowledge is. Instead, it is substantiated in the opinions of others or ultimately in a collective consensus (cf. Postman, 1951).

The issue we are dealing with here, of evidence as criteria for the acceptability of statements, makes a distinction between beliefs and propositions appear useful, as for example Goodenough (1963) suggests for the belief systems of peoples. By propositions we understand statements which have the peculiarity of being able to be either true or false, whilst opinions are statements that are considered to be true. The truth of propositions is accordingly established by the (not superficially social) evidence of sensations. 'The entities we perceive are what we perceive them to be, and those propositions about their mutual arrangements that we are able to verify by direct observation are true. Other propositions that follow logically from these are presumably also true . . . What is true and what is false is a function of our percepts, the categories in terms of which we habitually perceive things' (Goodenough 1963, p. 55) Opinions, on the other hand, would be statement systems which are socially handed down and cannot be directly derived from sensory experiences. They are established as propositions on an abstract level, and for the most part concern nonperceptual entities and classifications.

This distinction appears questionable, however, if one takes into account the perception-orientating effect of cultural belief systems. Of course, enculturation ensures that the senses and sense-like processing instances of the cognitive apparatus are precisely 'programmed' to culturally relevant objects, thus making the conceptualities of the culture the immediate view. For example, the casuar[7] is an animal in the culture of the Karam (New Guinea) which is very closely linked with tribal mythology, and metaphorically related to brother and sister (Bulmer, 1967). This relation can be explained by the particular physical and cultural living conditions of the Karam, and has consequences for the way that these birds are encountered, how they are hunted, and which parts of their bodies may be eaten by whom. Consequently, this animal is separated, even in the local zoological classification, both from other birds and the other vertebrate animals. If a tribal member encounters a casuar, his perception and judgement will be determined directly by the position which the bird takes in his cosmology. But this blurs the boundary between the immediate perceptual process, which should verify the claim to truth made by a proposition, and the handed-down belief system, which makes an opinion be experienced as true due to its social evidence (for other examples, see Douglas, 1966).[8]

Differentiation between propositions and opinions according to their proximity to things might best be understood as a continuous dimension between these two poles. A reference to this is the finding by Nida (1964) that taxonomies differ in a more strongly intercultural manner at a higher level, that is, in more abstract conceptual areas, than at a more concrete, percept-closer level (in Black, 1973, p. 514). If one starts from the premiss that there is for all cultures a common world of natural things which is accessible to perception, then that world necessarily restricts the freedom of human diversity of classification. Experiments in hypothesis theory have shown that attitudes as to what one is expecting can 'guide' perception up to certain limits (cf. e.g. Lilli, 1978; Neisser, 1974).[9]

## Social comparison

Social comparison theory also recognises the distinction between verification processes, which proceed using 'the object', as it were, or by observing reality, and social comparison which takes the opinions of others as its model; with the effect that the aforementioned critique refers to Festinger's second postulate (Festinger, 1954). This asserts that individuals endeavour to validate their opinions about themselves and things in the world. They view direct observation of the objects as a primary source for validation. If this is not possible, individuals will refer back to social information and compare their opinion with the opinion of other reference persons. Social comparison theory is thus an approach to illustrating the process of social validation and evidence.

Festinger's (1954) theory of social comparisons is a final synthesis of a social-psychological tradition which investigated the influence of collective convictions on individuals' attitudes and opinions (cf. Singer, 1980). Before him Newcomb (1943) showed in a field study of political and social convictions of student groups that these convictions, whether liberal, radical or conservative, preferentially followed the collective views of reference groups (Hyman, 1942), whether of the family or of the community of fellow students. Sherif's (1936) works proved the influence of experimental opinion monopolies on the development of individual standards even more impressively.

Festinger (1954) stresses that if people do not have objective – non-social – means at their disposal, they will evaluate their opinions and abilities by comparing them with the opinions and abilities of other people. The primacy which Festinger concedes to objective, virtually physical observation as opposed to social comparison in his second postulation can only be understood with difficulty. It will normally always be easier to prove an opinion by social validation than to make observations independently, even if there were no problem with their accessibility: 'Both in the history of the science of our culture and in the knowledge systems of other cultures there are numerous examples of the opposite process; i.e. these cultures do without using "material" means for checking which in principle are available, since there exists a very high (or absolute) consensus about the character of a phenomenon.' (Tajfel, 1975, p. 371). Tajfel therefore ascribes to social comparison theory a much greater field of application than Festinger wanted to admit.[10]

All the same, the distinction between validation by objective or empirical means and validation by social comparison is not as clear as it seems to be. It does not even become any more understandable by taking into consideration the different perspectives of the subject and the researcher. If Tajfel (1978, p. 65) means that social reality is just as objective as physical reality, or conversely, that physical reality can appear just as social as the originally social world, then this depends on the point of view. The first statement appears unavoidably true for the involved social subject, whilst the second formulation appears more valid to the observer. Social participants will not experience their world as a 'social' one, but as what it is, and this in naive understanding is objective and true, regardless of whether social relations or a mountain are intended; or, expressed differently, social forms in their 'natural attitude' appear just as natural and inevitable as a rock or the sun.

If, however, individuals within a culture demarcate the virtually physical validation of opinions from validation by asking others, then this expresses something about the culture and its social representations in the individual who makes this distinction, but nothing about the objectivity or non-objectivity of the checking. If a society allows an experimental examination of the truth content of a statement to be viewed as harder, more credible and more reliable than social comparison, then this differential judgement of the validation methods is a consensual act, and therefore conventional. If a different society prefers to rely on interpersonal validation and affords physical 'experiments' less credibility, then this too is the consequence of social agreement. It is not enough to take on the aloof perspective of the researcher, either by decreeing that everything is social, including 'objective' experiments (as Tajfel does), or that there is an objective reality checkable by the methods of the sciences, which confronts the social world (as Festinger does). Both are the consequence of the point of view of the observer, which is not the standpoint of the people involved. What is called for is interpretation and judgement of the two validation methods in the context of social practice, in the way that it is represented for individuals within the cultural interpretation schemata of their society: Does culture make an explicit distinction between physical and non-physical reality? And if so, what status do validation actions of the one or the other,[11] or perhaps even a third kind, have? Thinkable third methods could include, for example, asking an oracle in the case of the Azande (Evans-Pritchard, 1976), or an astrologer or palm-reader in our culture. Such methods are neither a physical means of checking in a strict sense, nor do they come under the processes which social comparison theory touches on, since it is not the majority opinion which is tapped. Rather, the random contingencies of other phenomena are symbolically interpreted, thus their outcome is neither physically predictable nor substantiated in the consensus.

## Social projection

It is not absoltuely necessary for test participants to communicate with each other in order to initiate social comparison processes (Gerard and Wagner, 1981).

*Method.* Test participants in same-sex groups of four to five people took part in the experiment. They were presented with two judgement questionnaires whose fictitious results were subsequently reported back to them. The fictitious reporting was about the homogeneity or heterogeneity of the judgements (much similarity, little similarity, no information). Afterwards they read a story about a delinquent boy whose punishment for an offence was to be decided at the end individually by the test participants. Before they passed their judgement, they were informed about an alleged debate to come with other test participants in which they would have to defend their position. This debate was set either immediately or for a week later or was not mentioned. This manipulation varied the immanence of action linked to the decision. The test participants were additionally asked as to their opinion about what judgements they suspected that the other people present had made, half of them before and the other half after they had made their own judgements (priming yes or no).

The results show that on occasions when the other people are perceived to be generally similar in attitude, thus constituting a reference group to a certain extent, judgements are given more extremely and with greater certainty than in groups that are perceived as unsimilar in terms of judgement. The effect of extremes was further reinforced by the manipulation of the priming, that is to say when the opinions of the others had been considered before one's own judgement, thus directing attention to the group.

Following Allport (1924) the authors explain this effect by the tendency of individuals to project their opinion on to others (insofar as they can accept these others as partners to relate to). Thus they implicitly compare themselves with the others socially. If the test participant first of all assumes, in a way conveyed by the projection, that others share the opinion in question (which the answer to the question about their opinion confirms), this increases their own certainty of attitude without any opportunity for direct contact. Figure 3.1 shows a path diagram of this process.

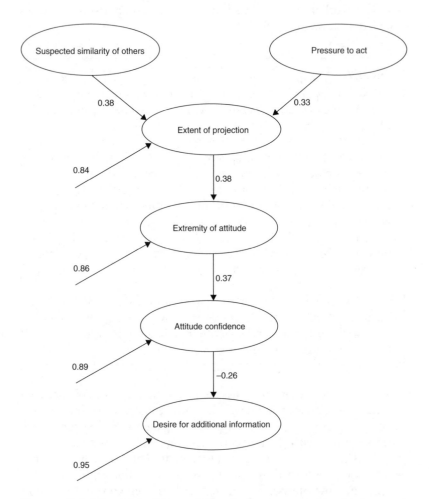

FIGURE 3.1 Diagram of the relation between social projection and extremity of attitude (data from Gerard and Wagner, 1981)

The negative path from the variable 'certainty of attitude' to 'need for additional information' in Figure 3.1 is particularly interesting. It shows that the demand for new information about the domain of attitudes has been reduced by the process of opinion validation, through implicit social comparison via projection and the higher certainty of attitude derived from it. This is an important indication that extremes of attitude are a cognitive effect, and not principally an affective one or the consequence of a heightened level of arousal. The study presented here was carried out using judgement-related attitudes as a dependent variable. The effect of projection and extremes of attitude following from it is also considerably greater with judgement-related contents than with fact-related ones (W. Wagner and Gerard, 1983b).

Holtz and Miller (1985) demonstrate the same effect. Their experiments also show that projecting the opinion on to the members of an ingroup increases the certainty of attitude, particularly with contents which the test participants consider to be important. However, it is also conversely the case that the higher one's certainty is, the more one's own opinion is likely to be attributed to other people (Marks and Miller, 1985).

## Reference

In order for social comparison processes to be activated, it is necessary for individuals to be able to establish consensus within their reference group. Assuming intersubjectivity is one of the fundamental requirements of everyday social living, since assuming a reality only appears to be sensible as long as it is seen as the same by all those taking part in everyday life (Pollner, 1974). Similarly, actions only appear to be sensible as long as the individual can accept that they would also be taken by others in the same situation. This produces the 'false consensus' effect (Marks and Miller, 1987; Ross, Green and House, 1977; van der Plight, 1984).

As the experiment by Gerard and Wagner (1981) indicates, via the backdoor, as it were, it is not a trivial matter *who* shows consensus. Test participants expect only the same judgements as their own from fellow participants. Given fictitious reporting, these could be viewed as similar in judgement, and thus comparable with themselves in their social orientation. This may also explain why many studies of the role of consensus in attributional and social

deduction processes show a consistently negligible influence from
the consensus information available (McArthur, 1972; Nisbett and
Borgida, 1975). Even if the absence of this effect appears to be
explicable due to the low vividness of statistical and therefore
abstract consensus information (Nisbett and Borgida, 1975; Wells
and Harvey, 1977), other, more social reasons can be expected.

It might not be primarily essential that consensus exists at all,
but matter who shows consensus. Festinger (1954) already indicates this when he remarks that social comparison with members
of a group of higher or lower status very seldom takes place. If it
involves validating one's own opinion and social identity as a result
(Rijsman, 1983), the views of the reference people in one's own
group are decisive. If it involves establishing differences, as for
example in the case of suspected social disadvantage in the social
allocation process, then it is necessary to compare oneself with
other groups (Tajfel and Forgas, 1981; J. Turner and Oakes, 1986).

## Evidence by sheer perception?

The evidence experience has been called one of the essential features of common sense, conveying the power of the sheer perception of things. 'The world is the way we see it' is the motto of
everyday orientation. This principle apparently contradicts explanations of evidence criteria conveyed by the collective.

When Asch (1956) carried out his well-known experiment on
group influence and conformity, he created a situation in which
personal perception contradicted the collective judgement. When
individual test participants in a group of experimental informers
had to judge three lines which were perceivably of considerably different lengths, the other apparent participants in the experiment
contradicted the convincing view by giving a judgement about the
line which, although false, was consistent. One can imagine the distress of the genuine participants by looking at the photographs in
a text by Asch. The facial expressions of one test participant show
a confusion which is worthy of sympathy.

As many test participants, at least in a public situation, finally
gave into group pressure and adopted the false judgement, Asch
saw the experiment as an illustration of the influence of the majority in experimental situations. Alternatively, Moscovici (e.g. 1979b)
in his works about minority influence interpreted the imitation

effect of the test participant as a consequence of the influence of a consistent minority (compared with the great majority of the population not present in the experiment). Both interpretations are agreed that collective judgements and opinions are in a position to destroy the evidence of sheer perception. Direct perception for us is only valid as criteria for veridicality as long as we know ourselves to be in harmony with the weight of consensus of the anonymous collective of our reference group.

## Locality and universality

In the cycle of life in our culture we encounter many different possibilities of obtaining evidence. Validating one's own views and opinions by social comparison is only one of many options. Let us think of the ideology-forming influence of parents and other relatives, as well as, for example, teachers and powerful people in general. It is often enough for the remarks of individual recognised 'leaders' to impart an evidence experience to 'the masses'. How else could it be explained why some decades ago 910 men, women and children in the village of Jonestown in the Guyanan forest committed collective suicide without excessive force having to be applied against them? Similarly, Reverend Jones succeeded years before in creating a religious community more or less from scratch and many of his disciples followed the instruction to commit suicide (see Cialdini, 1984). Was it just the persuasive power doubtlessly exercised by Jones or (of equal importance) the evidence experienced through his words?

Evidence is realised at different times, at different places and in different cultures in different forms. Authoritative evidence can provide intuition, introspection, external observation, meditation, the testimony of the Holy Scriptures, the prophets, the seers, the monks or the ancients (Shweder, 1986, p. 181). Just like thought contents in the form of metaphors, analogies and models, as well as the classification categories for natural objects, the criteria of evidence are variable quantities. We can join Shweder (1986) in speaking of 'divergent rationalities' which are at least 'softly' consistent and acquire local truth via their innate evidence. Elias's (1978b) dictum, that the only thing people universally share is their variablility, applies to this as much as to any other cultural phenomenon.

In this chapter we have defined the formal framework which will give us room to explore in the discussions which follow. The theory of social representations is one of the contemporarily important social-psychological approaches to represent forms of everyday knowledge and take them as determinants of psychological phenomena. Social representations are interpreted as that part of epistemological knowledge which is subject to the dynamic changes and mechanisms of consciousness production in our modern society. As a result the same defining elements apply to them as were designated for content-rational systems. They must follow the pragmatic efficiency demands of the cognitive 'miser', that is, the pragmatic imperative, in order to satisfy the practical orientation needs of everyday life. This concerns the reference to the concrete, the heuristics of similarity, the need to explain, and the criteria of local consistency derived from them. Further, they are subject to the evidence criteria of consensus, and are relative to the times and places in which they are formed and have an effect.

# Chapter 4

# Introducing Social Representations

## 4.1 On the concept of 'social representations'

### 4.1.1 Delimitations

The history of scientific concepts is littered with abandoned and half-forgotten concepts, and associated theories that have not withstood the 'test' of new generations of scientists and their research. This is particularly, but not only true in the social sciences. The social sciences are a distinctive field, because their history and progress are tightly linked to the political and societal history of civilisation. New societal conditions bring with them new problems in people's lives, and new political structures that need to be accommodated in social scientific theory building. What is considered progressive in one decade is condemned as conservative in the next, and vice versa. Hence, the development of social sciences resembles less the image of cumulative progress with occasional 'scientific revolutions' (Kuhn, 1970) than a never-ending search for the one and only theory. Theories in the social sciences die with the retirement of their authors more often than in other sciences. This theoretical discontinuity has the consequence that new theoretical approaches sometimes mimic old ones, without giving due credit to their forefathers.

Another characteristic of social theory is its qualitative format. By qualitative format we mean the fact that most social science theories are not, or cannot be expressed in mathematical terms, unlike those in the so-called hard sciences. Even biology, which has been qualitative for centuries, is currently on the road to mathematical reformulation, thanks to the progress made in genetics, evolutionary modelling and computer simulation. Social theories escape easy mathematical formulation due to the complexities of social life, the 'illumination effect' (Habermas, 1968) and the near impossibility of defining reliable and reproducible measures, particularly of discursive events. Once a social theory becomes known among the general public, the people, being at the same time the objects and the 'illuminated' knowers of the theory, ever so subtly change their behaviours, thereby defeating the theory. The problematic of defining measures has to do with the highly complex and involuted nature of meaning in everyday discourse, where syntax, pragmatics and variable cultural conventions combine to determine the meaning of an utterance. These problems are unknown to natural sciences; and they justify, in a way, the widely qualitative and natural-language-based format of social theories. The result is that theories in the field of social sciences are hard to compare, and also hard to evaluate in a reliable way. It is much easier to compare mathematically accessible theories. This fact often leads to confusion in social scientific theory building, also in social representation theory.

As a consequence, several theoretical approaches compete in the field of a more societal psychology, including discursive and constructionist psychology, Vygotskian sociocultural approaches, anthropologically inspired cultural psychology, Marxist and critical psychology and social representation theory. Each of them has its own merits, shortcomings, blind alleys and explanatory potential in its own area, such that a decision for or against one of the theories is often more a matter of personal taste and sympathy than rationality or pragmatic justification. Targeting very similar social and cultural processes, they are more often than not complementary in a global sense. This book is about social representation theory, but the authors are aware of the other theories' value as complementary approaches.

The concept of social representations was first internationally mentioned about 40 years ago in an *Annual Reviews* article about attitude research (Moscovici, 1963). The theory was originally intended as a dynamic social counterweight to the individualised concept of attitude, which appeared too static and asocial for modern social psychology. Its historical proximity to the classical concepts of attitude and opinion, however, resulted sometimes in its being erroneously used as equivalent to these terms.

There are quite a few concepts which may be understood as anticipating one or another aspect of social representations. Attitudes and opinions have already been mentioned. Other candidates include attitude systems or attitude hierarchies as structured cognitive contents; structured knowledge in the form of story grammars; and propositional hierarchies such as macro-propositions (van Dijk and Kintsch, 1983); schemata, scripts and scenes (cf. J. Mandler, 1984); and cognitive maps (Milgram, 1984). It is true that such cognitive top-down processes correspond to the concept of social representation with respect to capturing structured knowledge. However, the knack of social representation theory is to link this knowledge to societal processes. It is this aspect and its implications that set social representation theory apart from traditional approaches. In fairness, we do not dispute that the classical concept of attitude has some legitimacy, especially in applied areas. Attitudes are relatively easy to measure and are therefore of high pragmatic value in some areas of research.

What is common to theoretical constructs explaining top-down processes is that they are viewed as cognitive representations of reality, being subject to the *a priori* limits which the respective culture or society imposes on its members (e.g. van Dijk, 1980). Whether a cognitive entity is seen as an integrated superstructure or as a local cognitive element in the research process depends on the particular standpoint of the researcher. The classification of part and whole is a direct result of the particular science's research interest, formulation of the question, and available methodological and conceptual inventory, as well as its traditions of interpretations. Global constructs are not necessarily restricted to intraphysical cognitive processes. They can be extended just as well to models of interaction between people and the social organisation constituted by them (e.g. Berger and Luckmann, 1979), to vocal comments, dialogue, conversations and written texts; and to the organisational forms of social-structural phenomena like kinship systems, religion and art (e.g. Lévi-Strauss, 1967).

## Roots

The most direct forefather of social representation theory is the sociologist Durkheim. When he debated the theory of symbolic systems using the example of religion (Durkheim, 1981), he noticed that such systems constitute a means for a society to become conscious of its self, and objectify its rules of social intercourse. He characterised it by defining the concept of the 'collective representation' which he contrasts with 'individual representations' (Durkheim, 1967).[1] He points out that social facts cannot be reduced to psychological facts by making an analogy with the irreducibility of psychological facts to neurophysiological ones. The external nature of social facts as far as the individual is concerned, especially social facts of an obligatory nature, justifies viewing them as autonomous superindividual collective constructs. They express themselves, not in individuals, but in their combination (Durkheim, 1967 p. 72 onwards). As a result, they gain partially autonomous reality (p. 78 onwards).

Moscovici's crucial step was to adapt Durkheim's conceptualisation of collective representations to render it more dynamic, applicable to modern societies, and accessible to social-psychological inquiry (Moscovici, 1963). In doing so he intended to make traditional social psychology, with its emphasis on the individual, more culturally and socially relevant (Farr, 1986; Moscovici, 1972). The contemporary version of the theory of social representations has, in addition to those by Durkheim, other roots which will not to be dealt with here. These include the work of Lévy-Brühl (1921) and the dynamic attitude concepts of Thomas and Znaniecki (1918) and of Piaget (Doise, 1987a). These theories have important parallels with social representations. Their historical relationships are dealt with in the context of the history of ideas by Deutscher (1984), van Ginneken (1989) and Moscovici (1989a).

One important point of social representation theory is the intimate relationship between the subjective and the objective. It is a logical premiss that the complement of the subjective cannot be the physically objective. Individual subjective phenomena, in the social psychological approach, contrast not with objective physical conditions, but with the intersubjectively Given. The individual's own idiosyncratic experience only appears subjective and individual by taking into account the background (virtually the projection screen) of collective intersubjectivity. Why would individuals want to compare their own conceptions with external natural objects, which too are only accessible to them via their own senses, thus subjectively? Individual perception is 'perceiving the truth' and therefore objective for individuals.[2] Only communication and the cultural matrix acquired in the socialisation process make it possible for one's own opinions, ideas, feelings and impulsive experiences to be compared intersubjectively and make it possible for doubt of the truth of subjective events to be raised (cf. Tyler, 1978, p. 146 onwards). A 'socialised' social psychology cannot therefore, for both logical and pragmatic reasons, close its mind to the collective environment and its representation in the individual, even if it conceives itself as being individual centred.

In this aspect social representation theory and other modern approaches are at odds with traditional social cognition theory. Social cognition juxtaposes the subjective inner experience and the objective outer world. This world is populated by physical objects with attributes 'which would be registered on mechanical recording devices' (Ostrom, 1984, p. 9). A person's inner experience is called 'subjective' because it may be either a veridical or a wrong representation of the outside world. In fact, 'subjective' is often used as a synonym for a wrong belief. By manipulating physical objects, social cognition researchers maintain, people can validate their subjective representations. This definition of 'subjective' versus 'objective' assumes that the sensory data resulting from manipulation are somehow less 'subjective' than the sense data by which a person attained his or her representation in the first place. This assumption is unwarranted, though, because both sets of sense data (i.e. their interpretation) belong to the subjective world. As Putnam (1990) puts it: 'The idea that we sometimes compare our beliefs directly with unconceptualised reality has come to seem untenable' (p. 121). Traditional social psychology's 'mystery act' of opposing the subjective to the physically objective (p. 121) follows from the individualist framework. The model of the 'lonely cognizer' separates the person from the wider interpersonal environment – that is, society and culture – which therefore appear as a superfluous embellishment of psychological theory.

Figure 4.1 depicts how social representation theory acknowledges the fact that knowledge is social in origin and in general not the product of individual cognition. The person's epistemic relationship to an object is defined and mediated by his or her relevant others. The group, through its system of representations elaborated in discourse and in the service of communication, sources the individuals's understanding of, and interaction with, the world.

In the following parts of this chapter we will elaborate some global views on the concept of social representations. This will be done by emphasising three aspects of the theory which are fundamental in our opinion: first, the descriptive function as a way to ascertain the everyday knowledge of people and groups; and

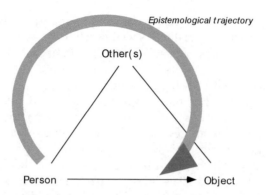

FIGURE 4.1 Illustration of the epistemological trajectory of a person's understanding of social objects

second, dynamic aspects on a collective level; and finally, the metatheoretical aspects of the theory.

### 4.1.2 A preliminary definition of social representations

By giving a preliminary definition of social representations at this point, we run the risk of artificially separating the individual and collective elements in representations. We hope, however, that the research examples given later in this book will correct this impression.

### Individual knowledge systems

The first aspect characterising social representations is as the: (a) structured, (b) cognitive, affective, evaluative and operative, (c) metaphorical or iconic 'portrayal', of (d) socially relevant phenomena. These can be 'events', 'stimuli' or 'facts' (e) of which individuals are potentially aware and which are (f) shared by other members of the social group. This commonality between people represents (g) a fundamental element of the social identity of the individual. The above definition could do with come elucidation, and what follows elaborates the indicated points:

*(a)*  A representation forms a structured, multi-dimensional portrayal of the subject area – that is, a whole set of statements related to one another as a theory-like construct. This stands in contrast with attitudes and singular opinions of a one-dimensional nature.

*(b)*  Although linguistically accessible, social facts are probably, in the majority of cases, represented in iconic, image or metaphorical form. The particular character of iconic and metaphorical forms links them to affective experience since they relate to phenomena which directly affect individuals in their everyday lives. For the same reason, a representation is evaluative because social facts affect the well-being of individuals in various ways. Finally, and as a consequence of their evaluative character, social representations also encompass bodily and verbal actions.

*(c)*  As such, a social representation is not a portrayal in the sense of a proposition which can be either true or false. Instead, it can be understood as an elaboration of ideas or facts, which has a fiduciary truth. Being symbolic in character, representations mediate between the individual and the social world and endow objects and facts with their unique social meaning. Thereby they convert brute facts into the social objects that populate the life space of groups.

*(d)*  Phenomena that may become socially represented can be brute facts, that is, processes and relations between people, animals and things, but they can also be ideas that have a bearing on a person's life. The distinction between real and imagined entities is somewhat artificial, since each object can only become socially relevant to the extent that it obtains imagined meaning at the same time. But what is social relevance for an object? Is a tree, an animal, or a stone a social object, or must the tree have been planted by people, the animal domesticated, and the stone broken by humans? Is an assistant in a shop, my neighbour's child, or the head of state a more social object than the things of inhabited and uninhabited nature? What feature differentiates social from non-social objects?

The answer from the social cognition perspective is that social objects are physical or imagined people, that is, the cognizers themselves, or others. Social cognition investigates how people try to understand themselves and others (S. Fiske and Taylor, 1984, p. 17). People are different from other entities, in that they actively influence their environment, remember and are influenced by others. Their traits or characteristics cannot be directly observed, but only ascertained;[3] they change over time and are complex (p. 16 onwards). Ostrom (1984) amplifies this by stressing the degree to which social cognition is related to action. This tradition categorises objects (albeit roughly) according to traits which are meant to permit a definition of an object as a social or non-social one.

In contrast to this, social representation theory defines socially relevant phenomena and objects not according to any traits inherent to the objects, but according to the relation that exists between people and the objects and the events represented by them. There are cats and holy cats, blocks of flats and imperial buildings, and there are people who are only seen as natural objects when, as patients, they are treated by some of their doctors (Moscovici, 1982, p. 117 onwards). It is the meaning of the things in, and for, the lives of people which makes them a social object.

(e)   The potential consciousness of the social idea is a theoretical prerequisite as well as a theoretical necessity. It follows from the nature of the genesis of social representations in social discourse. Unconscious contents could not be the object of collective discourse, and in addition, unconscious contents would not be ascertainable using the methods predominantly applied by researchers working in relevant areas. As will be discussed later, this characteristic demarcates the social representation from sociological concepts such as 'habitus' (Bourdieu, 1987).

(f)   Ideas should be considered social representations only if they are predominantly, but not necessarily entirely shared by the members of a group that is culturally distinct in society. This does not necessarily require complete consensus, as is sometimes critically remarked (e.g. Potter and Litton, 1985), but rather extensive agreement by the partners of a social group in the sense of modal representivity. If individual group members ignore the discourse or are prevented from participating in it, this does not negate the meaningfulness of speaking of a shared representation.

*(g)* Since these shared ideas contain both judgemental and action-directing elements, they orientate the way members of the group act, both between one another and with respect to outsiders. The background knowledge shared by members of the group distances it from other competing groups and individuals, who lack the associated interpretative schema. The relative uniformity *vis-à-vis* others lends the group member security and identity. At the same time, the social representational system essential for the social identity of groups reinforces the marginalisation of others, and justifies discrimination. In this way, social representations also play an important role for intergroup behaviour.

It is nonetheless linguistically ambiguous to speak of objects whose representation directs the dealings people have with these objects. The distinction between an object and its representation is only accessible to the observer – the social psychologist, for example. Only from the outside do bearers of a representation appear to be confronted with an object existing independently of them. Only the observer can make the decision as to whether to describe and localise the object physically, chemically or in some other natural-scientific way – that is, whether to select whichever scientific form of representation permits real objects to be distinguished from imagined ones and natural objects from artificial ones. The social protagonist, on the other hand, is not offered the object independently of its socially represented form, either in perception or action. Strictly speaking, the social protagonist does not interact with the object itself, but with its represented form. It is therefore linguistically incorrect to speak of objects and their representation if an internal view of a community is intended. The reader should keep in mind that speaking of the 'social representation of an object' is always a shorthand for the aforementioned complex relationship (W. Wagner, 1996).

### Societal discourse

Second, the term 'social representation' identifies the process of the origin, change and elaboration of the iconic portrayal of things in the discourse of social groups discussed above.

Social ideas arise and change whenever people discuss them and collectively exchange thoughts about them. One could also say that a group engages in a 'project' of coming to terms with a new phenomenon (M. Bauer and Gaskell, 1999). This, however, is not necessarily a purposeful process which always and immediately follows real social needs, even though social discussion is doubtless initiated by real needs, problems and conflicts. Using the analogy of the spread of disease, we can speak of epidemiological processes, in the course of which new or altered social representations become established in the knowledge system of group members (Sperber, 1990).

Social discourse, as understood here, is not only a small-group process, such as a conversation or discussion between people at certain locations, such as the pub, but also a collective phenomenon or social institution. The media also play a decisive role here. One can therefore casually speak of the 'thinking' of a society or organisation (Douglas, 1986).[4] Additionally, discourse in our understanding is not only verbal, that is, any talking or writing done in a social situation. As a social action (van Dijk, 1997) discourse subsumes also any overt (bodily) action in a social context, which by virtue of its semiotic powers conveys meaning to other social actors. Through the communicative function and/or consequence of any such discourse, people sharing a social setting construct a particular reality that is true for the actors at a given time and place.

## Macro-reduction

A third way of understanding social representations on a meta-theoretical level is as a concept which enables the social and the individual level of analysis to be related to each other. Thus, it allows us to construct explanations of individual and interindividual processes by using social conditions as explanatory devices.

Unlike theories of the form 'if x, then y' or 'x explains y', whose explanatory concept (x) and explained concept (y) derive from one and the same level of analysis (such as the individual intrapsychic level, for example), theories whose concepts are not located on the same level of analysis are logically problematical in science.

One can conceive the theory of social representations as an attempt to transpose or translate social-structural facts as a 'macro-reduction' (Friedman, 1981) into forms of thinking in order to make possible top-down explanations from the social to the individual.

If, in this preliminary definition and subsequent chapters, we speak of social representations as being simultaneously individual knowledge contents and social discourse models, then we mean to understand this separation more as an analytical than an actual duality. It is difficult not only in everyday life but also in theory to look at both sides of a coin simultaneously – to use a long-serving metaphor. Of course both viewpoints refer to one and the same phenomenon, namely the circular translation of superindividual conditions into a pattern of individual behaviour, whose togetherness and concertedness reproduce, but can also change, the superindividual conditions. Separate treatment of the individual and social side is a result of the methodological difficulty of, on the one hand, conceptually grasping both sides at the same time, and on the other, the handed-down premises of 'if-then' social-scientific thinking.

The problem of simultaneously dealing with different levels is not new. It is often dealt with in the social sciences. It is possibly the consequence of a deeply rooted cultural conception in the developed and science-orientated societies of the West: a fundamental representation which prohibits us from thinking of society and the individual as being in anything other than confrontation (cf. Duveen and Lloyd, 1986).

## The term 'representation'

The German and English semantics of the term 'representation' comes across as something that describes a thing. An image represents something and is simultaneously something that can be touched, a screen, a sheet of paper, a photographic plate. In a system consisting of an object and its representation, we are dealing with two material things according to popular belief. In such contexts 'representation' is rightly an ontological concept.

In early philosophy and psychology, 'representation' was used from Schopenhauer and later Wundt to describe the idea as recalling something not present (Schmidt, 1969). In this sense the concept takes on an epistemological, or non-ontological character which comes closer to our use of the term.

In some of its variations, the concept of representation poses a philosophical problem (Collins, 1979; Maze, 1991). For example, in a discussion of the concept of belief as a representation, Collins

(1979) criticises the idea of wanting to understand an opinion as either a physical state of the nervous system (the materialistic view) or a state of an immaterial mind (the mentalistic view). Both views lead to the same problems, even if they shift the metaphysical reference:

> The presence of a mind-state, like that of a brain-state, cannot be identified with belief *that* p because its existence will be patently independent of the truth of p, and this independence will have to be recognized by the believer. The independence of 'Such and such is present in my nonphysical mind,' on the one hand, and 'Caesar crossed the Rubicon,' on the other, must generate the same inevitable difficulties for mentalist theories of belief that we have already traced in materialism.
>
> (Collins, 1979, p. 242 onwards)

Without going into Collins's detailed reasoning here, it seems to me that he is indicating an important point which affects the use of the term 'representation' when it involves the material location of representations. Although Collins's criticism refers to individual opinions and brain-states, it also fits the understanding of 'représentation sociale' as a collective phenomenon. That too refers, in analogy to the individual idea, to the condition or state of a social construct, the expression of which is a particular belief system 'p', which is realised in the actions of collective protagonists.

In the present context we understand the term 'representation' to be a theoretical construct, which is used to describe a mental state or social process of whatever nature, by which physical or ideal objects are designated. At the same time, we do not imply any particular physiological nature and material location of this condition, neither in the individual nor the collective domain.[5]

We can speak of a representation R at the precise moment when an observer, for example a social psychologist, establishes through observed linguistic or other behaviour that: 'The observed individual or collective protagonist A possesses representation R about a real or imagined object X', without having to make any correspondence to a physical or mental realisation of representation R. It is not whatever the protagonist says or does, for example, which is the representation, but term R in the model sustained by the observer. If we say the following: 'Protagonist A possesses representation R', it is to be understood as 'Protagonist A behaves as though he possessed representation R'; or, expressed differently:

'The protagonist behaves as though he lived in a world whose objects (that are essential for him) are represented in him, in such and such a form' (cf. Friedman, 1981, p. 9). The term 'representation' is a construct that plays an explanatory role in theories referring to socially related individual and collective behaviour. The term does not explain anything by itself, but is used as a way of talking about observed individual or collective behaviour in particular contexts.

### 4.1.3  An anthropology of modern societies

In a discussion about the incompleteness of artificial languages Wittgenstein (1969) asks:

> whether our language is complete; – whether it was so before the symbolism of chemistry and the notation of the infinitesimal calculus were incorporated in it; for these are, so to speak, suburbs of our language. (And how many houses or streets does it take before a town begins to be a town?) Our language can be seen as an ancient city: a maze of little streets and squares, of old and new houses, and of houses with additions from various periods; and this surrounded by a multitude of new boroughs with straight regular streets and uniform houses.
>
> (p. 296)

If we extend this idea to the system of our cultural and everyday knowledge (according to Geertz, 1983), then social psychology is only just starting to chart those suburbs with uniform houses which are the social heritage of a historically late time. It ventures only hesitantly, if at all, into the cultural old town, which is traditionally reserved for cultural anthropology.

In the 'suburbs' of everyday knowledge, the social life of people in developed countries, but increasingly also in the economically more developed regions of the world, is undergoing permanent reconstruction and change. Some districts remain incomplete, because social-economic activity changed too early, before this part of modern mentality was completed. Other, older districts fall victim to more recent fashionable trends: the 'zeitgeist', whose wind direction in modern societies hardly knows any continuity. A certain constancy is demonstrated by the shopping malls, the factories of consumption of the new districts, in which, though the brand names of the wares and consumer goods may change, the actual product produced in these factories – the consumer – does not. It is not only material goods which are consumed, but ideas, scientific theories and modern eclecticist mythologies of the so-called psychoscene.

The suburbs of everyday knowledge, or better: the everyday knowledge of the suburbs, comprises the knowledge learned from parents and the values shaped during primary socialisation, much like our school knowledge and that professional knowledge which is becoming more relevant in the household as well as the workplace (for example technical abilities, or knowledge of using computers and operating software). Even the most modern knowledge very seldom confronts us with a cultural-historical heritage in a really new and unconfused way. Rather, all knowledge acquired in this way constitutes a cluster of traditional and recent elements that are hard to unravel: 'There is nothing in the suburbs (of knowledge) which would not first have appeared in the old town' (Geertz, 1983, p. 262).

We accept and take on information offered to us via the mass media and speak with friends and acquaintances if we want to know more about one of their special fields. This knowledge and these values, in part, have undergone a long historical development so that they have become a part of our culture. Religions and their value systems, especially, have penetrated and formed societies during the course of history, in a way that makes it impossible to separate them from a particular culture either practically or theoretically. In fact, they *are* this culture, and form the institutions and ways of organisation of their societies. They shape how facts can be experienced as problematic. All these stores of knowledge and ways of experience are an integral component of human identity, with its cultural, national and kin-related subdivisions.

Over the past 100–200 years, a new field has developed in addition to classical sources of everyday knowledge. The significance of this new field has now almost reached the level which the religious and ecclesiastical institutions could claim in earlier times. It is the field of natural-scientific and technical research and development. The same, perhaps less clearly, applies to the social sciences. Because of the logical structure of science, only propositional and instrumental knowledge can be produced – that is, knowledge that excludes value components in principle, but integrates them nonetheless into real societies and the ideological and political discourses where value judgements are currency. This integration affects the transfer of scientific and technological thought systems into everyday knowledge. Thanks to the judgemental neutrality which is implicitly, if not always practically, attributed to them, scientific statements and theories obtain an image of solidity which makes them appear particularly useful for underpinning ideological argumentation in practice. The credibility and truth previously ascribed to elders or religions is nowadays to a large degree attributed to science. Many conversations by the 'man or the woman on the street' can be observed in which reference is made, implicitly or explicitly, but always in an abbreviated manner, to the supposed findings of the system of science. Published, and above all popularised, scientific knowledge enters everyday discourse, and forms points of view, argumentation strategies and ways of allocating blame.

In appropriating elements of scientific knowledge and practices common sense adapts science for use in the domain of everyday life. It is being adapted according to the criteria dominating everyday practices, social relationships and communication. In this understanding the theory of social representations does justice to common sense in delineating the marked differences and the commonalities between scientific understanding and everyday thinking by highlighting their respective realms of validity (cf. Foster, 2003; Purkhardt, 1993).

All these areas are potentially subjects of social representation research, so the heterogenous majority of relevant empirical works does not surprise us. On the contrary, it is much more surprising that so many cultural areas have not yet been investigated. It seems that the more we implicitly or practically know about a social world, the less we tend to question things and relations, or make them the subject matter of scientific work. The closer we are to an object, the greater the necessary effort becomes to get it into focus as a research problem (cf. W. Wagner, 1990).

What immediately catches the eyes of anthropologists in a foreign culture, hits the blind spot of their theoretical eyes in the researchers' own culture and society. The task for a psychology of social representations does not differ practically from that of anthropology. Hence this social psychology is not by coincidence called an anthropology of modern society (Moscovici, 1987a, p. 514) – that is, of societies where culture has attained a new sort of dynamics and autonomy (J. Alexander, 1995, p. 146).

## 4.2  Research fields

The range of empirical works on social representations can be structured on the basis of two aspects, the contents and the methods used.

### Research topics

The first aspect relates to the importance which is given to various collective phenomena. It is orientated towards the contents, or rather, the real and imagined objects, relations and institutions which are represented. We would like here to distinguish primarily between cultural objects, social phenomena and conditions, and scientific theories. Cultural objects in this context are such as were formed by long-lasting historical processes and would rarely gain the acute topicality of, for example, ecological matters. Examples of cultural objects include bodies, sickness and health, psychological states, children and adults, or the idea of time. Scientific theories well known to many people include: psychoanalysis, which is very often a popular synonym for psychology; the theory of relativity; Marxism as a theory of society and economy; or new technologies. Social conditions which frequently gain economic relevance to the present include employment and racial conflicts, school and education or ecological problems.

The question can be raised whether one should demarcate cultural contents, such as the body or sickness and health, from other social contents like work, school and new technologies; or whether these are entities that are comparable in principle. The distinction made here is chiefly substantiated by the two following differences. On the one hand, the core forming the basis to social representations has historically grown along with cultural representations. It is therefore doubtless more stable than more transient representations, formed in short- or medium-term historical processes, which adapt to the relatively fast transformation of technology and living conditions. Cultural representations are closely linked to ideas of 'Weltanschauung' and religion and in part are even identical to them. We can therefore accept a greater homogeneity of cultural representations, with the effect that they are shared by larger collectives within a society than, for example, knowledge about technology. Of course, objects that do not easily lend themselves to clear demarcation can be found in the continuum which is opened thereby.

## Methods

The second aspect differentiates empirical research methods. These mainly consist of document, text and media analysis, the use of questionnaires and free or structured interviews, focus-groups and, finally, social-psychological experiment. These will be presented in more detail later in this book.

Although the different formulations of question and forms of understanding which one can come up with studying social representations appear to demand a multi-methodological approach (Flament, 1981), the majority of investigations are limited to a single empirical method. The consequence of this is that only one side, for the most part the individual representation of collective ideas, is being recorded. Comprehensive analyses which combine individual interviews and questionnaires with analysis of discourse, documents and media are rare. It is naturally even more difficult to link field and experimental studies. But it is only studies such as these which would permit the interaction between the micro- and macro-dynamics of the representation process to be shown.

## 'Primary' and 'secondary' representations

The content areas of social representation research demonstrate a dilemma in the use of the term. In the original works the term 'social representation' is found as a substitute for popularised scientific theories. In actual fact the subject matter of one of the first investigations was of course the popularisation of psychoanalysis (Moscovici, 1961/1976). Cultural imagination, such as 'bodies' (Jodelet, Ohana, Bessis-Monino and Dannenmüller, 1982) or 'sickness' (Herzlich, 1973), increasingly became the subject of research in later works. There is a gap between these two research lines in their usage of the term 'social representation'; in the first case as a more or less simplified theory, as an everyday metaphor for a scientific statement system; in the other case as a 'subject matter' to which the content of the social representation refers (cf. de Rosa, 1994, p. 274).

In the case of representations refering to long-term cultural or short-term social objects the relationship between representation and referent is relatively easy. There is a social object or phenomenon such as a child, a school system, illness or war whose meaning is elaborated and socially represented in the way people relate to these things. There is no other template against which the veridicality of the representation could be judged, except it seems perhaps an analogical representation elaborated by another group. But the very fact that the other group is different and lives in a different cultural world impedes direct comparison and judgment, not least because the other group's analogical but different representation implies a more or less different social object. We may want to call such representations primary.

In the case of popularised scientific theories the situation is slightly different. We have a natural phenomenon that has been investigated by the scientific community resulting in the respective scientific theory. Any popularisation of this theory, hence has as a referent not the original natural phenomenon, but its first-hand scientific representation, that is, the theory elaborated according to the methodological and language standards prevailing in a particular scientific community. In this case any representation elaborated by and within a wider public as a result of vulgarising or popularising the theory is secondary – a re-representation of the original scientific representation. As such, and in contrast to primary representations, we are – in this case – in a position to judge the popular version by comparing it to the scientific version. Although the scientific community is often considered a group by itself, it is also an integral part of the wider social system, particularly in modern societies where scientific expertise takes the place of former priesthood. The game of judging popular representations of scientific findings as erroneous, as well as blaming the man and woman in the street as ignorant in scientific matters, is well known and has been discussed in an earlier chapter of this book. In fact, a whole scientific entreprise called 'the Public Understanding of Science' makes a living from this 'game'.

Primary social representations offer an interpretation schema or a cultural definition of a relevant object. Let us take as an example the simultaneously social and private object of the human body. Studies on the representation of the body investigate how the body is understood, constructed and 'lived' in the discourse and practice of our society (Jodelet, 1984a). Knowledge of our bodies in this case is not at all second-hand knowledge. It consists of the original mental categories: the cognitive and normative models which control the lived experience and knowledge about the body, as well as its use (p. 214). In dealing with the body, the representation integrates daily experiences with the collective norms and practical routines of a social group.

Cultural representations are appropriated differently from popular science representations. They are based on cultural *a prioris*, the continuity of which is established by socialisation and enculturation, and which possess priority over the object. The contents of these representations reflect the social conditions of their genesis, as a result of the handing-down process. The underlying idea here supposes that the cultural object originates only in the process of everyday construction by the collective protagonists. It is constructed over and over again, as implied by the social representation. Cultural knowledge possesses an immanent relationship with the objects it describes; it is their prerequisite and gives them existence. As a result, they do not constitute a model of reality, but a model for reality (Geertz, 1973; Moscovici, 1961/1976). Without knowledge about the cultural objects of everyday life, one cannot speak of them or relate to them.

If scientific theories become the 'object' of representations, then the source of this second-hand knowledge, that is, the scientific publication, is not part of individuals' everyday lives. Scientific theories are a product of an institution relatively isolated from life lived everyday – universities, laboratories, academies and research establishments are only marginally accessible to a reconstruction by outside subjects.[6] In any case, the possibility of access by individuals is very much more restricted than in the case of cultural objects: scientific theories cannot be directly constructed in their practice.

Such representations appear as an explanatory system of statements which offer models of explanation for understanding facts. A social representation of popularised theories must demonstrate 'how the things work'. Here laypeople are easily prone to cross over from the 'what?' to the 'how?', and from there to the 'why?' (Moscovici and Hewstone, 1983, p. 113). Even if a scientific theory was originally purely descriptive, such as the works on hemisphere dichotomy in the brain for example, in everyday usage (as second-hand knowledge) it becomes an explanatory schema where hemispheric dominance is used to explain behaviour tendencies (p. 114).

Once a scientific theory exists in its popularised version, it becomes integrated into the entire complex of cultural background knowledge without being able to influence directly the institution of science as an actual source. It becomes a part of the social representational system and cultural imagination. Therefore, the features of theory-related and object-related representations can be demarcated only in a fuzzy fashion and continuously overlap each other.

# Chapter 5
# The Topography of Modern Mentality

## 5.1 Popularised science

### 5.1.1 Recycling science

We have already seen how science has become an important source of everyday knowledge during the past 100–200 years; especially in connection with the secularisation of everyday life across broad social strata. It has become an authority for legitimisation and justification of political-ideological decisions. The more that classic moral authorities lose their influence, the more science takes their place; providing social living with the seemingly strict rationality of scientific thought and decision.

It is an ironic feature of history that science has to appear as a moral authority. According to its principles and metatheoretical premises, science reveals what is the case and not what ought to be the case. Making science into a moral authority for justification in the everyday understanding of lay people (including politicians), and hoping thereby for a greater rationality of political judgement, overlooks the fact that a value dimension must first arise externally, following social and cultural rules which are not scientifically, but socially rational. One only needs to think of the racial theory of National Socialism with its horrific consequences for Jews, gypsies and other 'unworthy' peoples to see an illustration of this. Improper combinations of scientific findings and political value judgements can also be found in debates on ecology, biotechnology, abortion and the like.

It is, for whatever reason, the very scientific theories that prefer to be popularised which have most appeal to everyday life and the experiences gathered there or which can be transferred to platitudes or common sense. Let us think, for example, of psycho-analysis, the theory of relativity, the philosophy and economic theory of Marxism, medical knowledge and so on which all lend themselves to popularisation. An example of the topical process of propagating and collective appropriating of a science might be the one that we are experiencing just now, in the form of the great public interest being shown towards artificial intelligence research and the daring extrapolations of its advocates (Stähelin, 1991; Weizenbaum, 1990). It is to be expected that this recycling of science as common sense does not in fact result in a reasonably faithful reproduction of the scientific meaning of a theory. Instead, it is mainly those components that are immediately accessible to everyday understanding which are selected (Thorngate and Plouffe, 1987) and reduced to a 'figurative schema' (Herzlich, 1975, p. 391).

In spite of initial resistance to Freud's psychoanalytical theory, some of its basic ideas became established very quickly in the world of everyday wisdom. The resistance of many leading voices in Freud's time, and also later, was a sign that the statements of the theory could not be transferred to everyday knowledge in a linear manner, since they in part contradicted fundamental moral ideas. For example, the term 'libido', on account of its often being mis-understood and reduced to sexual desire and sexual drive, repre-sents such a difficult to integrate concept. As a result, the scientific concepts are selected and taken out of context so that in the fol-lowing stage they can be joined back together in whatever specific elaboration (Herzlich, 1975). The 'figurative schema of psycho-analysis' that is created in this way: 'concentrates on some simple, and easily concretisable concepts, on a point of view of the psyche, in the centre of which stands the conflict between the internal and the external, the manifest and the obscure – they are the meanings which are allocated to the designations of "Conscious" and "Unconscious" – and the availability of a harmful mechanism of "repression" which forms the basis of all evils, the "complexes"' (Herzlich, 1975, p. 391; see also Chapter 7).

One can view everyday theory as a caricature of the name-giving original theory as well. It is no longer a complete theory in the actual sense, but a functionally fragmented construct that corre-sponds to the needs and knowledge guidelines of the culture, as the omission of central concepts, such as 'libido' in the case of psychoanalytical theory, shows. The pragmatic relevance that the original theory has for the particular group determines which parts and concepts appear useful in the framework of existing knowledge. For groups which are accustomed to markedly intellectual discourse, it is essential to adopt the theoretical structure more or less entirely. But for cursory everyday remarks without intellectual claim, all that is needed is knowledge of the foreground of meaning of a few concepts which do not collide with the value guidelines of *a priori* knowledge. The concepts and theory fragments which survive popularisation are not without connection to the original theory, and do preserve some of the concept's structural coherences. Nevertheless, the original content of the psychoanalytical theory is more of a roughly sketched image or metaphor than a reasonably faithful portrayal in its 'recycling as common sense' (Moscovici, 1961/1976).

## Concepts coming home

How does it happen that we can use representations deriving from science and its theories in everyday life, where science is generally seen as abstract and far from everyday domains? A lot of the social sciences use concepts in their vocabulary whose names are borrowed from an extended everyday understanding. These concepts are designated with words which already have a generally comprehensible meaning. Scientific usage, of course, changes this meaning, and assigns the words a specifically theoretical sense in their context which has less to do with the everyday synonym. Which everyday term, for example, could designate and simultaneously illustrate the psychic process of repression more effectively than the one used by Freud? In the process of assimilating scientific theories in the course of popularisation, we therefore arrive at a 'return' of words or concepts previously borrowed from everyday life. With reference to Freud's native German, the note and convincingness of the apparent understanding of psychic processes gained in this manner can be gleaned from the example of the German word for repression, *Verdrängung*. This suddenly changed from its everyday concept of physical *Verdrängung*, meaning ousting, displacement or the pushing and shoving that occurs, for example when boarding a bus, and became applicable to forgetting processes.

Above all, one should be able to expect of such theories that they will result in popularisations and a development of social representations which are suitable for a metaphorical understanding of everyday life. This includes psychoanalysis, and to a somewhat lesser extent Einstein's theory of relativity, which is cited as the authority for the assertion that taste and many other things are relative. It is open to doubt in such cases whether the everyday user of the term 'relativity' has any idea of what the curvature of space and the speed of light actually mean. In fact, the theory of relativity may have become established in everyday discourse more as a result of its having been imparted by the prototypical genius of Einstein. Above and beyond his actual theories, the man symbolises the power of the word: the sheer idea which comes to fruition in the 'historic equation' $E = mc^2$ (Barthes, 1964, p. 25).

A second, albeit trivial precondition for assimilating science is often forgotten. Not all groups in a population possess the same will to assimilate, or have the same chances of being confronted with scientific statements, however popularised they may be, or of understanding them (cf. Thorngate and Plouffe, 1987). This often restricts such knowledge and the development of representations to limited strata of population, depending on the degree of popularity of the theory, and the range of attention it is given by the media. G. Jahoda (1988b, p. 203) points out that it is mainly the more educated strata which possess representations of psychoanalysis. This puts them in a position to compare the theory with a religious belief system, which is something less intellectually orientated strata do not do. This argument refers to the thesis that representations are used among other things to make the hitherto unfamiliar familiar, for example in the way that the formerly unfamiliar psychoanalysis has been interpreted pastorally. In order to be able to make such a comparison, people must first get to know the new theory to a not insignificant extent, which is probably only possible for strata which are more open intellectually.

## Labels

Using the names of theories and theory-bound concepts in everyday discourse – as with the theory of relativity – does not always indicate a collective assimilation of significant parts of those scientific theories. This appears to be the case with Marxism, the social representation of which has been investigated at the École des Hautes Études en Sciences Sociales in Paris. General knowledge about the philosophical and economic theory of Marxism is much lower than about psychoanalytical theory, and at the same time shared out much less homogeneously. Explicit knowledge about theoretical contexts and concepts is markedly limited even amongst the ranks of unequivocally Marxist-orientated political groups like the French Communist Party.[1]

It seems that these, and also other theories of high political import and social symbolic content, are not assimilated primarily for their explanatory value. I. Bauer (1988) illustrates this in a comprehensive interview study of the political and everyday history of the female workers at Hallein, a tobacco factory, during the interwar period. Although all the workers declared themselves socialists and the social democratic party of the time explicitly defined itself as Marxist, the women interviewed did not possess even the simplest background knowledge of Marxist theory: 'To be a socialist was . . . for these women obviously . . . less a question of ideology, of great political principles, utopias and designs for society at the back of the head. It was much more something to reinforce one's sense of belonging to the workers.' Marxism and social-democratic models of orientation were for these women 'in a very general sense points of reference for identity, self-assertion and stability' (p. 205). In such cases, the use of theoretical names and terminology does not act as a model for explaining social reality, but more as labels and symbols for determining one's own social identity.

There are many areas of scientific knowledge which seem to be suited for popularisation as social representations. These include the sciences of psychic phenomena and behaviour (e.g. Deconchy, 1987; Furnham and Wardley, 1990; Mugny and Pérez, 1988); natural phenomena (e.g. Nascimento-Schulze, 1999); psychiatry, psychology and the profession of psychologists associated with it (e.g. de Paolis, 1990; Gigling, Guimelli and Penochet, 1996; Thommen, Ammann and von Cranach, 1988); biology and medicine (e.g. Buchhotz, 1991; Deconchy, 1990; Fraisse and Stewart, 2002; Herzlich, 1973; Joffe and Haarhof, 2002; Lucchetti, 1991; Markovà and Wilkie, 1987; Moloney and Walker, 2000, 2002; Páez, Villareal, Echebarria Echaba and Valencia, 1991; Schmitz, Fillipone and Edelman, 2003; W. Wagner, Elejabarrieta and Lahnsteiner, 1995); new technologies with potential risk such as biotechnology and novel food (Bäckström, Pirtillä-Backman and Tuorila, 2003; W. Wagner and Kronberger, 2001; W. Wagner, Kronberger and Allum et al., 2002); and risk in general (e.g. Joffe, 2003). The object of these scientific disciplines is the human being in various manifestations: as a subject that acts and a body that suffers through disease or natural phenomena such as earthquakes (Yamori, 2001) . They are close to everyday peoples' conception and experience of themselves, which provides reasons for the intensive interest in the insights of these sciences.

These sciences build on very old (in part even palaeolithic) prescientific cognitive systems, represented in all cultures by specialists (cf. e.g. Beals, Hoijer and Beals, 1977; Herzlich and Pierret, 1984). They are the basis for modern representations of the body, health, illness, psychology and intelligence, and the way that medical or psychological knowledge – almost as an extension of the culture's concept of the human being (see Heelas and Lock, 1981) – forms the keystone of a foundation that has existed for a long time (Moscovici and Hewstone, 1983, p. 116). Such representations form an amalgam of culturally traditional knowledge and new scientific insights which is hard to disentangle, as is shown by Herzlich (1973), for example, in a study of everyday images of health and illness (cf. also Augé and Herzlich, 1984).

## The genesis of representations

A relatively short time ago, a particular disease acquired sudden publicity which it has maintained until today. The debate about the disease described by the abbreviation AIDS enables us to reconstruct the steps to the topical genesis of a social representation (cf. Apostolidis, 2001; Joffe, 1995; Lucchetti, 1991; Markovà and Wilkie, 1987; Páez, Echebarría Echabe, Valencia et al., 1991).

The debate in the media bears a detailed resemblance to public discussions about syphilis in the second half of the nineteenth century. From the outset of the AIDS debate there was a predominant tone of the threatening and uncontrollable, which led to a moral debate. AIDS was not viewed as an individually contractable contagious disease, but as a stigma and 'divine scourge' of minorities with devout sexual practices. Rather than considering how the disease came about (which was already known at the time of the first bout of publicity, and was no longer restricted to the at-risk groups to homosexuals and the drug scene) the moral – or moral-ising – majority's resort to moral judgements represents the first defensive reaction to protect their self-esteem.

At the same time, such a frightening, inevitable, and simultaneously 'just' (Gruman and Sloan, 1983; Lerner, 1971) phenomenon like this disease – which apparently only strikes others – confirms the correctness of one's own way of life. It required several years of discussion in the media before the details of scientific knowledge began to structure public consciousness. It was only then that we could deal pragmatically with the phenomenon of AIDS, which as almost all of us now know does not spare women and is not limited to particular sexual practices. But general enlightenment does not prevent this field of disease being used as a strong social metaphor, 'behind which are concealed fears, conflicts, taboos and projections' (Lucchetti, 1991, p. 146). There are thus two general types of representations which reflect the extent of integrated scientific knowledge developing, which depend on the possibilities of coming into contact with HIV-infected people. More scientifically correct knowledge exists to a greater extent in a 'liberal' representation, for example, than in a 'conservative' one (Páez, Echebarría Echabe, Valencia et al., 1991).

Using data from policy analyses, media analyses and a Europe-wide survey about public perceptions of biotechnology, W. Wagner, Kronberger and Seifert (2002; W. Wagner and Kronberger, 2001) showed how a country's population develops an everyday understanding of a new technology which has been construed as potentially harmful by the media. The study emphasises the importance of the public relevance of an issue which encourages the genesis of menacing images and representations of a potentially threatening technology, such as genetic engineering. Although the media set the agenda in alerting the public, it is the people who, in their discourse, develop an understanding of the technology as metaphorical beliefs. These image beliefs are relatively independent of pre-existing popular science knowledge, and they are functionally equivalent to scientific knowledge in providing judgmental confidence and reducing self-ascribed ignorance. In the case of genetic engineering, it was the shocking news of biotechnology altering how life was assumed to work in lay understanding. The public were particularly prone to resort to such representations in countries where the news broke after relatively little previous media reporting on the issue (cf. also Gaskell and Bauer, 2001).

## Group differences

A second focus for empirical investigations concerns theories about social processes which are to do with the economic existence of humans, as well as with changes that imply the applications of computer science to the world of work (e.g. Furnham, 1986; Grize, Vergès and Silem, 1988; Lewis, 1990; Vergès, 1989). We are dealing here with an area whose prominence can be explained by the meaning of economic knowledge, which leading voices credit for how our economic system functions. Everyday representations in this case constitute a cognitive construct which reduces highly complex economic theories to a few core concepts, which owe their intelligibility to the everyday semantic connotations of the words used. If test participants associate savings with banks, shopping and earnings with family, and taxes with the State, this knowledge appears less as a recycled science, and more as a set of concepts to which the semantics gained from everyday experience are applied (Vergès, 1987).

Vergès (1987, p. 290ff.) therefore sees three sources of economic knowledge: daily practice, the cultural interpretation matrix and ideology. Daily experience constructs the form of economic-related discourse, which often comprises personal experiences and the influences and limitations placed on behaviour by specific situations to which the individual has been exposed. On the other hand, culturally developed conceptions of history, about how the money economy works, for example, often form the matrix within which contemporary economic phenomena are understood.

The ideological dimension to the representation of economic processes can be shown in the clear differences that exist in this field between social groups (Vergès, 1989). Industrial cadres prefer a functionalistic image of the phenomenon of economy which isolates processes as 'machinerie', functioning independently of political contexts. Contrary to this, militant workers stress the continuous link between politics and economics. 'The analysis of economic mechanisms is often mediated by their social and political correlates. The economic givens are not conceptually proper but an extension of the dominant political practice' (Vergès, 1987, p. 401).

No unified image of economy can be identified in the case of dedicated social workers. They structure the subject as being in conflict with ethical ideas, in which the central concepts of economics – money, consumption, market – represent the negative pole of moral dimensions.

Studies such as those cited show that social representations do not constitute proper knowledge of the meaning of the original theory (Grize, 1989, p. 160). Rather, their organisation follows a practical logic of orientation and communication which has nothing to do with the logic of explanation usually adopted by scientific statements. Such representations therefore cannot be described as knowledge analogous to theory either. The factioned concepts and parts of theory are at best clichés in an interpretation system subjected to everyday demands.

## 5.1.2 Explanation versus legitimisation

### Super explanation

Explanatory models of attribution theory usually draw on the causal understanding of current phenomena if the behaviour of a friend, for example, is conspicuously outside of the usual framework. Popularised science as a social representation, by contrast, offers explanatory models which also transcend the immediate situation. It is not the primary task of such representations to explain the minor events of everyday life, in the sense of me ascertaining that 'this stone smashed the glass because it was thrown by that child'. Rather, representations make 'super-explanations' available which go far beyond everyday relevance. They tell us why things are as they are, how they are, explain the existence of the objects identified in them, name surviving aspects of our lives and society, and justify value judgements and moral opinions. Their statements are not part of the causal order of the world, but part of its moral order (Harré, 1981b). Normal explanations help to control chance by reducing the variety of possible causes. Super-explanations explicate the invisible reasons behind the visible manifestations (Moscovici and Hewstone, 1983, p. 122 onwards).

This aspect is demonstrated very neatly by Herzlich's (1973) reduction of the social representation of sickness and health to elementary super-causal relations in such a way that the individual is to society as health is to illness. According to this research, individuals are the bulwark of health, which can only be maintained by them and constitutes their personal property. Never is health something outside of the individual. Illness, on the other hand, comes from outside and results from the reaction of the individual to the pressures of life (Herzlich, 1973 p. 91ff.). The explanations about mental illness produced by the inhabitants of a village in which mentally ill persons are being hosted similarly constitute such super-explanations (Jodelet, 1989b). This can be shown particularly clearly when the 'mentally ill' condition is put down to a lack of attention and nourishment in the broadest sense, or when a patient's level of education – unusual as far as the villagers are concerned – is supposed to have damaged his or her nerves. Similar examples easily come to mind.

The super-explanations of collective conspiracy theories take on especially clear forms, which can be observed in history time and time again with clockwork regularity. In the rarest cases, conspiracy theories can be put down to an actual threat by the collectively marginalised group. The development of these 'collective metaphysical delusions' (Groh, 1987, p. 7) follows the following schema:

1.  An initial trigger in the form of political unrest, economic crisis, agricultural catastrophes, etc.;
2.  a consequent crisis of consciousness, aiming to understand the seemingly mad world as a cognitive reorientation under stress;
3.  a search for the reasons for an event results in identifying guilty people or groups, preferring those which have already aroused attention by being different;
4.  if 'guilty' ones are found, there is a concretisation of a conspiracy theory, which can be released in collective action in order to overcome the evil.

Pogroms of this nature are countless. The self-affirming consequence of such punitive actions is particularly tragic since the sufferings of those affected becomes interpreted as a retrospective validation of the theory in the sense of the 'just world hypothesis', according to which everyone gets what they deserve. Such explanatory models do not resemble what is generally understood by the explanation of a phenomenon. Rather they are metaphysical substantiations of relatively stable relations and conditions, or macrosocial facts, and so go beyond the explanatory function originally intended by the popularised science. Conspiracy theories, according to Moscovici for example, do not pursue the purpose of explaining an event by its cause, (Moscovici, 1987b, p. 157). They are more of a response to the necessity of integrating the image of society into a single 'super-cause'.

Against the example of historical conspiracy theories (which can be found from time to time even today) as illustrating popularised contemporary science, it has been argued that at their time there were none of the knowledge systems which conform to the science of today and which attempt to present us with a more or less rational image of the world. Although the argument is superficially correct, it is nevertheless false. When contemporary science in industrialised society takes on the function of an authority in things to do with explaining the world, then it is precisely that function which it has in common with other historic and pre-scientific explicative-moral authorities, such as the ancients and religious leaders.

Science is an authority today because of its indisputably great achievements, which make everyday life visibly pleasant for many people. This is a consequence of its inherent rationality. On the other hand, however, it is also an authority for non-rational reasons – that is, for the role it plays in modern politics and for the complexities of its doings that escape most people's understanding. The condition and structure of scientific reasoning is hardly accessible to the 'man and woman in the street'. If that reasoning nonetheless lends credence to its findings, then this occurs on account of its definitorial authority.

Desautels and Larochelle (1987) investigated the spontaneous conceptions that adults have of science in general. They observed in many cases that specific definitions of scientific knowledge turned out to be very vague, and were restricted to the descriptive aspects of phenomena. The ideas of scientific methodology, objectivity and knowledge production remain foreign concepts to students as well (Desautels and Larochelle (1987, p. 169).

The answers by respondents in their study reflect the helplessness with which they tackle the question of what science is: 'It seems to me that I have heard talk about it, but I am not sure', 'I can't say, I don't know much, I just heard of it'. Only in a few rare cases could people make the link to scientific rationality and method. This allows us to conclude that science is recognised as a justification system due to its socially attributed authority, and not because its structure distinguishes it from pre-scientific systems of evidence. As a result, assimilating quasi-scientific knowledge into everyday knowledge can be understood as modern myth making, legitimised by its social authority.

## Legitimisation

One of us conducted a small study to investigate how scientific statements are used by supporters of a belief system (W. Wagner, 1984).

*Method.* Eight participants in a seminar on transcendental meditation (TM) were asked in partly structured interviews how to explain the changes of awareness and phenomena of perception attainable via meditation and related techniques. The interview was disguised as a conversation out of personal interest, so that those interviewed did not recognise the interview character, making them assume that the interviewer could be a possible future supporter of TM. None of those asked were qualified scientists, even though some were students of mostly technical vocations.

The Asian philosophy underlying transcendental meditation offers in itself consistent explanations for altered states of consciousness, which can be experienced by meditation. To this extent it is a unified system whose explanations require no external aid whatsoever. During the interview, supporters of this philosophy and technique initially expressed themselves enthusiastically about this technique and the metaphysics associated with it. But questions about how to explain the phenomena were answered in contradictory terms. There was initial predominance in most interviews of the philosophy-inherent explanations and conceptualisations, which are acceptable if one knows and assumes the original vocabulary. However, this did not satisfy six of those asked, and they offered additional explanations, mostly without prompting questions on the part of the interviewer, in order to underline the positive consequences of the meditation method. This occurred with five of the people as the conversation took an explicitly missionary turn, with the aim of convincing the conversation partner of the value of the method. These secondary explanations referred to findings of general psychology and medicine. They were obviously seen as more authoritative by the respondents than the original Asian philosophical explanations and were used to legitimise their 'exotic' interests. These quasi-scientific explanations would remain undisputed if psychologists could not identify them as a one-sided selection motivated by proselytising interest.

What function is adopted by popular psychological theory in this example? Superficially, they explain phenomena in that they provide good, even scientific grounds for their occurrence and the consequences for their practitioners in terms of psychological and physical health. But the supporters communicated more than that. The philosophy, which undoubtedly sounds esoteric to European ears, was not enough for them to substantiate the doctrine and its positive aspects convincingly. For this, they tried clichés from outside science completely foreign to its doctrine. Although the conversation was carried out with someone not initiated, there are reasons to suppose that the secondary explanations also reinforced their own certainty of belief. The half-assimilated science performed an ideological function of justification.[2] Similar functions of the assimilation of popularised science are shown by studies on the everyday understanding of biological phenomena (Deconchy, 1990) and intelligence (Mugny and Carugati, 1985). The same concern was also pursued by the Catholic mass media in France, taking theoretical statements out of the overall context of psychoanalysis and promoting only those that seemed fit for the church's own interest (Moscovici, 1961/1976).

To summarise: declarative, instrumental and explanatory functions can be ascribed to popularised science. The declarative aspect describes and names the area of the phenomenon, and the instrumental aspect gives instructions on how to deal practically with the object or fact. But its most important function is explanatory. It consists, as we shall attempt to show later, of three parts. First, of the immediate causal explanation of a fact, which is still closest to scientific understanding; second, the super-explanation of the metaphysical reason for a social fact; and third, the ideological justification, or secondary substantiation, of existing doctrines.

## 5.2 Social structures and political events

### 5.2.1 Social conditions

If the previous section was about the social representations of scientific theories, then that classification stressed such representations as can be explicitly attributed to fields of science and their theories. The works summarised in this section, on the other hand, deal with knowledge systems about social conditions that do not have such a clearly identifiable origin. In many cases, the spread of scientific knowledge may have a central part to play here as well; but the cultural, and particularly the subcultural tradition as it has formed in social classes of Western societies is just as important. Therefore these works are related to the social problems of developed countries.

Relevant studies in this field predominantly refer to the representation of social conflicts. Themes stretch from the perception of social structure and inequality (e.g Augoustinos, 1991; Emler and Dickinson, 1985; Hewstone, Jaspars and Lalljee, 1982); xenophobia and migration (e.g. Chryssochoou, 2004; Hraba, Hagendoorn and Hagendoorn, 1989; Windisch, 1982); intergroup conflicts (e.g. Augoustinos and Penny, 2001; Bar-Tal and Antebi, 1992; Byford, 2002; Echebarría Echabe, Guede and Castro, 1994; Orr, Sagi, and Bar-On, 2000; Philogène, 1994, 1999; Valencia, Elejabarrieta, Páez, et al., 2003); protest movements (e.g. DiGiacomo, 1980; Orfali, 1990; Reicher and Potter, 1985); aggression (e.g. Campbell and Muncer, 1994; Kornblit and Petracci, 1996; Tapper and Boulton, 2000); community life and the public sphere (e.g. Campbell and Jovchelovitch, 2000; Howarth, 2001; Jovchelovitch, 1995b; Levin-Rozalis, 2000; Pirttilä-Backman, 2000); the reconstruction of democracy and the rise of individualism in the former socialist countries (e.g. Markovà, Moodie, Farr et al., 1998; Markovà, Moodie and Plichtova, 1998, 2000); to the abortion debate and the womens' movement (e.g. Faina, 1984; Harbridge and Furnham, 1991); the issue of human rights (e.g. Clémence, Devos and Doise, 2001; Doise, Spini and Clémence, 1999; Molinari, 2001; Spini and Doise, 1998); and school and education (e.g. Emler, Ohana and Moscovici, 1987; Ivinson, 1998; Monteil and Mailhot, 1988; Orr, Assor, and Cairns, 1996; Rangel, 1977). Recently the European Union and the formation of a European identity have received widespread attention (e.g. Breakwell and Lyons, 1996; Chryssochoou, 2000a, 2000b; de Rosa, 1996; Licata,

2003; Rutland, 1998). The topics of work, unemployment and money (e.g. Capozza, Robusto, Squarza and de Carlo, 1995; Kirchler, 1991; Mannetti and Tanucci, 1993; Meier and Kirchler, 1998; Oberlechner, Slunecko and Kronberger, 2004; Penz, and Sinkovics, 2001; Salmaso and Pombeni, 1986) takes up a prominent place. Although this theme should doubtless be seen in the context of economic theories, the research mentioned here is less concerned with the global theory-orientated image of economy as discussed earlier. Rather the concern is with current social problems, which justifies separating this area from representations of economic processes.

## Orientation and evaluation

Research into the collective coping with social conflicts highlights the relevance of representations to group and identity formation more clearly than the analyses of popularised science. Hewstone, Jaspars and Lalljee (1982) identified the auto-stereotypes and hetero-stereotypes of pupils at elite schools and pupils at state schools, who differed markedly in their family backgrounds. Those attending elite schools recurringly came from rich families which belong to the economically dominating class in the United Kingdom. The other group came from middle- to working-class families. As had been expected, the prevailing stereotypes found in the study clearly differed between the two groups. More fundamental, however, was that the two groups' attribution models for success, and lack thereof, at school differed systematically. Pupils at elite schools differentiated themselves from the others through attributions of effort and ability, while the pupils at normal schools attributed their exam experiences more to luck – thus choosing an uncontrollable, unstable and external attribution dimension. Attributions at this level seem to have rather more to do with the consensual background knowledge of social classes than with abstract causal thought (Augoustinos, 1990, p. 264).

If causal explanations for success and failure in school contexts determine the self-image in both social groups, and have something to do with action, then we may also infer a low level of social mobility between the groups. Attributions of luck certainly do not warrant good prognoses for intergenerational mobility, even though the comprehensive schoolboys appeared to have hopes: 'It seems that (comprehensive school) boys engage in intergroup

differentiation more than (public school) boys, a finding which may
be tentatively explained by reconsidering secure and insecure social
identities (Tajfel, 1978a) and also by considering some of the characteristics of these two "natural" groups . . . We have classified the
(comprehensive school) boys as consensually "inferior", but perceiving "cognitive alternatives" and thus challenging the present
system' (Hewstone, Jaspars and Lalljee, 1982, p. 263).

The function of social representations that establishes identity
and directs action is also illustrated by an investigation about a
student protest movement at the University of Louvain (DiGiacomo, 1980). Analyses of the political self-images of participants
and the leadership committee of the protest movement showed
serious differences between the two groups. The consequence of
this was that the mass of students did not subordinate itself to the
committee, even though both shared a close proximity to the political left, with the result that the movement was a failure altogether
(p. 340).

Social representations in this area are always and above all a
product of a constant social process of judging people and facts.
Representations about short- or long-term social events are formed
with surprisingly great consensus. The representations are based on
evaluative criteria which are evoked in the milieu of a social group,
and lead to the development of structured and value-laden beliefs.
This spontaneously created value system helps to interpret the environment and other groups, and determines how one deals with
them (p. 341). Therefore, social representations are more than a
system of culturally inherited images. They are the result of the
encounter of a group with its current environment and with the
group's reference system (DiGiacomo, 1985; Käes, 1968).

## 5.2.2 *The echo of historical experience*

Representations of events and social conditions can soon be forgotten if the events are transient, temporally short and irrelevant
in the long term to the lives of individuals – such as a student
protest movement. But on the other hand, a long-lasting effect can
be expected from historical events which are drawn out over a
longer period of time and above all touch individuals in their existence. As the introductory chapter noted, it is the collectively experienced past which is condensed into dominant images and

interpretation models, and can thus form the everyday knowledge of whole generations. Research in this field is scarce despite its importance for group identities and contemporary politics (cf. Kalampalikis, 2002; Liu, 1999; Liu, Wilson, McClure and Higgins, 1999).

## Collective memory

Jodelet (1992) used the war crimes trial against Klaus Barbie 1983/4 to analyse how historical events and their topicalisation can become symbols of social facts. The statements of witnesses during the trial and the rhetoric of the prosecution, defence, court and mass media in this case show how collective memory is reconstructed (cf. Shotter, 1990). Collective memory needs living images which evoke and mark recall. The representations of collectives mix past and present, and put the images thus created in place of reality. The strength of such historical knowledge comes from the symbolic weight of the images of the past projected into the present (Jodelet, 1992, p. 239 onwards). In this way, collective historical experiences leave behind their moral and affective traces, in the everyday schemata which help to judge contemporary events. Experiences are concretised into symbols which coalesce into interpretive stereotypes.

In India, in 1992 a call was made for Hindu volunteers to assemble in the city of Ayodhya. Millions, from all over India, assembled.In the ensuing fray a Muslim mosque, the Babri Masjid, was demolished in five and half hours of frenetic activity and its debris thrown in a river. The reason for this demolition was to liberate the supposed birthplace of the Hindu Lord Ram from Muslim dominance, and to construct a Hindu temple instead. After the demolition, massive riots took place all over India. As a later consequence to these events, which deeply hurt Indian Muslim feelings, the Godhra incident took place in 2002. Voluntary workers coming in a train from construction work at the Ram temple in Ayodhya were massacred by supposed Muslim terrorists.

Who the perpetrator of this violence was is a moot issue; but what is of significance is that a powerful historical symbol was used to provoke the dormant embers of Hindu militancy. As before, the symbol of the mosque Babri Masjid at Lord Ram's birthplace was used to activate Hindu volunteers. The train 'surfeit with death' is an evocative symbol, associated with the partition of India in 1947 into what today is India, Pakistan and Bangladesh, when such trains would arrive from Pakistan. It immediately brings to mind the horrors of the partition and the brutality of Muslim–Hindu encounters.

The political use of such symbols was investigated in an interview study with Hindus and Muslims by Sen and Wagner (2004). They show how history and the representations that emerged from past events that were painful for one or another group exert a powerful influence on collective action, and have accordingly been used by politicians for decades. Such representations, condensed into icons, are the symbolic template according to which present-day intergroup relations are politically tailored and intergroup feelings maintained.

Social representations of historical events thus adopt a peculiar ambiguous position. On the one hand they represent these past events as content. They come to mind through any key word which produces a link to history. On the other hand, they constitute explanatory knowledge which shows great similarity to the social representations of scientific theories. As is stated before, we know that the main function of popularised theories lies in their power of explaining (repetitive) everyday phenomena, whilst object-related representations mainly have an interpretive function. Just like popularised theories, representations of historical experiences constitute a condensate of events, that is to say, the causes, reasons and consequences of past facts. Causes, reasons and consequences, much like the causal statements of quasi-scientific theories, form a stereotyped network of explanatory models which legitimise them for application to similar events in the present. While popularised science for everyday people draws its evidence from the authority of the institution of 'science', and representations of cultural objects draw their legitimacy from apparently inert tradition; historically substantiated explanatory models justify their evidence using the affective weight of their own immediate experience, which, replicated millions of times, forms the mentality of entire peoples (Namer, 1987; Radley, 1990).

## Memories of the Nazi era and the Second World War

An important collective historical experience is represented by National Socialism and the Second World War in the case of

Austria. These events play a great role in the political and every-day discussion of the Austrian population, but are also used as an explicative representation. It was especially during 1988, the fif-tieth anniversary of Austria's so-called *Anschluss* to Nazi Germany, as well as in the aftermath of the internal political disputes arising from Kurt Waldheim's standing and subsequent election to the post of Federal President a short time before, that these issues obtained an everyday presence seldom achieved by other issues.[3]

The cognitive and affective framework which is applied to these events by the collective memory of Austrians developed over the course of time into terms of reference: a system of quasi-theoretical interpretation and an image within everyday under-standing which far exceeded the original form of a simple episodic memory content or a memory of one's life. The contents of this collective memory took on the form of a social representation, an interpretative schema which allows current events, people, politi-cians and their politics to be understood.

It is an interesting question how it it is that historical events, or the collective memory of them, become a theoretical framework of everyday understanding. As this report only refers to the end-product of this process, namely the social representation of Nazism and war, the question cannot be pursued more closely. It may be enough to point out that the ideological contents that were con-veyed during the Nazi period were spread by a wellnigh perfect propaganda machine, which understood how to target its audience using contents in an affective-emotional manner as well. This pro-paganda success was reinforced all the more by the fact that the time itself was experienced, or better, had to be experienced, with a high level of affective arousal, whether positively or negatively. Immediately after the *Anschluss*, Austrians experienced an ephemeral economic development which could be interpreted as an upturn. In the subsequent period, the war provided the affec-tive background which made the trials and tribulations associated with it unforgettable, and made them a part of individual histori-cal identity. This phenomenon may perhaps make one think of a temporally more prolonged version of 'flashbulb memory', with all its veridical and distorted elements (Winograd and Neisser, 1992).

After the end of the war and the construction of a new Austrian state, these issues were discussed further, interpreted, invoked, made absolute and relativised. Public discourse was led just as intensively by electronic and printed media as by those formerly affected. In this way, the basic structure of these historical events was also conveyed to the postwar generation not so much in the classroom, but rather by the primary authorities of socialisation in an appropriately emotional context.

This system of the social representation of Nazism and the Second World War has been investigated in Austrian citizens (W. Wagner, 1989a). It was assumed that experiences from the time of the *Anschluss* and Second World War constitute not only historical knowledge, that is, the contents of an episodic and semantic memory system reflecting the person's own idiosyncratic experiences in the sense of abstract conceptual knowledge about the events; but, above and beyond this, that they constitute a social representation. It was further assumed that the declarative and implicit process knowledge summarised therein has an important part to play in understanding, explaining and interpreting current, and in the broadest sense, political events.

*Method.* Forty people were investigated. The people formed a 'convenience sample', being mainly selected according to their accessibility to the interviewers. Half were women and the other half men. In addition, one half of the people had been born between 1945 and 1955, so that they did not associate any personal experiences with the time in question, while the other half had been born between 1915 and 1925 and had therefore experienced the period in question personally. Due to a technical glitch two of the interview recordings were acoustically unintelligible and had to be excluded.

The interviews were structured in parts, according to seven groups of themes: (1) *Anschluss*, Austria's incorporation into the German Reich, invasion; (2) Second World War; (3) system and ideology of National Socialism; (4) persecution of the Jews, anti-Semitism, racism; (5) biologism, heredity, fate of humanity; (6) general consequences, inferences and lessons from the events; and (7) political leanings of those questioned.

Three aspects were touched on within each theme area. First, a general image of opinions about the group of themes, plus views and memories (content opinions). Personal judgements of the events and memory contents were also touched on in such a way that those questioned gave information about positive and negative aspects (valency). Finally, the participants were also asked about their entirely personal opinions of the causes, reasons and aspects of guilt (cause attribution).

The participants were contacted either in person or over the telephone to see whether they were prepared to participate in a scientific study by the university. Interview times were arranged for those prepared. The interviews lasted between one and one-and-a-half hours and were carried out in the private homes of those being questioned. The interviews were recorded on cassette recorder, with the permission of those being questioned, and were coded afterwards.

The patterns of discourse on this subject distinguish more clearly between generations than between social groups or affinities to political parties. It is the personal experience and emotional involvement which differentiates the representation of the older interview subjects, making them appear contradictory whilst simultaneously forming a cohort of solidarity to deny younger people the right to pass judgement. Yet the content of the following qualitative description of the representation should not be understood as a modal value, for the sample was small. It is merely meant to demonstrate the possibility of an underlying representational structure.

## Order and chaos

The discourse of older interviewees focuses on two complementary concepts: order and chaos. The political system of National Socialism appears as an incarnation of order. There was no crime, but there was work; decent people had no downsides to fear, which affected only the undisciplined. Life was felt to be a burden because no criticism was tolerated, and that could lead to difficulties; but whoever kept to the rules of the game could lead a peaceful life – so peaceful that it could still appear to be desirable even nowadays. Upheavals in the apparent order, such as ethnic persecutions, the need 'to keep one's mouth shut', and the emergency that became acute during the course of the war appear as peripheral phenomena in this context. They were seen as secondary symptoms and not as belonging to the general order. 'The ideology was good', only its execution was wrong.

The disorder or chaos came in the form of the war. This was understandably perceived to be a threat. But even the war might be understood as an orderly phenomenon if it had not been badly executed by one person – Hitler – or a small group of 'power-hungry' people. Hitler is without exception accorded a psycho-pathology which ultimately seems responsible for the degeneration of the war into chaos. If the scope of the war had not become unruly, the war could have been won, even though most of the people interviewed were not sure as to whether a German victory would have been desirable.

## Ambivalence

An ambivalent attitude towards this time arises from the interplay between desirable order and menacing chaos, which can often become visible within one sentence. For example, the persecution of the Jews is felt to be wrong, whilst it is stressed at the same time, however, that only the poor Jews became victims whilst the rich ones carried on 'buying everything up', which makes hatred of the Jews appear 'justified';[4] or 'maybe nothing would have happened if there hadn't been any Jews here . . .'; or the war is rejected as terrible and simultaneously described as the cause of full employ-ment; or 'I was afraid, but it was your own fault if you opened your mouth'; or 'democracy is good, but a certain mixture of dic-tatorship and democracy might be even better'. Comparable inconsistencies in the interviews can be found on all the themes mentioned. They result from a dialectic of order and chaos that has not been cognitively confronted.

The maintenance of the self-image of the older and involved respondents mandates an allocation of causality and guilt for the union of Austria to the German Reich and the persecution of dis-sidents, as well as for the outbreak of war either to circumstances or other people and powers. However, this is not the place to find out whether this foreign attribution is the lasting consequence of the propaganda of the time, or has only developed in hindsight.

## Those born after the war

In contrast to this, the interviews with younger people born after the war are understandably marked by distance. The interaction between desirable order and terrible, hard-to-avoid chaos is rarely mentioned, if at all. Thus any deep-rooted ambivalence in their statements does not apply. Their reasoning appears less aimed at protecting self-esteem, but equally related to the situation and actors of that time.

If the representations of these historic events are applied to today, it is the lessons of order which are to be preserved or re-established. The chaos which inevitably accompanied 'order' is cognitively separated. If 'too many' political parties are felt to be bad; that democracy may be good, but people may be unsuited to it; and that there must sometimes be war to 'challenge the people' (a positive and orderly aspect to war), then the social representation of personally experienced historical periods has the effect of an anchor and reference for today.

## Cohort identity

Social representations of current and historical events, as well as social issues, have different functional focuses by comparison with popularised science. The examples of 'second-hand' knowledge and assimilated science show that their main functions are orientated towards explanatory, declarative and instrumental aspects. By contrast, collective knowledge about political events and social structures informs social identity or, in the case of a cohort, historical identity. Collectively shared interpretation of the social environment and its history becomes the precondition of social categorisation. This applies to the interpretive models of the German and Austrian war generation just as much as to the 'siege mentality' of Jewish communities and Israeli citizens (Bar-Tal and Antebi, 1992), even if they may not necessarily be homogeneously distributed in the communities affected (Nadler, 1992). It is a process that summarises social objects or events in such a way that they correspond to the actions, intentions and belief systems of the individuals (Tajfel, 1981, p. 254). The social identity derived from them enriches the individual's self-concept with knowledge of their social belonging and historical origin; and implies common value dimensions with their accompanying emotional significance. This orientation system, in the form of a 'polemic' representation (Moscovici, 1988, p. 221 onwards), defines the subjective place of the individual in society (p. 255).

Comparison with other groups is a cognitive consequence of social identity. Social comparison is sensitive to the relative deprivation of one's own group as compared with others. We have seen this process in the investigation into the auto-stereotypes and hetero-stereotypes of schoolchildren, in the analysis of the course of the student protest movement, and in the consequences of a shared historical experience: The middle- and working-class children in Hewstone, Jaspars and Lalljee's study (1982) saw themselves (correctly, one is tempted to add) at a disadvantage *vis-à-vis* the promotion and career prospects of the pupils from elite public schools. Accordingly, their causal attributions also inform them about failures and successes in the university context. In the second example (DiGiacomo, 1980), the differences in judgement and different self-images of the group of activist students and the organisation committee led to a loss of contact and influence on the part of the committee. In the third and fourth case, the shared experience of intergroup violence by antagonistic groups as Hindus and Muslims in India (Sen and Wagner, 2004) and the common experience of National Socialism and war in older Austrians led to perpetuated intergroup hostility in the one case and to intragenerational solidarity in the other (cf. also Hraba, Hagendoorn and Hagendoorn, 1989; Liu and Hilton, forthcoming).

## 5.3  Imagination and cultural knowledge

The variety of subject areas that one could describe as cultural objects is reflected by the great number of relevant studies. These studies record a social and cultural form of expression which allows us to describe the mentality of social groups. Through it we gain an insight into the implicit codes, value systems, models, comprehensive ideologies and interpretation systems which a society pursues and applies as spontaneously 'natural' and true to the events of life and its protagonists (Jodelet, 1984b, p. 22). They describe the content, objects and concepts which make up the field of content-rational knowledge in its culturally handed-down core, the 'old town' of everyday knowledge. But before going into examples of investigations, we need to mark out the boundaries to the term 'culture'.

## 5.3.1 On the term 'culture'

The term 'culture' usually plays a subordinate role in social psychology. Culture is 'a blank space, a highly respected, empty pigeonhole', as Mary Douglas (1982a, p. 183) puts it. It often constitutes just a residual category, which goes into the error variance of quantitative studies (LeVine, 1984, p. 67). Views about what culture is are almost as numerous as the researchers who busy themselves with it. Far back in 1952, Kroeber and Kluckhohn counted a total of 175 mutually distinguishing definitions. These definitions can by and large be divided into two complementary classes (Vivelo, 1981), the totalistic and the mentalistic point of view, from which the latter is primarily useful for the needs of social psychology.

### The totalistic approach

The totalistic point of view describes the entirety of things, events and features produced by humans as culture. 'Culture' is the generic term for that non-genetic and metabiological human phenomenon. It includes all phenomena whose existence is due only to the life of the human species, and which is not any direct consequence of genetic heredity (Weiss, 1973, p. 1396). A cultural system consists of a 'set of material components (human and non-human), a set of modifications (neural and physical), and a set of organizational relationships (social and technical).' (Weiss, 1973, p. 1397).

This comprehensive definition of the term culture as a totality has the disadvantage of depending on the non-explained terms of 'genetic' and 'biological'; and assumes they are known. Yet the boundary between biological and non-biological phenomena cannot be defined if neither of them can be precisely specified by its consequences. The subject matters of sciences are of course primarily defined by the methodology of the sciences themselves: the material procedures and non-material constructs of which help the subject matter to reach an ontological status. The fact and manner of managing subject matters depends on the methods available. This gives rise to the inherently blurred boundary between biological and non-biological phenomena which so hampers social-scientific debate about many of the observations by ethologists and sociobiologists (cf. the discussion in Casti, 1990, p. 189ff.). In fact, an in-depth analysis of human cognition and behaviour makes the distinction obsolete between what can be considered merely genetic and what merely learned (Barkow, Cosmides and Tooby, 1992; W. Wagner and Wagner, 2003). The historic debate between Noam Chomsky and Jean Piaget in 1975 in the Corral of Royaumont in France, about the biological or social nature of elementary grammar, is an eloquent example of this (Piattelli-Palmarini, 1980). A somewhat more managable totalistic definition is provided by Cohen (1968). He makes reference to the function and organisation of ways of life as an adaptation process. According to him, culture is the whole of all material and non-material means which help people to adapt to the conditions of their habitat and make effective use of the available energy potential (p. 41). This approach also embraces the entirety of all tools and instruments, actions, thoughts and institutions in their functional context as an adaptation mechanism.

## The mentalistic approach

The mentalistic approach stands as a counter-pole to the totalistic way of viewing 'culture', referring only to a partial quantity of the totality of cultural phenomena: the realm of knowledge and belief. 'Culture' in this sense denotes 'an organized body of rules concerning the ways in which individuals in a population should communicate with one another, think about themselves and toward objects in their environments. The rules are not universally or constantly obeyed, but they are recognised by all and they ordinarily operate to limit the range of variation in patterns of communication, belief, value, and social behavior in that population' (LeVine, 1982, p. 4). These rules establish the *a priori* concepts according to which the members of a culture regulate their perceptions and experiences and make decisions. They give meaning to 'acting in this way and in no other' (Vivelo, 1981, p. 51). The code is an internalised model for behaviour – that is, the underlying reason why individuals act in a particular way – and not a model of behaviour which could be identified externally, as it were, without consulting the individual. It corresponds to standards of correct behaviour and not to real behaviour (Frake, 1964; Schneider, 1976; W. Wagner, 1997).

Cultural behaviour in this view falls within the category of rule-directed behaviour. A rule for behaving is an instruction for a particular class of protagonists on certain occasions to carry out certain actions or refrain from them (Cheal, 1980, p. 39). It is concurring behaviour for which the person acting is in a position to give reasons (p. 45). Those reasons, which imply the rules for behaving, are the actual cognitive and affective content of cultural knowledge. The requirement that the protagonist should be in a position to give these reasons for rule-directed behaviour does not exclude behaviour proceeding in a routinised way. Such habitualised behaviour patterns are often the ingrained results of an earlier explicit following of rules and self-regulated action sequences (Harré and Secord, 1972, p. 140). By contrast with purely biologically regulated behaviour, for example, habitualised acts of behaviour must be able to become known to the individual as rule-directed (p. 141, 176). The mentalistic concept of culture excludes material artefacts from any consideration. They are only part of 'culture' inasmuch as they are part of the mental representation, and can be interpreted, understood and appropriately used by individuals.

Schneider (1976) identifies two consequences or functions of culture. The first – the integrative function – is where culture binds the disparate parts of a social system into a significant whole. The cultural system gives significance in a global context to the most varied behaviour patterns and endows them with meaning. In the second – the generative function – culture provides the 'primal principles' according to which new meanings and contents can be generated and integrated into the existing system. 'New meanings are established with reference to old meanings and grow out of them and must be made, in some degree, congruent with them; and exchange, whenever and wherever it occurs, must be articulated with the existing system of meanings' (p. 204 onwards). Integration and generation establish the continuity and coherence of the entire cultural system of symbols and meanings.

### 5.3.2 Representations and cultural objects

Cultural imagination[5] is the idea of the real. It does not create reality in a physical sense as a product of material objects. But it gives physical conditions the reality that is essential to the lives of individuals. It integrates things into real life by naming them and allocating them meaning, and by making them parts of culture and society. The term 'imagination' is meant to describe exactly this process: the transformation of an *a priori* formless physical world – since form is in the eye of the beholder – into a social world, of which one can say that it is ultimately intelligible only to the members of the culture, and with which only they are able to interact. The interaction at the same time constitutes the subjects as bearers of the representation and makes them the complement of the objects created by them (K. Gergen, 1982; W. Wagner, 1998). Led by cultural ideas, the physical dealings people have with physical objects illustrates the social meaning which is intended for those objects within the bounds of practical forms of intercourse. Ultimately, this transforms them into cultural objects, in which one can see their origin.

The potential themes of cultural imagination are just as inexhaustible as the cultures and subcultures from which they originate. They range over wide areas: defining the everyday interaction of bearers of roles and gender roles (e.g. Aebischer, 1985; Corsaro, 1990; Flores Palacios, 1997; Furnham and Taylor, 1990; Kruse, Weimer and Wagner, 1988; León Zermeño, 2003; Lloyd and Duveen, 1990; Lorenzi-Cioldi, 1988); children (e.g. Behar, 1988; Carugati, Emiliani and Molinari, 1990; M.-J. Chombart de Lauwe, 1971; D'Alessio, 1990; Feuerhahn, 1980; K. Gergen, Gloger-Tippelt and Berkowitz, 1990; Molinari and Emiliani, 1990, 1993); elders (e.g. Liu, Ng, Loong et al., 2003); God and religion (de Sa, Bello and Jodelet, 1997; Lindeman, Pyysiäinen and Saariluoma, 2002); anomalies of life such as mental illness and psychological problems (e.g. Courtial, 1999; de Rosa, 1987; Foster, 2001; Jodelet, 1991b; Krause, 2002; Kronberger, 1999; Morant, 1995; Petrillo, 1996; Schurmans, 1984; W. Wagner, Duveen, Themel and Verma; 1999; Zani, 1993); being disabled (e.g. Giami, Assouty-Piquet and Berthier, 1988); sexuality (e.g. Giami, 1991; Giami, Humbert-Viveret and Laval, 2001); and the human body as a reference point of individual experience (e.g. Boltanski, 1971; Costalat-Founeau, Picot, Hauchard et al., 2002; Jodelet and Moscovici, 1976; Jodelet, Ohana, Bessis-Monino and Dannenmüller, 1982; Moloney and Walker, 2000, 2002). One topic, disease, health and life has attracted a host of research activities and revealed interesting aspects of social representations that build upon culturally old thoughts (e.g. Dross, 1991; Flick, Fischer,

Neuber et al., 2003; Goodwin, Kozlova, Kwiatkowska et al., 2003; Herzlich, 1973, Krause, 2003; Markovà and Wilkie, 1987; Nascimento-Schulze, Fontes Garcia, and Costa Arruda, 1995). Another topic attracting continuing interest is the idea of intelligence, which is situated right at the crossroads of modern psychological science and cultural conceptions (e.g. Poeschl, 2001; Räty and Snellman, 1995; Snellman and Räty, 1995; Srivastava and Misra, 1999).

## The body

Jodelet, Ohana, Bessis-Monino and Dannenmüller (1982), in a comprehensive study about the representation of the human body in the French population, show the cultural forms of thought of and about dealing with one's own body. The authors cover four areas which define the image of the body in modern French society. First, the perception of the biological condition, the perception of organic conditions and their categorisation. Second, the structuring of the contact and experience with one's own body which by and large appear in two forms as a hedonistic-active and a rather functional-passive manner. It is shown how social norms regulate dealings with desire and hierarchalise permissible emotions. Third, the external image of the body as mirrored in clothing and cosmetics. Fourth, the regulation of the manifestations of the body via social relations and reference groups.

The process of integrating social relations and private experience is reflected in a more pointed manner than many other cultural objects in dealings with the body and the image of the body. On the one hand it is personal feeling that makes the body a reference point for individuals in their lives. Desire and pain are two deeply personal realms. Social norms and cultural demands regulate the range and quality of experience, even when individuals withdraw into the non-public areas of their everyday environment:

> On one hand it is the object of the immediate personal experience, the place where one's subjectivity is inscribed and where affects and psychological investments are being projected upon. On the other hand it is the object of a sort of social thinking ruled by prescriptions of how to maintain and present it as well as involved in how one sets oneself in scene. Therefore the body constitutes a priviledged realm for studying the interaction of

individual and collective processes in the elaboration of social representations.

(Jodelet, Ohana, Bessis-Monino and
Dannenmüller, 1982, p. 340)

## Children

Closely connected to our perception of Self, in addition to our body, is gender identity. Children are born into a world which is already structured by the representations circulating in the communities into which they are born. Growing up to become actors and participants in these communities implies a developmental process through which these representations become as much a part of children's sociopsychological landscape as they are for their parents and elder siblings. Among the representations which structure children's lives, gender is central, both because it is one of the earliest social categorisations which children acquire and which they use to anchor much of their knowledge of the social world, (cf. Duveen and Shields, 1985) and because it provides one of the first forms of social identity which children acquire. Indeed, as Rubin, Provenzano and Luria (1974) demonstrated, a gender identity is first extended to the child as a new born infant, and only subsequently is the meaning of this social act of categorisation internalised by the child.

Children, then, come into a world which is constituted in a complex web of cultural meanings, a web which both structures the ways in which others interact with them and also provides frames of meaning through which children come to structure their own understanding of this world and their place within it. A series of studies (reviewed in Lloyd and Duveen, 1989, 1990) traced the early development of gender identities in pre-school children through observations of their play with other children. The observations took place in a room furnished with toys with specific gender markings, so that toy choice could be taken as a relevant indicator of the extent to which children regulated their activity in terms of gender. By the age of 4, a clear asymmetry emerged, boys (whether playing with other boys or with girls) showed a clear preference for masculine-marked toys and avoided choosing feminine marked toys, while girls (again irrespective of the gender of their play partner) selected masculine- and feminine-marked toys equally frequently (this asymmetry does not imply that girls at this age lack a gender identity, only that toy choice is not the medium through which they seek to express it). In spite of this asymmetry, when these same children were given simple cognitive and linguistic tasks their responses indicated that they shared more or less the same knowledge of the gender marking of toys.

As they reach school age, children have already become independent actors in the field of gender to a certain extent, but the context which frames this activity is the domestic setting of home or pre-school. At school they encounter representations of gender embedded in a new context, and one in which gender plays a much more focused structural role in the organisation of classroom life. In the first year of schooling, it was discovered that clear descriptions of the pattern of gender organisation in reception classrooms was virtually absent (Lloyd and Duveen, 1992).

Childhood, therefore, offers a distinctive arena for the study of social representations, since those cultural things which are most familiar and taken for granted in the adult world are themselves the focus of children's cognitive reconstructions. What has already become habitual for the adult is the object of active elaboration among children. This developmental process, however, is not a simple or linear process of acquisition. Just as Piaget's studies showed the difference in young children's thinking, so too one can see the influence of children's own cognitive elaborations in their representations of gender in the representational work which is at the centre of their reconstruction of social representations (cf. Duveen, 1997).

The cultural object of 'child', together with the cultural construct of 'childhood' has only been around for a relatively short period in history. In European history, the term 'childhood' as we understand it only appeared in the nineteenth century, just as 200 years before that 'youth', and in the twentieth century 'adolescence'. Before then, these periods of one's life virtually did not exist in everyday language and in the domain of everyday life. There was just as negligible existence of the cultural objects described by them, children, youngsters and adolescents (Ariés, 1975). When we nowadays speak of children, we are describing a social artefact whose definition and demarcation has been created artificially within the course of a person's life and is produced on a daily basis in the dealings over the years of their parents (especially their mothers) along with their offspring, and conserved by the media (M.-J. Chombart de Lauwe, 1984).

The different studies carried out on the social representation of 'child' and 'childhood' provide an illustration of its genesis. Molinari and Emiliani (1990) investigated 80 mothers for the images that they had of their own and other people's children, as well as looking at the consequences of these images for their style of dealing and talking with children. If mothers see their children as being intelligent and autonomous, or at least able to be formed to this end, then they deal with them in a more narrative style of conversation than if they feel their children to be dependent. A dialogical style of conversation predominates in this case. The dialogical style deals with the comments of the child through questions, confirmations and points of clarification which convey day-to-day knowledge of life. In this way, children may be able to take part in everyday life, but they are also monitored and guided in their understanding. The narrative style is marked by a predominance of descriptive elements, for example of objects or events, wishes and feelings, as well as components derived from them (p. 104). This form of conversation emphasises a didactic matter and wishes to offer knowledge and provoke the drawing of the child's own conclusions. If mothers see their children as autonomous and perceptive, then it does not therefore appear necessary for them to check their children's real understanding. Rather, they presuppose it and give the children a passive role in the interaction in which they never become active narrators of stories: 'The definition of the child's level of comprehension, and therefore of their cognitive skills, derives from the representations which adults construct of them' (p. 195).

## The declarative function

From the very outset, representations of cultural objects constitute declarative knowledge. They determine, at a fundamental level, the subject matters to which they refer, structure their characteristics and establish their significance in a social context. They make one 'know what is the case' – which things belong to the social world and which do not (W. Wagner, 1998).[6] They therefore adopt a more fundamental function than explanatory representations of popularised theories or evaluative, instrumental and identity establishing representations of social conditions. If cultural imagination plays a role in action, it does not do this because one might be able to substantiate why one should act in this way and in no other. This gives no prescriptions for dealing with objects where there is an element of choice, such as in the kitchen for example, where one might choose according to the taste one prefers to indulge in a meal on any given day. If cultural representations imply ways of action, then they do this as a direct consequence of the declarative function of the object because so long as the definition is accepted, one can only tackle it in this way and in no other. If a way of action requires substantiation, people often resort to secondary scientific knowledge which can be used as an explanation.

Molinari, Emiliani and Carugati (1992) questioned over 400 Italian mothers of children aged 4–8 about possible explanations for different characteristics in their own children and children in general, such as independence, intelligence, liking for neatness and tidiness, and obedience. The results show which models of explanation were preferred according to the target person (their own or someone else's child) and the characteristic to be explained. The explanations range from genetic reasons, to the child's internal motivations and the affective attention of parents, through to social surroundings. Theories used come from biology, psychology and sociology. While, for example, intelligence in children is generally viewed as being independent of parental interaction, it appears as a natural gift and internal motivation as far as one's own children are concerned. The models of development which mothers see realised in their children differ accordingly. What is crucial here is that the social representation of the child contains various images and bits of all the theories of development: the innatist theory, which refers to individual will; the interactionist theory; and finally that of environment, role and values.

At the same time, selecting explanatory popular-scientific models is useful for protecting the self-image. In contrast to children in general, mothers prefer to apply such theories to their own children: they reduce their own responsibility in raising them. This need-orientated variation in the choice of developmental models points to the secondary character of quasi-scientific explanations in the representations of cultural objects.

Finally, but not least, fragments of popular science have an important part to play in the media's marketing of the myth of the 'child' as consumer. This publicity uses authoritative scientific justifications from medicine and psychology to extol the virtues of products which allegedly do justice to the needs of the cultural object 'child'. This is used to spread knowledge on the one hand and, on the other, to transmit scientifically 'authorised' education measures and integrate them into the contemporary image of the child as consumer (M.-J. Chombart de Lauwe, 1984, p. 196; Feuerhahn, 1980). This final economic refinement makes cultural imagination 'modern' and is a reflection of the social condition from which it emanates.

# Chapter 6

# The Organisation and Structure of Social Representations

## 6.1 Iconic form and metaphorical organisation

'If you ask a Russian mother to describe her children "sharing", she will describe children playing with a toy at the same time. An American mother, however, will describe children taking turns playing with the toy' (Adler, 1990, p. 9). Clearly an invitation to share a toy offers all sorts of possibilities of interpretation. More importantly, it gives rise to widely different images of ideas which can be associated with it. The image of an American child engaged with a toy for half an hour before letting the next child play with it does not just illustrate the understanding of the term 'sharing' in American culture. Its meaning and roots lie concealed more deeply in the conception that the everyday life of the accompanying culture has of itself. It can only be from a culture that is able to understand 'sharing' not as a joint experience, but as a temporary appropriation by an individual of an object or condition. In actual fact it is not even the most succinct image that one can make as an example of individualistic behaviour, but only a relatively marginal one. Although in itself it contains all the typical characteristics of such a style of behaviour, 'sharing a toy' should be in the periphery of a much greater and more fundamental cultural representation. It does not belong to the centre of gravitation of everyday ideas and action of an individualistic style. Yet it is, albeit typically, casually attributed to it in this way; such that it could be replaced by other images at any time. The actual centre and the core of the idea-guiding images is – in the case of American society – the ideological complex of 'individuality' (Lukes, 1973) which is predisposed to alloting everybody the responsibility for their own actions.

The previous example shows two cognitive systems at work, which are intricately linked. The first is an operative system, which draws more or less logical inferences from the invitation to share, and which evokes images of ideas and differentiates instructions for the right course of action. This system takes effect within a quasi-cognitive 'metasystem' which is a direct expression of the underlying global social representation, and channels, conducts and controls the activities of the operative system. The metasystem is rooted in the social and restricts what is thought to what is thinkable. One can suppose that the American mother, as a representative of an individualistic yet cosmopolitan society and after lengthy reflection, is also perfectly capable of coming up with the idea of 'sharing by simultaneous co-operation', just as the Russian mother could think of 'sharing by temporarily exclusive use'. What is crucial, however, is that the spontaneous production gives rise to precisely the aforementioned stereotypes and no other images.

On the other hand the example shows the relationship of the centre and periphery in social representations which, as structured mental 'objects', unite the most different of stated views and the complexes thereof, as well as their derivations, into a whole. Just as the sun is indifferent as to which planets orbit it as long as there is a balance of gravitation, so also we can distinguish in systems of social representations the stable core area from the interchangeable and dynamic peripheral areas.

## 6.1.1 Images and metaphors

The concrete form that content-rational knowledge and social representations adopts in the heads of its bearers can best be compared with images and metaphors. Thinking by way of images, icons or metaphors is closely related, if not identical, in its underlying structure. In the present context we consider metaphorical analysis more easily accessible and useful, but maintain that what is being said about metaphorical structure by and large also applies to images as vehicles of thought.

A metaphor, as we understand it here, consists of three parts (Lakoff, 1987): a target domain, a source domain and a relation defined between target and source domain. The source domain is an iconic and concrete mental content. This domain is closer to personal experience than the domain to be understood and, because of its experiential basis, immediately comprehensible. The source domain provides the mental image by which another less comprehensible concept, theory or phenomenon becomes intelligible or 'explained'. This means that the source relates to widespread experience, is pervasive, well known, well and simply structured, and represents a well-demarcated part of everyday life of social actors. (Lakoff, 1987, p. 278). The target domain is always farther away from experience, more abstract and less iconic and, because of this, less comprehensible. Source and target domain are linked by a mapping which defines a structural correlation between the two. The mapping is the result of a constructive effort in communication and discourse and establishes relevant structural similarities between target and source. The relationships between the elements of the abstract target domain thereby become intelligible in terms of the experiential relationship between the elements of the concrete source domain. In this sense, a metaphor is an iconic illustration of an initially non-iconically accessible target domain. It 'transports' or 'projects' the structure and meaning of the source on to the target. A metaphor, therefore, represents a kind of reference fixing which is not a definition, but resembles the concrete operation of ostension (cf. Kripke, 1972). Whereas, however, ostension refers to real objects, metaphorical reference indicates the structural properties of phenomena 'rather than features of internal constitution' (Boyd, 1979, p. 358; see Figure 6.1).

### Transport and conduit metaphors

Some typical kinds of metaphors are the transport or conduit metaphors, orientation metaphors and ontological metaphors (Lakoff and Johnson, 1980). The basic structure of transport and conduit metaphors results from the conception that ideas or meanings are objects; that linguistic expressions constitute containers; and that communication has to do with conveyance: 'I gave you that idea', 'I can't get my opinion across (to the listeners)', 'Try to fit more into fewer words', 'His views don't contain anything really important', 'His words are hollow'.

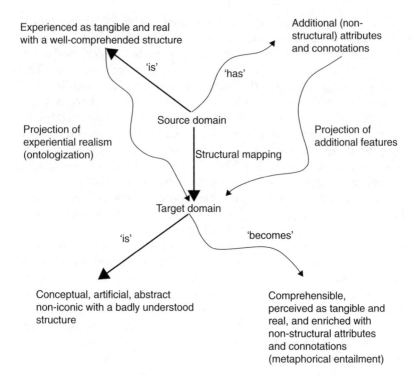

FIGURE 6.1 Schema of metaphorical structural mapping and entailment

NOTE: Straight lines denote relationships to do with structural mapping, snake-lines denote metaphorical entailment.

## Orientation and ontological metaphors

The 'up versus down' orientation in orientation metaphors is applied to states of mind (happy is going up, sad is going down): 'I'm feeling on top of the world', 'My spirits are high (are at rock bottom)'; states of consciousness (conscious is up, unconscious is down): 'He fell asleep'; states of health (healthy and life is up, ill and dead is down): 'She sank into depression', 'He is in top form'; states of control (having control or power is up, being subject to control or power is down): 'She has control over him', 'You're on top of the situation'; physical size (more is up, less is down): 'His income went up'; status (high status is up, low status is down): 'She's at the bottom of the company'; judgement (good is up, bad is down): 'His work was below standard'; reason (rational is up, emotional is down): 'The discussion descended to an emotional level'.

All the examples of this category have a physical basis: an upright or slumped posture. People sleep lying down and are upright when awake; illness and death is associated with lying down; physical size usually correlates with physical strength; adding substances makes the height of a quantity in a vessel rise; status is to do with power, and power with status; pleasant and healthy conditions are judged as good; and rationality is felt to be control, emotion as being controlled. The physical basis or source domain of such metaphors is ultimately humankind's experience with their body (M. Johnson, 1987; Lakoff and Johnson, 1999).

In ontological metaphors non-material entities are ontologised and become linguistically manageable by attributing to them perceptible, visible and even 'touchable' characteristics: 'Your neuroses are making you ill', 'We're fighting on the side of peace', 'IBM has a lot of power', 'Her ego is fragile', 'His self-esteem fell apart'.

## Tropes and metaphorical entailment

These examples illustrate an important feature of language, which could not express the vast variety of human experience without recursive metaphorical relations and metonyms. The important part in our context is the relation between the source and target domains: (a) what determines the choice of a well-structured source domain?; (b) what determines a suitable pairing of a source domain with a target domain?; and (c) on what do the structural details of a pairing between source and target domains depend? (Lakoff, 1987, p. 276ff.). This will be investigated using the orientation or verticality metaphors (more is up, less is down) as well as the 'purposes are aims' metaphor.

If we say 'the stock market has fallen' or 'my savings are on the up', we are using verticality as a source domain in order to portray a change in quantities (the target domain). It is easy to see why verticality is a suitable source domain. Verticality as an idea, the course from up to down and from down to up, is independent of the metaphor itself, since it comes from both individual and evolutionary ongoing experience of gravity, and its effect on our body and other objects. The suitability of pairing verticality and quantity is based on the experience that a heap of fewer stones is lower than a heap of many stones, or that an increase of fluid in a vessel results in a higher level of fluid. The pairing is conveyed by experience, too. The image of verticality and its application to quantities is entirely rooted in our experience.

If we think 'if I put an intention into practice, then that equals achieving a geographical goal', then we are employing the purpose-aim metaphor. An explanation of the closeness to experience lies in the idea of a special case of putting an intention into practice – that is, in travelling and the means of transport associated with it. Travelling requires – normally at least – establishing a travel destination, which is then reached after applying proper effort, whether of a physical or material expenditure. This, of course, is only another expression for – in most cases – preceding effort and work. In the same way, when small children crawl to a new place, they put the intention into practice, achieve an aim. In this special case, source and target domains are identical. The transfer of 'movement between places' to the psychic and physical effort that enables an intention or purpose to be realised is immediate.

The means–end schema is, on the one hand:

> one of the most common structures that emerges from our constant bodily functioning. This schema has all the qualifications a schema should have to serve as the source domain of a metaphor. It is (a) pervasive in experience, (b) well-understood because it is pervasive, (c) well-structured, (d) simply structured, and (e) emergent and well-demarcated for these reasons. In fact, characteristics (a)–(d) provide some criteria for what it means for a structure to 'emerge' naturally as a consequence of our experience.
>
> (Lakoff, 1987, p. 278)

On the other hand, there is also a direct correlation in terms of experience between the motion and the achievement of an intention. As a result, associating the target domain with the source domain appears natural and direct. Similarly, the structural relationship is preserved since in both cases the starting point, means and end can be portrayed on a topographical or abstract mental map.

In almost all languages, the forms of everyday knowledge by and large follow the pattern of metaphorical understanding. Many languages use concepts of different areas of perception to describe psychic states, for example perceiving taste (Asch, 1958). In

Hebrew it is said that praise 'is sweet for the soul'; in Chinese 'honey-sweet words' are those that flatter but can be dangerous; in Thai 'to be sweet' means to faint; in Haussa one does not feel any 'sweetness' when one feels bad; in Burmese one has a 'sweet language' if one has a pleasant voice; and so on. Similarly, there are also metaphoric usages of other areas of taste, such as 'bitter' and 'sour', and also of tactile perceptions like 'hard', 'soft' and the like. Asch sees the usage of physical characteristics[1] for psychic states as the result of observation and experience of direct interaction with other people (p. 91). Our knowledge of others is transmitted by physical energies which exchange interaction partners, so that the 'physicoid' form of psychological concepts is no surprise. We experience interaction as a force emanating from people that wishes to bring about a change in some Other and meets resistance whilst so doing: 'The hardness of a table and of a person concerns events radically different in context and complexity, but the schema of interaction is experienced as dynamically similar, having to do with the application of force and of resulting action in line with or contrary to it' (p. 93). The procedural basis of these mental operations is not reduced to an abstract logical generalisation of common features when interacting with physical and personal entities. Rather, it involves concrete mental operations which help us to understand, in a naive way, events and similarities between events.

A metaphor appears natural when our experiences imply the structural correlation of the two domains through language. Schemata of physical experience are understood preconceptually and have a very simple non-linguistic logic. But in addition, the immediacy of social structures and relations that are felt to be 'natural' offer them as original source domains for sociomorphic metaphors for understanding; such as dominance and subordination, or the asymmetrical relations between the genders that prevail in most societies, which provide a pervasive source domain for metaphorical mappings. A further example of this can be found in accounts of the interaction between sperm and ovum in sexual conception (W. Wagner, Elejabarrieta and Lahnsteiner, 1995; cf. Haste, 1993).

Preconceptual structural correlations in experience give rise to secondary metaphors, which project this logic on to more abstract areas (Lakoff, 1987, p. 278). Through metaphorisation, a target domain is experienced as tangible and ontologically real like the source domain. Furthermore, and this is an important point, the 'experiential realism' of the source is projected upon the target. That is, besides the structural similarity which stimulates the use of a specific source, non-structural experiential properties, such as affective and moral connotations, are also generalised on to the target (Fernandez, 1974). This 'metaphorical entailment' (Lakoff, 1987, p. 384) impregnates the target with characteristics which originally pertain to the source. The overwhelming number of metaphorical references in all languages can be taken as an indication that understanding does not constitute a purely cognitive process, but also comprises iconic, affective and synaesthetic dimensions (Figure 6.1).

## The expressive function of metaphors

Metaphors cannot be described only by their cognitive function. The study of metaphors and metonyms handed down over time shows that their potential functions exceed it by far. They play emotive, expressive and behavioural roles (Fernandez, 1974; V. Turner, 1974).

Metaphorical mapping not only projects the structural features of the source area on to the target area, but also the affective connotations which mark the source area as the horizon of immediate experience. Examples of this include the widespread swear words of animal, excremental and genital origin; positive prepositions meant as praise; and general cultural and religious comparisons, such as 'the lamb of God', 'menacing clouds', or 'mercy . . . droppeth as the gentle rain from heaven' (T. S. Eliot, in Fernandez, 1974, p. 123). What literal definition of the word 'mercy' could better characterise its meaning than this comparison?

Finally, there remains the domain of the ritual organisation of action central to each culture, which is conveyed by metaphors. Examined this way, a ritual appears as a sequence of organising images or metaphors, which are realised by a series of superordinate and subordinate ceremonial scenes. Each of these scenes has its specific task in the context of the graphic process (Fernandez, 1974, p. 125). One need only think of the ritual components of Christian communion which metaphorically comprehends the mystical embodiment of Christ via purification of the soul by confession, subordination by kneeling, bible-reading and the eucharist. Examples more common to the lay world include rites of passage, by which an individual mutates not only in a symbolic but an almost real way from being a child to a youth, and from a youth to an adult. Birth, marriage and funerals can similarly be understood metaphorically (van Gennep, 1960). Through rituals and ceremonies individuals themselves either become a metaphor or objectify it in their interaction (V. Turner, 1974; cf. also Kimmel, 2002). The cognitive, expressive and action-guiding functions of metaphors produce connection between the world, individual experience and social representation. In the broadest sense, that which we describe as 'the world' therefore turns out to be a product of mutual accommodation between language and experience (Kuhn, 1979, p. 418).

### 6.1.2 The figurative schema of social representations

In the previous chapter, we outlined examples of research fields whose forms have been adopted by everyday knowledge about scientific theories, social events and structures and cultural objects. In so doing it was noticeable that representations often show a simple form even if, or all the more so when, the subject matter is actually really complicated. The basic symbolic form to which social representations can be reduced has traditionally been called the 'figurative schema' (Moscovici, 1961/1976, p. 116). These schemata can be analysed in terms of metaphors.

### Psychoanalysis

Moscovici's (1961/1976) work about the image of psychoanalysis amongst the French public, for example, shows how the relatively complex details of original Freudian theory are condensed into a simple image or figurative schema in everyday understanding. The image in Figure 6.2 is, accordingly, a schema for the effect of psychic forces.

Two entities, the conscious and the unconscious, have such an effect on each other that certain psychic contents and strivings are repressed, and as a consequence create a psychic complex. The metaphor in this case consists of several parts. It ontologises on the one hand by making objects out of psychic forces (PO: 'There are two things: the conscious and the unconscious'); and personifies by proposing to view objects as homunculi (PT: 'the study of the uncontrollable being.'). It also calls upon the orientation idea of physical repression or suppression (PL: 'generally suppressed ten-

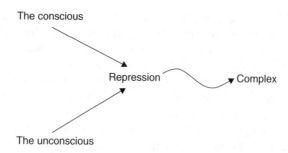

FIGURE 6.2 Figurative schema of the social representation of psychoanalysis (adapted from Moscovici, 1961/1976, p. 116)

dencies'); and is thirdly based on the container metaphor, since everything is going on in one individual head (PM: 'a state of tension in a living being with problems'; PT: 'the uncontrollable being that is in a subject').

Which approximation of experience does this image adopt as a source domain? The idea of two homunculi repressing, oppressing and suppressing unwanted thoughts and strivings seems to be directly borrowed from the experience of physical repression and the impenetrability of bodies. The 'repression contest' of the two homunculi and effective tensions and conflicts produces a new entity, a complex, which all (neurotic) people possess and which governs their strange behaviour.

Mapping the target domain on to the source domain is somewhat harder to justify. It can be assumed that all individuals have had experiences of the most secret strivings and thoughts (generally of an interpersonal or sexual nature, antipathies, etc.) and that they have been forced to keep them hidden from the public (PL: '. . . that which is most secret in us . . .'). The endeavour to conceal these thoughts is often associated with unpleasant feelings of expenditure and strain. This implies the idea of an internal conflict between the wish to give in to those secret thoughts, and fear of the reactions of Others which would be the consequence of making them public (PO: 'Psychoanalysis is useful in recognising what one cannot express and what one dare not say'). Many people have experienced the often uncontrollable consequences of such conflicts in their behaviour – feelings of ambivalence, slips of the tongue, mistakes, abrupt changes of action and physiological reactions such as blushing.

The personalisation and ontologisation of the conflict is the ultimate concrete structural correlation – to perceive the internal forces to which one feels exposed as more or less autonomous entities, which in the sense of the orientation metaphor are 'below', that is to say, in the 'depths of the psyche', out of one's own guiding grasp, and are effective from there. The whole image appears to be a transmission of a 'fight' idea realised in a source domain, the terms of which are made available, by Freudian psychoanalysis,[2] to one's own psychic experience. The terms of the unconscious and the conscious follow a logic which often uses strange contradictory concepts, such as involuntary/voluntary, internal/external and so on. The popular idea associates them with concrete images and implies a dynamic inherent to every contradiction. Because psychoanalysis is seen as a science of the unconscious with its effects on conscious experience, its image simultaneously reproduces elements of Freudian theory with a pre-existing cultural conception of human existence (Moscovici, 1961/1976, p. 116).

## Health and illness

The figurative schema of the representation of health and illness is a comparably clear metaphor (Herzlich, 1973, p. 91). The author's findings from interviews can be reduced to several metaphors. For Herzlich (p. 92), illness arises from the conflict between society (ontologised as lifestyle) and the ability of the individual to resist (ontologised as their reserve of health and part of the individual – retention metaphor). The conflict results in the victory of one or the other. Accordingly, 'society' is to 'individual' metonymically what 'illness' is to 'health'. As a further consequence, society is placed as the equivalent to illness and the individual to health. Health brings integration into society via activity; illness excludes the individual from social life via forced inactivity (ontologisation and personification). Illness can appear in the discourse of individuals as a state, external object or as the behaviour of the ill person. Health appears either as a state – an object belonging to the individual – or as the behaviour of the healthy individual. At the same time, however, the object idea predominates both with illness and with health.

The figurative schema of this social representation constitutes a fact which in itself implies great closeness to experience. The metaphorical projections are already largely outlined – they are not characterised, as in the case of the image's psychic phenomenon, by the psychoanalytical conceptualisation initially foreign to the individual. 'I possess great powers of resistance', 'Society makes me ill', 'I have an illness' are metaphorical statements which describe the possession of objects (resistance, illness) and the negative influence of personified forces (society). Its origin from the personal field of experience is immediately apparent.

## Imagining a complex technology

In a study aimed at uncovering the interaction between media reporting and the resurgence of popular images of biotechnology, W. Wagner, Kronberger and Seifert (2002) show the elements of implied metaphors. Figure 6.3 depicts a photograph that captures the basic ideas about genetic engineering and which appeared half a year after the researchers established the existence of such ideas in the public.

FIGURE 6.3 An obviously staged photograph illustrating the popular conception of biotechnology
SOURCE: SALZBURGER NACHRICHTEN, 19 March, 1997. Printed with permission © Erwin Johann Wodicka.

In this study, questionnaire items captured three underlying ideas relating to the figurative schema of biotechnology, which a considerable number of Europeans found plausible. These were: only genetically modified tomatoes possess genes whereas natural ones do not; by ingesting a genetically modified fruit, the person's genes might also become modified; and genetically modified organisms are always bigger than natural ones. Focus groups also produced similar ideas, as witnessed by the following respondent:

*Respondent*: Well, I mean . . . we are all living well, and . . . we are not experiencing hunger, and . . . I don't know why we then still need *larger tomatoes* . . . it is certainly healthier, if we do this by the normal way . . . instead of *mixing something* to it [the vegetables] or *injecting something* [genes] . . . I don't know.

(Wagner, Kronberger and Seifert, 2002, p. 332)

Why is it that the tomato captured the public's imagination in Europe? Tomatoes were certainly not an arbitrary choice, although different icons may be expected in different cultures. In many countries, photographs of tomatoes were used in weeklies, newspapers and television to illustrate articles about novel food. Whatever other images might have circulated at the beginning of intensive press coverage about genetic engineering, these images converged easily on the enigmatic icon of the innocent tomato being manipulated by injecting foreign substances, in this case the 'genes'. This metaphorical closure is justified by the fact that the manipulation of organisms is known from medicine and chemistry. People generally know that foreign substances can be injected into organisms, such as in the case of inoculations, and it is not far-fetched to use this source domain when trying to understand genetic manipulation. Consequently, genes, in this context, are presented as something foreign to the manipulated organism: genetically engineered tomatoes should possess them, while naturally grown ones do not. The associated belief in infections follows. Foreign substances, such as bacteria, are known to pass from one organism to another. Hence, genes might very well do the same. Finally, the belief in the monstrosity of genetically engineered organisms is related as well. The topic of '*Frankenstein foods*' is not far from these ideas and in fact frequently came up in interviews. Just as tomatoes are good to eat, they are also good to think with. These images and metaphorical projections capture the 'What is it' and the 'How does it work' part of popular imagination about 'genetic engineering'.

## 6.2 The structural features of representations

The foregoing section highlighted an integral view on the organisation of social representations by using metaphor theory in the analysis of its figurative schema. This approach allows the inclusion of affective and evaluative aspects of the figurative core, as shown by the process of metaphorical entailment. The present section outlines a structural approach to social representations.

### 6.2.1 The central core

The core–periphery or structural approach to social representations analyses the figurative schema in terms of its cognitive functions. The concept of the central core was introduced by Abric (1984), to highlight those elements of a representation that give the representation its significance and coherence (Abric, 1987, 2001).

According to this view social representations are not unitary, homogenous mental constructs. Instead, they embrace a set of beliefs, evaluations and attitudes which, in combination, form an orderly hierarchical structure of mutual dependence. The central core is the starting point in the structure. It has an organising function, determining the nature of the relations between the hierarchised elements (Abric, 1984, p. 180). Through this, the elements gain their meaning and value within the system, and allow us to derive conclusions. The author refers to this as the core's creative function.

Cultural knowledge is not just an accumulation of readily formulated propositions. It is also, in large parts, knowledge that can be derived from a small number of generative rules (D'Andrade, 1987; Quinn, 1982). In this way, an existing representation or its core enables inferences to be derived which are not part of the directly available trove of knowledge, but are implied by it. These derived opinions, attitudes and evaluations are the consequence of the generative function of the central core and can be referred to as 'virtual' elements. They mark the generative function, generative potency or normative dimension (Abric, 1987) of the central core. The elements of the core differ, not according to their degree of consensus, but in their significance for the whole structure. Beliefs and features that belong to the central core of a representation show a greater number of associative connections to the other elements of the core than to the so-called peripheral elements (Guimelli, 1991).

An experiment using the representation of 'ideal groups of friends' (Flament, 1982) illustrates the role of the core (Flament and Moliner, 1989).

*Method.* Fifty-eight students described a friendship group of four people, and were asked what the likelihood was that in this group there was: (a) no hierarchy; and (b) a great convergence of opinions. Both elements showed high consensus and were shared by over 95 per cent of the subjects. The sample was then divided into two groups of the same size and a group of friends was described in detail. One of the groups that had been divided received the information that Pierre, one of the friends, takes the lead in difficult situations. The other group was informed that the friends had fundamentally different opinions in many areas. In the one case it was the absence of hierarchy, whilst in the other it was the consensus of the group which were questioned.

The results show that when the absence of hierarchy had been put into question, only 21.5 per cent of the test subjects considered this an ideal group of friends, whilst in the 'divergent opinions' condition, the group was still considered 'ideal' by 73.3 per cent of the subjects. We know from preceding investigations (Flament, 1982) that the absence of hierarchy constitutes one of the central features of a group of friends that students would consider as ideal. One can view it as a relevant element to the central core of the representation which gives meaning to all other elements. The feature of 'shared opinions', on the other hand, belongs at the periphery of the representation, even though, as in this experiment, it receives just as much approval. Although the degree of approval in the pre-test of the two features 'no hierarchy' and 'consensual opinions' was equally high, the absence of one or the other of the two elements influenced judgement in different ways. If the element was a part of the central core, the group of friends lost their ideal character. If the element was a part of the periphery, the group continued to appear 'ideal'.

The central cognitive position and organising function of the core can also be seen in a memory experiment by Abric (1989).

*Method.* Almost 100 student experimental subjects had the task of learning a list of 30 words. The words referred to characteristics of the term 'artisan' and had been collected in a previous study. Some of the characteristics belonged to the central core, others to the periphery of the representation of craftsman. Half of the subjects learnt a list of words which included the terms belonging to the central core, whilst the other half's list did not contain any words belonging to the core. This variation of condition was crossed with a variation in the instruction. The test subjects were told that they would either learn a 'word list' or a 'list with craftsman features'. After presenting the list, the memory of the test subjects was tested either immediately or an hour later.

As might be expected, the results show that both immediately and an hour later, and independently of the experimental condition, the elements of the central core are better recalled – that is, they are recalled more frequently, than peripheral elements. Above and beyond this, however, we can see a differential effect of the priming through the instruction to expect a 'list with craftsman features' or a 'word list'. When the instruction primed the subjects to expect a representation of a particular object (the craftsman), elements of the central core (the definition of a craftsman) were 'recalled' incorrectly – that is, added – significantly more frequently than peripheral elements. The number of incorrectly 'recalled' central and peripheral elements was considerably smaller without priming and roughly equal. Furthermore, more central elements appear with delayed testing. This experiment illustrates the organising function of the top-down processes guiding memory and categorisation.

This feature of internal organisation, however, does not yet clearly distinguish social representations from other cognitive structures such as schemata and scripts. The findings of this experiment only replicate what has long been known from social schema theory (S. Fiske and Taylor, 1991). In this sense, Abric's (1989) experiment does not differentiate. The state of affairs is different in the experiment by Flament and Moliner (1989) described earlier. It would be hard to understand why the attribute of 'consensual opinions' should turn out to be less relevant than 'absence of hier-archy' in an ideal group, when both were rated equally frequently as important in the first part of the experiment, if one did not explicitly take into account the *social significance* of an 'absence of hierarchy' in a group of friends. The central position of elements defining a representation are not primarily determined by numeric consensus, but by social marking (de Paolis, Doise and Mugny, 1987) – that is, from their social meaning and action implications (in this case interaction with friends) and their stability *vis-à-vis* new information. The meaning of an 'ideal group of friends' would be rescinded if it were organised as a social hierarchy. This would negate desirable forms of intercourse between friends. On the other hand, although diverging opinions may be regarded as disturbing, they do not contradict ways of interaction and communication between student friends.

## 6.2.2 Self-reference, functions and hierarchy of elements

### Reference to the Self

The central core of representations, as an essential part of the social identity of the individual, is marked above all by its implications for values and its affective charge. Its structure depends on: (a) the individual characteristics of the subject, especially its relation to the object of the representation; (b) the social features projected upon the object, that is, its integration into the system of norms and values of society; and (c) the explicit and implicit aims of the person in a particular situation with regard to the object of representation (Abric, 1987, p. 69).

Several authors have studied the development of relevant rep-resentations in and of experimental situations (Abric, Faucheux, Moscovici and Plon, 1967; Abric and Vacherot, 1975–6).

> *Method.* In a prisoner dilemma game, experimental partici-pants were informed about the nature of their fictitious game partners (either human or computer), their status relative to the test participant (higher vs. equal status) and the nature of the task (game or problem-solving). The dependent variable was the representation of the situation ascertained according to the game.

The results show that representations of the experimental situation differ when information varies. The social features of the test participants, their social relationships and ideologies went into the system of representation to the same degree as the anticipated game partner and his presumed social relationship with the test subject, as well as the task to be solved. The social characteristics brought into the laboratory by the test subjects in each of the experiments played a crucial role in the unfolding of behaviour in the experimental situation, and the associated representation.

## Periphery

In an experiment similar to the preceding one, Abric and Kahan (1972) illustrated changes undergone by social representations during the course of a prisoner dilemma game. If a human partner (supposedly a fellow student) behaved rigidly during the experiment, he or she was described by the test participant (as compared to what had been assessed before the game) as more competitive, opposing and irrational. If he or she behaved in an adaptive manner, then his or her representation appeared to be more flexible, co-operative and rational. What did not change was the characteristic of honesty that is obviously close to the core of the representation of fellow students. Representations are a means to adapt strategically to reality. They achieve this by providing reality with meanings such that it agrees with the cognitive and ideological universe of the individual. In this sense, the representation system of an individual is an essential factor for maintaining and defending his or her identity (Abric, 1982, p. 92 onwards).[3]

The foregoing studies, as well as others, establish that the cognitive elements of a social representation do not only differ with regard to their degree of centrality – that is, belonging to the core or not – but also with regard to the role they play. Some elements are functional in the sense of orienting behaviour and being constitutive for definition, while others are normative in the sense of allowing evaluative judgments (Abric, 1987; Moliner, 1992). Moliner (1995) shows that in the representation of a commercial enterprise or firm, the beliefs that enterprises are hierarchically structured and make profit are more central than those about enterprises to do with research and development and serving personal fulfilment. That implies that they cannot be dispensed of or negated without changing the character of the representation. However, each of the two elements of the core and of the periphery serves different functions (Figure 6.4).

The results depicted in Figure 6.4 show that from the two core elements (hierarchy and making profit) an enterprise having a hierarchy is considered by the majority of subjects as an essential part of its definition, and therefore descriptive; while making profit is considered by many as simply desirable and an enterprise making no profit remains a possibility, although undesired. Among the peripheral elements (research and development, and serving personal fulfillment) a majority considers research and development as an essential descriptive element, while personal fulfilment of employees is desirable, but not often given.

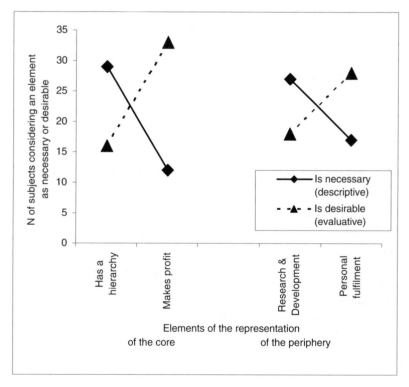

FIGURE 6.4 Results of Experiment 4 by Moliner (1995, p. 37) on the functions of central and peripheral elements in the representation of an enterprise

Besides fulfilling different functions, the elements constituting a representational system stand in hierarchical order with respect to one another. The relations of representations to others, as well as their changeability following new experiences, depend by and large on two parameters: their generality and their normativity (Codol, 1984). In a representation, those elements with the greatest influence on the whole structure are those which show the greatest generality and the greatest situation-dependent relevance to action (functionality) in a given context.

In an experimental game Codol (1974) varied how the task was formulated, the representation of the other players, and that of the group as a whole. The representational system of these elements was organised with descending generality from the representation of the self-image, the task, the group and others. The predominant generality of the self-image (cf. Greenwald and Pratkanis, 1984, p. 145ff.), as well as the function of the element for the task in the game, determined the elements' position within the hierarchy. After the test participants had focused on the task, their thoughts about the group and about others were only of a secondary relevance compared to self-image (Codol, 1984, p. 250).

## Context stability of the core

Whereas the majority of these reported studies aim to uncover the structure of representations at a purely cognitive and individual level (for a critique see Banchs, 2000), a study by W. Wagner, Valencia and Elejabarrieta (1996) focused on the role of societal discourse in structuring social representations. In line with Moscovici's original proposition that conflict is the source of representations (Moscovici, 1988), they argue that well-structured representations can be expected in groups with an ongoing and conflictual discourse, whereas no such well-structured representation can be expected about domains that are not a recurrent discursive topic.

*Method.* People from Spain and Nicaragua responded to a word-association task about what comes to mind when thinking about war and peace. At the time of the study Spain was at peace, but Nicaragua was engaged in a bloody civil war and US intervention. In a preliminary study, it was established that in a country at peace, war was a frequent topic of discourse because of the ongoing Yugoslav war being a regular topic in the media, while peace was not. In Nicaragua war as well as peace were frequent topics in both the media and personal conversations. The design was such that half of the respondents in each country wrote down their ideas about peace first and in a subsequent association task their ideas about war. The other half of respondents wrote down their ideas in the inverted sequence, i.e., first about war and then about peace. This design was used to introduce a context effect from the sequence of topics. If the associations derived from well-structured representations being topics of ongoing discourse, the structure of the associations, that is, the interrelationship between them, should not be affected by context. Associations deriving from less well-structured representations not being a regular discursive theme should be affected by context.

The findings confirm the expectation. Figure 6.5 shows the results of a modified correspondence analysis of the data.

The two convex hulls in three of the four graphs comprise associations that show context-independent interrelationships among them, and which determine a stable core of the representation. This stable core is missing in the structure of the associations about peace in the Spanish sample. The data also show that associations constituting the stable core are more likely to be 'hot' words, that is words that have an affective and evaluative connotation, whereas words outside of the stable core were more frequently 'cold' intellectual and cognitive ideas. The data also confirm on the group level of analysis what Flament and Moliner (1989) have shown for the individual level: that the mere high frequency of a word is not sufficient to determine its centrality to a representation. The words constituting the stable core were not always the most frequent. Without an object or topic being salient and relevant for a social group and hence entailing a public discourse and symbolic elaboration of the object, there is not much sense in expecting an elaborated and well-structured social representation.

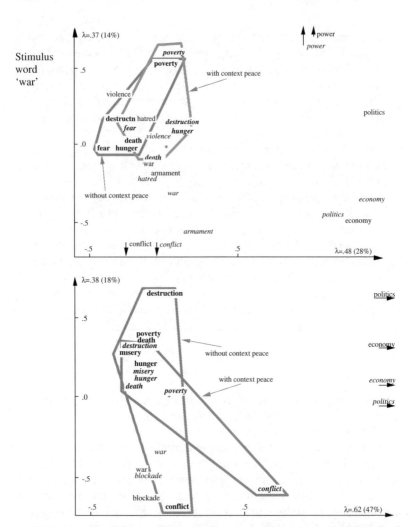

FIGURE 6.5 Clusters of words related to war that are structurally stable (convex hull) in Spain (top) and in Nicaragua (bottom) across different contexts (data from W. Wagner, Valencia and Elejabarrieta, 1996)

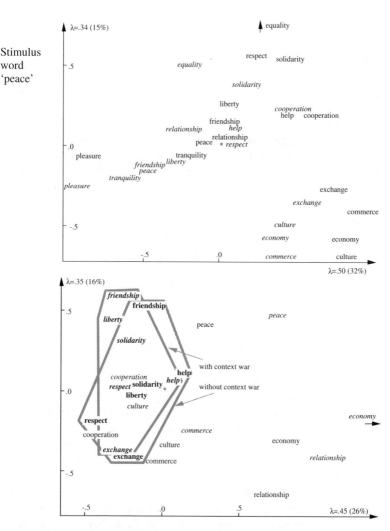

FIGURE 6.5 continued. Clusters of words that are structurally unstable in Spain (top) and stable (convex hull) in Nicaragua (bottom) across different contexts.

## 6.2.3 The protective function of the periphery

The structure and function of social representations as an ensemble of a core and a periphery can be understood analogously to the structure of scientific theories (Lakatos, 1974). Lakatos distinguishes the 'hard core' and the peripheral 'protective belt' in research programmes. The hard core is a system of stated views, which is preseved during 'normal scientific progress' (Kuhn, 1970). It holds the general theoretical basic assumptions of the programme. Every theory when applied is confronted with anomalies which cannot be explained by the central assumptions of the theory. These anomalies would falsify the core if it were not prevented by a negative heuristic rule. The negative heuristic rules out the possibility that the fundamental assumptions of the core may be challenged or relinquished because of a negative result. The representatives of the research programme must therefore make a series of additional assumptions which have the task of explaining the anomalies, and thus forming a protective belt around the core, preventing the core being refuted.

Lakatos's (1974, p. 130) idea that the core of research programmes is 'irrefutable' due to the methodological decision making of its protagonists is a conceptual forerunner to Abric's cognitive approach (cf. Gaskell, 2001). The central core of social representations appears to be hard and 'irrefutable' due to its affective link to the holder's self-image, and also due to a protective periphery. The protective periphery of the representation contains additional assumptions supporting the core under varying circumstances, and justifies it (Flament, 1987).

In the previous chapter we referred to the function of popular scientific theories to legitimise everyday belief systems such as belief in transcendental meditation. Scientific evidence is perfectly suitable for legitimisation due to its acknowledged societal status. However, the integration of scientific evidence into existing representations proceeds selectively, and the relationship between the culturally inspired central core and the peripheral assimilated science remains fragile. Due to its historically gained and affectively proven evidence, the cultural core maintains priority over secondary and assimilated scientific knowledge in ambivalent situations (Billig, 1988).

This relationship can be shown in some of Deconchy's (1990) work. The author investigated collective images which exist about the field of biology and biological processes, and in particular about biological causality. New knowledge about the biological must, of course, be incorporated into representations of biological and cultural objects which already exist, such as the human body. But in this way, new knowledge can in some circumstances endanger the integrity of beliefs and the self-image of people holding them.

*Method.* Experimental participants were presented with fictitious scientific investigations, which they were to judge according to their theoretical, technical and ethical aspects. After describing the structure of the investigation, two alternative fictitious results were presented to each test group. One half of the test participants were informed that if somebody held certain religious ideas, then a higher concentration of a 'salivary acid' could be observed in the blood. The other half was told that if there was an increased concentration of salivary acid in the blood, then certain religious ideas appeared in patients. The author manipulated the direction of causality portrayed in the fictitious results, either from the biological to the cultural/mental, or from the cultural/mental to the biological.

Deconchy's participants consistently judged that research reports in which the direction of causality was from the biological to the cultural/mental more negatively than that in which the direction of causality was the reverse. The finding was confirmed with different samples.

The resistance shown here and in other experiments against accepting biological influences on mental being, as well as the cultural belief of a difference in principle between human and animal (Deconchy, 1990, p. 298), reflects the difficulties people have in bringing the biological nature of their own bodies into harmony with cultural images. If the views of science collide with fundamental cultural knowledge, popular scientific knowledge, although being part of the representation, becomes dissociated in order to maintain the consistency of culturally informed images of human 'nature'. The culturally inspired image of what it means to be human (the *Menschenbild*), as a central core of the representation, maintains priority over peripheral supplementary knowledge. It is as though scientific 'additional assumptions' contradicting the core (e.g. the 'false' causality going from the biological to the non-biological in Deconchy's experiment) evoke resistance in the service of cognitive immunisation (Deconchy, 1990, p. 281) of the central core of the *Menschenbild*.

# Chapter 7
# Dynamics of Social Representations

## 7.1 System and metasystem

Social representations and schemata provide our orientation in a manifold and complex social world. They give meaning, weight and structure to phenomena that are relevant in everyday affairs. Meaning and structure give certainty, and thus positive affect (S. Fiske, 1982). Positive feelings arise from the congruence between our expectations – the available schemata – and the evidence offered by interacting with the world (G. Mandler, 1982, p. 20). The unfamiliar, undefined, unexplained and unreasonable remains outside and has to be integrated into the existing cognitive and representational system if it is to become a part of our personal world. As long as it is outside, it is perceived as a threat, which is sufficient reason for initiating a discourse to construct suitable interpretations, schemata and categories which will endow the unfamiliar with meaning.

In fact, the dynamics of knowledge systems such as social representations, schemata and beliefs have their roots in the processes of communication and discourse of social groups rather than in the contemplating individual mind. This has been alluded to briefly in Chapter 4 and Figure 4.1 and will be discussed in detail in Chapter 8. There are some aspects of social representations, however, that have a bearing at the individual level and which justify a separate treatment in this chapter.

The content-rational system discussed in Chapter 3 defines the limits of what is conceivable, the realm of the admissible. It constitutes a metasystem which determines and restricts the course of admissible cognitive and evaluative processes. Social-cognitive processes operate within available bounds. They are the operational system which comprises thought processes following the logical rules of everyday life (Doise, 1990; Forgas, 1983; Moscovici, 1961/1976). The combined metasystem and system establish a top-down process in individual cognition.

## Schemata and top-down processes

Under normal everyday circumstances, one can think of hardly any situation in which the individual does not act according to his or her expectations of further consequences. Indeed, this is at the heart of any action (as opposed to general behaviour). He or she has expectations, the content of which is delimited by the socially pre-set content-rational system, and the system's modifications on the basis of his or her individual past experience. If people go strolling in the town centre, they will expect houses, streets and pavement, but certainly not cornfields or brooks. Even if they were deliberately to expect 'nothing' in an unfamiliar situation, that idea of 'nothing' is not empty in any way, but probably just another term for openness and tolerance towards future events.

Top-down and schematically controlled processes guide everyday activity and cognition to a large degree (Rumelhart, 1984, p. 170 onwards). The resulting expectation, for its part, is controlled via stimulus information, which is more likely to activate a schema the more culturally salient it is (Forgas, 1985; Higgins, King and Marvin, 1982). This is the basic idea of the schema concept in cognitive social psychology, with its conceptual relationship with research on artificial intelligence (e.g. Minsky, 1975; Rumelhart, 1980). By a 'schema' we understand mental structures and processes which form the basis of 'molar' aspects of human knowledge and abilities. They contain abstract 'generic' knowledge in a modular way, whereby various cognitive areas possess schemata with different structural features (W. Brewer and Nakamura, 1984, p. 140 onwards).

Schemata appear – as do social representations – as theory-like structures which serve to categorise and name experience. Both complement our imperfect perception and evoke affect (Billig, 1988; W. Brewer and Nakamura, 1984; S. Fiske, 1982). They are the prerequisite for allocating meaning and for understanding social phenomena. Bartlett's 'war of the ghosts' experiments (1932) showed that even the content and structure of overheard or read stories changes as they are adapted to the individual's schemata. Anthropologists observed that non-European informants often reproduced Western stories in a radically different way, in order to satisfy their indigenous understanding of nature and society (Rice, 1980, p. 156).

The social-schema approach places schemata in their individual cognitive context, referring less to the social and cultural conditions that give rise to them. Leading schemata are therefore individually learned abstractions or stereotypes, retrieved in a step-wise fashion to identify and interpret personal experience. Schema theory neglects the social function of higher level knowledge (Semin, 1989).[1]

Social representation theory allows a more general view of top-down processes. Social representations are understood as leading schemata rooted in the discourse and social structure of groups, which makes them a socially shared construct. Their being rooted in the social and cultural background of the group makes them relevant for the identity of its members, both on the level of self-identity and on that of social identity (Codol, 1972). According to this view, a top-down process is therefore not just the individual use of some knowledge schema, but is initiated in the social position that the individual takes in a group. The individual's place and embedding in its social group determines the content and structure of the available representations. One can say that because representations identify groups, and because they carry implications for an individual's social 'self', the top-down process actually begins outside of the person on the social-cultural level.[2]

In a study with Australian and Chinese students, Forgas and Bond (1985) show the cognition-guiding influence of the metasystem 'culture'. The experimental participants were students, and thus lived in a relatively comparable milieu of everyday interaction and rational study of science at their university. They were asked to scale and classify social episodes of their shared life at university. Despite agreeing on the situations, the participants in the two samples constructed significantly different episode spaces. Interindividual differences determined each style of perceiving the episodes, but the nature of the relationship between the style of perception and individual differences was clearly controlled by the cultural metasystem. Differences in how the episodes were perceived could be attributed to the specific features of the underlying culture (cf. Bond, 1983). On a somewhat more general level, Nisbett, Peng, Choi and Norenzayan (2001) explain the different styles of either analytic or holistic thought in Western and Chinese people through their different underlying metaphysical systems and tacit epistemologies, which emanate from radically different social systems in the two regions.

Just like the cultural supersystem, representations that correspond to any particular social situation of individuals or a specific formulation of tasks also determine the details of the concrete course of cognitive processes: 'The exigencies of the metasystem vary with regard to the situational position taken by individuals; They may, for example, imply a rigorous logic during scientific work, or a fierce defence of in-group cohesion in the event of a conflict with an out-group' (Doise, 1990, p. 115 onwards). Different social conditions: in the one case, such as the need to have scientific rationality, and in the other the need to resolve conflicts and secure one's self-image in social disputes; imply the adoption of various individual cognitive processes (Doise, 1989).

## Social marking

The way that social representations function as a metasystem is illustrated by studies of 'social marking'. Social marking is a process whereby social conditions are 'tacked on to' cognitive operations in dealings with particular objects (de Paolis, Doise and Mugny, 1987, p. 11). Put differently, social marking consists in a correspondence between the cognitively produced relations between objects and the norms which govern the real or symbolic interaction between individuals (Doise, 1990, p. 122). Studies of the interaction between the content and process of cognitive operations, mentioned far back in Chapter 2, consistently show that logical tasks such as the 'Wason Selection Task' are correctly solved more quickly and with greater probability if they are presented in contexts which are exchange oriented (Cosmides, 1989), everyday pragmatic (Cheng and Holyoak, 1985; Cheng, Holyoak, Nisbett and Oliver, 1986) or culturally significant (D'Andrade, 1989), as opposed to abstract or unfamiliar contexts. This interaction between socially significant content and cognitive operation is an example of the significance that social marking has in cognitive operations on knowledge.

The results of the Wason tests can also be replicated with entirely different cognitive tasks. For example, Roux and Gilly (1984) used transitive inferences offered to test participants in different contexts.

> *Method.* Children between the ages of 12 and 13 were presented with the task of identifying a hierarchy between objects. The objects included on one occasion bricks with different features (form and colour) and on the other occasion pictures of people varying by gender and age. The bricks and pictures were to be organised according to a predetermined transitive context. The predetermined rule for organising the bricks conformed to an arbitrary non-social context, whilst the rule for the people corresponded to the conventions of greeting them according to seniority, thus constituting a conventional social rule.
>
> (de Paolis, Doise and Mugny, 1987, p. 22ff.)

In accordance with the hypothesis, the task could be solved correctly more often when it was socially marked. This effect of social hierarchies can also be found with children as young as 6 years old (Doise, Dionnet and Mugny, 1978). In that study, the children were also able (after appropriate instruction) to transfer the advantage gained by their social knowledge to contexts that were not initially socially marked.

Such results cannot be exclusively explained by different levels of familiarity with the material (De Paolis, 1982), nor by the degree of abstraction of the tasks (Girotto, 1985a), and nor also by the presence of social models, giving an implicit clue for the correct solution (Girotto, 1985b; in De Paolis, Doise and Mugny, 1987). Rather, what suffices is the social marking of inanimate objects which often also convey social norms and relations in everyday life.[3]

## 7.2  Categorisation and anchoring

### Anomalies

Identifying stimuli by assigning them to categories is one of the main tasks of representations and social schemata. If the categorisation of a new stimulus succeeds, then the process is completed and entails a positive affect. But there are several possibilities for

TABLE 7.1 Relationship between the congruence of schema and
stimulus and accompanying affect

| State | Ensuing process | Accompanying affect |
|---|---|---|
| Congruence between schema and evidence | Successful categorisation | Positive affect of very minor intensity |
| Minor incongruence between schema and evidence | Assimilation of the stimulus | Positive affect of minor intensity |
| Considerable incongruence between schema and evidence | Choice of an alternative schema | Positive affect of higher intensity |
| | Successful accommodation of the schema | Positive or negative affect of very high intensity |
| | Unsuccessful attempt at accommodating the schema | Negative affect of very high intensity |

SOURCE: Table adapted from G. Mandler 1982, p. 22.

dealing with the problem occurring if experience contradicts the available schemata and representations (G. Mandler, 1982, p. 22; Table 7.1).

If there is only limited congruence between a stimulus and the available schema, the stimulus is assimilated, but possibly neglecting any deviating features. If the incongruence is considerable, then either an alternative schema can be adopted, or the schema applied must be adjusted and adapted to fit the new experience.

The latter case, in which an anomaly is interpreted by accommodating or altering the representation or schema, is particularly interesting for social representations. We have characterised the organisation of social representations as a set of central core and peripheral elements (Chapter 6). If the task of the peripheral elements of a representation is to protect the core from being challenged, then a highly incongruent stimulus will involve changes or adaptations primarily within that protective belt of assumptions.

It has been assumed that the elements of the periphery can be changed and accommodated relatively easily in order to be able to do justice to such cases of unusual events. The successful attempt at accommodation will be restricted just to these elements. The outcome is a representation whose peripheral assumptions have been exchanged for newly generated features, which do not contradict the central organisation. The existence of the core and its meaning to the representation can therefore be preserved. In the experiment by Flament and Moliner (1989) cited in Chapter 6, the participants amended their representation of the ideal group of friends with a newly generated peripheral element. This allowed for friends having different views on things, even though the participants had not considered this option spontaneously. This process represents an individual adaptation strategy for classifying phenomena that are incongruent to experience (Table 7.2).

TABLE 7.2 Adapting representations to new stimuli and circumstances

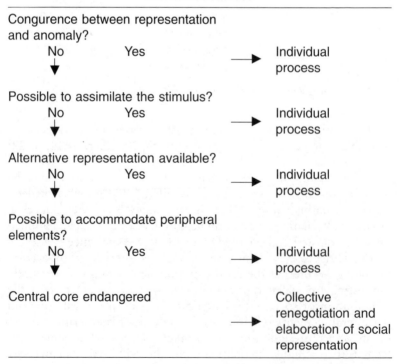

Congurence between representation and anomaly?

No      Yes      ⟶   Individual process

Possible to assimilate the stimulus?

No      Yes      ⟶   Individual process

Alternative representation available?

No      Yes      ⟶   Individual process

Possible to accommodate peripheral elements?

No      Yes      ⟶   Individual process

Central core endangered      ⟶   Collective renegotiation and elaboration of social representation

If the anomaly cannot be successfully integrated into the category by accommodating the periphery alone, then there is a much more fundamental problem. The new experience jeopardises the validity of the representation as a whole. In such a case, the individual will refer to significant members of his or her reference group: comparing his or her interpretation with those of the others. If this fails, the process necessarily moves on to the collective level. New interpretations will be developed in debate and discourse, and negotiated to form a new representation. This process exceeds the bounds of the individual, and will be dealt with in Chapter 8.

The theory of social representations thus exceeds 'classical' schema theory, in which attempts at unsuccessful accommodation go no further than strong negative affect for the individual (Table 7.1). The inherently non-social character of the schema concept means that it does not exceed the bounds of the individuals. It withholds the social solution to such a problem, and 'abandons' the individual in 'depressive contemplation'.

## Prototypes and polythetical categories

If we, like researchers of the 'central core and periphery-approach', conceive of social representations as cognitive structures in the individual mind, they appear similar to many categorical systems that have been a topic in cognitive psychology for a long time. This poses the question of how representations understood as categorical devices are structured with regard to classification processes. Taking into account the complexity and multi-dimensionality of stimuli in the social world, they can hardly be characterised as Boolean sets with a 'Yes–No' membership. For this case, either the theory of fuzzy sets (Zadeh, 1965) or the theory of polythetical classes offer themselves as models.

Fuzzy categories permit an object to be classified on a continuous scale between 0 and 1, according to its membership value of belonging to a category. This model has been successfully applied to human categorisation and decision-making processes (e.g. Rosch, 1975; Rosch and Mervis, 1976; W. Wagner, 1980). The most typical representative of a class or its abstract cognitive image (Posner and Keele, 1968) constitutes the prototype to which classification can be directed. The more similar a stimulus is to the prototype, the more quickly and confidently it can be assigned to the respective category.[4]

If stimuli possess a large number of attributes, then one may also observe two objects being classifiable to the same category, even when they have only a few or no features in common. This is called polythetical classification. Think, for example, of the category of games. There are football games, chess games, children's games, role games and the like which lack some or even most overlapping attributes, but which can nevertheless be grouped together. It is enough for the elements in the class to share a few attributes, and for some elements to share no attributes at all. The unity of the category is maintained exclusively by the fact that some intermediate elements exist which gradually overlap with the disjunctive elements, in the form of serial similarity. In other words, elements are linked like a chain in which adjacent links touch one another. Elements in polythetical categories are grouped together according to their family resemblance (Wittgenstein, 1969) and there is no central prototype uniting most attributes of the class, as is the case with fuzzy categories. Shweder (1977) gives the following definition: 'To be an element in a grouping (category, class, etc.) is to possess a large number of the relevant attributes (features, properties) of the grouping, under conditions where the following is also true: (a) each member of the grouping possesses a large number of the relevant attributes of the grouping; (b) each relevant attribute of the grouping is possessed by a large number of the elements of the grouping; (c) no relevant attribute is possessed by every member of the grouping' (Shweder, 1977, p. 646); Table 7.3 illustrates this relationship.[5]

In Table 7.3, element B is forming the bridge between the disjunctive elements A and C. Such categories are not definable by

TABLE 7.3 Serial similarity in polythetical classes

| Set of attributes and characteristics | | | | | | | | | |
|---|---|---|---|---|---|---|---|---|---|
| Element A | p | q | r | | | | | | |
| Element B | | | r | s | t | | | | |
| Element C | | | | s | | u | v | | |
| . . . | | | | | . . . | . . . | . . . | . . . | . . . |
| Element N | | | | | | | | x | y z |

SOURCE: Adapted from Needham, 1975, p. 351.

intension, that is by giving an exhaustive list of attributes that an element must possess, nor can their elements and grouping rules be unambiguously computed by the rules of classical formal logic (Feldman and Toulmin, 1975; Shweder, 1977).[6]

These two models allow for fuzzy and ambiguous boundaries that can quite frequently be observed in human categorisation behaviour, as well as in experimental research on the structure of social representations. In research reported in Chapter 6.2 we observe, for example, that in Moliner's (1995) study on functional elements in the central core and periphery of the representation (category, in this respect) of a commercial enterprise, the average difference between scores for central (hierarchy, profit) and for peripheral (research and development, personal fulfilment) elements in the representation of the enterprise is a mere 0.98 on a six-point scale (Moliner, 1995, p. 32). If central elements of a representation were indeed unambiguous determinants of class membership, one would expect much stronger statistical effects for the classification of the object 'commercial enterprise'. The weak statistical effects may have to do with the exclusive focus on cognitive instead of affective, emotional and figurative elements of social representations in this kind of study. It may well be that social representations, due to their cognitive, affective and figurative multi-dimensionality, allow for fuzzy or polythetical classification which blurs statistical effects.

## Anchoring

Social representations, as systems of concepts, classes and theory-like relationships, permit or even demand social objects and stimuli to be classified into the existing system of understanding. This mechanism enables us to anchor foreign ideas into known contexts, by reducing them to commonplace categories and images, classifying and naming them (Moscovici, 1984, p. 29 onwards; Doise, 1992).[7] While things or phenomena remain unclassified, they have no meaningful existence, as it were, for the members of a group. Alternatively, they are perceived as a threat, insofar as they cannot be negated. The logic of social knowledge and interpretation prohibits refraining from classifying and naming the novel, or declaring one's neutrality towards a new object (Moscovici, 1984, p. 30).

According to Billig (1988), anchoring is a universal feature of social knowledge systems.

The logic of polythetical or prototypical categorisation permits classifying the new according to its greater or lesser similarity with the conventional. It knows no sharp boundaries and so makes classification possible in a manner analogous to the model of fuzzy sets and degrees of membership. The categories are enriched with new elements in this way, whilst at the same time a process of assimilation furnishes what is new with old features, conventionalises it, and adapts it to the cultural given. The traditional and conventional appears to be more important to social thinking than discriminating perception and intellectual reason (Moscovici, 1984, p. 26).

Posner (1969) has shown that when irregular patterns of dots have become associated with the dot pattern of a tree, they are later recalled as being closer to the tree prototype than without this anchoring. Their recalled form is biased towards the 'figural halo' of the prototype (Posner and Keele, 1970). In the case of social representations, new stimuli are, so to speak, 'accommodated' by a similar process. They are assigned the social attributes of already existing representations while being anchored to them according to the model of metaphorical entailment presented in Chapter 6.

An impressive illustration of how old categories and ideas are used in anticipating the new can be found in Stanislaw Lem's novel 'Solaris' (1972). The story is about a science-fiction future of space travel, in which all the functions of space stations are supervised and controlled by computers. In spite of this thoroughly organised electronic world, Lem pictures the ambience of the spaceship by using images of bookshelves and piles of hard-back books in the ship's cabins. Under this condition it is quite natural that the hero – 'with the thick, stiff spine on his knee' – begins to flick through a voluminous monograph. The fact that we are offered such a familiar sight in a time of space travel (when text will surely only be found in the form of probably more advanced electronic and magneto-optical media of high-memory density than we know today), can only surprise us if we do not consider the force of the known, the power of conventional images. The anchor of the familiar imposed itself even upon this prime author of science fiction – perhaps as a central core of his representation of literacy – in an otherwise phantastically imagined world. The fact that it is the world of books, of all things, that survives in Lem's science-fiction future may be explained more by his profession than by the fact that the novel was written around 1960. It can be assumed that it is because his writing profession is strongly associated with the affective charge of literature, in the classical form of hard-back books, that the author did not conceive of electronic media. This barred him from more realistic extrapolations to the future, even though the rest of his novel can still be regarded as believable science fiction today.

Processing new information in the context of social representations is not analytical. It does not take as a starting point an object with attributes that are investigated for their 'suitability' or not in a categorisation. Instead, the process runs the opposite way, in the sense that the available concepts and their features are applied to the new phenomenon. The end result is given before any analysis so the certainty of customary category systems does not have to be forsaken (Moscovici, 1984, p. 30). If a student in a university decides to categorise somebody unknown as a professor, this implies the attribution of many additional characteristics beyond the reach of perception, including rules of behaviour governing the appropriate interaction with persons of authority.

The anchoring and integration of new elements also amends those features defining categories and representations. The inhabitants of the village investigated by Jodelet (1989b), in which mentally ill patients had been accommodated, tended at first to use current categories such as 'idiots' or 'fruitcakes' to describe the newly arrived patients. Over the course of time, however, that did not prevent them from adapting their categories. Representations were enriched by quasi-medical terminology and metaphorical elements, in order to do better justice to the everyday impressions given by the patients. The villagers also diverged in their opinions, which is a characteristic of the collective process of renegotiating a representation.

It is clear that metaphor theory's mapping of a target domain on to a source domain captures the cognitive and iconic aspects of anchoring the new in the familiar. The variety of source domains is, however, not arbitrary, but limited by the frame of a common culture (Bangerter, 2000; Bartlett, 1932; Kashima, 2000). One's culture provides the symbolic resources that can be put to use as nuclei in the ongoing construction of new meanings and representations. Zittoun, Duveen, Gillespie, Ivinson and Psaltis (2003) illustrate this process in their work on symbol use in developmental transitions and of tourists facing a foreign culture. Further, and on a more general level, within and across many cultures there exist a series of basic source ideas, image schemes, archetypes or 'themata' (Moscovici, 2000) to which source domains can be traced. Examples are the dichotomies 'right–left', 'man–woman', 'good–evil' and other constants of human experience (cf. Kimmel, 2002; Lakoff and Johnson, 1999; Markovà, 2003; Needham, 1973).

Two fundamental consequences arise from the anchoring process (Moscovici, 1984, p. 36 onwards). First, an anchoring understood as a cultural assimilation process does not warrant using the term 'bias' or 'error of categorisation' for diverging classifications of one and the same object. Since representations are always orientated towards the social needs of a group and conform to its daily life, different groups can possess different representations of the same social field. Deviation therefore does not mean that there is an epistemic deficit, but rather that different representations are being applied. Second, anchoring is not simply categorisation and naming. It simultaneously enriches the object by projecting additional and virtual qualities that are implied by the category, beyond the information given. In the same vein, the tendency in everyday life towards explanation and rationalisation (Chapter 3) has the consequence that the targets of attribution – people, objects and situations – are attributed intentions and meaning which channel future interactions with them. Only through this do the new phenomena become an ordinary and customary part of everyday practice.

## Self-positioning

An easily overlooked consequence of anchoring and categorisation as well as of the identity-related function of social representations is that social actors, besides putting order to the world of things, also assign themselves a place within the social world. The relationship between representations and categories and the social position of those using them is entirely reciprocal.

Classical social cognition research understands categories as information about a class or grouping of objects, events and qualities (Lingle, Altom and Medin, 1984, p. 78ff.). As discussed in Chapter 4, these can be either social or natural categories according to whether human behaviour is of interest, that is, 'what does it mean for people?', or whether one focuses on the relations between humans and other life forms, for example plants, animals, mammals, primates (p. 77). This approach to categories refers to the intensional definition of concepts and categories through ahistorical attribute sets, and refrains from taking account of the common reference point linking subject and object. The reciprocal relationship between *who* does the classification and *what* is being classified is disregarded.

By contrast, the theory of social representations broadens our horizons. Both the classified object and the classifying subject are linked through the social field embraced by the representation and its relation to other representations (Giami, 1989). The reference for classification and anchoring is to be found neither within the object nor within the cognising person, but in the social field that comprises both. The content and sophistication of representations depends on the social position of their bearers. If individuals subsume an object into a category, or interpret it with reference to a particular representation, it is not only the result of sophistication in cognitive activity, but equally an expression of the relation of the cogniser to the object: their identity and their belonging to a social group (Duveen and Lloyd, 1986). Just as the water level in communicating vessels changes when the content is altered at only one point, the act of categorising an object similarly places the individual in his or her rightful place, like a bilateral lever arm whose axis is fixed in the social field common to both (cf. Clémence, 2001; Elejabarrieta, 1994; Harré, 1981a; Harré and van Langenhove, 1999; Schiele, 1984). Hence, none of the two sides takes priority, they go hand in hand (cf. Brewer, 2001).

All this is not to say that categorisation, naming and anchoring occur inside the mind of a lonely cogniser. Positioning is by its very definition a relational concept, and makes sense only in a social context. It is located in the space of interaction and discourse unfolding among a group of people, as van Langenhove and Harré (1999), in line with social representation theory, convincingly argue.

## 7.3 Objectification and the socialised mind

One function of anchoring is organising the world in terms of the classification and assimilation of objects and phenomena into social representations and categories But a second essential function is the process of objectification. The term 'objectification' in the literature of social representations identifies a many-sided process. In general, objectification is the process which transforms the Unfamiliar and the yet Unknown into 'conceivable' reality (Moscovici, 1984, p. 38).

Objectification is a mechanism by which socially represented knowledge attains its specific form. This process has been described differently by different authors. In his assessment of French society's representation of psychoanalysis, Moscovici (1961/1976) describes the process by which scientific psychoanalytic knowledge impregnated everyday thinking. As a result of this process, naive recipients take these concepts and their signification literally, and attribute physical reality to them. The ideas are detached from their social sources, that is, from the theory as a scientific construction, and from the psychoanalysts as its practitioners; and turned into a reality confirmed by the senses (Doise, 1993, p. 163; Moscovici, 1961/1976, p. 109f). Instead of relating to a theoretical construct which depends upon the social fabric of science and its methodological grounding, everyday thinking relates to a series of empirical phenomena, such as slips of the tongue, forgetting (displacement), neuroses and so on. These are taken as *being* the theory and its concepts: words and logical relationships become physical reality, in the view of the recipients. At this sociocognitive level, objectification consists of constructing an iconic aspect for a new, difficult to grasp concept, theory or idea, which makes it literally visible (Farr, 1986; Moscovici, 1984, p. 38; for a critical position see Billig, 1993).

Take atomic theory, for example. When Bohr and his predecessors developed the concept of the atom in physics, it was not much more than a relatively abstract, mathematically provable consequence of certain physical experiments which, among others, showed that neutrons passing through a metal demonstrated a different dispersion pattern from positively charged protons. This result from physical experiments (actually not much more than a parameter in a mathematical function) became Bohr's atomic model during subsequent theory development. The theory became popularised partly through simplifying metaphors of the atom as a 'ball-shaped thing' with a hard core and orbiting electrons, a metaphor which was spread by Bohr himself. In the thinking of non-physicists, this image of the atom became popular through a decades-long public discourse, and media reporting that made the originally purely mathematical term into a visually conceivable entity of almost tangible reality. Nowadays, almost every child and the great majority of the adult population of developed countries are able to imagine an atom and talk about it as though in principal it were nothing more abstract than a knife and fork on the dinner table.

This understanding of objectification refers to holding a representation and attributing ontological reality to its associated beliefs. By doing this one behaves towards the world *as if* these ideas existed outside of the mind (cf. Moscovici and Hewstone, 1983). Scientists, when thinking and talking about their theories, also use images and metaphors and in their empirical work. They also act – and with good reason – as if there were some material counterpart of their ideas. But they are usually aware of the ontological limits of these ideas. Experts use scientific information differently from novices. By virtue of their expertise, they are aware that the empirical objects of the world are constructions, dependent on their theories or descriptions, their methods and assessment procedures (Dee-Lucas and Larkin, 1986).

The picture changes when scientific ideas become assimilated by scientifically naive lay people. Novices think in concrete terms, and do not usually differentiate between bits and pieces of scientific information. They are likely to take their assimilated ideas as real, that is, not just as a logical and epistemological construction, but as a thing in the world outside of their minds. (Jost, 1992; Moscovici and Hewstone, 1983). This difference between lay and scientific knowledge does not imply, however, that folk knowledge may not be perfectly valid for its purpose as a means of understanding and communication in everyday life.

'Becoming concrete' in this way, the metamorphosis from the abstract to the widely shared concrete image comprises the social process of communication and collective discourse. It also comprises the origin of meaning and shared images, as a consequence of discourse and communication.[8] An example of this process is the existence and the use of 'money' in all societies. Money, as we know it, appears as a thing which gives substance to the pure idea of exchange value. Like ideas which allow us to connect such divergent things as bread and apples, elephants and a human life, refrigerators and ecological disasters; money makes everything which exists in the (economic) world of mankind commensurable in terms of value. Since the contemporary forms of money have no utility value of their own, their existence depends completely upon the ideas or representations associated with them (e.g. Doise, 1990, p. 143f; Moscovici, 1988, p. 315ff.).

What, then, is the essence of objectification? On a general level objectification is a sub-theory about the people's implicit *convictions* about the relation between their *beliefs about the world* and the supposed *outside world itself*. If people take money to *be* value instead of symbolising value, a psychic complex to *be* a thing in the head instead of a pattern of thoughts assessed in psychoanalytic sessions, and madness to *be* a contagious substance instead of a 'deviant' state of mind (Jodelet, 1991b), they implicitly make a statement about the relationship between their beliefs and reality.

For an idea to become a general item of knowledge, it must first be aligned with already existing elements of knowledge and made into a concrete thought that can be expressed in everyday talk (Moscovici, 1984, p. 39). The social representation of psychoanalytic knowledge would not have spread in the way that it has, had it not been for its applicability in many private and public domains. This wide-ranging use rendered it independent of its previously scientific roots; and it became an unquestioned item in the form of its metaphorical structure (Figure 6.2). It is the everyday pragmatic imperative of concreteness which motivates this metamorphosis, and makes the formerly abstract idea part of the objects populating the world and discourses of everyday life.

Everyday representational knowledge, in the form of images and metaphors, plays a similar role; as do other forms of knowledge. Like technical, scientific and school knowledge, representations reduce ambivalence and provide confidence in personal judgments about the world, as well as confidence when participating in public discourse (cf. Guerin, 2001). Both forms of knowledge are equivalent in terms of replacing ignorance; as was shown in the recent debate on biotechnology and genetic engineering in Europe (W. Wagner, Kronberger and Seifert, 2002). This study used survey data from all over Europe in 1996, where respondents indicated the plausibility of items, which more or less described the representational image of genetic engineering (Figure 6.3). In countries where the new technology was not yet an issue – in other words, where the media had not picked up the biotechnology debate – a high number of people responded 'don't know' and a rather low number found the image either plausible or not, depending on their general background knowledge. In Austria, among other countries, a hot debate surged due to recent political events concerning technology regulation. In this situation many people immediately adopted the representation and its image as plausible, and the number of 'don't know' responses fell considerably in comparison to pre-debate countries (Figure 7.1).

The reason for this, the authors argue, is that ignorance is experienced negatively amidst heated debate and media reporting about a controversial issue. With no idea about an issue, people will not understand the media discourse and cannot participate in

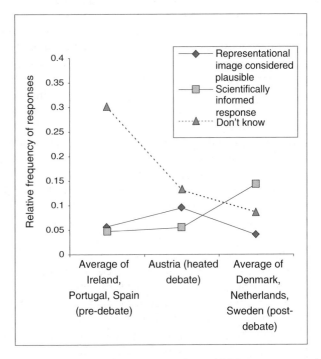

FIGURE 7.1 Frequency of responses in a 1996 survey considering the representational image of genetic engineering (on a very conservative measure) as plausible, not plausible (scientifically informed), and don't know in three country groups, respondents with lower level of school and science knowledge (data from W. Wagner, Kronberger and Seifert, 2002)

conversations about that topic. Developing a representation and objectifying the issue in metaphors and image-related beliefs comes quite naturally in such a situation.

Note that in these two types of country there is no significant difference in the number of people who reject the image as erroneous. The frequency of more scientifically minded people rises steadily in countries where no heated debate and fierce argument raged in the media. These were primarily countries with a longer and more intense history of media reporting about biotechnology. The findings illustrate two aspects of objectification and representation. First, the equivalence of representational and scientifically informed knowledge in reducing self-ascribed ignorance; and, second, that objectification occurs during and through periods of public debate of a novel issue (Moscovici, 1988).

We argued in Chapter 6.1 that source domains in the objectification of unfamiliar issues are most likely to be close to everyday experience and widely accessible in a group. In other words, source domains are part of local culture. The following study about the representation of sperm and ovum in conception illustrates this (W. Wagner, Elejabarrieta and Lahnsteiner, 1995). Fertilisation is a natural process which is described in biomedical terms: anatomy, cytology, physiology and endocrinology. In scientific understanding, it is a complicated process stirred by complex biological relationships between gametes and ovum within the chemical ecology of vagina, uterus, Fallopian tube and ovary. The fundamental event is the meeting and merging of two entities, the sperm and the ovum. This fact has been known in medical science since the end of the eighteenth century (cf. Darmon, 1977).

In the industrialised world, contemporary folk knowledge about procreation takes the form of vulgarised scientific knowledge transmitted in school, by parents and by the media. People with a standard level of schooling know about the two entities, sperm and ovum, involved in procreation. Knowing that sperm and ovum exist is the scientific part of folk knowledge in large parts of the world. The only problem that has to be solved is to elaborate an image of how these two entities function, meet and interact. It was hypothesised that people would use a social metaphor in order to make the natural process intelligible in anthropomorphic terms. This metaphor of an anthropomorphic sperm and ovum also appeared in a public advertising campaign for a brand of mineral water (Figure 7.2).

FIGURE 7.2 Advertising campaign for a mineral water in Paris, 1993, using a metaphor of anthropomorphic sperm and ovum
SOURCE: © Wolfgang Wagner.

The experiment was as follows:

*Method.*  A total of 169 participants in an interview and questionnaire study with an experimental design were presented with metaphorical comparisons for the role of sperm and the ovum. The metaphors were comparisons, which made reference either to gender roles (e.g. 'The role of the sperm towards the egg cell during conception corresponds to the role of men courting a woman') or to other, non-human domains (e.g. 'The role of the ovum towards the sperms resembles that of a cat catching a mouse'). The combination was cross-cut with a second dimension in which either the active role of the ovum (not a gender-role stereotype) or of the sperm (gender-role stereotype) was emphasised. The participants were asked to indicate their agreement with these metaphorical comparisons. In addition, they were asked for judgments on characteristics

continued

of the two cells on a polarity scale, half of which comprised adjectives related to gender stereotypes (big–small, weak–strong, submissive–dominant, etc.) while the other half were less so (important–unimportant, negative–positive, ugly–pretty, etc.).

The preferred form of objectification of the activity of sperm and ovum, as expected, was sex-role behaviour and not any other source domain. Additionally, the sperm and ovum cells were discriminated on gender-stereotypical adjectives, but not with non-stereotype related adjectives. The essence of these results was replicated in a study where some participants read a scientific statement about sperms and ova, which they had to relate to other participants in a serial reproduction chain. After five generations, the reproduction gave the sperm subject status in sentences, rising from about 50 per cent to 85 per cent per cent. Reproductions which referred to the sperm as 'travelling' rose from zero to about 60 per cent (Bangerter, 2000).

The reason for choosing this source domain in objectifying conception is that public and intimate sex-role behaviour is a pervasive experience for most people. For these reasons it is well understood, not least because the rules regulating this behaviour are a central topic of informal socialisation and a frequent topic of conversation. In fact, sexual behaviour is a preconceptual domain close to bodily experience and cultural habitus. It has a simple logic and can be thought of without the use of language. Additionally, of course, the respective cells originate in men and women, implying a kind of metonymic principle where the part stands for the whole (cf. Rozin and Nemeroff, 1990). Therefore it offers itself quite naturally as a source, first to anchor and then to objectify conception.

In the present context, however, the fact that people's preferences and judgments differed in accord with their local culture, that is, whether they adhered to conservative or liberal gender-role styles in relationships, is more important. Gender-role conservatives judged the sperm's characteristics to be more stereotypically male (i.e., as stronger, harder, more active and more dominant etc.) and the ovum's attributes to be more female (i.e., weaker, softer, more passive and more submissive etc.) than gender-role liberal

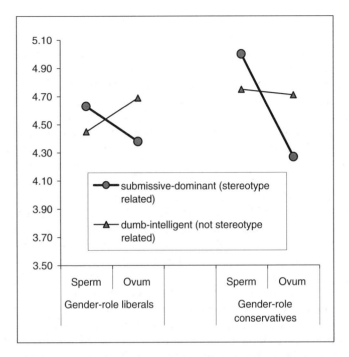

FIGURE 7.3 Degree to which sex-role liberal and conservative subjects attribute dominance and intelligence to sperms and ova. The higher up on the scale, the more dominant and intelligent, the lower on the scale, the more submissive and dumb the biological cells are judged (data from W. Wagner, Elejabarrieta and Lahnsteiner, 1995)

subjects. This cultural effect was independent of the participants being men or women (Figure 7.3).

By comparing the characteristics and behaviour of natural cells with men and women in social and sexual life, the process of fertilisation becomes objectified as being as intelligible, 'real' and 'tangible' as sexual interaction and intercourse in real life. The previously abstract entities of sperm and ovum known from popular science become converted into concrete entities with specific attributes. The cells, invisible to the unaided eye, become part of our everyday world. The cells created by this objectification are social objects with new attributes unknown to biologists, forming the natural part of the moral domain (Harré, 1981b). Their moral attributes make sense only in the consensual universe of everyday thinking and discourse. They are good to talk with, as was vividly illustrated by the comment of an eminent Spanish professor of gynaecology in a class in the 1960s, who commented that 'Contra esperma vigoroso no hay óvulo que resista' (There is no ovum that resists a vigorous sperm).[9] The same representation is communicated by the author of a newspaper story about 'subzonal insemination', whereby a single sperm is artificially injected into an ovum, who titled his story 'Le viol de l'ovule' (The rape of the ovum) (Nau, 1994). The reader will easily remember one or the other advertisement alluding to this representation.

Moscovici and Hewstone (1983, p. 112) list three transformation processes characterising objectification. These are personification, figuration and ontologisation. The study illustrates the first and the third of these overlapping processes.

As might have become clear in the meantime, anchoring and objectification are intricately linked. Confronting an unfamiliar phenomenon or idea, people initially link or anchor, and in consequence explain this phenomenon by reference to their available categories and schemata. Anchoring has a social dimension such that people in a group do not revert arbitrarily to categories and schemata. One might suggest that the categories and schemata primarily used for anchoring the unfamiliar are those which are particularly well-known and/or appear in some way to be functionally or structurally related to the unfamiliar, just as sexual relationships are functionally related to fertilisation. This initial anchoring of something unfamiliar to a familiar domain – often occurring during childhood (Duveen, 1993, p. 175) – can in due course result in the subsequent process of objectification, where the prior anchoring category, schema or experience serves as the source domain to objectify the unfamiliar.

Billig (1988) argues that the concept of objectification, by contrast with anchoring, is not a universal process. In religious belief systems especially, it is likely that concrete objects are, and have been, enriched with transcendental contents extracted from the field of normal everyday practice. He uses the example of the burning bush which Moses encountered in order to accept the presence of the sacred even in such lowly things as a shrub (Billig, 1988, p. 7). Whilst, therefore, objectification is about conceiving the abstract in everyday images, religious 'transcendentalisation' would produce a non-material consciousness from ordinary things. To consider religious belief systems as social representations, however, is debateable (Billig, 1988, p. 8).

With the process of objectification, its function, images and metaphors, the circle of argument of this chapter links back to Chapter 6, the organisation and structure of representations. Existing social representations are used initially for understanding the unknown by categorising and anchoring it. But if the accompanying discourse keeps the topic on the agenda, this leads to a new representation being created. It is assigned a source domain which objectifies it and makes it familiar as part of the life-world.

# Chapter 8

# Discourse, Transmission and the Shared Universe

## 8.1 Dialogue, discourse and doxa

It took until the middle of the twentieth century for two long-separated paths to cross: that which relates to the physical world by way of communication, and the more recently discovered one which relates to the world of communication by way of physics. The whole process of human cognition thereby assumes the characteristics of a closed system. Furthermore, we remain faithful to the inspirations of wild thinking if we acknowledge that the scientific mind, in its modern form, and through an encounter that only it could have foreseen, has contributed to legitimising the principles of this thought and putting them back in its rights.

(Lévi-Strauss, 1968, p. 310)

To take communication as a prerequisite and collective debate as the source of individuals' practical everyday knowledge is something that has been accepted within social psychology, by the theory of social representations and others. For this, it is necessary to leave the individual level – the processing of social information in the heads of people as an exclusive level of investigation – and to place social processes, as of right, as preconditions for individual psychic existence. These collective conditions remain an unassailable companion to the study of the individual structures of social representations, whether they be the reflex of popularised scientific theories, influenced by current social processes and historical orientations; or established in the broader cultural environment.

## Conversations

Social representations constitute a phenomenon which is related to a special way of acquiring and communicating knowledge (Moscovici, 1981, p. 186f.). The manner of acquiring and communicating is bound to a social system which allows individuals to feel themselves of equal value and indispensable. This enables a relatively unrestricted discourse in which, at least in principle, everything can be open for discussion: politics, medicine, education, and such other relevant topics as are offered by a society and might interest its members. The universe of conversations constructed in this way is suitably illustrated in the question and answer by Clov and Hamm in Beckett's 'End Game': Clov: 'What is there to keep me here?'; Hamm: 'The dialogue' (quoted in Moscovici, 1981, p. 187). It forms the fertile background in, and against which, everyday knowledge in the form of social representations is subjected to a continuous process of formation and transformation. The communication process creates and elaborates those social objects which are the prerequisites of social behaviour and of one's self (Moscovici, 1963, p. 251). In this universe, no member of society occupies an exclusive position or authority. Each participant in the discourse can be awarded whatever authority may be required in a situation (Moscovici, 1984, p. 21). All are simultaneously 'curious observers' and 'amateurs' in all the areas in which they wish to give their voice (cf. Markovà, 2000, 2003).

For the following paragraphs let us agree on what we consider to be dialogue and what discourse. Dialogue, according to the Encyclopedia Britannica (DVD edition, 2000), is originally a 'form [that] has long been used [by writers] as a vehicle for the expression of ideas. It is especially cherished by authors eager to eschew the forbidding tone of formality that often accompanies the expression of serious thought.' As an element of fiction, it is the 'recorded conversation of two or more persons'. In our more general understanding, dialogue shall be the surface form of conversation, debate and argument among people. Discourse, on the other hand, shall be understood as the total of dialogues in particular situations or on a particular topic. As a form of social action (van Dijk, 1997) it may also comprise any overt (bodily) action in a social setting, which by virtue of its semiotic powers conveys meaning to other social actors. It has a structure and content that goes beyond the sentence and beyond a concrete dialogue or conversation.[1] A universe of discourse, then, is the class of entities that is tacitly implied or explicitly delineated as the subject of dialogues, theories and statements. When we talk of discourse, therefore, we are primarily referring to the entire universe of entities implied by the topic; when we talk of dialogue, we are referring to the concrete instances of ongoing discourse – that is, its surface form.

The significance of discourse for the (inseparably linked) creation and spread of social representations warrants a 'rhetorical' approach, as is suggested by Billig (1987, 1988) amongst others. Although contradiction and dissent are implicit requirements for any dialogue, Billig (1988) criticises their lack of emphasis in the social psychology literature; dialogue does not just consists of repetitions and amendments; contradiction and conflict are just as important (p. 14; Markovà, 2003). Rhetorical and conversation analyses[2] stress the contradictory topics forming the cultural and ideological life of modern societies (Potter and Wetherell, 1987; Windisch, 1990).

This raises the question of which social-cultural conditions must be met if we are to be able to speak of social representations at all. In other words, we must establish those places and times which permit this kind of discourse and the origin thereof.


## Doxa

In archaic societies there is probably less arbitrariness in the subjective organisation enacted by the members of a society or of an ethnic group in their daily lives. This borderline instance of the relative coincidence of subjective and objective principles of organisation represents the ideal of monodoxical experience (Bourdieu, 1976).[3] In such a society, thought and perceptual schemata produce objectivity

> because they make the boundaries of cognition, which they enable, unrecognisable. Through the Doxa they align their life and state of being with the world of tradition which is felt to be 'natural' and taken for granted. In such a case, the means for recognising the social world are (objective) political means which contribute to reproducing that social world; through an immediate agreement between the world and thoughts about it, which is accepted as convincing and unquestionable. They are means

which are the product of this world, and which continually reproduce and transform its structure.

(Bourdieu, 1976, p. 325)

Although societies in which the Doxa represents the dominant knowledge establish a shared universe, they exclude critical discourse and debate about their foundations. The exclusion of this debate is not even an active political measure, since even to think of it seems impossible due to the 'naturalness' of what exists. In such societies and early historical times the term 'social representations' does not seem applicable.

More developed societies, not only contemporary modern ones, open the boundaries as to what can be discussed. Such societies, whether orthodox or heterodox, include a knowledge and acknowledgement of the possibility of different or antagonising convictions (p. 325 onwards). It is precisely this possibility of contradictory experiences and knowledge which is the prerequisite for that form of collective discourse that permits divergent everyday knowledge and common sense. In so doing, it does not seem important whether the rulers of orthodox societies – such as the Church and clergy in the Middle Ages and the Renaissance, or the fascist and communist rulers of the immediate past and present[4] – try to prevent critical discourse through repression or control it for their own benefit. As soon as political measures become necessary, then knowledge of other possibilities already exists amongst the public and the more vehemently they are officially denied, the more interesting they appear.

## 8.2 Sharedness, situatedness and functional consensus

### 8.2.1 Intra-group variability

The use of the notion of consensus for content-rational systems, and therefore also social representations, never fails to arouse criticism in scientific debate. The term 'consensus' seems problematic if one understands it as literally meaning close to 100 per cent agreement in a social entity (e.g. Potter and Litton, 1985) – an interpretation which can always be empirically refuted with great certainty.[5] Therefore Augoustinos and Walker (1995, p. 158 onwards) argue that even if individuals show considerable variety in the elements of representations they hold, it still makes sense to talk about shared representations at the collective level (cf. also Rose, Efraim, Gervais et al. 1995).

In psychology, in fact, exist a great number of general statements, that is, statements applied to the whole of a population, which really have only a probablistic character, and therefore do not apply to each and everybody. But the probabilistic character of the statement does not contradict its universal claim, if it is theoretically tenable or imperative. A well-grounded theoretical claim overrides the empirical verification of a false literal understanding. In addition to this, in most cases it is not possible or useful to investigate the population as a whole. In practice, that reduces the problem to identifying as high a modal value as possible.

The concept of 'consensus' gains theoretical sense if we stand back from statistical considerations and emphasise its function. Social entities are defined and exist through the orderly living together of their members. Social protagonists possess largely shared ideas about how interaction is to be organised such that the structure of the group and its institutions is either preserved, or continually socially reconstructed. Consensus must therefore be assumed, to the extent that the existence of the social entity is safeguarded through co-ordinated interaction. Yet just as a social entity under normal circumstances must always be able to deal with deviance and ignorance, we do not need a statistically 100 per cent consensus. There need only be a functional consensus in each group, the numerical size of which depends on the extent to which the members are faithful to the rules and the dynamic of their institutions and self-organisation.

The problem of which questionnaire data from a sample may be taken as an expression of collective commonality is one which social psychologists share with anthropologists, in the sense of the reliability of informants. Both cases are about identifying which answers are the modal ones related to a population, and can thus be taken as a reflex of a functional consensus, and what significance should be attached to deviations.

Variance, such as in the analysis of variance models, or range, such as is used for non-parametric measures, is often interpreted as 'error', and a deviation from the central tendency. This interpretation of variation as deviation from the average or modal value has only very recently given way to the view that heterogeneity has an important part to play in social systems. Intra-group variability, in behavioural repertoires, cognitive and emotional reactions, and in knowledge, plays a much greater role in social adaptation processes. Just as the genetic variation of a gene pool is the prerequisite for possible adaptation to changing ecological conditions, so social change only becomes possible through the variability of the cognitive and affective behaviour pool (Pelto and Pelto, 1975). Differential participartion in culturally shared knowledge occurs for a variety of reasons. These reasons are to be found in the conditions of division of power, amongst other places, and, linked to this, in possibilities of accessing sources of knowledge which result in the positive and negative discrimination of certain bearers of social and gender roles. This is similarly the case with the acquisition of knowledge dependent on age, and symbolised by rites of passage and stages of life (Holland, 1987; Mathews, 1987). Knowledge is often shared in a complementary fashion as it is with gender roles, where neither the male nor the female part can be interpreted on its own, let alone have any claim to modal value. Although in a society structured in such a way there will hardly be 100 per cent consensus about cultural knowledge, it would be theoretically unproductive if one wished to attribute variability to probabilistic error alone. It is irrelevant, in this context, whether one understands cultural knowledge as a quantity of individually available knowledge 'chunks' or as implied by a number of rules (Boster, 1987, p. 152 onwards).

Expertise about content-rational knowledge, on the other hand, is only possible if culture as a whole is a coherent system. Representatives of a culture do not only give comparable answers in a questionnaire or in an interview, but also produce almost identical answers in word-association tests. This would not be possible if the acquisition of idiosyncratic personal knowledge were not subjected to social control. Here, it is the better educated and more intelligent informants whose answers most correspond to the modal value (D'Andrade, 1987).[6] The apparent 'bias', to which informants appear to be subject, is on closer analysis geared towards the probabilities and norms which underlie a topic: 'Subjects will be ... biased, but they will be biased in the direction of providing accurate descriptions of the underlying structure that is our true focus of interest' (Freeman and Romney, 1987, p. 331).

Romney, Weller and Batchelder (1986) developed a mathematical model to calculate the extent of consensus and the reliabiltiy of informants in sampling tests. It is based on three basic premises:

1. Common Truth. There is a fixed answer key 'applicable' to all informants. This simply states that it is assumed that the informants all come from a common culture, that is, whatever the cultural reality is, it is the same for all informants in the sample.

2. Local Independence. The informant-item response random variables satisfy conditional independence (conditional on the correct answer key).

3. Homogeneity of Items. Each informant has a fixed 'cultural competence' over all questions. This is a strong assumption that says that questions are all of the same difficulty level. In most situations a weaker assumption is warranted, namely, that the informants who tend to do better on one subset of questions will tend to do better on another subset of questions. This might be called the monotonicity assumption and is related to ensuring that questions are drawn from a coherent domain.'

(Romney, Batchelder and Weller, 1987, p. 165)

Applied to different sets of data, this model has proved to be useful and correspondingly robust with small samples (for applications, see Romney, Batchelder and Weller, 1987; Weller, 1984, 1987). It appears to be important in discussions about the meaning of intra-group variablity because it does not interpret it as variance and statistical error, but as something meaningfully interpretable and accessible to content analysis.

## 8.2.2 Situations and sharedness

The data that social researchers, social psychologists and anthropologists use in their scientific work – be it interviews, focus-groups or replies to questionnaire items – are utterances of people in particular situations; they are situated beliefs, opinions and attitudes. Therefore utterances may not only vary between subjects, but also vary between situations.

### Situatedness

Mugny and Carugati's (1988) investigation of the social representations of intelligence illustrates this issue. Whether parents refer to the intelligence of their children – or the lack of it – as a natural gift or as the result of their educational work depends largely on the context within which they think and speak. When parents refer to the intelligence of their children as a natural or divine gift, they reject responsibility which they would accept if they saw it as a result of their educational work. Such variation in rejecting or accepting responsibility is perhaps less of an indicator of the existence of different competing representations of intelligence, than it is an indicator of divergent modes of talking in different contexts and situations that stimulate divergent strategies of accounting for one's own behaviour (W. Wagner, 1995b). This point has repeatedly and rightly been made by discourse analysts (e.g. Potter, 1996, p. 213).

More explicitly than in Mugny and Carugati's (1988) research, the series of investigations by Schurmans and co-workers show how the conditions of an interview exert an influence on how people talk about an issue. Respondents refer to social indicators and identities more explicitly, when the interviewer emphasises his or her own pertinance to a group, than when they do not. The examples of the interview topic given by repondents clearly illustrated their relevance to a system of knowledge that was assumed to be shared among interviewee and interviewer. This difference is due to the situation and interview context, rather than to intrinsic differences between the interviewees. (Fournier, Schurmans and Dasen, 1994, p. 163).

Lloyd and Duveen (1992) give examples of how representations of gender imply situated self-referential talk and behaviour in children. Having a clear representation of their gender makes children self-aware of any violation of their identity in terms of relating with others, their proper clothing, and the toys they choose for playing. Their gender-related talk and behaviour is a situated expression of the representation they are holding.

## Sharedness

In a study of a literary work, Arthur Miller's 'The Crucible' taken to be a model for live everyday interaction, Wagner and Mecha (2003) analysed the unfolding conversations and dialogues, from the initial events triggering witchcraft accusation, through the court proceedings, to the final execution of some villagers. The village people conversed about witchcraft in different ways, depending on whether they talked to other villagers or in an institutional setting. Their utterances ranged from rejecting that witchcraft was at work, to accusing others of it. Their particular statements were motivated by their interests: that is, when they accused others, they were fuelled by greed, jealousy, hatred and love. Despite their situationally divergent talk, however, all villagers implicitly referred to one and the same shared representation of witchcraft. That is, beyond their divergent dialogues, they converged on enacting one single representation (cf. Verheggen and Baerveldt, 2001).

This brings us to the crucial point: that we need to discriminate between the level of beliefs, attitudes and accounts as the material of dialogue and conversation, and the underlying representations as guiding discourse. In this sense, representations are patterns in discourse which embrace shared background knowledge, and which are true in the group's world and minimally situation dependent. On this level, they are group specific and locally rational, delimiting the discursive space of what can or cannot be said in particular situations. It comes as no surprise, therefore, that the representation derived from a set of interviews – for example, about food and eating – can be squarely aligned with the food and eating related material contained in encyclopaedias, which collect a culture's reified universe of knowledge (Lahlou, 1998)

This is the reason why we prefer to call the universe of representations underlying discourse a *shared*, but not a *consensual* universe; just as it sounds right to call the objects populating a local world shared, but awkward to call them consensual.[7] The system of representations is the shared underpinning of groups, which enables a group's members to converse about topics and issues and express divergent opinions about them. It delimits the possible dialogues which can unfold in the group's living space; but does not prevent them – more often than not – from being controversial.

Consensus and dissent are characteristics of dialogues and conversations. What is being consented to or dissented about, are beliefs, attitudes, evaluations and judgements in particular situations. These discursive forms are derivations and conclusions from the underlying shared rational system of representations; and they are the means by which individuals bring their specific interests and idiosyncrasies to bear. Each individual in a social setting is subjectively free to express whatever he or she desires, but they cannot exit from or dissent on their shared discursive, that is, representational space.

Sharing a world-view in the form of collective and social representations is a characteristic of groups. It is the epistemological means enabling communication. Under regular conditions, doubt and argument exist on the level of beliefs, opinions and attitudes, and not on the level of representations. Doubt about other's or one's own beliefs is brought to the fore in interaction, argument and dialogue (Duveen, 2002). We are not in the position to doubt the very epistemological basis that has emerged from our history of interactions.

Note that to define a group in the present context we need – contrary to most text-book definitions – a minimum of four persons. We call a social group any set of a minimum of two persons sharing a set of representations which enables a meaningful communication. But in order to know whether two or more persons are sharing their epistemological space, they must confront at least one other group. Because a group is a subset of a universe of people, it can only be conceptualised within a universe which is itself composed of social entities, that is, at least one other group. Social groups are distinct in terms of their understanding of social phenomena, which in turn constitutes their social identity. The shared understanding of their world and of the objects composing it must be different from an outside group's understanding. Therefore a minimum of two groups mutually provide the background against which each group can be distinguished. Otherwise, talking of social groups would not make much sense.

To summarise this point: Social representations are shared (if they were not shared in a group, they would not be social representations), but cannot be called consensual by their very definition. Beliefs, attitudes and the whole range of equivalent rhetoric devices may be called consensual if two or more people agree on a belief, or controversial if they do not agree. It must be added that the afore mentioned difference between opinions, beliefs, attitudes as rhetorical devices and social representations as their epistemological basis is always gradual. We suggest that representational systems become more irrefutable the more *cultural burden* they carry.

A nice example of the role of cultural burden is Saito's (1996) study of Zen-Buddhism. She shows that the knowledge of Zen in Japan, even among people not practising it, differs notably from the knowledge of Zen found among believers in Britain. Japanese respondents produce a coherent, well-structured and proximal account of Zen which is strongly connected to all walks of everyday life. British followers of the Zen movement produce a fragmented image which is relatively isolated from other practices and which can easily be challenged.

The more ingrained that representations in a group's life become, the more epistemological entailments they imply – in other words, the more burden they carry in making the world intelligible – and the less they can be subject to doubt and refutation in discourse. Usually this correlates with their duration of enactment, in a historical perspective, in a group's ongoing discourse. This also explains why mentalities always lag behind social change (Le Goff, 1989).

## 8.3 Epidemiology, culture change and cognitive polyphasia

### 8.3.1 Culture change

#### Epidemiology

The process of forming, spreading and changing social representations resembles, to some extent, the spread of a contagious disease (Sperber, 1985, 1989). Medical epidemiology uses mathematical models and pathological findings to study the preconditions contributing to the transmission and mass spread of pathogenical germs like viruses, bacteria and so on, and how each disease is communicated. In an epidemiology of cultural and social representations forming the consensual universe, we are dealing with something similar. We are trying to identify the mechanisms that take effect at the start as well as in the course of transmitting the new ideas which produce collectively accepted representations.

Three questions appear relevant here. First, which cognitive and emotional contents are predestined to be experienced by a majority of individuals as attractive or useful? Formulated differently: which mental structures make individuals receptive to one idea, but not to another? Second, when, where and under what circumstances do social representations come about? And third, which paths and circulation routes are used for transmitting them?

An epidemiology of social representations therefore lies precisely at the interface of an ecological way of looking at social processes and individual cognitive and emotional mechanisms. Just as the pathology of individuals is an essential building block for understanding receptivity to and thus the spread of illness, so a social-ecological viewpoint requires knowledge about individual psychological mechanisms (Sperber, 1985, p. 74 onwards).

The answers to the three questions differ, depending on whether it is a matter of historically long-existing cultural contents and ideas which define the character of a culture and society (its cultural 'old town', to use Wittgenstein's metaphor) virtually endemically; or whether it is a matter of historically transient representations such as appear in each generation, spread rapidly and disappear just as quickly without finding a place in the realm of tradition. Transient representations appear without doubt to be more relevant to the social psychology of modern societies.

Possible answers to the first question – the characteristics which predestine the spread of a representation – have already been aired in those parts of Chapters 5 to 7 relating to the metaphors and images which people are more or less likely to absorb. These discussions also touched on aspects which are responsible for the change and elaboration of representations. Chapters 5 and 6 have given a partial answer to the second question by showing some conditions under which new representations evolve in modern science-orientated society (cf. also Sperber, 1990). In the majority of cases it will be the emergence of novel phenomena (e.g. Wagner, Kronberger and Seifert, 2002) and the associated conflict that motivates a group to engage collectively in the elaboration of a new representation (Wagner, Valencia and Elejabarrieta, 1996). In other cases it can be shown that rumour plays a role in creating and spreading representational thought (Lorenzi-Cioldi and Clémence, 2004).

## Change

Changes in conditions of living and behaviour necessarily lead to the transformation of conventional representations in groups. These may be practices such as the introduction of new technologies or social and political measures. One only need think of the rapid spread of electronic media at work and at home, of the recent technologies introduced in medicine, or of the ecological debate which makes nature and technology appear no longer as two separate areas, but as systematically integrated. Or they may be social conflicts, such as the distribution of public services and goods as a consequence of so-called globalisation, the solution to which must be thrashed out by interest groups and their representatives. Such conflicts and negotitations may appear on the surface to be primarily about the key to distributing whichever material amount is in dispute. However, the collective redefinition of available representations and justifications which symbolically conform to the new living conditions, and can be accepted as just, is at least as important to the outcome. The justifications and reasonings that members of a group can understand and accept determine whatever is considered right (cf. on this Boltanski and Thévenot, 1991). In this way new objects arise in the form of social representations.

These collective and individual adaptation processes can cause incompatible representations, both within generations and between them. The literature shows that there are mainly two adaptation and transformation mechanisms of representation systems that have been discussed. One concerns transformation processes which abruptly tackle changed conditions via a new representation. Such transformations consist in a dispersion of the elements of the central core, which is virtually 'divided' and therefore results in a relatively new representation (Flament, 1987). On the other hand, transfromation processes can be observed which constantly adapt the old representation system to the new conditions, leading to a gradual transformation without a 'break' (Guimelli, 1989; Guimelli and Jacobi, 1990).

Flament (1987) refers to an empirical investigations which illustrate how new representations come about. It first relates to the introduction of new forms of agriculture in traditional areas of Cameroon during colonial times when, as an alternative to the traditionally predominant cultivation of millet in a barter economy and as a way of being able to integrate the farmers of Cameroon into the monetary economy, the colonisers introduced rice production (Domo, 1984). This radical change in the agricultural base and the economy linked to it resulted in the development of a new social representation in a relatively short time. The new representation of agriculture was grouped around a core which consisted of elements of the old core. By virtue of the fact that both idea systems prevailed for a long time in parallel and with almost equal rights, they often contradicted each other in the everyday discourse of those affected (Flament, 1987, p. 147). Conversations could in the same breath describe the new rice economy as menacing in accordance with the old idea, or as a source of wealth in accordance with the new: 'Le riz, c'est la richesse!' (Rice, that's wealth!) versus 'Le riz, c'est la mort!' (Rice, that's death!). Such contradictions could be observed in the entire population. It looks as though the central core was 'split' and divided in its elements. The meaning of each element then changes according to an innate logic and can ultimately be refound (modified) more or less centrally in a new representation.

In 1993 the tanker Braer shipwrecked at Garths Ness, on the main island of the Shetland archipelago, and spilled 85,000 tons of light crude oil into the sea. Due to strong gales and high waves many of the island shores were badly affected by the spill and inland was covered by oil spray and vapours carried by the wind. This accident effectively destroyed much of the natural habitat on and around the islands and left most of the inhabitants – crofters, farmers and fishermen – deprived of their livelihood for some time. Just a newspaper headline for us, but a disaster for the Shetlanders, this incident triggered a process of collective coping which promises profound changes in the prevailing representation the islanders have of their nature. Gervais (1997) observed and analysed this process of 'culture change' and social reconstruction of a local world.

Before the oil spill the Shetlanders had an 'organic' view of nature. Their 'personal biography, collective memory and the physical world are all intimately linked' (Gervais, 1997). The author gives the following description:

> Walls, dykes, bays and hills are known by the names of those who built them, fished in them, or dwelt on them. The lines of demarcation between Nature and Society tend to become blurred, as rocks carried and carved by one's ancestor become imbued with meanings; as everyday activities are shaped through and through by the land, the seas and the winds; as ancestral knowledge is kept alive in bodily movements which no one can recall ever having learned and yet knows to be distinctly Shetlandic.
>
> (p. 270)

In their daily practice and talk the representation of nature was continuously re-created. As they attempted to address the devastating consequences of the oil spill, Shetlanders were confronted with opposing world-views. Technicians, scientists, journalists, green activists and lawyers from the 'outside world' introduced 'mechanistic' and 'cybernetic' representations of nature that were at once picked up and contested by the local media. These representations, shared by non-Shetlanders, gained a foothold in the local community because they were based on an instrumental rationality which made them functional in the context of the oil spill; they were actively resisted by many local residents, however, for the very same reason. Those who most strongly opposed the novel representations penetrating the community were the so-called 'real Shetlanders' whose entire livelihood was bound up with the land and the sea. They lived by 'organic' representations which are predicated upon an experiential knowledge of the dwelt-in world. By contrast, 'mechanistic representations' favoured a rapport of mastery and exploitation in relation to nature, whereby nature is reduced to being a set of resources to be used for human purposes; they were nevertheless adopted by local people when such aims were sought. 'Cybernetic representations', which suggest a relationship of mastery and protection with respect to nature, were activated mainly in order to address the concerns of environmental activists and foreign journalists (Gervais, 1997).

### 8.3.2 Representations and polyphasia

In the aforementioned cases, the existing representational system is rarely plainly contradicted. It is amended with a new representation. For a certain period, at least, change results in the simultanous coexistence of (frequently logically incompatible, but socially acceptable) competing representations, embedded in various discourses. W. Wagner, Duveen, Themel and Verma (1999) showed this process in action in India, where old representations of madness based on ancient Indian philosophies are being amended by modern psychiatric conceptions of mental illness. There, traditional representations of madness focus on the idea of spirit or ghost possession, or heredity, which also marks a clear shift in the representation of the person. In the family context, where mental illness results from frustrated desires, it is the person's own thoughts and feelings which are responsible for their mental affliction. The person here is implied as a psychological agent of their own condition. The same Indian respondents from the middle and upper classes are presently engaged in representational work to objectify psychiatric treatment and a new view of mental illness introduced by modern life and Western influence. This process can be seen at work in the mass media, particularly films and TV, and in the everyday conversations and experience of people as they engage with these new phenomena. In the long run this process of objectification can be expected to produce a more elaborated image of psychiatry and madness. One can already see an emphasis on the effectiveness of their treatment of the mentally ill and the mad in the emerging social representations of the psychiatrist contrasted with the ineffective treatment of the traditional healer. The authors found both representations to exist simultanously, but enacted in different contexts.

## Cognitive polyphasia

Similar findings can be found with emigrants who settle in a foreign culture. Jovchelovitch and Gervais (1999) show how Chinese people who immigrated to Britain use their traditional thinking about healing and diet alongside the new (and contradictory) representations and discourses about healing and diet they confront in their Western host country. These seemingly contradictory views are not resolved at the cost of one or the other. They continue to exist side by side because their representations and discourses are enacted in separate social contexts – for example in the family or in public (Castro and Lima, 2001; Jovchelovitch and Gervais, 1999; W. Wagner, Duveen, Verma and Themel, 2000).

Even in the earliest studies of social representations, it was clear that everyday thinking frequently embraces representations which carry contradictory meanings. These contradictions are not usually disturbing as long as each representation is locally consistent and they are not simultanously expressed in conversation. In fact, it is unusual for people to express utter contradictions in discourse because they do not live in a single homogenous world, but in many worlds, each of which requires its own distinct form of talk and thought. It is in the context of different situations that holding on to 'contradictory' representations makes sense. As noted before, representations are not more or less veridical reproductions *of* facts in the world, but above all they are elaborations *for* social groups, serving as epistemological resources for their particular life-world. They are bound to social contexts, to groups and their life-worlds, and to situations and events occurring in these life-worlds that demand specific forms of thinking, talking and acting. Apparent contradictions between representations in common-sense thinking can be explained if their situated use is taken into account.

Moscovici (1961/1976, pp. 279ff.) observed this coexistence of different, and even contradictory, modes of thinking in his research on psychoanalysis. In contemporary societies people are 'speaking' medical, psychological, technical, and political languages. By extending this phenomenon to the level of thought he suggests that 'the dynamic coexistence – interference or specialisation – of the distinct modalities of knowledge, corresponding to definite relations between man and his environment, *determines a state of cognitive polyphasia*' (p. 286, emphasis in the original).

The author rejects the notion that cognitive systems habitually develop towards equilibrium, that is, towards a state of consistency. Instead, judgements are based on representational terms being dominant in one field of personal or group interests, while playing a subordinate role in other fields. Contemporaries in Western and non-Western societies alike face a variety of situations where particular modes of reasoning fit better than others. Some are more useful in the family and in matters involving relatives, others are more apt for solving problems in political, economic, societal, religious or scientific matters.

Different modes of thinking and talking, and the representational systems on which they are based, are interrelated and at the same time specialised. While they are the product of cognitive development, they do not represent different stages of validity or value for people's lives, as normative social cognition researchers have suggested. In this sense, the forms of everyday thinking, or common sense for that matter, open a way of establishing a link between representations and the social conditions in which they are engaged. If people need to conquer different sectors of their life-space, and all are relevant for their social and even physical well-being, the different modes of thinking associated with each one must be considered equally relevant and of comparable worth. As long as people live their lives in everyday spaces there is no reason to expect that any one mode of reasoning, such as the scientific one, could or would become the only one in historical development (Moscovici, 2000; Yang, 1988).

The concept of cognitive polyphasia highlights two important research areas. One is to identify and make explicit the social characteristics of situations and the exigencies that determine specific forms of reasoning and discourse; instead of treating thought and language as though they were independent of their realms of use. Representations are social precisely because of their articulation with the context of their genesis and enactment. The other is to pay attention to the processes of change and transformation in representational systems. Just as a contemporary society's culture is constantly in flux and transformation, and rarely in equilibrium, so are the modes of thought and representations within it. What was a dominant mode of reasoning in a realm of life yesterday, can be relegated today to an existence in a marginal sector of life if it is replaced by another dominant form.

Cognitive polyphasia emerges primarily when members of groups are coping with new conditions during their life-time. Transformations between generations have been shown in a study about 'foresting' and 'hunting' and its relation to the image of 'nature' (Guimelli, 1989). The new generations of hunters and foresters integrate a wide-ranging understanding of ecological contexts into their professional self-image, which enters the traditional idea not as a contradiction, but as an addition. These new elements were already there in a different form in the classical image, albeit relatively marginally. In this way, the representations' comparability regarding content in principle remains preserved, even though they are so sufficiently varied as to speak of two different systems. Access to new practices has an important part to play in transforming social representations. In the act thereof practice and representation change almost simultaneously, as a constant process, with the effect that after a period of constant change one is confronted with a new representation, which has emerged without grossly contradicting the old (Guimelli and Jacobi, 1990, p. 331).

Continuous transformation, therefore, runs mainly between generations. This phenomenon is a reminder of the function of anchoring. As displayed in Table 7.2, radical differences between experience and representation leads to the system being collectively negotiated afresh. Such cases are above all likely to be expected when new practices become necessary within a short space of time, so that individuals are personally affected by them. If these new experiences prove impossible to integrate, it remains only to create a new system, which may be organised around parts of the elements.

The transformation and adaption may proceed differently either if the new conditions appear assimilable, so mainly affecting only the peripheral aspects of a representation; or when a subsequent generation of individuals grows up amongst the new conditions. In such cases it is more of a continuous transformation process. As far as the new generation is concerned, the handed-down representation no longer has the same degree of relevance to present practice as it did for the previous generation, with the effect that the representations carry a less affective and cognitive epistemic burden, thus allowing their re-elaboration.

## 8.4 Transmission and media

The third question on the 'macro-dynamic' of social representations concerns the mechanisms of spreading, simplifying and adapting. The shared universe of a society may, especially in pre-industrial times, have been formed chiefly via word-of-mouth rendition and interpersonal communication. Nowadays, whether with friends and locals in the famous pubs in Britain or in the coffe houses of Paris and Vienna, as well as the so-called 'Bassena' conversations in Austria,[8] conversations are likely to play only a rather subordinate role. New life-styles and the structure of contemporary urban architecture and town-planning contribute particularly to this.

### Communities

Conde Rodriguez (1985) investigated such a transformation process in patterns of interaction regarding the district of Tepito in Mexico City. The original dwellings bordered in pairs on a communal courtyard which had to be crossed by all inhabitants who wanted to get on to the street. The architecture of these *vecindades* (neighbourhoods) forced friendly contact and communication, as well as joint games and events in which all inhabitants of a *vecindad* traditionally participated. After the demolition of some of these neighbourhoods and the construction of new, 'modern' buildings, the common centre provided by the *vecindad* was suddenly missing. In accordance with industrial modernity the houses and dwellings had been psychosocially 'privatised', that is, the living space in the form of *condominios* was constructed entirely around the needs of the nuclear family, and isolated from the other residents. Although it was the same families who uprooted to these new buildings, there was no more development of a neighbourhood in the way that had taken place previously. The number of friendships, contacts and joint undertakings decreased, a state of affairs which was felt to be a strain by those interviewed.

In modern societies the mass media replace the prime role of personal conversations, taking on the key role in the macro-social discourse. The position which in earlier societies was occupied by appealing to the 'elders' whenever there was a question about the credibility of myths is now partly taken up by the institution of 'science', as well as the ideological trustworthiness of various mass media.

## Mass media

What interests us here are three different styles which can be observed in how the mass media and their representatives deal with new knowledge contents. These styles reflect the forms of symbolic exchange between social protagonists, the communicators and recipients of public(ised) opinion (Doise, 1990, p. 116; Roiser, 1987); and can be understood as one of the contemporary epidemiological mechanisms in the moulding of modern mentality. In fact, the quantity and intensity of media reporting is directly related to the emergence of metaphorical understanding and the objectification of representations (W. Wagner, Kronberger and Seifert, 2002; see Figure 8.1).

Moscovici's (1961/1976) analysis of the popularisation of psychoanalytic knowledge in society investigated the dealings of three sectors of the French press with this science. The sectors of the press examined were from not explicitly ideologically bound mass-circulation publications (e.g. *Le Monde, France-Soir, Marie-Claire*); publications close to the Catholic Church (e.g. *L'Aube, La Croix, La France Catholique*); and the rather militant press in the broader catchment of the Communist Party (e.g. *L'Humanité, Ce Soir, La Pensée, Libération*). The three press groups showed a specific approach to converting and spreading psychoanalytical knowledge: diffusion, propagation and propaganda.

## Diffusion

The first sector of the press transmitted the new knowledge in a neutral style, in the sense of a mere rendering of information. The authors of these articles saw themselves, just as much as their readers, as recipients; and thus restricted themselves to the diffusion of competent opinions by experts. Their articles were restricted to comparing existing varying opinions, and so gave the impression of psychoanalysis being a knowledge system in itself. The presentation was concrete, attractive, quick and geared towards the interest of the readers. Even if not all authors agreed with all elements and statements of the theory, psychoanalytic interpretations were attempted in the daily work of editing whenever it involved, for example, reviewing and criticising cultural events.

The diffusion process is characterised by the following features (Moscovici, 1961/1976, p. 330 onwards):

(a) The source of the information does not recognise any particular intentions in dealings with it and takes on a stable orientation.

(b) If psychological advice is issued, then it always relates to precisely demarcated areas of behaviour, and excludes both the relationship between communication itself and behaviour, and the relationship between the communicator and recipient.

(c) The public as a reader appears not to be a well-structured group.

(d) The transmitted contents are distanced and portrayed nonreflexively. This makes identification of the audience easier.

(e) The distance makes the different relevant contributions of one and the same press release appear relatively autonomous and independent of each other.

(f) Even if the articles do not make an obvious effort to force anything upon their readers, diffusion can be thoroughly effective.

## Propagation

A somewhat more complex form of media dealing with novel issues is represented by propagation, in the way that it can be found in newspapers and magazines which are close to the Catholic Church. It is a relatively well-structured group within a society with a just as well-organised *Weltanschauung*. It has belief contents to defend and nowadays strives to integrate new phenomena and scientific discoveries into its system. The matter is exemplified by its dealings with psychoanalytical knowledge, the spread of which is subordinated to this aim.

Propagation is characterised by a selective approach to new knowledge. Divergence from other authorities is suppressed, insofar as it conflicts with the unitary image of a cognitive system supporting the belief system. Elements which support individual matters such as educational measures, the priority of feeling, spirituality and symbolism are stressed, selectively spread and elaborated. At the same time it either neglects or suppresses the predominant world image of psychoanalysis (in this particular case) and the significance of the libido.

In this way, knowledge about psychoanalysis spread in this press creates the impression of its own continuity within a world full of new scientific insights. It is an endeavour to create a common knowledge base for all Catholics and to reconcile doctrinal principles with the – selectively appraised – views held by psychoanalysts (Moscovici, 1961/1976, p. 373 onwards). The newspaper articles propagate norms selectively, and use the views of science as secondary justification of their belief systems (cf. W. Wagner, 1984). A summary of propagation is provided by the following (Moscovici, 1961/1976, p. 374):

(a)   The primary aim is relatively restricted and clearly defined.
(b)   One tries to classify the new social phenomenon into a pre-existing context by denying uncomfortable elements and contradicting elements.
(c)   The aim is to provide a dominant conception and interpretation, (in this case) valid for the whole group of Catholics.
(d)   The aim is not to provoke any new ways of behaviour and thought, but to shore up the existing ones and strengthen norms by providing new meanings.

### Propaganda

The communist press nurtures a colloquial style which is derived from its aim of political enlightenment. It emphasises processes of conflict deriving from social history. In this terminology, psycho-analysis as a form of 'bourgeois' knowledge mainly represents an ideological system, which unfortunately seems to come from the USA. It is therefore ideologically necessary to distance oneself from this new science; and since it also lays claim to a comprehensive explanation of social phenomena, it appears to be a rival to the Marxist system (Moscovici, 1961/1976, p. 408ff.). In a metatheoretical perspective, the propagandist approach of the Communist Party press tends to explain this new phenomenon as an outflow of capitalist US society, and to relativise the theoretical views as a result.

Two main functions can be ascribed to propaganda: the regulatory and the organisational function. In its social-regulatory function propaganda endeavours to produce and consolidate the identity of the group. It does this by denying or eliminating internal contradictions and emphasising the external threat. Through this radical polarisation and opposition, a member of the group is presented with the choice of either wanting what is good by wholeheartedly sharing the aims of the group, or playing into the hands of the enemy. Therefore, propaganda in the case of psychoanalysis during the 1950s could only intensify its rejection (p. 441 onwards).

In its organisational function, propaganda pursues the purpose of permanently adapting its world-view to new situational demands, or in reverse, of assimilating the phenomena by frequently 'tilting' its interpretation in that world-view. These press articles appear set on transforming psychoanalysis (for example) via its concretisation as an 'instrument of the class enemy', into a perceptible threat. In the course of a propaganda campaign one tries to create a target which complies with the conditions of the social field, whilst simultaneously toeing the party line by using this specific *organisation* of 'information' (p. 438ff.).

In our context, therefore, propaganda appears to be a form of expression of the discourse of a group, in a situation pregnant with conflict. It appears as an instrumental elaboration of the target, in conflict with one's own ideology to evoke counteraction (p. 442 onwards):

(a)   Propaganda is thus simultaneously an expression of the group identity, and an instrument of manipulation.

(b)   The elaborations stress the controversial sides of the object represented, implying thereby both problems and social relationships.

(c) Propaganda is a particular cognitive organisation of communication, which explains the symptoms of a conflict and simultaneously proposes well-tried models of action.
(d) Propaganda is ultimately meant to evoke action.

There has been relatively little research on the role of the media in social representations (cf. Rouquette, 1996). Evidence for the reporting styles of media has been found in studies about the recent elaboration of the social representation of biotechnology in Europe (W. Wagner and Kronberger, 2001; Wagner, Kronberger, Gaskell et al., 2001). There it was found that the tabloid press – being partisan with the anti-genetic engineering movement – followed a propaganda style of reporting about biotechnology, whereas the broadsheets' style fell broadly in the category of diffusion.

## Myths

The mechanisms shown here of the different communication styles of the press vary in the extent to which they produce 'scientific myths' of public everyday knowledge. 'Scientific myths' are not only about psychoanalysis, but also such things as ideas about the nature of entropy and the so-called 'heat death of the Universe', popular opinions about the laterality of the cerebrum, and views expressed on DNA, heredity and evolution, genetic engineering and so on. Journalistic simplification and use of metaphor (e.g. Figure 6.3), partisanship and other political interests authorise the generalisation, commission or omission of apparently non-essential parts of a theory. This results in widely shared representations of a mythologically transfigured science (Moscovici, 1992a).

A prime illustration of how scientific myths are promoted by media reporting is the so-called 'Mozart-effect' (Rauscher, Shaw and Ky, 1993). This suggested that listening to classical music enhances spatial intelligence. The finding, made with college students, met high media interest and was reported repeatedly all over the world. During the years that the media referred to this effect, it was generalised ever so gradually to be effective with children and babies in enhancing intelligence in general, and not just performance on a spatial test (Figure 8.1). By the end it had became a scientific myth that even triggered serious suggestions for preg-

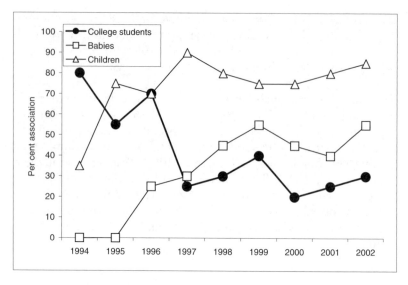

FIGURE 8.1 Percentage of newspaper reports associating the 'Mozart effect' with college students (as in the original publication), children or babies (redrawn from Bangerter and Heath, 2004, Fig. 2)

nant mothers and parents to expose their babies and children to classical music (Bangerter and Heath, 2004).

We have seen that diffusion, propagation and propaganda are three fundamental processes in the social discourse of groups. They have been analysed in our context here as the forms in which the press of different social groups voice opinions. It can, however, be suspected with great certainty that these forms also characterise large parts of the dialogues people have with each other and the forms of personal conversation. Those individuals addressed by the various press releases and other mass media doubtlessly orientated their personal approaches and those contents worth communicating in line with the styles of communication and argumentation of their preferred media.

As evidencing the distanced nature of liberally accepting new phenomena in the context of diffusion by media that appear ideologically neutral: the critically operational nature of propagation by the orthodox, yet willing-to-assimilate, Church press; or the radical, polarising propaganda of party organs that are orthodox in their politics.

The individual social representation of a phenomenon is therefore ultimately not only a 'purely' cognitive, conative and affective system of knowledge about a social object. It is also burdened with a form of communication, complying with belonging to a group. This form of communication determines how the contents in a discourse are transmittable, and whether they can be discussed in an endeavour for consensus and compromise, or only as confrontation. Co-operation and confrontation are just two of several possible forms of interaction which objectify a social representation as social reality.

# Chapter 9
# Action, Objectification and Social Reality

## 9.1 Action and objectification

### 9.1.1 Social representations guiding action

Representations guide the individual's processes of understanding and interpretation with respect to the social and 'natural' world. It would be hard for us to understand the behaviour of others if we did not possess conventional knowledge of which actions are appropriate or correct in whichever situations we encounter in everyday life. Understanding the behaviour of others makes us assume that they possess the same conventional knowledge as we do. Without communality of knowledge, there is no meaningful interaction. This means that social representations have to do with action and interaction in a way that makes us competent participants in society and culture and – quite literally – moral actors (cf. von Cranach, Kalbermatten, Indermühle and Gugler, 1980).

In the following, we will outline the action-guiding aspects of social representations using experimental and quasi-experimental examples. The first set of examples concerns studies using experimental games; the second group comprises investigations under more realistic conditions.

### Games

Numerous experimental games have looked into the regulation of action as a consequence of social ideas. In a zero-sum game, similar to the prisoner dilemma, Faucheux and Moscovici (1968) manipulated the expectations of the test participants *vis-à-vis* their game opponents.

*Method.* Two alternatives of action were available to the test participants which enabled them to make both co-operative and exploitative moves. Before the game, one half of the test participants were informed that they had to play against a random programme, whilst the second test group of opponents was supposedly playing against 'nature'. The terms were not explained any further, with the effect that the test participants were entirely reliant on their representation about 'random' or 'nature'. In actual fact the programmes in both cases were the same.

The results revealed a marked influence of the representation system on how the game and the moves by the test participants were understood. The students who believed that they were playing against 'nature' activated the idea of a relatively good-natured and predictable opponent. The 'random' participant group, on the other hand, felt they were not able to predict the opposing moves which would have allowed them to estimate the chances of winning in risky situations. By contrast with the 'nature' test participants, 'random' test participants understood the logic of the paying-out matrix much more poorly. Whilst the nature group could successfully maximise its winnings and demonstrated exploitative behaviour, this did not come as easily to the random group, even though their opponents' games were the same in both cases. Anticipating a relatively predictable and thus controllable opponent – who only existed due to an *a priori* representation being primed in the individuals – obviously made a more determined game possible than anticipating uncontrollable moves would have done.

A study by Abric and Kahan (1972) is comparable with the previous experiment. If individuals in a prisoner dilemma game expected to play against a person, in this specific case a fellow student, they implemented co-operative game moves much more frequently than if they suspected a computer programme as their opponent. A test beforehand had shown that the programme was expected to be more rigid, competitive, dishonest and unfriendly than a human opponent. Honesty and co-operative flexibility made the human opponent subjectively more calculable than the programme.

In another game the task was manipulated differently (Abric, 1971):

> *Method.* One of two groups was presented with the experiment as a test of creativity, and the other as a problem-solving investigation. The real task corresponded to either a problem-solving or creativity task, which was factorally crossed with the preceding manipulation. Four test participants worked jointly on one problem.

The number of correct answers by the groups depended directly on the experimentally induced representation of the formulated task. If the representation and the actual task were concordant, then test participants were more successful than under discordant circumstances. In the same way, the degree of group communication depended on the concordance of the conditions and expectations.

The problem of concordance between the representations available to the participants and the actual kind of problem was also used in an investigation by Haroche and Pêcheux (1971):

> *Method.* Participants from various social positions and different educational backgrounds (workers and students) had to solve a logical task which was presented in various contexts. The contexts were taken from different realms of life that were either proximal or not in the participants' personal experience.

As had been expected, both workers and students solved the task more correctly when the context of the task conformed to their actual life experience and they could draw on representationional background knowledge.[1] Abric and Mardellat (1973–4) came up with comparable results in the reaction of students and workers to social conflict. The social position of the test participants was just as important for how they dealt with a situation and the representation of a task as for the behaviour derived from them. 'Thus the objective elements which constitute the situation can only be meaningful if they are analysed in terms of their relation to the individual or group that is dealing with them.... The representation, subjective and personal transcription of the object for the subject, is the leading and motivating factor of his behavior' (Abric, 1971, p. 324). Similarly, the reactions of individuals to the interactive game moves of their partners only partially depends directly on their behaviour. The initital expectation or representation, on the basis of which a partner and his or her reactions are understood and judged, appears to be more important (Abric and Kahan, 1972, p. 147).

The micro-dynamics of action and its cognitive preparation has also been addressed by Valsiner (2003; Valsiner and Capezza, 2002). Social representations enable individuals' actions – guiding them towards their future – on one hand, while on the other hand they also restrict their thinking and acting. This tension can be said to enable a coping process on the side of the individual that involves, under certain circumstances, the modification of the representation in the service of the individuals' future projects (Valsiner, 2003). Research on the interrelationship between thinking about the future in the light of the present and impending action is in progress and promises insights into the micro-dynamics of everyday experience.

The following studies generalise these experimental results to real-life contexts such as health management, home management and professional intervention. Experience and learning forms the knowledge that we possess in the course of our lives, changes existing knowledge, and makes it possible to adapt our behaviour to change and to make new discoveries. This takes place both in the formal process of education in schools and universities, and in daily contacts with mass media, family, friends and colleagues.

## Personal health management

Farina, Fisher, Getter and Fischer (1978) investigated this process of behaviour change via new knowledge in an 'unobtrusive' experimental setting.

*Method.* One-half of the student participants were informed that psychological problems should be viewed as an illness, just as much as pneumonia or flu. The other half learnt that psychological disturbances are consequences of a history of learning and personal experiences. This manipulation was applied in three experiments under varied, but always inconspicuous, conditions. The test participants later answered different questionnaires containing behaviour-relevant questions relating to the nature and awkwardness of psychological illnesses.

It was continuously demonstrated that the manipulations were successful and had an action-controlling effect. Both in self-related questions and in questions which related to the therapeutic and everyday behaviour of third parties, the test participants tended to include their newly acquired knowledge in their judgement.

The consequence on behaviour becomes even clearer in the following experiment (Fisher and Farina, 1979).

*Method.* During a university seminar, two groups of students were confronted with the information already described above about the medical/biological or social/psychological causes of psychological problems. Four months later they filled out a questionnaire about their own health-related behaviour.

The students who had been informed about the biological roots to psychological problems in the preceding class, and therefore viewed such problems as a physical illness, pondered their own small problems less frequently, thought more frequently that they were unable to do anything about their difficulties, and were more likely to reach for alcohol or drugs in order to ease their problems than those students who had been taught to interpret psychological problems as a history of learning. One can say that both student groups had acquired different social representations about the internal or external causes of psychological 'turbulences', and orientated their future behaviour in accordance with them.

## Home heating management

Housekeeping involves a large number of technically orientated activities which require a basic understanding of physical, chemical and technical contexts. Knowledge about such contexts almost always exists in the form of popularised and therefore very simplified, if not outright wrong, theories. Contradictory everyday ideas about how particular appliances in our often very technologised homes work often circulate against each other, with differently effective consequences for how we go about behaving towards these appliances.

Such a technical area is how one deals with heating systems, in particular with automatised, thermostat-controlled equipment. There generally exist two theories about the way that thermostats in heating systems work: the 'control' theory and the 'valve' theory (Kempton, 1986, 1987). The essential features of the control theory correspond to the actual technical guidelines. It takes the thermostat as a instrument of control which essentially consists of a sensor, a comparator and a control element. The appliance constantly measures the temperature, feedback from which triggers the heating. Although viewed globally this idea is correct, it is nevertheless based in many cases on false ideas about radiation, heat loss and insulation. For example, the majority of the people interviewed are convinced that room heat simply 'dissolves in the air', is dissipated, and is not diverted away via the outer walls. According to the false idea, heat loss and the quantity of heating directly depends on the volume of the room and not on the area of the adjacent outer walls. Admittedly, this offbeat idea has no influence on operating the heating system, since its predictions about heat loss and heat quantity in reality largely correlate with the predictions of the physically correct theory. The idea about the 'heat simply dissipating into thin air' might come from the domain of cooking that is closer to experience. In cooking, hot meals do indeed lose their heat to the surrounding cooler air, with the effect that the everyday idea about heating a room appears to have been concluded from this source domain.

The valve theory by and large reveals the same erroneous offbeat elements of the idea about heat loss as the control theory. According to the valve theory, the thermostat is a valve through which the user, as a temperature-sensitive creature and 'measuring instrument', regulates the heat. The temperature is no longer measured by the sensor of the thermostat, but by people alone. If one turns up the control switch, then more heat is produced by the boiler and the room thus becomes warmer more quickly.

Both theories have direct consequences for dealing with thermostat-controlled heating systems. Advocates of the control theory will use their thermostat relatively evenly, without great deviations upwards or downwards, whilst advocates of the valve theory show an erratic patttern of control, since when they register cold they want to get back as quickly as possible to the level of warmth that they feel to be pleasant and thus up the heating to a high capacity.

During one week, Kempton (1987) investigated the behaviour of controlling temperature in several American households after he had ascertained their everyday theories on heat loss and heating processes (Figure 9.1).

The recording of the control behaviour in two typical households, leaning either towards the control theory or the valve theory, shows typical differences. In the one case, there is a pattern of periodic adjustment to daily or nightly needs with few ups and downs, while the other case shows an erratic up and down. Accordingly, there were also differences in running times, intensity and fuel consumption in the heater: an indication of the the kind of consequences that everyday theories can have for domestic economics.[2]

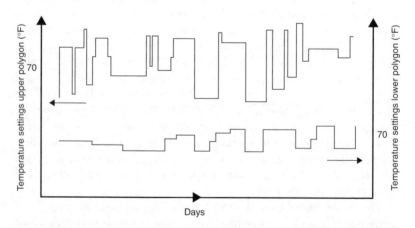

FIGURE 9.1 Eight days' thermostat settings for 'valve' theory (upper) and 'control' theory subjects (lower) (schematic redrawing according to Kempton, 1987, figs 4 and 5)

## Professional psychotherapy

In a large investigation, Thommen, Ammann and von Cranach (1988) dealt with the effects which social representations about methods of psychotherapy have on a sample of psychologists, working therapeutically and in the administration of their organisations.

> *Method.* Several representatives of two schools of therapy – non-directive and behaviour therapy – were selected. The representations of the two groups with regard to their therapeutic method was identified first, and some therapy sessions were observed and analysed. This was followed by confronting the therapists with some excerpts from the observed and recorded sessions.

Both therapeutic schools are based on a specific image of human beings, from which the respective theories and practical treatment steps are derived. In a very sketchy version, non-directive therapists base their representation on an optimistic image of humankind in which the ill person possesses the power for self-healing, whilst the outside world does not possess any influence relevant to healing. Most can be derived from the subjective world experienced by the individual. The aims of therapy follow these steps: a positive client–therapist relationship leads to opening up oneself, which leads to self-confrontation, which leads to psychological health (Thommen, Ammann and von Cranach, 1988, p. 116).

In contrast to this, and again with a broad brush, 'vertical' behaviour therapists see in their patients people who are coming to terms with information, who deliberately set themselves goals and seek to realise them according to their plans. Therapeutic intervention uses the behaviour of the therapist to produce those effects on the patient which are most likely to fulfil his or her goals (p. 120).

As a consequence of their image of humankind and their professional methods, there are clear differences between the two therapist groups, which can be demonstrated in their attributional behaviour. Non-directive therapists attribute more to the expectations and needs of their clients, whilst behaviour therapists refer more frequently to the cognitive processing of information: goals, traits and non-verbal behaviour. At the same time, the vast majority of all therapists refer to the conventionalised knowledge of their occupational groups, and only rarely to their individual knowledge (p. 142). These attributional patterns are closely connected to the interventions made during therapy (cf. also Augoustinos, 1990).

Strategies and therapy goals differentiate markedly between the two groups. The general goals of behaviour therapists in planning therapy, their derivation of the goals of the therapy from knowledge about their clients, and the directive influence strategy contrasts with the non-directive therapists, who set concrete and situation-related goals, derive the goals of the therapy from their theory, and pursue a strictly non-directive strategy. In this way, behaviour therapists follow a continual, goal-directed treatment process while non-directive therapists follow a discontinuous and reactive course of treatment.

It may come as no surprise that this example of varied therapeutic schools reveals such clear differences between the actual therapeutic practices of their supporters. Schools and theories are of course made in order to guide the behaviour of the members in complying with the theory. Therapeutic knowledge as an instruction for action is probably much more conscious and explicit than the operational everyday knowledge of individuals in general. The everyday person probably finds it harder than a therapist to make explicit the behavioural 'rule' implied by a particular representation. Yet it is precisely this which makes the example by Thommen, Ammann and von Cranach (1988) a comprehensive illustration of the action-guiding effect of social representations. In our opinion, it is not unlikely that one will also be able to observe therapeutically, relevant ideas in the everyday life of therapeutic psychologists. Unfortunately, however, this was not assessed.

All these studies show that action is subject to social control, which is internalised in the form of representations; that the representation and the expression of related behaviour is sometimes sanctioned by institutions such as psychotherapeutic associations (Genneret, 1990; Martin, 1990); and that the operational implications of representations extend right into the details of action and the patterns of attribution and thought.

## 9.1.2 Social representations as dynamic patterns in discourse and activity

In the last section, we presented research illustrating how action is guided by underlying representations. This way of thinking about the relationship between the mind represented by beliefs, opinions, knowledge, interests and attitudes and the like, and overt action is deeply ingrained in our professional psychological and everyday reasoning. Psychology textbooks dedicate whole chapters to models showing how norms, attitudes and intentions causally determine action and behaviour (e.g. Aijzen and Fishbein, 1980, to name just one theory). The research examples presented here, particularly the experiments, build upon a very similar version of this thinking when they observe and interpret certain behaviours or actions as a consequence of particular representations. This – as we would like to call it – naive causal approach to the link between the mind and behaviour has long ago (e.g. Smedslund, 1979) as well as more recently been attacked as inappropriate for the attitude–intention–action link (e.g. Greve, 2001) as well as for the social representation–action link (W. Wagner, 1994b). It is a serious problem for social representation theory that we will analyse and discuss in more detail in Chapter 10.

The concern about the epistemological aspects of the representation–action link is only one problem. A second problem relates to defining representations and discourse as the structure and form underlying the surface form of dialogue and action, as mentioned in the second section of this chapter. Let us discuss this issue taking Figure 9.1 as a starting point.

Kempton's (1986, 1987) research about heating management in households shows that people basically adhere to one of two theories about the working of thermostats, the 'valve' theory and the 'control' theory. Accordingly, in their handling of thermostats, they exhibit two patterns, an erratic up and down as mandated by the 'valve' theory or a much more technically correct and controlled up and down of as mandated by the 'control' theory. But where, in the graphs of Figure 9.1, exactly is the action? In fact, any single handling of the thermostat, that is, turning it either up or down, must be regarded an action, because it can safely be assumed that the person did it for good reasons, because he or she felt either cold or hot and intended to feel more comfortable temperature-wise. So far so good. However, if we wanted to infer the theory held by any of these persons, we would not be able to do this by observing only one, or maybe even a few, of the up- or down-turning actions. For our inference it would be necessary to have a string of observations that preferably stretch over more than a week. Only the pattern over time, as revealed in Figure 9.1, can give us a hint as to which naive theory the person implicitly subscribes.

What does this mean for our discussion of the relationship between representations and action? It means that verbal and bodily actions are an expression of social representations that reveal their meaning only in the long run of extended activity. Only a view 'from afar' on a series of social events and related activities exhibits a structure and form that a 'close-up' or a brief 'snapshot' does not.

According to this understanding, social representations can be considered as dynamic units in volatile talk, activity and interactions. Traditional units of analysis, such as a belief or an attitude, are conceived of as rigid, locally integrated mental entities with clear boundaries, whose definition is based on properties inherent to the unit itself. Dynamic units may be fuzzy and they are 'based on observing a *stable pattern of correlation* across the elements composing the unit'; its definition 'is *inseparable* from the *context of observation*: under different set-ups different units may be defined, each reflecting a different pattern of correlation'. Given this, 'it is *meaningless* to define the unit unless a specific context is given'. Dynamic units possess emergent properties, 'which are not present in the substrate from which the unit is formed'. In its relationship with the environment, the 'unit operates as a *basic-level* structure, on par with other basic units' and its interaction with the environment reflects 'the *system's properties as a whole* and not the properties of the individual constituents' (Mandelblit and Zachar, 1998, p. 230, emphasis in the original).

The constituents of representations understood as dynamic units are social actors and their doings in particular situations. There, social representations become real and tangible, as social objects that are enacted in situated talk and action between actors with individual beliefs, interests and motivations, who negotiate the state of an affair or relate to things such as thermostats, psychotherapeutic clients or their bodies and food (as in the case of health related behaviour). They are tacitly informed individual actors with ideas and beliefs about things and others, but it is only in their entirety and in extended activity, in which each person engages in his or her individually motivated interactions with others or things, that they enact a social object. The entirety of interactions and formal and informal talk shows a pattern of correlation across actors and across time. This pattern attains its meaning from, and is inseparable from, the particular situational context within which it is performed. The emergent meaning is clients being healed through non-directive interaction with their therapist or through directive behaviour modification (Thommen, Ammann and von Cranach, 1988), or psychological trouble being a biomedical or a learning problem (Fisher and Farina, 1979), or furnaces heating homes that are either valve-controlled or regulated by thermostats (Kempton, 1987). These 'objects': clients, psychological trouble and furnaces, exist at particular points in time, at particular places, and are the outcome of extended interactions. They emerge as a dynamic unit in the visible pattern of correlated behaviours across actors and situations.

In view of social representation theory as we conceive it, representations are patterns and features of discourse and extended activity realised by individuals with their own reasons and agendas. Just as Kempton's (1987) 'heating managers' did not act as they did because they wanted to realise their implicit assumptions about the working of thermostats, but because they wanted their house to be warmer or cooler, social actors do not act to bring a representation to bear on an issue, but because they want to achieve something concrete. The naive thermostat theories were merely the epistemological devices that allowed the 'heating managers' to adapt house temperature to their needs. In the same vein, social representations are the epistemological devices allowing social actors to reach their goals with rhetorical devices and specific actions that fall broadly within the space encircled by their group's representational system.

### 9.1.3 Objectification and social construction

The interaction ensuing within a functionally consensual collective creates realities which historically did not previously exist, and possibly may vanish again. It forms temporary realities or local worlds, which come about as historic phenomena due to shared belief and shared knowledge, materialise themselves in institutions, and become tangible to all involved. In this way, they justify retrospectively the correctness of the underlying way of thought and expectations. Even if the source of these worlds that have become material was initially immaterial social interaction, nevertheless the end product is about nothing less real than the ground beneath the feet of the actors. Numerous competent theoretical analyses exist on this issue which cannot be dealt with here, such as the classic works by Berger and Luckmann (1979), Searle (1995) or Shotter (1993).

In Chapter 7.3 we described one side of the objectification of a socially informed mind, which transforms the essence of the social representation into ideas close to reality and thus makes them into content 'perceptible' by the individual. Here, objectification remains on the semantic level of everyday life, but our present discussion of objectification refers to the interaction level of individuals, on which the apparent 'truth' of ideas is confirmed.

At this juncture we wish to distinguish two processes that are closely linked to one another. On the one hand there is the tendency of protagonists to validate their ideas and opinions through homogamy, that is, preferring to communicate with like-minded people and being selective with information. On the other hand there is the real process of constructing reality in interaction. An illustration of the latter is offered by works such as social-psychological studies on microcosms like the family.

In Chapter 3 we discussed the basic issue of evidence in social beliefs and came to the conclusion, in line with Elster (1983), that beliefs – and representations, for that matter – are rational and can be 'asserted with warranty' within a group (Habermas, 1985, p. 44f.), due to their available evidence and not because they correspond to a state of the world (for an extended discussion of this issue, see W. Wagner, 1996, 1998). Homogamic communication is a principle social mechanism providing evidence for this.

## Homogamy

We all know about the way we select our conversation partners. For example, political debates worthy of the name (i.e., conversations which are not set from the outset on confrontation and opposition, in which all participants already 'know' from the start that the arguments of their opponents are not to be 'taken seriously') can only be observed in the overwhelming majority of cases between people who, from the start, are of almost the same opinion; conservatives speak with conservatives, socialists with socialists and communists with communists. This homogamy of opinions, which prevents one's own opinion from being truthfully set against other views, is a widespread phenomenon. It can be observed all the more, the greater the certainty with which one can assume that one's own opinions are shared by the partners in conversation. If the partners reach a point where they have nothing new to say, then at least one can pleasantly feel that one is right in having such an opinion after all.

For example, Griffit and Veitch (1974) were able to demonstrate the prevalence of homogamy in communication in an experiment.

*Method.* They 'locked' 13 volunteer participants together in a relatively small room for 10 days. Before starting the experiment they ascertained the spectrum of opinions of the test participants. On several occasions during and after the experiment the test participants gave their sociometric choices.

The results show that the most frequent conversations and the closest relationships came about between participants with relatively similar patterns of opinon. According to Gonzales, Davis, Loney, LuKens and Junghans (1983), one can interpret such findings as a consequence of the effect of bolstering one's self-esteem by interacting with similar people, since interaction partners can expect to be perceived by the other person in a sympathetic manner as a strategy for easily validating one's opinion. Since we all know that being in the right is a thoroughly pleasant phenomenon, sympathy towards one's partner can also arise and appear as a consequence of the interaction.

Closely connected with the phenomenon of homogamy in conversations is the tendency towards selecting information in a purposeful and opinion-bolstering manner. Such bias in using information suitable for supporting one's own self-image concerning personal views (Swann, 1983) was investigted in a series of experiments by Swann and Read (1981a; 1981b), who showed that a selective approach to taking on information is commonplace.

Both whenever the test participants had the chance to see information and whenever they had the choice of showing off their expertise in a behaviour – that is, acting in a manner consistent with the self-image as opposed to being inconsistent to the self-image that does not correspond to their expertise – they were much more likely to select both the consistent information and the behaviour they were strong in.

## Reality construction and interaction

Providing evidence by homogamic communication and selective information choice is the first step in creating a reality. The second step is to enact beliefs derived from representations. In field experiments, in which students' orientation towards psychological disorders and turbulence was manipulated, once in the direction of physical interpretations and another time in the direction of situative and social interpretations, if the participants geared their auto-therapeutic behaviour according to the manipulation, one can assume with great certainty that their efforts produce success (Farina, Fisher, Getter and Fischer, 1978; Fisher and Farina, 1979). They were able to solve their 'little everyday problems', and thus directly confirm the induced social representations as correct.

In the classic experiment by Snyder and Swann (1978), experimental participants who had been systematically misinformed about their game partners (the partners had been presented to them as competitive and aggressive on the one occasion, and as cooperative and friendly on the other) were actually able to 'produce' this anticipated reality through the manner in which they played an experimental game. The naive game partners showed the behavioural patterns falsely expected by them in a subsequent second round of the game, with new, just as naive and uninformed test participants. This experiment is a confirmation of the effect of self-fulfilling prophecies (Merton, 1957b). 'Social perceptions can and do exert powerful chanelling effects on subsequent social interaction, such that actual behavioral confirmation of those beliefs is produced' (Snyder and Swann, 1978, p. 157). Although the initial information was false (from the experimenter's bird's-eye view), they did not use a tit-for-tat strategy, which would have been more appropriate in a laboratory environment and would have permitted a more reliable test of the unknown partner (Axelrod, 1984).

Instead, they chose a strategy in accord with their initial misinformation: competitive in the one sample and co-operative in the other.

The interpretation given by the authors, that social perception had channelled the participants' behaviour in the situation, seems rather dubious. In our opinion this investigation illustrates not so much the effect of processing (false) information, as the effect of a social representation in the microcosm of an experimental game situation. One can assume that both game partners possessed a comparable prior knowledge of co-operation and competition, and about what a game is. Both were similarly aware of the fact that they were playing against each other as dyads in a laboratory (albeit separated spatially); and thus constituted a micro-group as gamblers. Both therefore already shared a lot of knowledge before the experiment. This knowledge was only changed asymmetrically to the advantage of one player by a relatively marginal experimental manipulation (the 'whispering' of an expectation). If the 'naive'[3] game partner is confronted by pronouncedly competitive or co-operative moves, according to the manipulation of his or her opponent, then this did not come as a surprise. Hence it is also no surprise if he or she maintained the strategy that had proved successful in the first round in a later game with a new partner. A single game in a doubtless unusual setting does not provide the 'naive' test participant with a sufficient base of experience to be encouraged to try variations in strategy. His or her perseverance in using the initially chosen strategy of competition or co-operation in a second round was sensible behaviour, given the unusual context and the involved social representation of games and competition. As a group, the participants merely enacted a pre-existing representation through the limited alternatives for action that were at their disposal. They did not create a *new* reality, as the authors would have it, but *recreated* a well-known facet of their daily life.

Comparable results have been found in a number of other experiments (cf. Darley and Fazio, 1980; Snyder, 1984). Historical knowledge guides people's perceptions in such a way that it ultimately appears confirmed (Snyder and Cantor, 1979; Snyder, Campbell and Preston, 1982), and individuals form and choose situations in a way that conforms to the hypotheses and purposes behind their actions. Expectation confirmation is strongest whenever the target person is ambivalent or not strongly committed in a specific situation (Major, Cozzorelli, Testa and McFarlin, 1988;

Swann and Ely, 1984). Almost all of these experiments can be interpreted in a similar way.

## Families

The macro-social processes of reification are not generally accessible to social-psychological analysis because of methodological limitations. In a social context, however, there are 'structural niches': substructures and subentities which are microcosms, replicating the processes of discourse, negotiation and the construction of everyday reality on a smaller scale. These structural niches are not completely isolated from their environment, but they are relatively self-contained, allowing the development of construction and stabilisation processes inherent to that subsystem. Small-scale organisations, companies, churches or political unions are all examples of this. The family is also an essential subentity. Its organisational processes have been studied sociologically and social-psychologically; and to a certain extent it can be used as a handy model for larger social entities (e.g. Berger and Kellner, 1964; Reiss, 1981).

Berger and Kellner (1964) view families as social structures which define and validate their world in an ongoing process of negotiation, like societies. 'The plausibility and stability of the world, as socially defined, is dependent upon the strength and continuity of significant relationships in which conversation about this world can be continually carried on' or 'The reality of the world is sustained through conversation with significant others' (p. 4 onwards). The relative autarchy of married or long-time partners in their interrelated construction work was a consequence of the Industrial Revolution in the Western world, which created the family as a more or less private sphere, withdrawn from public control. Even though the private sphere can include many different social relationships with shared interests, like friendships, neighbours, colleagues and so on, the conjugal family constitutes the focus of attention of all these relationship patterns (p. 8). 'From the beginning of the marriage each partner has new modes in his meaningful experience of the world in general' (p. 11), so that after this 'substantive break' in the course of life, each action of a partner must necessarily be correlated to the definitions of the relationship by the other one. This process is calibrated by ongoing conversation.

Often in the course of conversation, the contributions by the partners are discussed, problems 'repaired' and the life-world constantly furnished with new elements. The longer these 'negotiations' go on, the more real the objectified contents become for the two partners (p. 13). This even applies to pathologically 'derailed' families, no longer communicating, in which one can observe the continued existence of mutual relation, albeit at the historic level of definition before the breaking off of communication. In a way similar to the elaborations of diachronous pasts in oral societies mentioned in Chapter 2.2, families also jointly reappraise and thus change their 'collective memory' in order to give room in the family for both life histories (cf. on this Halbwachs, 1985, p. 125ff.). This is particularly conspicuous when a partner corrects the memory of the other one about his or her own past. The jointly elaborated past, and jointly constructed present then project the jointly planned future (Berger and Kellner, 1964, p. 16). Ambivalences are cleared up and possibilities of choice narrowed. In extreme cases, entire classes of events that really took place (e.g. jointly experienced positive situations) are denied in order to be able to maintain the fiction of an 'incurably' shattered marriage (Harris and Sadeghi, 1987).

A number of studies by Reiss (1981) have investigated the schema-governed interactive behaviour of pathological and normal families. His typology of shared constructs reflects features which also show macro-social constructs such as social representations. He identifies: (a) environment-sensitive constructs which, in principle, relegate the origin of problems outside of the reference group or family (such as the representations found in Jewish families who feel themselves surrounded by a threatening environment (Bar-Tal and Antebi, 1992) or southern Italian families (Strodtbeck, 1958) who feel their future to be unpredictable and uncontrollable); (b) constructs which are sensitive to interpersonal distance, since they (at least in families of the Western world) give the individual space for his or her own contributions, and relative autonomy as a result; and finally (c) consensus-sensitive constructs, which stress and safeguard those constructs that family members have in common and suppressing constructs of interpersonal distance.

Patterns of interaction corresponding to these constructs can be observed both under laboratory conditions and in natural and therapeutic surroundings. According to the predetermined familial 'paradigms', families are in a position to manage and confront crisis situations and turbulence. Everyday interaction often takes on the form of ceremonial and ritual acts which at the same time plays a central role in conserving the family paradigm. Many readers will know of such examples from their own lives, whether it is the Sunday lunch routine, afternoon tea or opportunities to show oneself off at family get-togethers.

Reiss (1981, p. 224ff.) identifies a ceremonial core which is emotionally charged, symbolic and episodic, and obliges all family members to participate. This core is used for the 'observance' and self-elevation of family life, but also sometimes for the denial and covering-up of conflict (Wolin, Bennett and Noonan, 1979). It is surrounded by interaction regulators, which embrace the routinised, non-symbolic and amenable to delegation, constantly enveloping ordinariness (Kantor and Lehr, 1975). The routines are used both for forming interpersonal distance and closeness within a group, and for creating relationships towards the outside. Ceremonies and interaction regulators structure space and time, locating them with relation to the hierarchical positions and relationships existing between family members (p. 232ff.). In their form and function, family paradigms come across as micro-social homologies of macro-social representations and cultural knowledge (e.g. Bourdieu, 1976; V. Turner, 1985).

Both psychological experiments if properly interpreted and the family as a model of large-scale social processes strongly illustrate the epistemological function of social representations in confirming social realities. Under normal conditions, no new reality is being generated, but one of the numerous possible realities is reconfirmed. Therefore, in the vast majority of interactions in everyday life, objectification is not the genesis of a novel reality. Realities and institutions are not created afresh in interaction. Rather, interaction patterns confirm and re-enact social facts in the collective concert of action, and this adds further validity and evidence to representations and derived beliefs. Representations are objectified when they are intrinsically evident; and true in a situation which is a fiduciary truth and does not need justification: 'the end of justifying the evidence is not that we see certain propositions suddenly as true, but our acting which lies at the bottom of the language-game' (Wittgenstein, 1984, p. 204). Our acting, the very way we do things and enact our discourse, co-constructs the things in our world and simultanously is the evidence for their 'truth'.

## 9.1.4 Domesticated objects

In their concerted interaction, families and other groups enact the objects that populate their local worlds. These objects do not exist for an outsider in the same way as they do for the members of a group. The reason is that the outsider does not share the representational devices defining their meaning and directing action towards them.

Let us first define what we understand by 'object'. According to the Oxford Dictionary an object is 'a . . . person or thing to which action . . . is directed, subject _of_ or _for_;. . . . Thing aimed at. . . . Thing thought of . . . external thing . . .' (Sykes, 1976). This definition tacitly presupposes the social convention in 'action', 'being thought of' and so on, which we discussed in other places.

A *social object*, therefore, is any material, imaginary or symbolic entity which people name, to which people attribute characteristics and values and therefore are able to talk about. An entity like a book, for example, is an object if it is named 'book', if people describe it as consisting of paper leaves (at least usually), a cardboard cover and text or pictures in it, and if two people can engage in talk like: Mary says: 'Today I went to the library to fetch that book' and Peter replies 'Thanks for reminding me, I need to go to the library as well'.

The name, the attributes, the use of the name in talk, and the behaviour associated with the object 'book' make an entity a social object. People who recognise an entity as a book will pick it up, put it down, open it, close it, leaf through it or read in it, but they will not sit on it and expect it to carry them to their parents. An object is always an object for a group, society or culture. A *domesticated world* is always a world *for* a specific group, while at the same time being the reason which makes a group specific.

By contrast, we shall call any material entity which members of a group have not named, which has no characteristics attributed to it, and where people are not in a position to talk about it, a *'something'*. A 'something' is not a social object for this group, but it might well be a named object for people of other groups. We need the admittedly awkward term 'something' as a token for all those events and things which may potentially affect the life and wellbeing of people although they are not yet recognised as named objects in their world. They are phenomenally given, yet unnamed; perceived, yet not depicted on the 'map' of the domesticated world

(Sugiman, 1997).[4] It has to do with what Searle (1995) refers to as 'brute facts'; and it is useful as a reminder that there are many things beyond socially constructed worlds.

Separating objects from 'somethings' allows us to relate these concepts to social representations. 'Somethings' become social objects whenever they are being elaborated by a community (Moscovici, 1963, p. 251) and endowed with meaning which means that the members of a social group concertedly act as if the object *had* exactly those characteristics which *it is thought* to possess. In constructive events the 'somethings' become social objects within the group's system of common-sense, and in the course of interactions engaged in by actors sharing a representation. These interactions may be bodily or verbal or both, and they are expressions of and inseparable from the representation. Human action demarcates the boundary between the 'world of somethings' and the world of domesticated objects (Figure 9.2).

Figure 9.2 illustrates schematically how different groups inhabit divergent worlds. In this sense, even science creates its own world, albeit with methods that are only partly comparable to the workings of common sense.

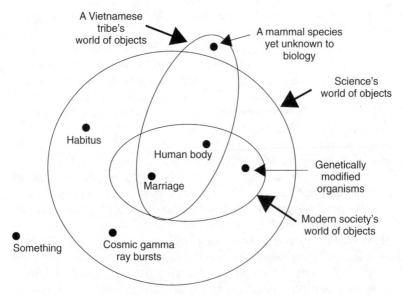

FIGURE 9.2 Schema of divergent group-specific worlds of domesticated objects

When a social representation exists in a group, it is never just a shared mental event, but essentially also the pattern of talk and action which 'selects and relates persons and objects in such a way as to meet the stipulation of the group' (Moscovici, 1988, p. 230). Social objects populating a local world are grouped to 'natural kinds' or 'human kinds' for that matter (Hacking, 1995). They are grouped under the description of a social representation, which disposes of the criteria of phenomenal or symbolic similarity between the objects.[5]

In many countries, the discourse surrounding disabilities and handicapped people has been undergoing substantive change in recent decades. In Sweden, for example, Gustavsson (1996, 1997) describes different levels of talk about intellectual disability in the context of a well-developed welfare system. The basic and more ancient level refers to intellectually disabled people as 'slow', 'weak', 'disabled' and 'disadvantaged'. This level is complemented by discourse about 'the right to special education, subsidised work', 'the right to an ordinary life among others' and 'the right to equality' which became more dominant when the state welfare system introduced a policy of integration 20 to 30 years ago. The social reconstruction of the object 'disability' towards equality and integration marks a fundamental change in discourse, and in the forms of interaction which affects the 'objects' of this representation – in this case, disabled people – to a considerable degree. Disabled people change their behaviour, their thinking and feeling about themselves, and thereby attain other characteristics than previously. They are socially constructed, in a historical process which shows clearly the analytical identity of representation and object in social life.

Social construction is not always an unintended outcome of communicative processes. Intended construction has always been a means of politics (Mehan, 1996). The 'politics of representation' creates 'guest workers', 'alien workers', 'foreigners', 'immigrants', 'asylum seekers', or awkward forms of 'political correctness'; with the aim of shaping social life according to the desires or assumed desires of an electorate. Equally, industry is under strong pressure to create favourable representations of their products. The biotechnology industry, for example, switched its language from 'genetically modified' to 'genetically enhanced' tomatoes, in the light of widespread resistance to genetic engineering in many European countries (cf. Gaskell, 1997).

A domesticated world is created through representations being elaborated and enacted. Because constructive events, that is, the discursive and overt acts of social participants, are physical events, a social object attains a near *physical* existence. This is true even of so-called imaginary objects like 'God', 'justice', 'beauty' and so on, which become physical and tangible in the web of physical behaviour of physical actors.

Consequently, it is utterly strange to speak about the *representation of an object*, The social representation is the very *raison d'être* of the object as such. In other words, the representation *is* the object it seems to represent and the world of domesticated objects *is* the 'local' universe of representations (cf. W. Wagner, 1996, for a more in-depth discussion of this problem, and Yamori, 2001, for a critique). Speaking colloquially of 'the representation of an object' is at best a conceptually incorrect formulation, and at worst an oxymoron.

## 9.2  Habitus and collective rationalisation

### 9.2.1  Social field and habitus

#### Intention and action consequences

The construction of the world of the family and the processes of conversation usually proceed without meta-reflection and are not known to the partners (Reiss, 1981, p. 226). As a result, they develop their micro-social and macro-social constructive power (Berger and Kellner, 1964, p. 17 onwards). The macro-social functionality of social actions exists despite, or precisely because of, the fact that it has not been planned. The real consequences of social action, such as political interventions, the strained effort to maintain family life and so on are by-products which are often very much removed from the wished-for consequences (Elster, 1983). This fact makes the process of social construction an adventure, and promises surprises.

If everyday theories had to be true, in a strict correspondence-theoretical sense, in order to be able to produce the desired effects of action, then neither the 'valve theory' nor the 'control theory' individuals in Kempton's (1987) example would be successful in domestic-heating arrangements. It would also be hard to understand how the variety of psychotherapeutic schools could show successes if their often conflicting theories claimed truth in this strict sense. These examples illustrate the relative independence between the contents of rational systems, such as those of social representations, and the effects which they entail both in individual action and collective interaction. However, 'ex falso quod libet'. Social representations are a necessary precondition for social functioning, but they may also be an arbitrary precondition for other purposes. Although the imagined objects constructed with their epistemic help are true in the immediate context of the community, the function fulfilled by these objects in social existence, and the rationality of the social phenomenon resulting from this, is not an intended consequence. Rational acting is not 'doing social construction' (W. Wagner, 1996).

Putting Bourdieu's theory of habitus into this context enables us to broaden our discussion. Bourdieu (1983, 1984b) developed an extensive theory about the multi-faceted economy of practice; taking his social and cultural-anthropological studies of the cabylic society of North Africa (Bourdieu, 1976) as a starting point and continuing with the large-scale study about the determinants of cultural consumption (Bourdieu, 1984a). This is not the place to go into the details of the theory, which have nothing directly to do with the concept of 'habitus' in question. Summarising accounts can be found in Bourdieu particularly (1987; see also Bohn, 1991; Eder, 1989).

## Social field

For Bourdieu (1980, p. 113), social space is a differentiated construct of many fields. These fields determine the practical possibilities of its protagonists. They express the horizontal sophistication of the social world, which includes positions and places. Such fields might be economic, religious, political, cultural and so on. Social spaces are established as a network of relationships (Bourdieu, 1985, p. 13) which can only be defined through their reciprocal relations, rather than from their immanent qualities (Bourdieu, 1983, p. 42ff.). These structured spaces exist in the form of institutions, thanks to the activity of protagonists who confront the objectified structures on an equal footing in constituting society. The entirety of the social thus encompasses 'history that has

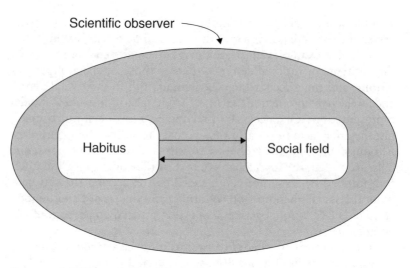

FIGURE 9.3 The relationship between habitus, field and observer (redrawn according to Bohn, 1991, p. 25)

become body and become thing' – the habitus of the protagonists and the social field (Bourdieu, 1985, p. 69). Figure 9.3 displays this context schematically.

## Habitus

Habitus can be understood as a system of lasting and transferable dispositions, that is, of schemata of perception, esteem and action produced by a certain social milieu. At the same time, the milieu defines the principle of generation, according to which practices and representations are structured (Bourdieu, 1988, p. 786). As an embodied structure of society, the habitus reproduces the conditions of its own genesis via social practice. Bohn (1991) establishes four central characteristics of the habitus:

(a) The incorporation of the social, which comes about through processes of conditioning and social learning, forms the 'basis of that presence in the social world which is the assumption of successful social action, in the same way that everyday experience by this world is taken for granted, without question' (Bourdieu, 1985, p. 69).

*(b)*   Whilst incorporation characterises the social protagonist as structured, habitus on the other hand is realised as a generative system of schemata and dispositions, determining perception, thought and action. This structuring side – the 'modus operandi' – determines the concrete form of the practical behaviour of people towards their environment. The execution of practice, conveyed via the schemata of judgement and perception, appears from the outside to be obedience of rules that are not known to the protagonists.

*(c)*   Therefore implicitness is an essential further defining element. 'Although the practical actions of walking, speaking and perceiving specific ways, tastes, and aversions brought about by the habitus all demonstrate features of instinctive behaviour, and automatism in particular; it is no less correct that a moment of partial, incomplete, discontinuing consciousness is constantly accompanied by actions and practices' (Bourdieu, 1976, p. 207). Dispositions refer both to and beyond the individual level of meaning (Honneth, 1986, p. 57), thereby forming an intentional system without conscious intention. This alone permits the regularities of the world to be mastered and the system's future predicted, without consciously having to construct the world as such (Bourdieu, 1988, p. 183 onwards).

This signifies neither total blindness on the part of the protagonists, nor complete awareness beforehand of practical actions. Reflection and awareness exist, either in the form of 'that minimum extent of vigilance which is essential to controlling the course of automatisms' or 'in the form of discourses which have to rationalise . . . those actions and practices' (Bourdieu, 1976, p. 207). All the same, that awareness must not extend to the point where people begin to ponder the rules of their practice, since this would negate the fundamental way that the habitus works as objective meaning without subjective intention.

*(d)*   In the reproduction of social conditions, stability is ensured by the tendency of the habitus towards hysteresis.[6] This inertness preserves its constancy, which the habitus seeks to ensure by fending off changes via its selections when given new infor-

mation; for example, by rejecting information that could question the accumulated knowledge whenever it happens to come across it or cannot avoid it (Bourdieu, 1987, p. 113 onwards).

The habitus protects itself from crises and critical questioning by the fact that the protagonists make a systematic choice between places, events and persons with which they have dealings. It creates for itself a milieu to which it is pre-adapted as much as possible, and thereby a relatively constant world of situations which are suitable for strengthening its dispositions, by offering to its products the market most ready to receive them (p. 114). This ensures that in habitus-controlled practice only those things which do not break the bounds of the conditions of origin without blindly repeating original conditionings can be freely perceived, thought and done. The bounds of the schemata are always wider than the conditions that created them (p. 102 onwards).[7]

### 9.2.2 Habitus, representation and rationalisation

We have characterised habitus as an embodiment of social structure, which in its realisation as practice reproduces time and again the structures which have created it. In order to achieve this, it is necessary to ensure intergenerational stability, and free oneself in large parts of conscious reflection: habitus is the 'illegitimate normal case of social reproduction' (Iser, 1983).

What relationship can be found between the theory of social representations of interest here, and the habitus approach? Some authors equate the two concepts (e.g. Doise, 1986a). In so doing Doise refers above all to the generative function, and the position in the chasm between the individual and the social which is attached to both concepts (Doise, 1990). Let us examine whether the two concepts are equivalent in methods, contents and the interests behind explanation.

First, the concepts – to a degree – differ on a methodological level. Whilst habitus is inferred from data which were gained by anthropological field methods and surveys, as being a structured quantity of tacit rules such as preferences, taste and behavioural practices; research on social representations largely, but not exclusively takes what individuals talk and do more literally. A social representation on this understanding does not exceed the potentially aware knowledge of people.

Second, this leads to social representations on a content level being understood as common-sense theories, evaluative models and operational indications of consciously controllable action. As action-governing schemata that can potentially be named by the subjects, they therefore underlie rational or 'natural' behaviour. Habitus, on the other hand, is characterised precisely by a lack of awareness of the rules effected by it. Those reasons for action available to the subjects are simply not part of the habitus. This means that representations are expressed in social discourse, in conversation, while habitus is realised in collective ritual and automatised practice.

Third, there is a different interest underlying explanation. The main interest of sociologists and anthropologists is aimed at the practices of social classes, societies and cultures. They stress the practical forms of expression, rituals and symbolic systems. It is the often ritualised practice of collectives which is explained rather than the collective action of individuals. The social psychologist uses collectively shared images about social objects in the broadest sense as a starting point, and correlates them with the rational actions and interactions of identifiable individuals. That is, individual action and thought is understood as a reflex of social conditions. When Doise (1986a, p. 91) criticises that when Bourdieu proposes the concepts of habitus and disposition, he does not describe the psychological processes that are necessary for their proper functioning in the individuals, he is demanding something which is just as little intended by sociologists, as social psychologists intend to explain macro-social conditions. For this same reason, Bourdieu's critique of social psychologists misses the point when he says that social conditions do not boil down to relationships between 'subjects' and their ideas about these relationships (Bourdieu, 1983, p. 23), and that social conditions must be analysed beyond inter-individual interactions.

The relationship between the two theoretical approaches is less an equivalence than a theoretical analogy on different levels and in separate realms of scientific discourse.

Figure 9.4 illustrates this relationship. The diagram does not display individual and social relationships and processes, but the conceptual realms of the two sciences. Within the circle, we are in the social-psychological universe in which theories describe how individuals are socialised and how individuals reconstruct their social world through interaction. The outer circle gives an account

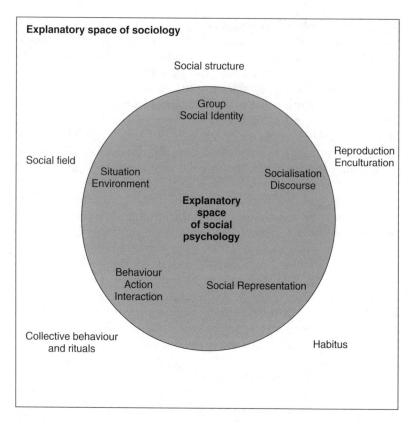

FIGURE 9.4 The analogous relationship between sociological and social-psychological explanatory concepts

of the conceptual relationship of an analogous process on a social level. Here, too, we begin with the social field whose reproduction is ensured by the forming of the habitus, and the collective practices and rituals resulting in a continuing social structure.

Although both theory systems speak about comparable processes, they refer to different levels of analysis. The adjacent terms may well constitute analogous concepts due to their varied theoretical histories and premises, but they are not equivalents that could easily be reduced to one another.

The position of social representations as collective discourse patterns refers, as has been shown, to a feature of this concept differentiating it from habitus. With the help of conversation, social actors make sense out of their environment, objects, their ritual and routinised patterns of interaction, and the exceptional situations which interrupt everyday life. In so doing, there is ample space for the subjectivity that social protagonists can and do bring to bear in their situated behaviour.

The topography of modern mentality takes on many forms and is comprehensive. There is hardly any area of life broached in social discourse which would not be subject to the elaboration 'machine' which constructs the shared universe. Content-rational constructs are subject to everyday actions as epistemological devices, and seem mostly to come up with the products of behaviour which the individuals intend to create. The requirement for this is the view from the inside, or that subjectivist[8] or 'emic' approach which takes the content-rational activities of the subjects 'literally'. From this point of view, these models of thought, ways of feeling and action orientations appear to be creative.

Even if theoretical analyses of social representations bring to light relatively abstract systems of ideas, these schemata remain accessible to subjective understanding upon questioning. This contrasts strongly with the dispositional system of habitus, that 'spontaneity without will and consciousness' (Bourdieu, 1987, p. 105), the revealing or reflection of which would interrupt the course of everyday practice.

By contrast, the outside perspective sharpens one's view on inconsistencies between intention and action result. For a research orientation which does not take individuals at their word, but looks at their undebatable forms of practice, social representations appear to be secondary constructions, that is, collective rationalisations which only connect with the structural features of social living rather indirectly. The contents of collective discourse – the beliefs – are ideological ideas and well-founded misconceptions, whose theoretical incorrectness and social function are only unveiled through a science of the objective relationships (Bourdieu, 1983, p. 24).

From this point of view, social representations appear to be *re*-presentations, a reflex of more global conditions. This make them secondary systems of allocating meaning, which interpret and rationalise what exists in subjectively comprehensible ways. Of course, these are not individual and idiosyncratic rationalisations such as the dissonance reduction strategies described in Festinger's dissonance theory, even though a certain family similarity cannot be denied. Much that is unintelligible and hard to reason also appears in macro-social life or everyday interaction, so that the 'apparent' explanation of such inconsistencies or 'dissonances' becomes a necessity for social living. 'Fluency' in conducting the course of everyday life will only be guaranteed when each individual feels the corners, cracks and dissonances of his or her everyday life to be natural and have *a priori* meaning, or at least be explicable.

## 9.3  The group and the public

In this section we outline a few consequences of the theory of social representations, which are corroborated with reference to the preceding text. These are: that it makes sense to restrict regular discourse and social representation to reflexive groups; that discourse and representations are public 'goods'; and that concerted interaction in groups requires representations to be inclusive, that is, to include some version of the others' perspective as well.

### 9.3.1  Regular discourse, reflexive groups and the public sphere

By a 'reflexive group' we understand a social unit which is defined according to the criteria of its members. Where the parameters of a social unit have been set solely by a criterion defined by an external observer, and does not determine membership or non-membership of the group in the opinion of its members, one can only speak of a nominal, but not a reflexive group. Austrians, for example, a national group defined by common citizenship, knowledge of the German language and other cultural features, form a reflexive group. Its members know that they belong and that, in some respects, they share a number of common features. By contrast, a group of introverted neurotics represents a nominal unit, as long as the features 'introverted' and 'neurotic' are only determined by an external diagnostician. Even if individual introverted neurotics were aware of their personality structure and could recognise others with the same behavioural tendencies, one still cannot speak of it as a reflexive group. The prerequisite for group consciousness emerges only when those affected organise themselves in, for example, a political party of 'Introverted Neurotics' or a self-help group of 'Neurotics Anonymous'.

It is of no consequence whether outsiders are aware of the group's existence or the membership of their fellow humans. Freemasons still form a reflexive group despite their ritual secrecy. Likewise, in many cultures, such as some of the African or North American tribes (Driver, 1975), there have always been comparable secret societies, 'sodalities', who choose to keep their organisation secret for other than political reasons. These groups are reflexive because their members can refer to their affiliation and describe their social identity collectively – that is, they are able to categorise themselves (cf. Hogg and McGarty, 1990; J. Turner, 1987). It is also not important how many members a group has, in order for a number of individuals to be meaningfully referred to as a group. In our opinion families and similar communities can also constitute a valid reflexive group, since sociohistorically they have developed from larger units whose social identity was frequently defined through the extended family. Clans, matrilocal or patrilocal kinship groups, or the hunter-gatherer families of African pygmies are all perfect examples of this. For the purpose of this discussion, only reflexive groups, irrespective of their size, represent a relevant social unit.

By 'regular social discourse' we understand the normal process of communication in a group which gives rise to, and elaborates on, the consensual rationalisation patterns of everyday practice. Discourse would not be regular, if, for example, it were imposed by a more powerful and external group, such as during the period of European colonialism. The colonisers did not generally acknowledge the differences of the divergent and various original social units, tribes, castes and ethnic groups which they combined into 'groups' and they governed colonies uniformly. For example, only the Europeans could coin the unifying term (American) 'Indians'; a label that amazed those to whom it referred (cf. e.g. Talbot, 1981). The communication between the invaders and those they colonised does not correspond in any aspect to regular social discourse. It never aimed for the shared view of reality which exists in a reflexive group, even when the direction of the discourse is determined by recognised and legitimate powers. By this we mean to say that regular discourse – as a prerequisite of collective rationalisation patterns and world-views – can only sensibly take place within reflexive social units.

We have already shown that the purpose of regular group discourse is to represent the foundations of ideology and justification on which communal actions are based. Members of a reflexive social unit interact according to a set of rules and in co-ordination with the relevant 'real and imaginary' objects, as well as with their fellow humans and institutions. This co-ordination would be at risk if a substantial part of a social unit were excluded from the discourse – that is to say, deprived of the knowledge and epistemic tools arising from it. The process of discourse, and in modern society also participation in discourse, is therefore public and, in principle, accessible to all. The minimum boundaries of the public sphere are determined by the size of the social units whose co-operation is under discussion. The minimum public sphere may consist of entire countries or nations, which may, for example, be considering future membership of the European Union, as is presently the case in Bulgaria, Romania and Turkey, or smaller groups, as, for example, the Catholic Church debating the issue of women priests. The influence of the mass media means that nowadays society sets no limits for the maximum size of the public sphere.

The public sphere as a precondition of social representation also helps to separate more traditional worlds dedicated to their doxa (Bourdieu, 1980) and collective representations (Durkheim, 1967) from the de-traditionalised modern world where the public sphere (Habermas, 1989) is the umbrella for a manifold of discourses. This point has been strongly made by Jovchelovitch (1995a, 1995b, 2001). The public sphere, in this understanding, is the cooking pot in which common sense, everyday knowledge and representations are created, resulting in the many shades of reflexive groups and their particular social realities in modern society.

## 9.3.2 Concerted interaction requires holomorphic representations

Concerted interaction is a prerequisite for regulated group life. Members of reflexive groups know what kind of socially relevant behaviour most everyday situations demand of them. That is, they know how to act towards represented objects, persons and institutions, and also what kind of behaviour they can expect from their fellow humans. Co-actors can only comprehend and derive meaning from social actions if these follow the framework defined by the representation – that is, if they are concerted actions.[9] This type of structured interaction is also required, in order to constitute the relevant objects socially during interaction with other people. Erratic and merely selective interaction does not objectify a social representation.

Even when a representation allows an individual actor several alternative courses of action, and even if an individual imposes their own preferences on it, every alternative will be in a homologous relationship with the others (Bourdieu, 1987; Doise, 1976). The homologous relationship between different courses of action sets the limit for compatible actions with regards to an object, a situation or a group without putting co-ordination at risk.

The concerted interaction of social actors with objects, people or institutions is guaranteed either by similar or by complementary actions of those involved, depending on whether they are facing each other as equals or act from different hierarchical positions. For example, interaction within a hierarchy conditions complementary behaviour patterns in the superior and in the subordinate actor. Although different, the patterns of action of those involved in the hierarchy complement each other in such a way that they create, or rather confirm, the social reality of dominance and submission. Another very common example of complementary interactions are the interactions between men and women in non-egalitarian societies. The correlating actions of both sexes – be it during courtship or in the course of daily tasks – complement each other in what may be termed the 'Dance of the Sexes' or the 'Dance of Life' (Henley, 1977, p. 124; LaFrance, 1981).

### Holomorphism

On an individual level, an inevitable consequence of the above is that every actor must not only be aware of their own available courses of action, but also have at least some general knowledge of patterns of perception and judgement, and the courses of action open to potential co-actors, even though the actor would never take on their role. Apart from the cognitive, affective and symbolic dimensions of the represented object, the distributive social representations, which can be determined on the individual level, must therefore also comprise their own action-relevant 'rules', as well as the rules underlying the actions of potential co-actors. We refer to this quality as the 'holomorphic' characteristic of social representation (W. Wagner, 1995).

A representation is holomorphic if it plays a constitutive role in the reconstruction of socially relevant objects and institutions, and orientates the actors' social behaviour towards each other so that concerted co-operation preserves and reproduces the social conditions. The term 'holomorphic' refers to the functional relation between the part and the whole in a society. If meaningful practice is to be established for the social whole (the group), one has to assume that its parts (the individual members) share a representation which contains the essential aspects of the entire situation, that is, the entire group. Without holomorphic representations the actors cannot meaningfully correlate their actions, and would have to rely on trial and error and erratic experiment. These experimental actions, however, do not arise during the regular course of social practice; nor could one ever reproduce the structure of the whole, of group life, of institutions, and so on by trial and error. Holomorphism is in this sense a functional necessity of collectively shared representations; it is a prerequisite of their socionormative function (cf. Backmann, 1979).[10] Holomorphism, however, does not imply that the representation is complete, but in the case of linguistic or intellectual division of labour, the social subjects themselves will know how and where to fill in the gaps.

The fact that the social discourse is held in public is a prerequisite for holomorphic representations. The public aspect guarantees that every group member can potentially participate in the social process of negotiation and its results. If some individuals decide not to participate in this process, or are prevented from doing so for sociostructural reasons; for example, due to a spell in prison or other sanctions, then this may cause serious problems for their integration into the group (cf. Kette, 1991). The uncertainty a released prisoner feels when faced with everyday demands and other people shortly after their release can at least in part be explained by their exclusion from society's process of negotiation. Newspapers, television and radio, which they may have been able to access at least occasionally during their term of imprisonment, do not provide a substitute. If future research were to show that passive media consumption as a means of conveying consensual discourse is not sufficient for an individual to acquire meaningful social representations for their actions, this would be another indication of the importance of informal communicative and interactive contacts for the development of holomorphic representations.

Research examining the processes of job-related or organisation-specific socialisation also highlights the importance of holomorphic group-specific representations. Teaching functional skills is only part of vocational training. It is at least as important to invest in partly explicit and partly implicit training, which imparts holomorphic knowledge about informal codes, linguistic rules, hierarchical relations, implicit communication channels and unwritten performance standards. These processes can be observed at all organisational levels: within an entire company, within departments and within teams. They convey to the new members of an institution not only the behaviour patterns expected of them but also those they can expect from their potential interaction partners (Levine and Moreland, 1991; Offe, 1970).

If a researcher is able to communicate with a few competent representatives of a reflexive community, it is possible to reproduce the socially essential behaviour patterns and demands of the group with their help. The holomorphic aspect of social and cultural representations is therefore one of the reasons why the method of interviewing informants – for example in the field of cultural anthropology – is, if properly conducted, a highly regarded source of information (D'Andrade, 1987).

If we adopt Moscovici's (1988, p. 221) distinction between hegemonic, emancipated and polemical representations, then even polemical representations arising in conflict and not being shared among the antagonistic parties need to embrace knowledge from the others'[11] world-view to some degree. If such polemical representations were not holomorphic to some degree, debate and argument in antagonistic discourse would not work (cf. Vala, Garcia-Marques, Gouveia-Pereira and Lopes, 1998).

The previous arguments, which have always referred to the structure-reproducing function of holomorphic representations, may give rise to the impression that the theory leaves no room for innovation and change. This is, however, not an inevitable consequence of the hypothesis. In our opinion every subgroup of a society or culture, irrespective of whether it forms a majority or a minority, is subject in principle to the same representational processes. As long as people define themselves as a unit and a reflexive group, and infer essential parts of their identity from their membership, the functional necessity of holomorphic representations remains with regard to the group as such and also to its relevant objects and institutions.

The difference between innovative minorities and conservative majorities can be found at a different level. As long as a minority is fighting for recognition and change by persuading and converting outsiders, group-relevant representations will manifest themselves more explicitly and be subject to constant efforts of ideological justification. A higher degree of awareness of the representational system corresponds to greater objective self-awareness on an individual level (e.g. Wicklund, 1975) and can cause the clearly recognisable intolerance against outsiders and dissenters which is easily observable in minority groups (cf. Abrams, 1990). This actively practised intolerance against deviation highlights the efforts spent on preserving the structure. The representational system of majorities will appear to be far more implicit and subliminal, thus achieving stability and the structural reproduction of the *status quo*.

### 9.3.3 Idiomorphic and social representations

Social behaviour in this context is any behaviour that originates in the socially represented structural and living conditions of a reflexive group, and occurs in concerted conjunction with other group members. This is a more narrowly defined notion of social behaviour than one would find in social psychology. Traditionally, social psychologists class all behaviour as social if it is directed at other people or is a result of the actions or the influence of others in any way; regardless of whether or not the interacting partners comprehend the behaviour of the relevant actor. If the interacting partner can comprehend, interpret and categorise the behaviour of an actor, then it is very likely that both share comparable holomorphic representations. Shared directive representations of this type form the basis for actions that will not surprise other group members, and virtually generate appropriate reactions. This conforms to the finding that public behaviour in structured situations reflects little of a person's idiosyncrasies (A. Buss, 1989). In the case of unexpected reactions, the actors will have to ask themselves whether they have activated an inadequate representation in the given situation. Such problems are usually resolved by conversation.

## Idiomorphism and subjective theories

Forms of knowledge shared by only a small number of people who do not form a group in the above sense, or by an individual, should be understood as 'idiomorphic' representations.[12] Thus they are a counterpart to holomorphic patterns of knowledge. Idiomorphic representations can at best be understood as actual individual representations. They may imply behaviour patterns, but to others these seem to be idiosyncratic, and disconcerting on a collective level. The content of an idiosyncratic representation, therefore, is not objectified by regular interaction. These private forms of knowledge may indeed form the basis for widely understood social behaviour, but they are meaningless as far as regulated group practice is concerned.

People, of course, possess extensive idiomorphic knowledge, subjective theories and a repertory of idiosyncratic behaviour; as well as holomorphic representations. Both aspects make up the sum of their present life experience. In the case of an individual and their comprehensive fund of knowledge it may almost be impossible to distinguish clearly – in a strict sense – between socially relevant holomorphic and idiomorphic representations. Instead, it would be better to refer to it as a continuous transition between the two poles.

In our opinion the differentiation developed above fulfils a significant diagnostic role in the analysis of social behaviour at group level, especially in the light of current theoretical efforts in the field of social psychology that aim to integrate the concepts of 'cognitive representation' (e.g. Mandl and Spada, 1988); 'subjective theories' (e.g. Scheele and Groeben, 1988); 'everyday understanding' (e.g. Furnham, 1988); 'common sense' (e.g. Giorgi, 1990); 'cultural models' (Holland and Quinn, 1987); and 'social representations'. For example, Flick (1991), in his collection of essays 'Everyday Understanding of Health and Disease', compares knowledge specific to an individual or a disease, as well as generally shared collective knowledge. His work shows clearly how the scope of explanations of idiomorphic subjective knowledge and holomorphic systems of knowledge, such as 'common sense', cultural models and social representations, differ from one another.

Subjective theories are used in the definition of a situation, the subjective explanation and justification of past events and the forecast of future events, as well as in the stabilisation of self-esteem

(Dann, 1992, p. 161; Flick, 1991, p. 15). Although their contents originate partly from personal life experience and partly from cultural patterns of knowledge, their scope of explanation, strictly speaking, refers to the behaviour of subjects as individuals and not to the behaviour of people seen as members of social units. When, for example, Angermeyer (1991) describes the explanation patterns of functionally psychotic patients, and Lucchetti (1991) gives an account of the coping strategies of HIV patients, then all these instances relate to private and subjective behaviour that does not require any agreement on a collective level. The particular actions of those concerned do not depend on whether their ideas can be validated by other people's opinions, or to a large extent on what others are expecting from them, or on a reflexive group, which shares their subjective everyday theories consensually. Strictly speaking, the scope of explanation of subjective theories does not relate to social behaviour.[13]

By reversing the previous line of argument, one can show that social, that is to say, holomorphic representations, strictly speaking, do not explain individual subjective behaviour. Their scope of explanation refers to collectively co-ordinated actions as the basis for everyday group practice, by providing a content-rational description of social conditions and thereby of implied behaviour.

If, therefore, both social and, to a degree, holomorphic representations do not explain subjective individual behaviour, does this construct still have the potential to resolve the issues arising in social psychology? Are the characteristics of holomorphism we have described here too narrowly defined? We do not believe so. Holomorphism is an attribute derived from the prerequisites of the theory. In our opinion it allows us to differentiate both theoretically and methodologically between social and subjective private systems of actual knowledge and experience. If this inevitably limits the scope of explanation of the theory if strictly applied, then this is not necessarily a shortcoming. The social behaviour of individuals and groups still provides important phenomena in human behaviour, and a challenge for research into social psychology. In the end, by overstating the theoretical approach one might offer a starting point for further examination and theoretical development.

# Chapter 10

# Epistemological Aspects of Social Representation Theory

## 10.1 Explanation and description in social psychology

### 10.1.1 The historicity and analyticity of social-psychological theories

The task of science in general and of psychology in particular is the production of knowledge about a defined subject area. Under 'knowledge' one subsumes, on the one hand, 'knowledge of facts and the way they are', and on the other hand, 'knowledge of the causes and functional relationships between facts'. The former is a description as an answer to the question 'What is the case?'; the latter an explanation and substantiation as an answer to the questions 'Why is that the case?' and 'How does this case come about?'. Both are requirements for prediction, which is frequently viewed as the essential task of academic activity.

In order to be able to make forecasts, one must, first, guarantee being able to identify and classify the relevant phenomenon appropriately – as a task of describing – and, second, able to derive the consequences of particular states and facts from knowledge about their contexts. The requirement for this is to explain and formulate theories.

Explanations chiefly have two forms in social psychology:

1. The causal explanation which represents the paradigmatic case of an explanation in the natural sciences and is also used in an objectively interpreted social psychology, and

2.  the explanation as (understood in a generalised way) a moral
    or teleological justification of the subjects in a more subjec-
    tively interpreted social psychology. The understanding of this
    concept, as has already been demonstrated, plays a central role
    especially in a social psychology of everyday life (see e.g.
    Fincham and Jaspars, 1980).

## The covering-law model

The covering-law model by Hempel and Oppenheim (Hempel,
1977; Popper, 1935) constitutes a causal explanation in the classic
sense in the way that it has been developed by the philosophy of
science for the natural sciences and, here especially, for physics
(Stegmüller, 1974). By this understanding the logical derivation of
a fact is to be explained in the form of a clause $E$ from some premisses. Premisses are for usually antecedent conditions, that is,
existing facts $A = \{A_1, \ldots A_n\}$ plus a set of law statements $L = \{L_1,
\ldots L_m\}$, the conjunction of which results in the explanatory clause
$E$. The law or law-like statements $L$ are required amongst other
things not to refer to particular places, times or individual objects,
and to be clauses that can be inductively confirmed by observations
– that is, synthetically and not analytically. In addition to this, the
clauses of set $A$ must of course be true. This results in law-like
statements being synthetic, essentially general 'if-then' clauses (von
Kutschera, 1982, p. 99). This model of explanation, on account of
its strict requirements, is valid essentially for natural sciences.

The two central conditions which are demanded from law
statements – the condition of universality and syntheticity in the
covering-law model – are not fulfilled or only partially fulfilled by
social-psychological theories. Concerning the universality, much of
the present-day subject matter of psychology is neither ahistorical
nor culturally invariant. The synthetic character of some psychological theories is also doubted by some authors.

## Historicity and enlightenment

People whose behaviour is being 'explained' in theories have access
to the theories concerning them, conveyed via mass-media popularisation of scientific discoveries. In this way, prescriptive tenden-

cies of social-psychological theorisation become general, seemingly objective values. One need only think of evaluatively relevant traits in personality psychology such as 'neuroticism', 'authoritarianism' or 'field dependency', which cannot be seen impartially by either the researchers or the participants themselves. On the other hand, popularised science can be used for consciously intended changes in behaviour, an effect which Gergen (1973) calls the 'enlightenment effect'. If people know why they act in such a way and in no other, they gain the freedom to decide on it arbitrarily, to the extent that it can be determined psychologically and is not a physiological determination. Foon (1986) was able to show how being enlightened about the theoretical backgrounds to psychological context ruins the results of an experiment.

*Method.* In an experiment investigating the halo effect in judging people, four conditions were created: a control group in which the test participants only saw a video of the person to be judged; a group with the video and an additional verbal description of the target person; an experimental group which had been enlightened about the halo effect before being offered the video and description; and a group which after being enlightened was additionally distracted by an irrelevant task.

In almost all judgement dimensions, the group of test participants which had been enlightened before they judged the target person differed markedly from the other groups. They did not show the expected halo effect which could be observed with the other groups.[1]

Social-technological knowledge is ultimately used for controlling behaviour, such as in organisational contexts which, upon being consciously experienced by those concerned, lead to reactance and the effort to get back one's individual freedom of behaviour.[2] All these effects change the validity of many psychological theories to a greater or lesser degree in the long term, and thus become views that are only valid locally and at particular historical times (cf. Habermas, 1968). To analyse such processes of change in a historically orientated social psychology might well help to capture this aspect of human behaviour (K. Gergen and Gergen, 1984); the objections made above, however, would remain untouched by this, since theories about 'enlightenment' can also be refuted by popularisation.

The cultural relativity of the inventory of concepts owned by psychological theories can be illustrated using one of the central concepts, that of the individual. The individual constitutes the atomic entity in the majority of psychological theories. Describing the subject being investigated as an individual or person also implies – in addition to alienating the human being from his or her environment as an autonomous unit of investigation – being able to identify intrinsic features or traits which are used for predicting behaviour (cf. Semin, 1987). This applies both to the everyday and the scientific usage of this concept. This tendency is also known as the 'fundamental' attribution error.

The works by Shweder and Bourne (1984), as well as by J. Miller (1984), illustrate how little reason there is to introduce this particular concept of the individual into scientific theories. Both investigations show that such an individualistic concept of a person cannot be fully reproduced in collectivist Indian culture, for example. A person, in the everyday understanding of India, is much more someone whose behaviour is explained less dispositionally than from his or her position in the social system and the social context (cf. Semin and Rubini, 1992). Elias (1977) identifies something similar in the courtly society of the Middle Ages: in the courtly 'art of observing people . . . the individual is always considered in how he is interwoven into society . . . as a man in his relations with others, as an individual in a social situation' (p. 375).

In Indian culture there is at least a concept of the person, so that psychological investigations can be carried out. Yet there exist other cultures in which the concepts of 'personality' and 'character' do not exist at all, such as with the indigenous people of Samoa, for example (Shore, 1982). Moreover, such people as the Baining in New Guinea refuse all conversations about psychological issues (Fajans, 1985). Thus the dispositional concept of a person and individual only turns out to be valid within Western developed countries.

The second demand made by the covering-law model, for the non-analyticity of law statements, is similarly problematical for social psychology. As the following will show, this too cannot be taken for granted in many social-psychological theories.

## Analyticity

Smedslund (1978a, 1978b, 1979, 1988), Brandstätter (1982), Holzkamp (1986) and more recently W. Wagner (1994) and Greve (2001) initiated a discussion which is about the problem of analyticity of theoretical clauses – those which establish the empirical connections between psychological variables. The argument of the authors is that: (a) claims of psychological theories which invoke rational reasons to explain actions (Greve, 2001; Holzkamp, 1986); or (b) theories which state empirically testable hypotheses, but merely describe relationships that are already embodied in the universe of everyday knowledge (Brandstädter, 1982; Smedslund, 1978a, 1978b; W. Wagner, 1994) are in fact not empirically provable. The stated relationships between thinking, intending, believing, on the one hand, and behaviour, on the other, cannot be subjected to experiment because the stated relationship is of a logical and not of a synthetic or contingent character. Such theoretical clauses are either a consequence of the very definiton of the terms, or *a priori* embedded in cultural and everyday knowledge.

The classic example of illustrating analytical or logical and synthetic or contingent connections in statements is provided by the clause 'bachelors are unmarried men'. This is part of the definition and not a fact that could be empirically verified. We have a different state of affairs with 'bachelors are blond persons'. This assertion can only be proven empirically by measuring the hair colour of bachelors in comparison to non-bachelors. The clause constitutes a synthetic relationship.

Concretely speaking, Smedlund's critique takes as a starting point Bandura's theory of self-efficacy (Bandura, 1977). This theory can be summarised as follows: 'A person will undertake a certain action if he or she is convinced that there is no reason why not to in the particular situation. Yet the person will refrain from the action if he or she is convinced that the opposite is the case. The probability of performing the desired action or refraining from it depends directly on the strength of the person's conviction.'

Bandura formulates his theory in a much more technical way than has been described here and goes on to define some peripheral conditions which do no affect the argument. In the everyday language in which the theory has been portrayed here, its message is surely nothing new to anybody. If one were to ask any random person in the street under which conditions they would sooner perform a certain action, then the essence of their views will flow into precisely this theory. It portrays nothing more than routine knowledge which is available to people. Precisely because of this, its logical structure is analytical in relation to the knowledge of those whose behaviour is meant to be described by the theory. If the peripheral conditions are provided, each person will draw exactly these conclusions and no others. The theory cannot even be refuted empirically if a few people react unexpectedly due to some arbitrary reason (cf. Shotter, 1981).

Fishbein and Ajzen's (1975) model of attitude, intention and action has also been accused of analyticity and its relatively good confirmation in experiment has been interpreted as a 'response bias', that is, a consequence of the devaluation of the theory due to the experimental participants already knowing about it. Budd and Spencer (1986) compared everyday ideas about motivated behaviour, using the basic views stated by the model, and identified great agreement between both systems of stated views. This already existing fore-knowledge of the test participants in the experiment can function as a response bias, which the participants bring in order to create consistency between parts of a theory when they answer questionnaires that measure the constructs of the model (Budd and Spencer, 1986, p. 109).

Similar problems confront the use of features of personality as *explanantia* of behaviour, since it can be shown that this construct is analytical to a certain extent. People are in a position to reconstruct intuitively both the meaning of items in personality tests, its factoral structure, and also their own position on the scales (Semin, 1987).

Research on volitional behaviour and self-report is a further indicator of the non-contingent, quasi-logical relationship between belief and action. In a word-list learning experiment on the validity of self-reports, Eagle (1967) asked one group of participants to use a rote-learning technique and the other group to use associative techniques. The associative technique was known to be superior to rote learning for the given task. After the learning phase the participants reported which learning technique they had actually used. The result showed that performance depended only on what the participants had reported. If they had reported using the rote technique, they had learned fewer words than when they reported having used the association technique. This effect was independent of the instructions given by the experimenter. Apart from the author's intention to show that people report correctly about what they think and do, this experiment also makes the point that participants in fact did what they thought or believed to be the best thing to do. Believing that the associative technique was the best thing to do immediately *obliged* the participants to do exactly this. It was *logical* to do what they considered best; their doing so was not contingently caused by their belief, but *necessary and rational* given their belief.

Research on volitional behavior or self-determination consistently shows that what people actually do depends significantly more upon what they believe and intend to do than upon objective situational determinants. Experiments on eating, heterosexual affiliation behaviour and so on revealed that the effect sizes of volitional control factors significantly supersede other effect sizes to an extent which can rarely, if ever, be observed in experiments with situational independent variables (Howard and Conway, 1986). This again is strong empirical evidence indicating that beliefs, intentions and action are integrated with each other beyond simple contingency.

The resistance of such theories to refutation by empirical proof has nothing to do with absent falsifiability in the sense of Popper (1935). There are likely to be exact conditions that could be formulated, in which a hypothesis derived from them could be refuted in the way demanded by Popper. Such a refutation in an experiment on Bandura's theory could consist of test particpants refusing to act despite favourable conditions. As such conditions can be reported, Popper's demand is met. They are resistant to refutation because it would simply be foolish of the test particpants to act differently than is formulated in the theories. The empirical character of such theories relate to their 'correctness or conformity with rules, and not to their factual truth. . . . We do not validate explications of common sense experimentally, but only consensually. . . . Explications of common sense have the form of implications, that is, they state what follows from what. Given correctness about what words mean in a given context, the propositions therefore cannot be false, that is, they are necessarily or non contingently true' (Smedslund, 1985, p. 77).

The problem, then, also appears if concepts refering to motives and needs come from everyday language use (cf. Danziger, 1997). As such core concepts of psychology are used to identify psychological forces of often rhetorical purposes, that is, are used as an instrument for justifying one's own behaviour (Lyman and Scott,

1970), one is well advised not to use them as a causal 'reason' in an objectivist psychology (Harré, 1990, p. 116 onwards). We call this effect the self-devaluation of theories. Self-devaluation is the mirror-image equivalent of the thesis of enlightenment mentioned above. According to this, views stated by social science devalue themselves when they become part of the trove of knowledge of the population investigated. The equivalence is a mirror image because the wrong claims of contingency in analytical theories come from investigations of the general knowledge of the population, and from the fact that the researcher has a close proximity to his or her participants and their cultural background knowledge.

In other words: social psychologists, as participants in their culture, already know too much about the thought and behaviour of their participants and have not sufficiently pondered this fact (Fletcher, 1984). Thus social psychologists implicitly assume that their participants know less about their everyday behaviour than they do themselves, even though the social psychologists have taken the basic structure of their theories from precisely that realm of collective everyday knowledge from which their participants also extract their rules of behaviour.

It must be remarked at this juncture that the criticism of analyticity from the authors mentioned can only be maintained in its strict form as long as one does not endorse Quine's (1961) argument of the undistinguishability in principle of analytical and synthetic clauses. What we describe here as the weak form of their criticism, however, remains untouched by this: it is the reference to the relative sterility of social-psychological, but also sociological, theories and methods whose structure and conceptualisation is a reproduction of the semantics of the subject, which ought to be their subject matter (cf. also Bourdieu, 1983). If models taken from everyday language flow into the formulation of social-psychological theories in an unpondered manner, this results in a substantialisation of relational concepts, ideologisation of theories, and objective reification of subjective facts (W. Wagner, 1990; Wagner and Elejabarrieta, 1992).

## 10.1.2 'Explanations' of rational behaviour

The preceding discussion showed some of the problems which can result from applying the strict covering-law model of natural-scientific causal explanations within social psychology. If a not inconsiderable number of social-psychological and social-scientific theories fail to meet the demands made on law-like clauses because of their reflexive relationship with their subject matter, or the only local validity of many concepts, then the covering-law model of explanation also remains only conditionally useful. Social-psychological explanations which attempt to formulate laws governing behaviour that is rational, governed by rules, or logical in everyday life, are right at the limits of the model. Meanwhile, Hempel's (1962, p. 27) reformulation of the covering-law model to include rational behaviour is also of little help:

*General law.* Every person who is rationally disposed will be more likely to do *X* in situations of the nature *C*.

Premiss 1:   Protagonist *A* was in a situation *C*.
Premiss 2:   *A* was rationally disposed.
Conclusion and explanation:   *A* did *X*.

The main problems of this model is how to establish what to understand by rational behaviour, and what its empirical form is. For decision theoreticians, behaviour is rational if the protagonist maximises the expected desirability of his or her action (Papineau, 1978, in Salmon, 1989, p. 395). This criterion is the result of estimating and comparing the chances of success presented by varied alternatives to the action, with the effect that a behaviour is rational if it conforms to this calculation, regardless of whether the protagonist actually undertook the calculation. If we assume that protagonists use objective data for calculating, in keeping with the model, then these data are of a probabilistic nature and are therefore not covering laws (Salmon, 1989). But not only that: 'Even if agents' beliefs are based on prejudice or ignorance, or if their desires are peculiar or hard to comprehend, their behavior can be rational. Moreover . . . to be rational in this sense, agents need not assign explicit probabilities to beliefs or quantify values, or even make rough or precise calculations of expected desirability. It is enough for agents to act as if they were maximising desirability, given their beliefs and desires' (p. 396). Neither a rational disposition nor following rules can be used in a meaningful sense as a causal explanation. People are not puppets of social systems of rules: if they were they would not break them. Causes differ logically from reasons for behaviour (p. 398; cf. Harré, 1989, 1990).

## Modal explanation

A softer model can be provided as a minimum consensus for the typical views stated by social psychology. As with everyday explanations, in social psychology we are often dealing with ways of giving reasons which, first, do not use any natural laws that can be described in a formalised form or as elaborated theories and, second, cannot justify any compelling deduction of the *explanandum* from antecedent conditions plus law statements (D'Andrade, 1986; M. Jahoda, 1989, p. 77).

As an alternative to the strict covering-law model there remains according to von Kutschera (1982, p. 101) the softer form of 'modal explanation'[3] as a model for social-psychological theories, which was presented in Chapter 2. In this model, one understands a phenomenon $q$ as a cause of $p$ precisely when $q$ goes ahead of phenomenon $p$ and if the following is valid:

$$q \text{ AND } (q \to_s p).$$

In this formula the bracketed expression is an if-then statement for which it is additionally true that the complement of $q$ (i.e., everything that is not $q$) likewise causing $p$ to be excluded:

$$q \to_s p = (q \to p) \text{ AND } \text{NOT}(\text{NOT}q \to p),$$

and the implication $\to_s$ is synthetic (von Kutschera, 1982, p. 101 onwards).

Probably the majority of statements, hypotheses and explanations of social psychology fall under the modal explanation schema rather than under the strictly interpreted covering-law model of scientific explanation. This model illustrates the logic of experimental research in social psychology, since by far the majority of experiments only show that a behaviour $p$ appears under an experimentally produced condition $q$, but not under the control condition $\text{NOT}q$.

By a further extension, it would in principle be possible to soften the condition of a strictly synthetic implication even more. Then one would not interpret the term $q$ as a cause, but the whole expression $(q \to_s p)$ as a description of a non-synthetic relationship. Under this condition, the 'if-then' statements analytical to everyday life could be subsumed as a context that is content-rational or logical in everyday life.

## Content-rational description of behaviour

The soft form of content-rational context statements makes it easier to formulate statements in a locally and historically bounded social psychology. Consequently such theoretical formulations would not be explanations of behaviour, but rather descriptions of behaviour. In a certain way one can formulate content-rational context statements analogously to the model of dispositional explanations (cf. von Kutschera, 1982, p. 105).

A person has a content-rational opinion $R$ precisely when he or she is of the conviction that

$$S \rightarrow_{\text{content-rational}} A$$

which includes $S$ as a situation and $A$ as an action which in $S$ is seen as sensible. The context logical to everyday life is symbolised by '$\rightarrow_{\text{content-rational}}$'.

A content-rational description of behaviour would therefore be a statement of the form:

$$\text{FORALL } P(S \rightarrow_{\text{content-rational}} A): S \rightarrow A$$

where the bracketed expression is a belief or representation R. This means that all people who are of the content-rational opinion $R$ will implement action $A$ when they find themselves in situation $S$. The implication of $A$ by $S$ is clearly no longer synthetic. The statement is no longer ahistorical either, since the content-rational convictions $R$ are of course variable both in a diachronous as well as a cultural perspective.

Let us compare the superficially similar form of the 'strict' explanation of rational behaviour according to Hempel (1962) – as was cited above – with the one presented here. Hempel's formulation assumes the general law that all people who are rationally disposed will be very likely to perform action $X$ in situations of the nature C. This 'general' law complies with our formulation $S \rightarrow A$, is identical to the required content-rational opinion $R$, and is therefore dependent on places, times and social groups. It is analytical in Smedlund's sense. Hence this law cannot be part of a covering-law model.

Furthermore, in our opinion, Hempel's formulation is tautological, since the partial requirement of 'being rationally disposed' in whatever culture or society whose content-rational, socially shared knowledge is being investigated is identical to the following part statement, 'in situation $C$ perform action $X$'. Being rationally disposed of course means precisely performing $X$ in $C$, since it is precisely this and nothing else which is sensible. The 'general law' can therefore be reduced to the statement, 'Every person who is rational acts rationally'. The concept of rationality, of course, produces a tight implicit connection between thought and action, so that being rational, that is, thinking rationally and acting rationally, does not, strictly speaking, constitute any distinguishable level of analysis. To our mind it is therefore impossible to apply the covering-law model, even in its reformulation, to explain socially sensible behaviour.

Strictly speaking, we are not dealing with an action explanation here. Rather, we have a 'behaviour description'. By 'description', however, we do not mean the description of a fact by an outside observer. A content-rational knowledge system with action implications constitutes a self-description of the observer's actions by the members of a social entity. The observer can then identify the correlation between ascertained content-rational knowledge elements and observed behaviour in a group, that is, interpret the knowledge system ascertained as a description of behaviour. But the observer cannot extract this knowledge for the logical reasons mentioned for causally explaining behaviour, and thus not for prognosis either (Duveen, 1994; cf. also Davidson, 1980).[4]

What are the implications of all this for social representation theory? One of us (W. Wagner, 1994) has summarised the implications of these epistemological problems for representation theory along the following lines: Social representations are not the causal antecedents of action, such that beliefs about home-heating control would cause heating-control behaviour, or that beliefs about psychotherapeutic methods would cause the therapeutic behaviour of clinical psychologists, or that beliefs in appropriate food would cause the food- and health-related behaviour of students (see examples in Chapter 9).[5] The meta-belief in psychological entities causing behaviour is a belief of everyday folk, just as is the knowledge about rain making you wet. Folk psychology serves social purposes in providing sensible accounts of actions and responsibility in a group. It is a set of rhetorical figures endowed with social meaning and is best investigated as such (cf. Edwards and Potter, 1992; Harré and Gillet, 1994). Hence, folk-psychology is an integral part of any representational system as far as it has action aspects (W. Wagner, 1997).

It would be wrong to make elements of folk-psychology part of scientific theorising in a supposedly objective psychology.[6] Along with all other beliefs, opinions, knowledge and representations, folk psychology is part and parcel of local culture and cultural behaviour. Social beliefs and representations are an integral part of everyday action, reflecting this action in cognitive, symbolic and iconic terms. By being part of social action, representations are intimately linked to co-ordinated practice and interaction. This also includes in many, but not necessarily all societies the folk-psychological belief that '*Thinking X makes me do Y*', while in other societies the formulation '*The ghost G makes me do Y*' would be a realistic alternative. Research about local systems of knowledge is well advised to take a descriptive approach and not to separate action from belief – that is, to treat 'belief as part of the action' (Douglas, 1982a, p. 200f.).

This connects closely with the notion of collective rationalisation discussed in the preceding chapter. Rationalisation is, of course, a description of action which embeds actions into a locally valid context of rationality, thus giving them meaning and establishing their place in the system of all relevant social beliefs. Comparable rationalisation processes have also been dealt with by social psychology, on an individual level in the theory of cognitive dissonance (Beauvois and Joule, 1981) and in the theory of 'self-perception' (e.g. Nisbett and Wilson, 1977). Cognitions can be viewed in every research design both prospectively, in relation to future behaviour, but also retrospectively, in relation to the variety of previous behaviour.

Such a view is rarely taken up by the acting subject, yet it might well be taken up by the external observer. One can infer from the fact that he or she rarely does so that the observer often lacks epistemic distance from his or her subject/object. Attitudes, behavioural dispositions, opinions, knowledge and social representations would then appear as a consequence of previous behaviour. The observer would hardly speak any more of the action-generating function of knowledge, but of an action-justifying one, or more generally, of an action-describing function of human knowledge. To our mind it is therefore more purposeful, both for epistemological and research reasons, to view social representations, systems of knowledge, values and norms as descriptions of socially relevant behaviour. Then they would be the mental side of two processes running parallel in a social context, the other side of which is behaviour.

## 10.2 Levels of analysis and macro-reduction

According to Allport, social psychology must not be at odds with the psychology of the individual, since it investigates individual behaviour relating to other people (Allport, 1924, p. 4), thus defining the individual as its subject matter. Nonetheless, other levels of social-psychological analysis can be found in social psychology. Levels of analysis also imply appropriate realms of experience, which restrict the nature of the questions which one can pose to the phenomena recorded in them. We shall therefore first present the concept of the 'explanation space' and, going on from this, the consequence for structures of explanation with levels of analysis.

### 10.2.1 Explanation space and objectivism

By a unified science one understands a philosophical school which was represented within, and in the wake of, the Vienna circle of positivism; and ultimately postulated the reducibility of explanations stated by so-called 'higher' sciences like psychology and sociology to the laws of physics. This direction, also known by the name 'physicalism', formulated the idea of the non-independence of all higher sciences, since their explanations were only pseudo-explanations, to be put on the same level as disreputable concepts such as 'vitalism' and 'psychism'. By contrast with this, Putnam (1974) believes that hypothetical knowledge of all necessary physical parameters does not in any way constitute a sufficient or valid explanation of phenomena of more complex units, such as psychic or social entities, because explanations are intransitive.[7]

## Intransitivity of explanations

An intransitive explanation can be illustrated using a mechanical example. There is a board which is provided with holes of varied sizes, and in these holes pens of different cross-sections fit (just like a well-known baby toy). Let us assume that one of the pens fits exactly into a particular hole on the board (fact 'C'). We might attempt to explain fact C by knowing the place and vector of momentum of all the elementary particles constituting the board and the pen, from which one can prove the impenetrability of the materials apart from the places where the solid material of the board is replaced by a substance of a different aggregate state, for example air in the form of a hole. The non-solidity of some of the areas of the board would ultimately be the explanation A for the fact C, which is that the pen can pass the board at precisely that place and at no other.

On the other hand, one could explain the fitting of the pen by comparing geometrical macroscopic measurement of the form of the board, its openings and the pen (explanation 'B'). In actual fact, the two explanations A and B could be interlinked, since the first one, the proof of solidity, is a precondition for geometrical measurement, whilst geometrical measurement ultimately permits the inference that the pen fits. Although this interlinking of 'if A then B' and 'if B then C' are each possible and meaningful, the transitive inference from this, namely 'if A then C', is inadmissable. Putnam (1974, p. 133) argues that: 'An explanation of an explanation (a parent of an explanation, so to speak), generally contains information . . . which is irrelevant to what we want to explain, and in addition it contains the information that *is* relevant, if at all, in a form which may be impossible to recognize. For this reason, a parent of an explanation is generally not an explanation.' The most interesting examples for intransitivity are, in his opinion, social and psychological systems, because they 'can have behaviors to which their microstructure is *largely* irrelevant'.

It is of course true that the laws of physics, chemistry, biology and neurophysiology are required for psychic and social phenomena to exist materially. But they do not explain their laws, since the 'higher' phenomena are realised via peripheral conditions which appear accidentally in the bounds of the 'lower'sciences (cf. Riedl, 1976).[8] These peripheral conditions can only be conceptually grasped within the 'higher' discipline of science:

The laws of the higher-level discipline are deducible from the laws of the lower-level discipline together with 'auxiliary hypotheses' which are accidental from the point of view of the lower-level discipline. And most of the structure at the level of physics is irrelevant from the point of view of the higher-level disciplines; only certain features of that structure . . . , and these are specified by the higher-level discipline, not the lower-level one. . . . [T]he laws of human sociology and psychology . . . have a basis in the material organization of persons and things, but they also have an autonomy just described *vis-à-vis* the laws of physics and chemistry.

(Putnam, 1974, p. 134)

The conceptual components of the explanation of a phenomenon, the theory governing the research and the hypotheses derived from it, must all be located in the same space of concepts if they are to provide an answer which is relevant to the question. This means that the possible explanation space (Putnam, 1975) is predetermined by the formulation of the question, the interest behind the question, and how prolific the answer is. The relativity of both the interest and the prolificness of the explanation for the formulation of the question places both pragmatic and methodological demands on research (Lugg, 1975). The popular idea of an ultimate explanation, analogous to Laplace, is the paradigmatic example of a non-explanation (Putnam, 1975, p. 296).

The relative autonomy of explanation spaces in sciences encompassing varied levels implies that an explanation for a human action, such as a question (c) posed to a psychologist: 'Why did $P$ commit the aggressive action $A$ against $O$?' must satisfy the demand for a homogenous explanation space. This explanation space is determined both from the way the question is formulated, and from the implied target person. They both express the implicit theory underlying the question and, as a result, the interest of the person asking the question.

The answer to the question (c) can therefore not consist of describing the electro-physiological patterns of discharge in the central nervous system and effectors of person $P$. Such an answer does seem in principle to be possible to this Why-question, especially if the target person is a medical doctor or neurologist, for example. However, as the question was posed to a psychologist it seems more obvious in answer (b) to give the meaning subjectively pursued by person $P$ – that is, his or her intention – whether these are conscious or (in the case of a psychoanalytic interpretation) sub-conscious. While the neurophysiological explanation is an answer to the question about the material and energetic causes of the action, the psychological explanation aims at the force behind the purpose, and so remains in the explanation space implied by the question. The conceptuality of the physiological answer (a) comes from the biological level of analysis, that of answer (b), of meaning or intention, has its roots in the psychological level of analysis. If neuropsychology knew which biological-physiological processes could be seen as a direct substratum of the psychic (Guttmann, 1972, p. 8), the answer (a) would indeed be able to explain fact (b), and fact (b) could explain the facts of the matter (c). But because of the logical intransitivity of explanations, (a) would not be an explanation of (c).

## Subjectivism and objectivism

If we ask 'why did $P$ perform action $X$?' in the above example, then we have not yet exhausted the explanation spaces possible in the social sciences. The reasons for action (c) were given by the intention of the individual, in other words, put down to internal processes in the person. Yet this substantiation can just as rightly be accompanied by an explanation (d) which refers back to the structural features of the social group whose member is $P$. Such an explanation, which puts the action by $P$ down to, say, the carrying out of a ritual, would not refer to the subjective reasons of the individual for justifying it, but to trans-individual attributes of the social group. Whilst (b) constitutes an intra-individual explanation which we will call 'subjectivist', (d) is a social and superindividual explanation which we will call 'objectivist'.

Both models of explanation, the subjectivist and the objectivist, can be found in the social sciences. Within sociology, disciplines such as ethnomethodology and symbolic interactionism produce rather subjectivist substantiations, whilst structuralist and functionalist sociologies aim for objectivist explanations (cf. Bourdieu, 1987). Both forms can also be found within social psychology, but they are often not clearly distinguished from one another. Reference to this problem has been made in the section on the critique of analyticity. By contrast with objectivist and subjectivist sociologies, which are explicitly defined as such on a metatheoretical level, comparable clear metatheoretical explications are rarely found in social psychology. Using these or those types of explanation is not linked to analogous 'schools' in this discipline. Instead, there is often a subjectivisation of objectivist concepts, resulting from, for example, behavioural patterns which follow the implicit norms of the cultural habitus being interpreted as behavioural preferences and intention in the individual. The actual legitimacy of assuming conscious intentionality in awareness of roles and norms often goes unchecked.

One can assume that this translation from objectivist to subjectivist vocabulary actually changes the content of the terms, even though the same words are used. The term 'norm', when used as an expression of the social reproduction mechanisms of a society, does not contain the same definitive content as the same term used to describe behavioural preference expressed by the subject and corresponding to his or her subjective reasons (or rationalisations). This problem for translation is also a problem for linking different levels of analysis, and will be discussed later in this chapter.

## 10.2.2  Levels of analysis

Doise (1980, 1986b) has proposed a schema which classifies theoretical concepts in social-psychological studies according to their conceptual origin. He defines four levels of complexity, which he does not wish to see interpreted ontologically, but as a consequence of different conceptual approaches to an otherwise continuously structured reality (Doise, 1986b, p. 11).

In the intra-personal level, Doise summarises theories which describe how individuals organise their perception, their judgement of the social milieu and their behaviour in this milieu. Such theories do not directly touch on the interactions of individuals with their social environment, but only on the mechanisms which help them to analyse their experience (1986b, p. 11). Explanatory concepts are restricted to phenomena in the individual mental apparatus, in a micro-genetic process. In this type of research, stimuli are provided in a relatively abstract form, for example as lists of features, without explicitly making reference to social a prioris in the explanation.

The second level of analysis concerns the interpersonal and situative level. In this level studies are mentioned which analyse the dynamics of the relationships existing between people in particular situations, but without taking into account the different social positions which the people occupy outside of the situation (p. 12). The third level refers to explanations which take into account the varied social positions of individuals that already exist before any interaction (p. 13). Theories and claims of relationships at this positional level include in their explanations relationships of social roles and positions which exist independently of the transient conditions of an experiment. The fourth, ideological level of analysis comprises all studies in which systems of ideology are invoked to explain attribution tendencies and behavioural patterns. This category includes, for example, works of cultural comparison which refer to cultural values and systems of norms to explain differences in behaviour.

If one looks at the typical examples of studies mentioned by Doise, then, first, it appears that the levels of analysis in the vast majority of the examples address the logical origin or conceptual source of the explanatory concepts, that is, the *explanans*, but not the level at which the explanatory phenomenon is assessed in research. Second, the level of analysis of the phenomenon to be explained, the *explanandum*, is not considered. With the exception of matrix game studies, cited as examples of the interpersonal level, all *explanantia* and *explananda* reside methodologically within the individual level. This is the case at the interpersonal level of analysis regarding actor – observer differences in attribution experiments (Jones and Davis, 1965; Kelley, 1967), where the *explanans*, the situational perception 'bias', is an individual cognition. In the case of the positional level of analysis where the group membership of subjects moderates attributions (Deschamps, 1983; Hewstone and Jaspars, 1982), group membership is an individual cognition. Finally, at the ideological level of analysis, the just-world hypothesis (Lerner, 1971) as *explanans* is also an individual cognitive representation.

In order to locate the concept of social representation metatheoretically, we propose a two-dimensional schema. In this schema, both the level of the *explanans* and that of the *explanandum* are considered and linked to each other in an explanation or a theoretical clause. This distinguishes three levels, an intrapersonal, a situative and a social-cultural level, which, although resembling Doise's levels, are explicitly understood as levels of assessment or aggregation levels.

*(1)* The intrapersonal level is intended to include all social-psychological concepts which refer to phenomena within the subjective world of understanding, feeling and desire in the individual person. These include perceptions, memories, attitudes, intentions, thought schemata, interests, states of feeling and so on, which can be interpreted as either individual representations of conditions and facts (cognitions) or as an individual reaction to past or current experiences (emotions, motivations). These variables are individually assessed and theoretically located within persons. The majority of all constructs used in social psychology fall into this class. This aggregation level, by and large, corresponds to the intra-individual level in Doise's (1986b) model.

*(2)* The situative level includes variables or concepts which describe transient facts in the immediate, individually perceptible and also mostly individually influenceable milieu of the person. This includes groups of whatever size, as long as the individual has an overview on them, and physical environments. Physical environments are transient elements of situations, insofar as the situation is influenced by the activities of other people, for example if members of an experimental group go their separate ways after the experiment has been concluded, or whether the participant has the chance to withdraw from the situation, or changes in physical conditions. What is important is the transient character of the fact within the person's daily routine, so that situative conditions can be distinguished from structures such as the social system, which are stable over the long term.

A construct at this level usually describes some attribute of the situation as a whole. Examples of this can be found in the social psychology of matrix games, in which a situation is artificially defined on the basis of the playing rules and predetermined pay-off schemes. A paramter that describes the game as a whole is located on the situative aggregation level. Such a parameter, for example, might be represented by a characterisation of a game as either a zero-sum game or a non-zero-sum game. In his monograph about groups and individuals Doise (1978b) introduces situative parameters whenever the aim of the experimental game is given as the individual or joint maximisation of winnings. Other examples, from group psychology, are concepts like 'similarity', 'group homogeneity', 'group cohesion' and the like; which define a structural network of relations between individuals in its entirety. What is common to these concepts is that they portray relations which cannot be reduced to features of individual people, but result from the patterns of relationships. This does not exclude an individual person from, for example, being able to dominate a situation and being almost exclusively responsible for the cohesion observed. Nevertheless, the situation variable does not refer to a single person, but to the network of relationships as a whole. It is the same with the term 'dominance' or 'power'. Even if an individual person can be described as dominant in the usage of everyday language, this actually addresses a situative variable, since dominance is reliant on at least two participants in an interaction (someone dominating and someone being dominated), and is therefore a relationship (cf. Rollins and Bahr, 1976; Scanzoni and Fox, 1980). The measuring unit for situative variables is the situation which comprises all those present and not a single individual.

Borderline cases are groups like families and work groups with some longevity and which play a central role in the people's lives. Work groups can still be counted as part of the interpersonal situative level, even though they are social structures that survive a relatively long time. In the family, however, the level depends on the concrete research interest. To the extent that the emphasis lies in the micro-genetic group processes, variables describing this process fall under the situative aggregation level. If norms and processes culturally regulated by society have a part to play, the relevant constructs will be subsumable to the third (social-cultural) level. This can probably be accepted as the normal case, since the family in almost all known cultures represents a central place of social reproduction and acculturation of offspring, thereby occupying an important status in the ideological system of every social order.

*(3)*   The variables and concepts of the socio-cultural level represent facts which appear to the individual as quasi-material *a prioris* – that is, as environments which are not subject to personal influence. They are entire societies and cultures, or sub-entities such as classes and subcultures. As with the situative level, concepts are also only to be assigned to this level if they refer to sociocultural structures as a whole. This includes various social institutions, economic phenomena, social-cultural norms, ideologies; but also constructs which identify relationships of power, status and position defined in a sociocultural way, and which are part of the social order. A role would be a position in a social system which sets out rights

and obligations and results in foreseeable behaviour (Merton, 1957a, p. 110). This environment is usually investigated using the research instruments of sociology, economics and cultural or social anthropology. As a result this class of phenomena is not directly accessible to psychological analysis.

### 10.2.3 Explanations, aggregation levels and reduction

In explanations, both explanans and explanandum can come from the three levels of complexity or aggregation defined above. This results in the following model for theoretical clauses in social psychology (Table 10.1).

In this model there are nine cells, of which the cells of the main diagonal line A, B, and C each constitue conceptually homogeneous explanations, where both the fact being explained and the fact to be explained are located at the same level. Cell A includes all psychological and social-psychological theories using intra-personal variables. A theory typical of this would be Anderson's (1974) information integration theory, whose constructs are cognitive elements and processes.

Characteristic of cell B are theories which address relationships between situational constructs. This cell can be illustrated, for example, by various studies on co-operation and competition as a consequence of certain game instructions and pay-off schemes in the social-psychological theory of experimental games. In these studies, both independent and dependent variables are terms which refer to the game situation as a whole. For pay-off schemes this is

TABLE 10.1 Schematic portrayal of the relationship between the *explanantia* and *explananda* of different aggregation levels

| | Level of *explanandum* | | |
|---|---|---|---|
| | Person | Situation | Societal |
| Level of *explanans*: | | | |
| Person | **A** | D | E |
| Situation | G* | **B** | F |
| Societal | H* | I* | **C** |

valid by definition, and likewise for the terms 'co-operation' and 'competition', because they are relational concepts. They refer to a relationship between several people and not to the behaviour of an individual.

Cell C comprises macro-sociological, macro-economic and anthropological theories in which concepts or facts of a high aggregation level are linked to one another. This is obviously not the field of social psychology, but of sociology, economics and some parts of social anthropology.

## Micro-reduction

Explanations or theories in which concepts and facts of lower aggregation levels as *explanans* are linked to facts of higher aggregation levels as *explananda* are what we shall call here micro-reductive explanations. In other words, a reductive explanation is a statement which explains the whole as a function of its parts. Such theories are covered by cells D, E and F in Table 10.1. Galam and Moscovici (1991), for example, use the mathematical-probablistic tool of solid state physics in order to describe the emergence of collective consensus and polarisation from the aggregate of individual reactions. Von Cranach (1992) proposes a multi-level model, with the aid of which the interaction between a social level and individual behaviour can be portrayed as a constant co-ordination of knowledge, cognition, emotion, action and learning.

We do not wish to venture into the details of the debate about reductionism in science. Discussion relating to this is dealt with elsewhere (see e.g. Alexander, 1981; Feyerabend, 1962; Friedman, 1981; von Gadenne, 2004; Hayes, 2002; Kim, 1993; Munro, 1992; Roth, 1981; Schurz, 1988; Spinner, 1973). At present it seems that Kim's (1998) physicalist theory of supervenience provides a particularly suitable model for dealing with reduction.

It seems important to us, however, to define micro-reduction as linking *explanantia* and *explananda* of different aggregation levels with one another at a synchronous level. The *explanans* coexists with the *explanandum*. When we say that the particular interaction of a set of elements explains the phenomenon of a system whole, then the link is 'here and now'. By contrast, some evolutionary theories or theories about development likewise link concepts and phenomena from different aggregation levels. They explicitly

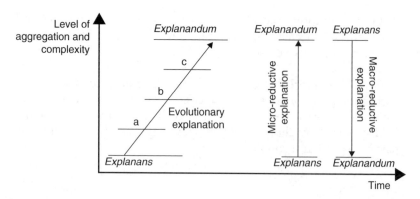

FIGURE 10.1 Evolutionary, micro-reductive and macro-reductive explanations

postulate a process which is relatively extended in time, such that the lower level *explanans* does not coexist with the higher level *explanandum* (cf. also Roth, 1981; and Figure 10.1). This is not just about describing evolutionary processes, but about giving a concrete description of the intermediate mechanisms, which in itself does not infringe the proviso of the intransitivity of explanations (Zilsel, 1976, p. 181).

An example of such an evolutionary theory can be drawn from biology, such as the 'hypercycle theory' by Eigen (1971; cf. also Stegmüller, 1987b). This theory explains the origin of more complex biological molecules from the physical-chemical interactions in a proto-ocean taking effect over a long period of time. In the social sciences, such explanations take on the form of historic or social-evolutionary theories, such as those developed to explain complex state structures and civilisations (e.g. Parsons, 1977; Steward, 1955).

Axelrod (1984) simulated such evolutions with the help of a multi-dimensional prisoner dilemma game; Galam and Moscovici (1991) use the mathematical-probablistic tool of physics in order to describe the emergence of collective consensus and polarisation from the aggregate of individual reactions; and von Cranach (1992) proposes a multi-level model, with the aid of which the interaction between a social level and individual behaviour can be portrayed as a constant co-ordination and folding of knowledge, cognition, emotion, action and learning.

It is clear that theories of the evolutionary type 'explain' the emergence of more complex structures by the preceding interaction of simple elements. At the same time, the explained phenomena – in contrast to the reduction – do not exist before the processes tackled by the theory have been brought into action. However, they do explicate, simultaneously and in detail, the interim elements (a, b, c, in Figure 10.1) accompanying evolution. In this way, they close the explanatory gaps which remain open in a micro-reductive explanation, and therefore do not infringe the proviso of the intransitivity of explanations. Whilst reductive theories hardly seem to prove their worth in the social sciences, evolutionary and historical theories enjoy a central status.

### 10.2.4 Macro-reduction and social representations

There is an odd case represented by statements in which concepts of higher aggregate levels are used to explain a phenomenon at a lower level, as in cells G*, H* and I* (Table 10.1). Such explanations are sometimes called 'holistic' (Alexander, 1981), but here we prefer the term 'macro-reductive' (Friedman, 1981). How can it be that a socio-cultural or a situative concept assumes explanatory power with regard to psychological intra-individual phenomena, as in cells G* or H*? What kind of articulation do we need to conceive for this relationship?

#### Cooking pots

Let us give a simple example to illustrate this problem. Imagine a cooking pot in which water is heated. The temperature can be measured with a thermometer, which is all that is important to us in the 'macro-cosmos' of the cooking pot. Yet if we look at the 'micro-cosmos' of the $H_2O$ molecules, we see them in chaotic movement which increases the higher the temperature measured at the macro-level of the pot. On the micro-level we cannot proceed with our thermometer measurements. At the micro-level, Brownian motion needs concepts other than those that are useful at the macro-level of the cooking pot for its description and explanation. Although there is a close mathematical relationship between temperature and molecular speed of movement, it would be nonsensical to say that molecules move quickly because they have a temperature, or because they are in this cooking pot with the certain temperature; even though this is of course the assumption. In anthropomorphic terms, the molecules are also not disposed to act according to the temperature. The difficulty of articulating between 'macro' and 'micro' is both a problem of measuring and of theory.

If the molecules were subjects, then it would make sense to speak of an intra-individual representation of the temperature condition. Members of a social group have plenty of implicit and explicit knowledge about the conditions of their 'group cooking pot'. This knowledge, be it implicit as a habitus or explicit as a system of rationalisation of, or giving reasons for, their behaviour, constitutes the objectivist (habitus) or subjectivist (reasons for behaviour) explanation for their behaviour at an individual level.

### Taxonomic priority

The significance of the 'cooking pot (macro-) condition' is formulated in philosophy as the taxonomic priority thesis (Harré, 1979, 1980). It means that states, processes, products and structures of lower aggregation levels can only be acknowledged and classified from the superordinate level, but not the other way round; and furthermore, that a particular state of the higher level must conform with one particular state of the lower level, whilst the reverse of the assertion is not true. Several states of the superordinate level can conform with one and the same state of the subordinate level.[9] This means that top-down mapping is unique whereas the bottom-up mapping is ambiguous.

This thesis denies the possibility of micro-reduction, while simultaneously calling for a macro-reductionistic approach in describing and explaining social phenomena. The specific behaviour and thought of individuals attains meaning when it is viewed in the context of social conditions.

Assume we were observing psychotherapists doing their therapeutic work. How do we explain the multitude of sometimes similar and sometimes divergent activities they exhibit? The pattern of individual behaviours constitutes the *explanandum*. The best explanation, indeed, would be to identify the therapeutic schools they subscribe to as an *explanans*; that is, to consider the taxon-

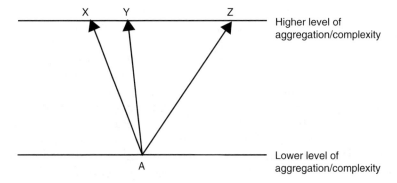

FIGURE 10.2 Taxonomic priority: homomorphic bottom–up mappings

omy and groupings on the superordinate level of social organisations structuring the field of psychotherapy. In doing so we are explaining a behavioral or psychological phenomenon $A$ by using a social fact $X$ under which it appears (Figure 10.2).

Such facts can be situative conditions, for example, the structure and the 'state of play' of an experimental matrix game, or the cultural and social-structural background of the population which makes up the sample. The subsequent 'explanation' would accordingly have the form '$X \to A$', where explanans $X$ and explanandum $A$ are not located within the same aggregation level. Strictly speaking, in this form we could not speak of an explanation but only of a correlation. Phenomenon $A$ constitutes a correlate of a state $X$ which lies outside of the intra-psychic explanation space of $A$. The explanatory context is only hinted at, but not demonstrated. In order to be able to view articulation '$X \to A$' as a strong explanation, it is necessary to project the essential parameters of the social condition $X$ into a state $X^*$, which is located at the aggregation level of the *explanandum*.

In our example it would be necessary to project the rules and prescriptions governing the psychotherapeutic behaviour of a school on to the level of the therapist in the form of a representation of therapeutic methods and/or professional identity. Only a theoretical statement of the form '$X^* \to A$' would represent an explanation in the strict sense. Taking no account of the interim step $X^*$ violates the intransitivity of explanation discussed above. Translating from $X$ to $X^*$ can thus have a thoroughly correlative character and $X^*$ can be a predicate of disposition. The relationship '$X^* \rightarrow A$' constitutes a content-rational description that we identified earlier as a non-causal explanation of behaviour.

Social representations have been defined on the one hand as individual theory-like mental constructs, and on the other as social processes of discourse which are closely connected to the social relationships within which they are formed and assimilated. As individual mental structures they are therefore a theoretical construct which: (a) satisfies the demand of taxonomic priority, since their definition and description demands that the trans-individual social context be taken into account. They are also a construct which can only be grasped taking the superordinate social level as a starting point, and thus simultaneously achieving: (b) the translation of sociostructural and cultural conditions into individual dispositions. If one understands the social condition of a social entity as an attribute of the entity as a whole – as a collective plurality (Harré, 1984) – then social representations are the mapping of this collective characteristic on to an individually accessible disposition that is distributed or shared across a group.

At the same time, understanding social representations as a social discourse constitutes a construct which: (c) virtually fills the intermediate processes between the individual and the sociocultural. The theory of discourse or the epidemiology of social representations, concerns the 'demergent' processes mediating between macro and individual aggregation levels. In this position social representation functions as a transformation process between individual and collective levels (Martin and Royer-Rastoll, 1990). The theory of social representations is therefore a macro-reductive attempt to grasp explicitly the articulation between the social and the individual, on a conceptual level.

## 10.3  A circular theory?

If one takes the theory of social representations literally and investigates its implications, it becomes evident that the constituent principles are mutually interdependent. We demonstrated that social representations emerge during the collective discourse in a social unit, that they comprise or describe the actions and interactions by social participants with real or imagined social 'objects', that they have to be potentially accessible to all members of a group (functional consensus), that they display holomorphic characteristics, and, finally, that they thus define the social identity of the group members, who are thereby able to regard themselves as an entity, that is to say, a reflexive group (Potter and Wetherell, 1987, p. 142 onwards).

The majority of these concepts, such as 'social representations', 'reflexive group' and 'social identity' appear to define each other mutually, and therefore constitute a set of recursive or circular concepts. Due to their close interdependence, the meaning of any one concept within the theory cannot be established independently of the others, with the effect that they resemble Sneed's 'T-theoretical' concepts (1979, in Stegmüller, 1986).

According to Sneed, a term $t$ is T-theoretical within a theory $T$ if the reading of $t$ assumes theory $T$ to be valid. Stegmüller illustrates this using the physical theory of the lever whose empirical examination assumes the existence of defined masses or weights. Yet in order to be able to determine weight during an elementary act of weighing, masses have to brought into balance using levers. The act of measuring assumes as fact the validity of the principle of the lever.[10]

In our case we could say that if the proposition 'that $t$ applies', where $t$ may be the concept of a reflexive group, assumes theory $T$, that is, social representation theory, to be valid, then we are presented with a (soft) t-theoretical form. For example, any social entity whatsoever could simply be defined as a group on the basis of structural and sociofunctional characteristics. But in order to ensure that one is dealing with a *reflexive* group, one cannot avoid establishing at least part of the members' representation system, since the representation system has a lot to do with social identity and the sense of belonging. While the first observation does not presuppose the theory of social representations to be valid, the second observation is very much based on it, since the representation system is itself a result of group membership. Consequently, social representations cannot be ascertained without prior knowledge of individuals' reflexive belonging; yet the belonging cannot be ascertained without at least elementary knowledge of the representations. The terms are theoretically interdependent (Figure 10.3).

Hence, if social representation theory were indeed circular, this would not necessarily diminish the heuristic value of the theory in describing and explaining empirical facts. Its circularity, however,

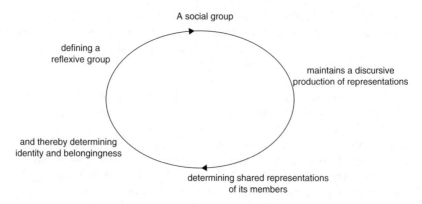

FIGURE 10.3 The soft T-theoretical circular structure of the theory of social representations

suggests that its concepts contain very specific meanings that are guaranteed only within the bounds of the theory. Such circular theories, in which theoretical terms mutually presuppose each other, do not occur only in the social sciences. Comparable theoretical structures are also found in the theory of evolution, as well as in the theory of relativity and quantum theory. Despite their high validity and prognostic power within their field of application, an accepted mathematical solution that combines both theories of physical science has yet to be found (Hawking, 1988). It seems that theories can be conceptually 'closed', yet be nevertheless of heuristic and empirical value. However, this does not mean that circularity should stay with us. In the long run, despite or because of its circular conceptual structure, social representation theory is well advised in trying to connect to one or the other theories flourishing in the social sciences so abundantly.

## 10.4 A note on reference populations and the concept of the 'individual'

### 10.4.1 Reference populations in social psychology

The sciences are distinguished from one another by greatly differing criteria. These can refer to the object, the method, or the historical or traditional derivation of a particular science. Whenever the social requirements, technology or political conditions which form the foundations of a particular strand of science change, then the names, contents and methods of this science, and the traditions supporting it, also change.

What general definitional criteria could apply to psychology, that is to say, to social psychology in particular? First, there is the type of object. On the one hand the object in social psychology is understood as: (a) the social animal (Aronson, 1980a) as distinct from the – not necessarily social – being in general psychology whose area of research may also include Kaspar-Hauser-types. On the other hand, the object in social psychology is often determined as: (b) the sum of all psychological processes with social content (e.g. Perlman and Cozby, 1983) or, in other words, as the 'science of the interactions between individuals' (Herkner, 1981, p. 16). Although both examples do not give an exhaustive account of all current definitional criteria, they do characterise the substantial aspect of this theme.

The problem arising from this determinative criterion of 'social psychology' is its indeterminability. If social psychology decides to make research into the characteristic features of the 'social animal' its objective, the parameters that delimit it from general psychology or human ethology exist at best in the methodology – for example, the use of questionnaires – but not in the content. As such, the theories of all these three sciences refer to the human species to the same extent.

A common alternative is to determine the object in social psychology with regard to psychological processes in which social contents, that is to say, other people, opinions about them, socially relevant facts and so on play a substantial role. This is, indeed, the most frequently employed criterion in the relevant textbooks. Allport (1924, p. 3) wrote: 'Social psychology is an attempt to understand and explain how the thought, feeling, and behaviour of individuals are influenced by the actual, imagined, or implied presence of others.' Accordingly, the object in social psychology is not the social individual in general, but certain processes, thought, feeling and behaviour which refer to specific contents and the actual, imaginary or indirect presence of others. All processes or their elements which process social stimuli are therefore part of social psychology. Things, animals and abstract entities, such as street lights, domestic birds in cages and the idea of mathematical terms, are part of general psychology.

In order to consider this further, the specific features of the theories adopted by social psychology need to be described using four dimensions:

1. The first dimension refers to the group of living beings – the population whose behavioural and other features are examined by human or social science. The population in social psychology is the species *Homo sapiens*.
2. The second dimension refers to the human phenomena and expressions of life which represent, as it were, the dependent variable of scientific examinations. These variables include, for example, features of social behaviour or psychological and experiential conditions. In theoretical explanations this dimension includes the number of possible *explananda*.
3. The third dimension consists of the set of criteria which allows categorisation of the field of independent variables. In 'classical' social psychology these are different stimuli situations, whose various effects on the dependent variables are of interest. In explanations these are *explanantia* or independent variables.
4. The fourth dimension describes the type of theoretical statement which can be inferred from the process of a specific research method. Since human and social scientific hypothetico-deductive research and descriptive research are always based on the comparison of at least two expressions of one independent variable, a theoretical explanation is always preceded by a superordinate theoretical statement which has to establish and consequently explain the relation between the categories of the independent variable. In social psychology these statements usually refer to differences in behaviour and experience derived from situational stimuli.[11]

In contrast to other social sciences, such as ethnology and certain orientations of sociology, this definition does not include an element which could describe the object or the problems of social psychology according to a criterion relevant to a population. For example, ethnology refers to the characteristics of different tribes, ethnic groups and cultures with regard to historical and developmental differentiation (Tischner, 1959, p. 7). By placing greater emphasis on the habitual and lasting features of society, anthropology takes an interest in the universal and also the individual characteristics of society (Beattie, 1964, p. 12ff.). Apart from being a description of the institutional and cultural characteristics of ethnic groups, differences between peoples can also be regarded as *explananda* which can be explained on the basis of general laws, formulated by cross-discipline research by cultural and social anthropology: the universalising branch of ethnology. The species *Homo sapiens* provides the framework in which tribes, ethnic groups and cultures are subjected to a comparative examination.

Social psychology, in the way it is usually understood, obviously deals with general human behaviour and experience, which depend on situational and other stimuli conditions. It is concerned with the universal aspects of the species (Lonner, 1980). Cross-cultural social psychology – at least in its classic incarnation – is no exception either. Its objective is to determine the intercultural field of validity of psychological phenomena which were initially examined in laboratories in the Western industrialised nations (G. Jahoda, 1970, Pepitone and Triandis, 1988). The search for universals, while being a legitimate and important objective, at the same time limits the potential field of social psychological research. Even where it claims to deal with society and culture, it only examines human nature (G. Jahoda, 1986).

Hence social psychology as already discussed in Chapter 2 represents a subfield of general psychology which relates to humans as a species. General psychology searches for obvious explanations for individual human behaviour and experience (Rohracher, 1966).

Behaviour first and foremost means activities and processes which can be judged objectively, that is to say, the isolated reactions of muscles, glands and other parts of the organism, and also the organised, directed external reaction patterns which characterise the organism as a whole. By the term 'behaviour' psychologists also understand internal processes, such as thinking, emotional reactions etc., which one person cannot observe in another but which can, nonetheless, be inferred from observations of external behaviour.

(Zimbardo, 1983, p. 25)

The reference population of general psychology comprises the whole of humanity, that is, the psychological and/or biological species *Homo sapiens*. Psychological explanations can refer to the entire human population or a part thereof, such as particular personality types. But even when they refer only to subgroups of the entire human population, the statements, as in ethology, can potentially be applied to the other units of the entire population. The statements of psychology cannot refer to infra-human beings meaningfully, apart from a few exceptions which consequently leave room for doubt as to whether they are really part of psychological theoretical language. By breaking this rule one will find oneself accused of anthropomorphism.

Hence psychology seeks the determining factors of human experience and behaviour. Differential ontogenetic and micro-genetic learning conditions can condition behavioural preferences and the disposition generally described as personality. The analysed mechanisms are, however, in any case principally valid for all members of a species, be they iNko-aboriginies or New York yuppies. Even though traditionally living iNko-people lack certain intellectual abilities – at a basic level this is knowledge of writing or abstract logical thinking – they are, in principle, capable of them if confronted with the relevant learning environment. Conversely, under suitable conditions, a European would also be able to learn the skills of reading animal tracks, finding roots, and coping with whatever life in the Kalahari desert may throw at them; if perhaps to a lesser degree.

In this context, the species *Homo sapiens* forms a biological and psychological unity. Because of the methodically desirable and theoretically demanded generality of psychological statements and explanations, it is a logical consequence that the specifically human biological, genetic, neurological processes which underlie psychological events have to be allowed to expand the language of psychological and theoretical explanations.

For example, neuropsychology, that is to say, biopsychology, is a typical case in point. It 'must deal with all biological processes that can be seen as a direct substrate of the psychological' (Guttmann, 1972, p. 7f.). The integration of biological terminology into the language of psychology does not deserve to be accused of biological reduction, so long as the terms describing biological substrates are only considered to be correlates and not *explanantia* (cf. Dewsbury, 1991). Nor does this expansion of the language necessarily imply a genetic determinism.

The stimuli used in general psychology often have social characteristics, such as the use of terms loaded with meaning in word association. The type of stimulus, whether social or not, is obviously not a sufficient differential feature of general as opposed to social psychology.

In order to investigate the social determination of individuals, it is not enough to examine the universal aspect of human social behaviour. What use is rough knowledge about psychological and behavioural dispositions which apply to the entire species in the characterisation of individuals who face us as specific subjects of investigation? Is the physiological ability of the liver to break down alcohol an explanation as to why we drink alcohol? Or is the anatomy of hand and arm an explanation as to why we eat with knives and forks? Physiology, anatomy and psychological capacities which apply to the entire species are a prerequisite for the differential formation of the specific subject. They are, however, no more than the framework within which human beings socialise and find their culture.

The *anthropos* as a representative of the species appears as a representative of a culture, a society, a social class, a family, a gender and so on – that is to say, as a member not only of the biological species but also of social groups. Therefore it seems obvious to suggest certain basic definitions of the object which are determined not only by the type of stimulus, but also the type of reference population to which any given human science refers. The comparative reference to partial populations, be they different social or ethnic groups, is an important basis for sociological and ethnological orientation. Their reference population, that is, the entire human population to which their opinions refer, seems compartmentalised into subunits, whereby the interpretation of behavioural differences is the basis for the development of superordinate theories. Generalised opinions stem from the empirically and theoretically determined comparison of populations.

Social psychology differs from this. The contents of this science are – as with general psychology – all theories and findings whose validity extends to the individual as a representative of the species *Homo sapiens* from the outset. By necessity, social phenomena that can be expected to apply to and are correct for the entire human species fall into the field of research of general psychology. This general claim for validity results from the lack of theoretically defined partial populations which could form the basis for comparative work. Comparison is to a large degree limited to situations and stimuli.

Consequently, the relevant reference populations of a comparative social psychology would be sociocultural subcategories of the species *Homo sapiens*. All theories and statements that – weakly formulated – cannot be assumed to be valid for the entire species, or that – more strongly formulated – cannot be shown to be valid for entire species but only for a subunit, a culture or society or the like would be the subject of a comparative social psychology. This results in the demand that the theories explicitly state the field of validity, that is, the reference population, and additionally state why this particular association and no other should display the phenomenon in the expected form. It requires a theoretical reference to a level of analysis which lies above individual aspects, and can describe and explain the differences between social units. For example, it is not enough simply to record that the explanatory theoretical statement X is valid for members of population P. It must also explain why X cannot be applied to population Q. This requires the concepts of sociology as well as general psychology, since both allow for general perspectives. Baldwin formulated a similar view: 'The need became apparent for a . . . social psychology, which would reveal the state of the individual mind in given social conditions' (1913, p. 106). In detail this refers to the relationship between individual and collective representations.

A replication attempt of recognised experiments carried out by Amir and Sharon (1988) etablishes the minimum demand for naming the reference population to which a socio-psychological statement refers further credibility. The authors chose a random 30 findings from a large number of articles published in important American journals and tried to replicate them in Israel, observing the original experimental procedures. They used experimental participants from the same social groups – in most cases students – as well as experimental participants from different groups than the original samples. Out of a total of 30 experiments, only six displayed intercultural and inter-social-class stability, four could be replicated only at the same social level, and the remaining experiments produced different outcomes.

If replication of narrowly defined experiments which do not even take into account the variety of everyday living conditions fails, and even when they are carried out in an economically similar society such as Israel, the claim for a universal social psychology is greatly diminished. They do, however, demonstrate even more pressingly that social psychology requires additional complements which are oriented along partial populations and a comparative viewpoint. This would warrant developing a differential social psychology. Now we would like to determine what is understood by the 'individual' in the context of a reference population.

## 10.4.2 The subjective individual versus social individuals

Generally, an individual is regarded as an elementary component of a superordinate unit that includes several people. This banal statement, however, directly implies that it is necessary to distinguish between several forms of individual being, because it requires the point of reference from the superordinate unit in order to define the concept 'individual'. If the superordinate unit plays an important role, then it is no longer immaterial which unit is at the centre of research interest.

On the one hand, an individual can be understood as a representative of the species *Homo sapiens*. This role suffices for the classic understanding of the individual whose mental processes provide the object of general psychology. The processes mentioned are processes in the strictest sense (cf. Chapter 2.2) and are derived from the common biological basis of the species. As an elementary component of the most general reference population, this concept is also the most abstract, since during our research we are never faced with an individual as representative of the species, but always as a representative of a particular social membership. As we have tried to show in Chapter 2.2 and the following chapters, research into the individual as an individual posits comprehensive comparisons between people with the most varied cultural identities. Only then is it possible to ascertain that the mental phenomena can be considered to be a constant of the species, and to be psychological processes in the strictest sense.

Strictly speaking, subjectivity, in the sense of 'subjective' or truly 'private' and idiosyncratic knowledge, can only be discussed in relation to individuals as conceptual complements of the human species. The singularity of an individual deriving from the understanding of subjectivity – their distinctness from all others – makes sense only on this very abstract level. The commonality of individuals as individuals stems from their sharing the same features of psychological processes. The content of these processes is arbitrary – completely peripheral – and therefore subjective, undetermined and singular.

The explanations of cultural psychology and of the theory of social representations refer to a different understanding of the individual. Here the reference population is a theoretically well-defined sub-unit of the species. Research focuses on the mental functions of representatives of specific groups whose parameters are defined by cultural or social criteria. The construct of the individual as a representative of a given social unit is found on a different level of the conceptual hierarchy, as is the construct of the individual qua individual.

The individual as a representative of the species, as a subjective individual, can be regarded as an individual being independent from others. This is not true for the representative of a group. Members of a group derive their specific features, the contents of their knowledge systems, their varying experiences of emotions and so on from the context of the other members and the structured life of the group. Their specific features, and hence their subjectivity as it were, can only have meaning in the context of the socio-cultural structure of their environment.

If the definition of the construct 'individual' is determined on the basis of which reference population we refer to, then the distinction also has a bearing on the question 'How can I explain the behaviour of any given individual?" Before this question can be answered, the reference population of the individual in question has to be clarified, since it is the only means of setting the parameters of the explanatory space. In looking at one and the same person it is vitally important whether the research focuses on the person as a representative of the human species, or as, say, a farmer in Brittany.

In our opinion, the question as to whether human behavioural determinants can be resolved by any given method is the subject of mostly unproductive discussions between some emphatically experimental psychologists and some of those demonstrably working with qualitative methods. The majority of these discussions can be traced back to a confusion of the above-mentioned interpretations of the concept 'individual'. The discussions deal only superficially with the method itself. It is rather a case of each side using a different level of formulation of the question as the basis for their discussion: on the one hand, the fundamental psychological processing characteristics of individuals;[12] on the other, an investigation of a specific socio-culturally developed actor. Each method has its own place in the correctly defined explanatory space. The importance given to ecological validity as a criterion for research methods also depends on this. The validity of a method can only be determined with regard to the formulation of the question, the abstractness of the understanding of the concept 'individual' and therefore the reference population.

# Chapter 11

# Methods in Social Representation Research

## 11.1 Defining and diagnosing social representations

In an earlier chapter we offered a definition of the term 'social representation' which became the basis for the subsequent text. The definition established the parameters of the field, proposing and substantiating the structure of the model through a logical integration of observations. To conclude this book we shall now attempt a definition which brings together the main statements and correlates of the theory according to the logic of the subject.

By a social representation, we understand a historical social process of elaboration, communication and dissemination of knowledge systems. This process is public and develops in heterodox societies, that is to say, reflexive groups who collectively rationalise their practice in the face of new and existing conditions in their everyday life in the context of their knowledge systems – that is, by the symbolic interpretation of their practice, or by explanatory justification and assessment. This knowledge system simultaneously embraces rules for practice which ensure the concerted co-operation of action and behaviour tendencies. It also provides the epistemic tools for coping symbolically with the novel. Opinions and judgements transmitted within a culture, popularised and therefore simplified opinions from scientific rather than every day knowledge systems, as well as experiences, judgements and justifications which stem from past political events and the sociostructural position of the group, all serve as content and justification elements. This collective knowledge system is on the one hand a social *a priori* for individual group members, but is, on the other hand, subject to continuous changes.

Group members acquire these epistemic knowledge systems by either actively or passively participating in the public process of social representation. They are distributed representations, which reflect an individual's thoughts, emotions and actions with respect to society. From a metatheoretical standpoint, their acquisition appears to be a macro-reduction of individual events to social events, since individual contents derive from the discourse proceeding on a social level.

The resulting knowledge system available to individuals appears to form a complex network corresponding to a theory. It has a structure containing core and peripheral elements, a specific form (usually in the shape of a figurative scheme or metaphor) and an epistemic function, allowing the interpretation of events and allowing the co-ordinated actions with interacting partners. Furthermore it is holomorphic because it provides the individual not only with their own alternative courses of action, but also with those that can be expected from the other interacting partner. Thus this knowledge system, whose collective basis is known to the social actors, forms the foundation for the social identity of the group members.

Social actors objectify or reify their representations through concerted interactions, and by seemingly orientating their social actions according to their social systems of knowledge – the distributed representations. Representations constitute the meaning and relations of real or imaginary objects. The relation between representations and behaviour patterns is more of a description than a causal connection between representation and action.

Defining a theoretical term and giving diagnostic criteria are two different tasks which allow us to comprehend the phenomenon which the term describes empirically. Criteria are also imperative for the differential diagnosis of similar theoretical constructs, such as, for example, opinions, attitudes, subjective theories and the like. There is no room here for a full discussion of this question, but we would like to raise a few points which follow compellingly from the previous line of argument.

A (new) social representation will be present in a group when the collective behaviour and thinking of all or the majority of members is markedly different from their previous behaviour and thinking (Himmelweit, 1990). The emphasis here is on the behaviour of a large number of people, belonging to a reflexive group with a representational project (M. Bauer and Gaskell, 1999). It is not enough for just some individuals to modify their opinions and their behaviour. In a fictive group, for example, if some people suddenly started their breakfast with muesli instead of bread and jam, we could only speak of it as a new *social* representation after those individuals had integrated this food preference into their implicit theory about a healthy and 'normal' diet; and had begun to regard themselves as a group, for example, one with ecological awareness. As long as this is not the case, the food preference is more likely to be a personal attitude.

In most cases representational work and collective symbolic coping will be initiated by societal conflict. The discourse instigated by the conflict provides the basic data for identifying an underlying representational structure. Hence, it is a good rule of thumb to identify the conflicting parties and reasons for dispute in any research.

Social representations usually refer to relevant objects or facts. They are relevant only if their emergence leads to a change in the behaviour of the actors or the collective practice of the group (Sperber and Wilson, 1986). If, for example, the pattern of interaction in several interacting partners changes when meeting a person with learning difficulties, then the fact of these learning difficulties is socially relevant. If the same actors meet an introverted person and their pattern of interaction does not change – apart from perhaps including the introvert in the conversation – then 'introversion' does not seem to be socially relevant in the given context. One can therefore speak of a social representation of learning difficulties, while introversion is not really an independent social object (apart, however, from its possible conceptual integration into an overarching representation of psychological phenomena).

As a consequence of public social representation processes, and because they function as models for socially orientated interactions, social representations are holomorphic. This adjective describes their characteristics: concerted interactions are only possible if socially interacting partners know not only their own, but also the alternative courses of action of their co-actors. If people co-ordinate their actions in a situation whose meaning is socially represented, an individual will not be surprised by another's adequate behaviour. Should the partners act in an unexpected way, then those affected will have to ask themselves if they are presupposing divergent representations. This is where actual subjective courses of action differ.

Representations also require holomorphic aspects so that they can become an important part of social identity. If a person identifies with a given group, that person will be aware of the system of justification and of the ideological foundation of the group's practice. The self-image of the entire group – its attitude to other groups, the ideologised image of its historical origin and so on – becomes a more or less complete part of the members' knowledge as relevant to their identity. Social representations thus comprise an image of the whole of the group – also and especially when they are distributively considered to be a characteristic of the individual: they are holomorphic. If a person is unable to state for which group their knowledge about 'correct' behaviour and important objects is valid, then that knowledge does not constitute social identity; and the loss or the change of knowledge – for example resulting from others trying to convert them – will not affect their social identity.

This brings us to the last criterion mentioned here: the necessity to identify a reflexive group whose interactive practice is validated by the social representation. It does not matter, for example, which individuals or group members can be observed to share a 'dislike of spinach'. Despite its widespread prevalence – we assume this to be true from personal experience – hardly anyone asked about it would be able to say which group would be typified by this preference in taste. The dislike is not tied to a reflexive group. Our extensive dietary belief systems, however, can instantly be related to a national and/or cultural (e.g. British cuisine, Indian cuisine, kosher cuisine), geographical (e.g. European cuisine) or quasi-ideological (e.g. vegetarian or macrobiotic cuisine) group.

The diagnostic criteria mentioned here make no claims to be complete. They emphasise aspects of the theory of social representations which arise on a theoretical level. Adapting them to suit empirical methods is quite another problem. Some of these criteria are taken into account explicitly during investigations. Most, however, are not, or only implicitly. Perhaps this incomplete list may prompt a clearer classification of the phenomena that are examined as social representations. We hope that this may prevent empirical papers which run the risk of examining nothing more than attitude patterns from coming under the banner of 'social representations'.

## 11.2  Methods in research

### 11.2.1  Research foci

There are many excellent textbooks presenting research methodology in social psychology which are also useful for social representation research. Some of these are on methods in general
(e.g. Breakwell, Hammond and Fife-Schaw, 1995; Hayes, 2000;
Langdridge, 2004); on qualitative methods in general (e.g. M. Bauer
and Gaskell, 2000; Denzin and Lincoln, 1994; Flick, von Kardoff
and Steinke, 2004; Hayes, 1997; Miles and Huberman, 1994;
Robson, 1993; Strauss, 1987); on computer-aided qualitative analysis (e.g. M. Bauer and Gaskell, 2000; Kelle, 1995; Weitzman and
Miles, 1995); and the long list of texts on quantitative methodology
of which multivariate methods for categorical data are the most
relevant (e.g. Greenacre, 1993; van de Geer, 1993a, 1993b; Weller
and Romney, 1990). Then there are a few sources with particular
emphasis on social representation research (Breakwell and Canter,
1993; Doise, Clémence and Lorenzi-Cioldi, 1993). An interesting
book suggesting bridges between qualitative and quantitative analysis is Ragin's *The Comparative Method* (1987).

In giving research examples in this section, we find it helpful to
order them according to the so-called 'Toblerone' model (M. Bauer
and Gaskell, 1999; and see Figure 11.1).

This model adds a time perspective to the person-group-object
triangle (Figure 4.1) and thereby completes the social process. The
circles in Figure 11.1 unite the parameters of three distinct research
orientations that can be found in empirical work on social representations: a focus on the persons' relationship with an object, that
is, the organisation and structure of representations; a focus on the
persons' role in group communication and discourse relating to an
object; and a comprehensive focus on the historical development
of a representational system. It is important to note, however, that
focusing on the first realm does not mean that research cannot
also take account of the other aspects, that is, group processes and
history. Our grouping is in this sense more an aid for orientation
than a strict categorisation. Further, we do not imply in what
follows that the methods presented in the context of a particular
research focus are exclusive to these foci. Each and every
method can be applied to all of the research interests, though with
caution.

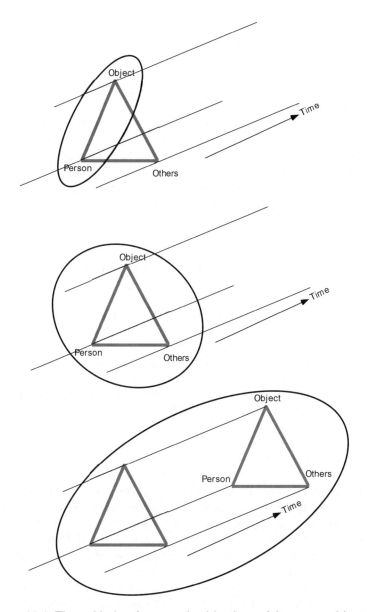

FIGURE 11.1 Three kinds of research objectives: (a) person-object dynamics; (b) person-object-group dynamics; (c) historical dynamics (adapted from M. Bauer and Gaskell, 1999)

At this point allow us a comment that is not specific to social representation research and has been extensively discussed in anthropology (e.g. Augé, 1982; Geertz, 1984, 1988; Spiro, 1990): This is the conspicuous absence of the researcher in the diagram of Figure 11.1. In all research having to do with culture and common sense researchers are more a participant than an observer in the research field and bring in their own culture and common sense. This makes them foreigners not only to other cultures but also to groups that are not their own, and challenges their interpretations of quantitative and qualitative results alike. Here is not the place to discuss this issue extensively (see Chapter 4), but only to draw attention to an issue that is all too easily overlooked (Arruda, 2003).

## 11.2.2 Persons and objects: experiments and interviews[1]

By far the most frequent research focus found in the literature is concerned with people and how they represent objects. The methods used range from psychological experiments, word associations and survey questionnaires, to qualitative interviews. After a brief discussion of experimentation we will present research on thinking about democracy in newly emerging capitalist societies and on thinking about androgyny.

### Experimentation

Experimentation poses a specific problem for research on social representations. Since representations are representations of local worlds and of actors; and because experimental situations, particularly in laboratories, themselves carry social meaning, the researcher necessarily becomes part of the subject's interpretation of the experimental situation. This problem is not unique to social representation research, but it is within the frame of this theory that its potential consequences become acutely important (Farr, 1976, 1984).

For experimentation it is necessary to have a detailed knowledge of the relevant semantics and symbolism, which can only be discovered by exploratory approaches. Due to their sharedness, and to their being part and parcel of social reality, social representations are not destined to play the part of dependent variables in experimental designs. It is virtually inconceivable that we could produce something which comes close to a representation by the short-term manipulations typical of experiments. The place where representations have entered experimental designs is as independent variables. Used as independent variables, social representations can be strictly tested for specific contents and characteristics. Experiments on social representation processes reveal their structure, organisation and action components. The results of such experiments are, however, never universal, but always limited to the specific population and group to which the subjects pertain. Several experimental studies have been presented in some detail in Chapters 6 and 7 to serve as examples.

Some experiments done in the structural core–periphery approach have a special status. They use lists of attributes of a supposed socially represented object and let subjects judge whether the object remains the same if one or more of the attributes is being negated (Moliner, 2002). These 'ambiguous scenario' or 'attribute challenging' techniques allow the separation of central attributes, that are crucial for the meaning attributed to an object, from attributes that are not, that is, those that are peripheral. We presented some of these experiments in detail in Chapter 6.

## Questionnaires

Survey and interview studies have been extensively used to extract a description of representations pooled across individuals. In this kind of study, it becomes clear that whenever we study individuals, we are simultaneously looking at how they relate to others and to their group. Markovà's and her collaborators' work on the understanding of democracy in the transition process from socialism to capitalism is a prime example. The main interest of this project was not political, economic and historical phenomena as such, but was how these different phenomena were represented in the minds of ordinary people, and how they were expressed in their language and communication. In view of these historical events the following questions were asked: 'Do people in the post-communist countries of Central Europe, after 40 years of totalitarian collectivism, still adhere to the values of the common European heritage?'; 'What is the meaning of "the individual" today, in Western democracies and in Central European post-communist nations?'; 'Which issues are important for the well-being of the individual and how do they relate to the political and economic circumstances of those individuals?'; 'What is the meaning of "democracy" in the nations with a traditional democratic system and in those who were subjected to totalitarian collectivism and who lived in "people's democracies"?'. It was conceivable that for people in post-communist countries 'democracy' could be affiliated with negative images of violence and force against particular persons and minorities.

Propaganda tries to transform ideology into culture, make it a part of common sense (Moscovici, 1961/1976; Moscovici and Markovà, 1998). When living in a particular social, cultural and political system, people unreflectively adopt the ideas and ways of thinking which are implicitly imposed upon them by that system. Even if they disagree and oppose that system at a conscious level, the system creates and defines their social reality and pervades daily language. Representations are expressed through language; and at the same time, language itself is an object of social representations. It is the interdependence between language and social representations that was explored in the following study.

The study used multiple methods (word-association tasks, rating scales, questionnaires, interviews and discussion groups) to capture different levels of awareness of the respondents (Markovà, 1996; Moodie, Markovà and Plichtova, 1995). The samples were from six European nations and comprised about 2600 respondents in each nation and from two generations. The older generation was born around the time of the communist take-over in Central and Eastern Europe. The younger generation was born around the period of the Soviet invasion of Czechoslovakia in 1968 and grew up during the period of so-called 'normalisation'. Data from word associations and rating scales were collected twice: in 1994 with a focus on individual and social-collective issues, and in 1996 with a focus on democracy and the individual.

In the word-association task, respondents were presented in both 1994 and in 1996, with political, ideological and economic terms. These particular terms referred to important political and economic phenomena in Central and Western Europe. Rating scales contained the same terms as the word-association tasks and respondents were asked to rate each of the items on the scales to find out how these terms were important for the individual, or for the local community, or for democracy.

Word associations were studied using semantic space analysis and content analysis. The former was carried out to represent the structure of associations, initially by calculating similarity matrices for the distribution of the frequency of associations to each stimulus word. Second, those matrices were subjected to multi-dimensional scaling, resulting in a two-dimensional graphic representation (cf. Spini, 2002). Terms with similar distributions of associations appeared close together, while unrelated terms appeared more distantly on the plot. The plot then represented a descriptive map of terms and their clusters. It was found that the structures of the representations of 'the individual', 'the community' and 'democracy' were formed, in all cases, by the core terms (freedom, justice, human rights, self-determination). These were relatively stable across all six nations. By contrast, the flexible periphery terms appeared to depend on the economic, ideological and political circumstances of the nations involved.

Content analysis of associations to 'the individual', 'the community' and 'democracy' corroborated the existence of a stable core, with 'freedom' being the most frequent association for all three terms. However, while for the Western nations 'community' was represented as a positive and meaningful concept (although often as something belonging to the past), in the post-communist nations, community was destroyed during the years of communist domination and was represented as a negative or meaningless concept (Markovà, Moodie and Plichtova, 1998).

These studies showed that social representations are structured and contain some relatively stable and some relatively flexible components at different hierarchical levels. It also became clear in the studies that these structures are not static. They are processes that are reconstructed in the socioeconomic conditions in which they take place.

## Word associations

As a further example we present a study on androgyny using, among others, the method of *word associations* (Lorenzi-Cioldi, 1994). The author postulates three conceptions of androgyny, according to an emphasis on the content or on the structure of the androgynous personality. The author suggests that these three types of androgyny have emerged not only among psychologists, but also in people's lay representations.

In one part of the study 48 respondents gave spontaneous answers to the question, 'What comes to mind when thinking about androgyny?'. Multiple-choice questions then invited the participants to specify which target people they thought of when responding to the open question. Questions were worded as: 'Did you think of a man, a woman, a person in general or anybody else?' and 'Did you think of someone in particular, for example an acquaintance, a famous person or anybody else?' Before the statistical analysis, the responses were slightly simplified and synonyms, singulars and plurals homogenised. The simplified responses comprised a total of about 700 words, with 40 per cent of them distinct. That was followed by the analysis of a matrix, cross-tabulating individual respondents of the 77 words mentioned by at least two participants.

The respondents-by-words matrix was subjected to a lexical correspondence analysis (Doise, Clémence and Lorenzi-Cioldi, 1993; Lorenzi-Cioldi, 1997). This method clusters words according to their co-occurrence. Specifically, two words stand closer in space if they are associated in the answers of several participants, and are located farther away from other words to which they are less associated.[2] Proximal words are considered a key to the contents of social representations of androgyny. Social and other attributes of respondents can also be projected into the word-correspondence space. The positions of these attributes relative to the word clusters provide information about which class of respondents produced which word clusters about androgyny.

The results show the opposition of a symbolic and abstract androgyny and a more concrete and personified one. The first pole includes 'neither masculine nor feminine', 'neither man nor woman' and the word 'non-identity', each of which characterise androgyny in a transcendent way. The passive variables attest to this: alternative androgyny being perceived as a sublimated wholeness. Androgyny appears here as the exclusive reference to generic 'persons'.

On one pole of the second dimension, there are words like 'harmonious opposite', 'entirety', 'archetype', 'totality'. Associated with 'ideal', these words disclose a positively valued androgyny. On the other pole we find words like 'notorious women', 'womanish man' and 'mannish woman', 'homosexual', 'ambiguous' or 'confusion' together with the qualifiers 'disturbing' and 'mysterious'. This contrast seems to fit well with a distinction between the interiority and the appearance of the androgyne. It is also a separation of its most abstract, positively valued, and most concrete, often negative, components. On the concrete side, androgyny is bound to everyday life and to the discourse of the media, and remains more of a paradoxical and even deviant unity.

Interesting facts emerge from the positioning of the passive variables (target people). References to a 'man' likened to a generic 'person' appear on the pole of interiority. Conversely, the 'famous person', as well as the exclusive reference to the 'woman' and the simultaneous designation of both sexes, appear toward concrete androgyny. Thus, the referent's prototype for the most abstract definition of androgyny is 'man' taken in isolation, or linked to a 'person' in general. When androgyny is in a way carved in the bodies and attitudes of famous people, the referents focus on the 'woman' or else on both sexes simultaneously.

A correspondence analysis brings to light very diverse structural principles of the social representation of androgyny. On the whole, it shows that androgyny cannot do easily without a concrete figure of the androgyne featuring an ambiguous and troublesome being, womanish man or mannish woman, or even homosexual.

There are several other methods that have been used for a structural decomposition of word associations and other questionnaire data. All start off from a similarity – or from the complement, a distance – matrix mapping words or questionnaire items. The matrices are then analysed by multi-dimensional scaling techniques (Purkhardt and Stockdale, 1993; Spini, 2002); network models (Capozza, Falvo, Robusto, and Orlando, 2003); graph-theoretical algorithms (Roussiau, 2002) or others. Methods based on 'Kelly-like' grid analysis have a slightly different structure, but fall broadly into the same category (Fransella, 1984; Green, Muncer, Heffernan, and McManus, 2003). Which of these methods is best for the present research purpose is a tricky question. Sometimes different techniques of structural decomposition do not converge on comparable solutions and give space to arbitary decisions (Bergmann, 1999). Whatever decision is taken, it will need to be well argued in theoretical as well as methodological terms.

## 11.2.3 Persons, groups and objects: ethnography, focus-groups, text analyses and media studies

When it comes to highlighting the interaction of persons within groups in the elaboration of an object and its representation, the most interesting and helpful methods are ethnography, focus-groups, interviews and media studies. In his classical study on psychoanalysis, Moscovici (1961/1976) used several of these methods to assess the form, function and transmission via media of the representation. Here, we present research on gender with children, the public sphere in Brazil, and madness as depicted in television.

### Ethnography

In a series of ethnographic studies Duveen and collaborators investigated the context of gender, toy use in the classroom behaviour of children (Duveen, 1997; Duveen and Lloyd, 1993; Lloyd and Duveen, 1992). Ethnography has been characterised by Geertz in terms of the distinction between thin and thick descriptions (Geertz, 1973). Descriptions can be said to be thicker the more they move from observations of the regularities of social life toward an interpretative account of the intentionalities of the actors engaged in the situation. Traditionally, ethnography as a method was used to investigate the social organisation of communities, with the ethnographer's interpretive categories emerging through their reflexive analysis of the data collected during fieldwork. In the present case, since the researchers came to classrooms with the aim of focusing on the role of gender in structuring classroom life, this approach was described as *motivated ethnography* (Duveen and Lloyd, 1993).

It is perhaps surprising that ethnography has not been more widely used in the study of social representations. Indeed, in spite of Moscovici's explicit definition of social representations as 'system(s) of values, ideas and practices' (Moscovici, 1973), the theme of practice has been relatively neglected, although Jodelet's (1991a) study is an exception. In the present study, ethnography was the first choice of method, not only because it enables the researcher to focus on structural aspects of gender in the classroom, but also because at this age children's practice is a much richer source of their representations than their reflexive talk. One learns more about children's understanding of their worlds through observation than through direct questioning in interviews and in this respect observations of children's pretend play is a very rich source (Duveen, 1997; Furth, 1996; Lloyd and Duveen, 1992). The ethnography of gender in the reception classroom served several purposes for the research as a whole. First, the structural description of gender as an organising dimension revealed precisely how children's activity was visibly regulated by gender. In particular, gender was important in children's peer associations, and in their use of the material culture and space of the classroom. On the basis of this ethnographic description, an observation schedule and a series of interview tasks were developed which allowed the researchers to undertake a longitudinal study of the development of representations of gender through the first year of school. These methods enabled tracing of the ways in which the gender identities which children brought into school gradually adapted to the specific characteristics of the classroom as a context for social life.

Second, ethnographic records provide the basis for a description of the social representation of gender elaborated among these young children. This is based on an image of bipolar opposition which crystallises a state of understanding for the child in which the form of knowledge (its categorical structure) is fused with the content of knowledge (the separation between things masculine and things feminine). All things masculine tend to cohere together and to separate from things feminine. As is noted in the ethnography, separation along these lines can come to characterise the pattern of interaction in the classroom. Once established in this way, the dynamic interplay of activity and understanding is capable of sustaining such moments over extended periods of time. Yet, as well as representing difference, the image of gender as a bipolar opposition also represents hierarchy, for the difference between the genders is also a relation of power. As much as the image is saturated with notions of hierarchy and power, so long as the difference between the bipolar opposites can be resolved, the hierarchy can be obscured. Sometimes, the researchers also observed how this sense of hierarchy produced moments of conflict and resistance among the children, especially among the girls.

Third, the ethnographic work also raised specific problems and issues related to the analysis of the development of gender identities. In particular, the researchers' daily exposure to life in the classroom highlighted the variability and heterogeneity among boys and among girls in how they expressed their gender identities. Generally, in developmental psychology, a contrast is drawn between girls and boys as though each of these categories were homogenous. This therefore obscures any variability within the categories. Again drawing on their ethnography, the researchers constructed an index of children's gender identity in terms of the proportion of time that they were engaged in single gender groups. Although this is a very imprecise indicator, since it uses a single observational measure to describe a very complex phenomenon, including this index in the analysis of the observational data from the longitudinal study nevertheless revealed the extent to which variability amongst boys and amongst girls contributes significantly to the patterns of gender activity in the reception class. In particular, these variations contributed considerably to the organisation of the local gender cultures distinguishing one classroom from another.

## Focus groups and the press

Quite another realm of study from children in the classroom is public sphere and public life in Brazil (Jovchelovitch, 1995a, 1995b). Taking the work of Habermas as a starting point, the debate about the public sphere in contemporary societies has focused on both the form and realisation of public life today, and their consequences for the future of democratic societies (Habermas, 1989). The discussion varies from country to country and, in Brazil the constitution of the public sphere is, and historically has been for some time, an urgent and pressing issue. Corruption in political life, absence of trust in politics and politicians, and violence, criminality and individualism in the streets, were just a few of the realities traditionally associated with the public sphere in Brazil.

Representations about the public sphere are a key factor in the overall constitution of public spaces (Jovchelovitch, 1995b). Symbolic constructions shape the contours of social and personal reality as much as historical, social and economic factors. While it is true that we need to consider history and social structures, it is also true that both history and social structures are constructed by social psychological people, who know, act, invest with affection and render with meaning the realities in which they live. In the Brazilian case, an investigation about representations of public life is informative of how the Brazilian community makes sense of, and relates to, public issues. This social psychological edge can contribute to a much needed assessment of the possibilities and limitations of the public sphere in many countries.

Social representation theory conceptualises these issues, first, in relating lay knowledge to the cultural, historical and social frameworks of the context under consideration. In this sense, lay knowledge is more than knowledge in the heads of individuals. Quite the opposite, it is knowledge produced by a community of people, in conditions of social interaction and communication, and therefore expressive of identities, interests, history and culture. Second, the theory is concerned with meaning and its interpretation. The symbolic dimension of social representations is central to understanding how people express identity, develop patterns of behaviour and engage with significant others. And last, but not least, because social representations are themselves symbolic phenomena produced in, and constitutive of, the public arena (Jovchelovitch, 1995a). The use of the theory in this project allowed for the establishment of conceptual links between social representations and the public sphere.

The research design sought to capture, at different levels of social life, the relationship between specific social actors and the public sphere, and how the logic of these relationships leads to representations about the public sphere. The public sphere was operationalised along two dimensions: the space of the streets (which corresponds to the 'natural', day-to-day settings of public life) and the arena of politics (which corresponds to the institutionalised public sphere). The mass media of communication are a key medium of the public sphere and were content analysed in relation to the above dimensions. Hence the empirical translation of the concept of the public sphere involved two dimensions – streets and politics – and one mediator – the press. Three others emerged from these dimensions, concerning the key social actors who re-enact the public sphere on a daily basis. The strategic social actors sampled were politicians, the ordinary 'citizen in the street' and the media. The media are also considered to be social actors, insofar as they are institutions which produce an effect in the web of social relations. These social actors do not belong exclusively to one space or the other. It is not the case that politicians belong only to the political arena while the citizen in the street belongs only to the space of the streets. Although they are predominantly associated with these spaces, they interact with, and produce ongoing effects on, each other. The media plays a fundamental role in this interaction: they mediate between the two and interact with each of them at the same time.

Content analysis of the press,[3] focus groups with different categories of lay informants[4] and narrative interviews with parliamentarians[5] comprised the range of techniques. The press analysis involved a selection of all articles related to the streets and to politics during May 1992, and the focus groups were centred in a discussion about the situation in the streets and in political life. The narrative interviews with politicians were conducted around the impeachment of the former Brazilian president, F. Collor de Mello, who on December 1992 became the first Brazilian president to be expelled from office on charges of corruption and misuse of public money. The impeachment was considered to be perhaps the most important event epitomising the conditions of public life in Brazil and this exemplary, and unprecedented, event led to its inclusion in the research. By contrast with other forms of in-depth interviewing, the narrative interview leaves the field completely open to the interviewee by simply asking subjects to tell the story of the event being studied (M. Bauer, 1996). Narrative interviews draw on the conceptual value of story telling as one of the most fundamental forms of human communication (Barthes, 1988) and have been considered a particularly useful method in the study of social representations (Jovchelovitch, 2002; Jovchelovitch and Bauer, 2000; Laszlo, 1997; Laszlo and Stainton-Rogers, 2002; Murray, 2002; Rose, 1996).

The analysis of the data was both qualitative and quantitative. It involved two general steps: data systematisation and data interpretation. Data systematisation was achieved by constructing coding frames for each one of the data sets that emerged. In the coding frame for the content analysis of the press, the articles were treated as stories and the analytical framework was an attempt to identify what the story was about – the event, who were the main actors, and which claims and justifications were present in the story. The discussion in each one of the focus groups was systematised through a coding frame which considered three levels of content: descriptions about life in the streets and in politics; claims and explanations made regarding such descriptions; and, finally, strategies of coping, relating and feeling developed in relation to the situations the groups were discussing. The coding frame for the narrative interviews followed principles of narrative analysis (Riessman, 1993) and identified themes in the stories, the qualifications and metaphors associated with the themes, the main actors in the stories, the reasons and explanations given in the stories as well as their consequences, and the aftermath of the stories. Once the full data set was coded, both qualitative and quantitative analyses were carried out. The qualitative interpretation was based on the logic of argumentation in the groups and interviews, the relations between the different categories coded, and on the previous literature related to the overall picture emerging from the data. The quantitative analysis was carried out using descriptive statistics, cross-tabulations and correspondence analysis. Correspondence analysis proved particularly useful with regard to the corroboration of the qualitative interpretations, as well as to the definition of the nuances and differences between the focus groups.

The analysis of the three empirical studies produced a strikingly similar representational field, marked by notions of fear, threat and individualism in the streets and corruption, self-interest and individualism in politics. These notions were brought together and explained by a central representation: the Brazilian character. It was this character, portrayed in the data as dubious, ambivalent, hybrid and of a 'contaminated' nature, which justified the situation in the streets and in political life. The objectification of the streets and political life into the Brazilian character suggests that the blurred and ambivalent relationship between self and other in Brazil lies at the very heart of social representations of public life. Old metaphors of corrupt blood and a contaminated, ill social body, provide the anchors to contemporary representations of public life. These are deeply ingrained in Brazilian culture and self-interpretation, whose quest for a defined identity has been consistently undermined by the encounters of different peoples that shaped the cultural trajectory of the country (Ortiz, 1986; Quijano, 1993). These results suggest that the workings of social representations are inseparable from the historical and cultural features of the society in which they develop; and from the processes whereby a community struggles to maintain an identity, a sense of belonging and a location in the world.

## Television analysis

Despite the fact that TV and other electronic media play a crucial role in the diffusion and elaboration of representations in modern societies, there has been little research using media other than the press. A remarkable exception is Rose's research on TV representations of madness (Rose, 1996). The author's focus is on British TV and how it portrays and represents madness, mental illness and people with mental health problems. The topic of madness and media has generated a huge literature by itself (Philo, 1996; Rose, Ford, Lindley et al., 1998; Signorelli, 1989; Wahl, 1992) but little within the framework of social representation theory. These studies uniformly conclude that mentally ill people are stigmatised in the Western media, especially through their association with violence.

The mass media are social in their production (Allen, 1992), social in their texts (J. Fiske, 1987) and social in their consumption (Livingstone, 1991), making social representation theory a suitable approach. There is also a much more specific reason for using social representation theory to analyse representations of madness *on television*. Many media are partially visual, yet have often been analysed as if they were only made up of words (for counter-examples see de Rosa, 1987; Wearing, 1989). Social representation theory permits us to look at the visual side of television through the concept of objectification. The observation that representations contain the dimension of the concrete and visible proved very helpful in the attempt to understand the structure and operation of representations of madness on television in a Western country.

The method used here has its roots in early content analysis (Berelson, 1952), and it allows the proper quantification of meaning in the present context. Taking up criticisms by deconstructionists, the method also acknowledges that what is *absent* from a text is just as important as what is present (Gervais, Morant and Penn, 1999). For the present purposes, it would be highly significant if, for instance, positively valued meanings were completely absent from the television text on madness. It also tells us that we should include meanings that we do not expect in a coding frame, as well as those we do. The formal instrument used in the analysis was a complex coding frame that cannot for reasons of space be detailed here.

The coding frame itself has a hierarchical structure and at the most detailed level of the instrument are a large number of semantic categories which can be allocated to analytic units. The reason for the large number of categories is to capture the idea that madness has multiple meanings. At the same time the coding frame provides the capacity to reject the hypothesis of multiple meanings. Common sense might say that 'mental illness' is represented in close proximity to the category of 'illness'. From the present point of view, it would then be expected that nearly all the coding allocations would fall in this category, which would show that the social object 'madness' is conceptualised in terms of the medical discourse 'illness'. This is not, however, what was discovered. A further point to note about the detailed categories is that positive evaluations are included. We do not want to pre-empt the idea that all representations of madness on television are negative. But if these categories are empty, it would be highly significant.

Representations are not pure content, nor are they only semantic. Stories in the media have a structure, just as Propp (1969) proposed with the analysis of folk-tales. The structuralist view that structure carries significance is put to use by the coding frame having a first level which allocates a narrative element each time a coding is made. For example, an analytic unit might be coded 'narrative description' as well as 'danger'.

The coding frame was applied to a body of data which were subjected to procedures that turn moving pictures and spoken discourse into a form amenable to content analysis. First, there are the steps to do with selection. At the start, a broad sweep of prime-time popular TV programmes was selected, including news and current affairs, documentaries, soap operas, drama serials and situation comedies. Over a two-month period in 1992, 157 hours of data were collected by video tape. A definition by Wahl was used for selecting extracts depicting madness along with his suggestion of searching for specific psychiatric labels, slang words or indications of receipt of psychiatric treatment within the media presentation (Wahl, 1992).

A further problem in selecting the dataset concerns metaphors. Mental illness terminology is routinely used to tease and insult, for example: 'you're a raving nutter'; 'who is this loony schizo'; 'she's mad about the boy'. These uses of mental illness terminology are important for the overall representation of madness on television. Metaphorical use of such terminology can be either tightly or more lightly connected with other representations of madness. That still leaves the question of what metaphorical uses to include. However, if language is a system, then signs belonging to one context will still carry some of the weight of the initial meaning, even when appearing in a completely different one. At first sight, the popular phrase 'she's mad about the boy', seems to have little to do with psychiatric disorder. But the term 'mad', generic for centuries, is still tinged with notions of extreme and excess, and even emotional danger, when located in its new context. Finally, both visual and verbal elements of the text were transcribed so that the transcript looked like the script for a play: in two columns, one describing the visuals and one the spoken text.

The unit of analysis was the camera shot. When the camera switched to a new shot, a new unit of analysis began (Rose, 1996, 1998). The visual transcription consisted of a brief description of the action, a note of who was in the shot, and a note of the camera angle. The verbal transcription was a 'verbatim' record of the spoken word.

Once transcribed, a coding was ascribed to each unit of analysis. For the visual dimension a number of technical details were coded, such as the camera angle, whether the shot was a single shot, a two-shot (two people in frame) or a group shot. A count was also made of the number of shots that used shadowy lighting, and of the number of times music was used and its nature. The verbal material was not, of course, coded independently of the visual. Spoken discourse is critical in making a decision about the codes to be allocated to each unit. Visual and verbal were taken together to provide a coding allocation for each unit of the appropriate narrative element, a subdivision of the narrative element and a detailed content category. The totals of the different codes in over 2000 units of analysis were then calculated. Besides quantification, the analysis also took note of the structural features of stories in order to properly assess the semantics of madness on television.

The resulting coding can be read like a map. It shows the points of emphasis and stresses as well as the points of lack and absence in the data (cf. Gervais, Morant and Penn, 1999). The numbers are not interpreted merely quantitatively. It would not be sensible to say there was 'twice as much danger as sickness' in a scene, although a metric reading of the figures would come to that conclusion. It makes more sense to say that danger dominated themes of sickness, and that the absence of themes of success and coping

TABLE 11.1  Type of shot and character in the soap opera
*Coronation Street*

| Type of shot | Mrs Bishop | Mr Sugden | Others | Total |
|---|---|---|---|---|
| ECU/CU | 45 | 8 | 9 | 62 |
| MCU | 42 | 33 | 41 | 116 |
| MW | 22 | 36 | 16 | 74 |
| OTHER | 22 | 9 | 3 | 34 |
| TOTAL | 131 | 86 | 69 | 286 |

NOTE:  Camera shots were described and a note made of the angle of each unit. The codes for monitoring camera angle were: ECU (Extreme close up), CU (Close up), MCU (Medium Close-up), MW (Medium Wide), WA (Wide Angle), Tracking (Camera follows action), Environment (Shot other than a person).

say something significant about how mental health problems are represented on the news. As semioticians have shown, what is absent is just as important as what is present.

It was possible, with the visual material, to employ a method of contrasts. Since both mentally ill and non-mentally ill people appear in the programming, their visual depiction can be compared. Table 11.1 shows such a comparison. It shows that the mentally ill character (Mrs Bishop) was much more likely to be filmed alone and in close-up than either the other main character in the story (Mr Sugden) or other characters in general. This finding was repeated for other genres, the news and drama. It carries the message of an isolated, emotionally scrutinised person. Others are filmed as couples or in groups, social shots that usually require a medium or wide angle.

A further important result was that structure carries meaning. In the present audio-visual material, structure has been conceptualised in terms of narrative form (Propp, 1969). Narrative structure on television is often open, for instance in soap operas, to keep up the suspense. But the analysis of narrative structure in the representation of people designated mad showed that lack of narrative closure was the norm. The analysis of narrative structure in drama programmes shows that the majority of sequences have either no ending at all or no restoration of social harmony.

These representations of madness and of people designated psychiatrically ill in the media carry multiple meanings and refer to an unstable concept. The visual representations marked off the mad person as different, and the semantics of the field are fluid and uncertain. This structure (or lack of it) of meaning poses a semiotic threat. It could be said that the mad person inhabits a realm of Otherness in popular imagination. Additionally and in contrast to psychiatric facts, it was found that in the news, 70 per cent of mentally ill people portrayed were associated with violence. This stands in stark contrast to the estimated 92 per cent of people with serious mental health problems who will never be violent, and to the fact that age, gender and drug and alcohol use are better predictors of violence than mental illness (Swanson, Holzer, Ganju and Jono, 1990).

Both visual representations and narrative structure are revealed as marking the mad person as different, through scrutinising visual shots and in a narrative which lacks the structure inferred as universal by narrative analysts. There is evidence that these portrayals affect the perceptions of the general public making the Otherness of the mental patient doubly relevant.

## Automatic text analysis

Media analysis, such as the one reported above, is very labour-intensive research. To date, there have been no viable computer-aided methods to deal with images, although there are methods to automatise lexical analysis for certain research questions. Using the *statistical text analysis* program ALCESTE, Lahlou (1998) investigated the meaning of eating in various discourses.

The method aims at spotting the basic nuclei of social representation in the discourse produced by an informed source. First, a corpus of statements – that is, sentences in natural language – about an object is obtained. A corpus can be any discourse that can be transcribed, such as a series of media articles, interviews, free associations, group discussions and so on. The whole corpus is then processed, with ALCESTE calculating the co-occurrence of words in predefined chunks of text and performing a top-down, descending cluster analysis on the correspondence table, yielding classes of statements that have similar lexical content. Classes are built on the principle of putting together statements or words which are close to each other within a cluster, and contrast with statements and words in other clusters (cf. Kronberger and Wagner, 2000; Lahlon,

1996; Reinert, 1990; Viaud, 2002). Another program for automatic text analysis is PROSPERO (Kalampalikis and Buschini, 2002). Note that many such sophisticated programs for automatic text analysis are only applicable to certain languages, mostly of Roman origin and able to be spelled in ASCII characters. Lahlou (1998) considered the semantic classes to be the basic nuclei of a social representation, and the pattern linking them as the structure (Beaudouin and Lahlou, 1993). This method is a kind of quantified content analysis. Being computerised it can – and actually should – be applied to very large sets of text, which are beyond the reach of manual analysis.

## 11.2.4 Groups and representations in history

The final class of research as characterised in Figure 11.1 takes account of groups, objects and the history of change in representational systems. There are only a handful of studies with such an embracing focus, of which we present a study on the media history of a scientific myth, and a series of studies on the representation of a newly emerging technology, that is, biotechnology at the turn of the millennium.

### Media studies

In their study on the previously mentioned 'Mozart effect', Bangerter and Heath (2004) conducted three media studies intended to show how the original scientific news was received and kept on the agenda of press reports over a decade; and how the intensity of reporting correlated with particular societal needs at the time. Each study was based on an on-line search for articles mentioning the name of the effect or the name of authors related to the original *Nature* publication in 1993.

The popularised version of the effect states that classical music enhances intelligence in children and even in unborn babies, while the original scientific report referred to college students who showed a significant increase in spatial cognitive abilities when exposed to classical music. The Mozart effect would probably not have received the attention it got, if it did not respond to a social need or desire to control and manage the level of intelligence in children, to the ages old conviction that certain kinds of music have a beneficial effect, and to the idea that infants' psychology is determined at an early age (Kagan, 1998). Responding to a social need is the prerequisite for a scientific myth to emerge and become popular.

In their first study, the authors were able to show that this particular *Nature* article received more media attention in the USA than any of ten other scientific reports published and mentioned in the media in the same year. Their second study is more interesting. There, they show that the biggest two predictors of media reporting intensity across time, taking US states as units of analysis, was the state's level of teacher salaries and the level of national test scores and pupil funding: the lower these two variables were – indicating serious problems in a state's educational system – the higher was the interest in the Mozart effect in local media. This corroborates the assumption that interest in scientific myths has to do with their promising a cheap way out of social problems. A final result concerned the reported generality of the Mozart effect. Over time, the original sample of college students was replaced more and more by children in general and by babies in media reports (Figure 8.1, p. 242).

## The public, media and policy

A comprehensive attempt at studying – among other things – the *development and form of social representations of biotechnology* across various countries and across time was made by Durant, Gaskell and Bauer (1998), Gaskell and Bauer (2001) and M. Bauer and Gaskell (2002) and collaborators. This series of studies involved on a grand scale longitudinal press-reporting intensity statistics; cross-sectional qualitative media analyses (media module); European-wide surveys in 1996, 1999 and 2002; focus groups and qualitative interviews (public perception module); and policy analyses (policy module) in 17 European and non-European countries (Figure 11.2).

The size of this research is unprecedented in the field of social representations. There will be few opportunities where researchers have the resources and most research will involve only one or two of the modules depicted in Figure 11.2; but it gives some hints as

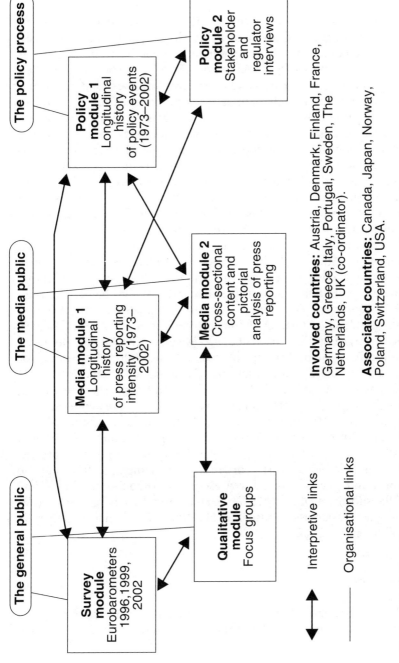

FIGURE 11.2 Modular organisation of 'Public Perception of Biotechnology' projects

to which factors are relevant in the social dynamics playing a role in social representation.

Representations have a history, they have a dynamic that is, to a certain degree, culture dependent, they involve media processes and one component of their dynamics is political, particularly if technology and its legal regulation is involved. The methods used ranged from focus groups and interviews with the broad public and specific interest groups such as farmers, students, mothers and so on; questionnaires given to representative samples in many countries; media statistics of the opinion-leading press across time and across countries; in-depth qualitative analysis of press reports; and the semiotic analysis of all sorts of pictures in the press during certain periods related to crucial events having to do with biotechnology (e.g. the first publication about Dolly, the cloned sheep); expert interviews with stakeholders and politicians; and a longitudinal study of political events related to biotechnology.

The results were manifold and a few parts have been presented throughout this book. In general, the results shed light on representational core-processes in the interaction between media reporting and public imagination (M. Bauer, 2001; M. Bauer, Kohring, Allansdottir and Gutteling, 2001; Einsiedel, Allansdottir, Allum et al., 2002; Gutteling, Olofsson, Fjaestad et al., 2002; W. Wagner, Kronberger and Seifert, 2002; W. Wagner, Kronberger, Berg and Torgersen, forthcoming); the role of the cultural heritage for anchoring new representations (Nielsen and Berg, 2001; W. Wagner and Kronberger, 2002; W. Wagner, Kronberger, Berg et al., forthcoming); the determinants of perceived risk, its representation and science (Gaskell and Allum, 2001; Gaskell, Allum, Wagner et al., 2001; Gaskell, Allum, Wagner et al., 2004; Sturgis and Allum, 2004); the role of political discourse in shaping representations (Einsiedel, 2001; Torgersen and Hampel, 2001); and the form and structure of the representation (Kronberger, Dahinden, Allansdottir et al., 2001; W. Wagner and Kronberger, 2001; W. Wagner, Krouberger, Gaskell et al., 2001; W. Wagner, Kronberger, Allum et al., 2002).

## Pictures

The use of pictorial analysis is a particularly fruitful approach given the focus on groups and a historical and cultural dimension. Much cultural material is transmitted across generations in pictorial form, and this represents an invaluable resource for understanding modern representations, which, as argued earlier, are primarily iconic as well as culturally informed. In a by now classic investigation, de Rosa (1987) studied the representations of madness of children and adults by having them draw a 'madman'. The drawings were then systematically analysed and compared to historical material. The results showed differences between age groups in emphasising either deviance or illness, and many drawings were remarkably similar to the cultural heritage. Similar cultural approaches were used in the study on biotechnology cited above (Nielsen and Berg, 2001; Wagner and Kronberger, 2002; W. Wagner, Kronberger, Berg et al., forthcoming).

## 11.3 Developing appropriate methodologies

### 11.3.1 Presence, absence and triangulation

It is clear from the foregoing sections that each research focus has certain methods that are better suited to tackle the question than others. Often, a multi-method approach is advisable. The researcher must decide from the beginning of his or her work whether the focus is on the form and structure of distributed representations, on group dynamics and the elaboration of a shared representation involving media, or on diachronic processes that highlight change in representational systems.

### Absence

In so doing, researchers are easily tempted to take what comes out as their results as the 'thing', but the *missing elements* may play an equally important role. What is absent sometimes points to shortcomings or lacunas in theory, method, data and interpretation (Gervais, Morant and Penn, 1999). Absence occurring from the one-sided use of methods can be remedied using multiple methods as shown in the next research example (Parales Quenza, 1999), but absence may also have important meanings for interpretation, as shown earlier in the media research on madness (Rose, 1996). In their research on perceptions of democracy, Joffe and Farr (1996) interpret the absence of knowledge about democratic institutions with younger Britons and women as revealing a structural deficit of the political system and not as revealing a cognitive deficit in some groups. The authors take the absence of a well-structured representation as being in itself a symptom of wider sociopolitical conditions and historical processes. Conspicuous absence and ignorance, therefore, deserve a heightened awareness in the conceptual and interpretive activity of the researcher (Gervais, Morant and Penn, 1999).

## Multiple methods

In his thesis on the representation of healthy eating in Colombia, Parales Quenza (1999) applied a multi-method approach including ethnographic participant observation, media content analysis, focus groups, and a structural analysis in the sense of the core and periphery approach. The results from this research on the well-delimited topic of eating show that some methods are superior to others in being able to reveal the contents and dynamics of representations. Participant observation, in which the author invited a few people to a restaurant and observed and discussed their food choices, revealed a whole range of contradictions between ideas, choice preferences and behaviours. Observing their choices in the light of the invitees' 'theoretical' ideas highlights that the representational field is much more complex than can be revealed by a one-shot assessment using verbal methods: 'The material reality is constantly reshaping the representation. Acting as a dynamo, it incites the movement from one structural array to another. The norms are in constant tension with the practices, determined, to a large extent, by the material conditions. All the subjects interviewed during the observation agreed that habits and opportunity are the most important elements in deciding what to eat' (Parales Quenza, 1999, p. 177). Hence, if they wish to address behaviour and action in representation research, researchers are well-advised to include situational determinants and habitual preferences besides the norms that usually emerge as the result of verbal methods.

The second method, analysis of focus group and media discourse, highlights normative elements and social stratification in the representation of eating, and links these to health, cleanliness and medical aspects. Informal and formal discourses are situated at the collective level and provide the pieces of a puzzle that jointly offer a comprehensive view on the ways a society conceives a social problem. The core–periphery analysis, in the end, presents the structure of the representation in a more formalised manner, allowing differentiation of the key words being associated with it by members of different social groups. In terms of content, the structural results are necessarily much poorer and also more normative than results produced by other methods. However, they do offer some insight into the hierarchical interrelationship between cognitive elements.

## Triangulation

Comparing the results obtained from different methods, the author was able to show that there are certain elements which surface in all of the data (Parales Quenza, 1999). This convergence when using multiple methods is a necessary condition, particularly in social representation research, which – by its very nature – is geared towards many dimensions and both individual and collective levels of data. It can be regarded as a form of triangulation, fostering the validity of results found with one method through the use of another (Kirk and Miller, 1986). Flick (1992b) gave this view a fresh interpretation by urging researchers to use triangulation, not only as a validation strategy, but simultaneously for complementing and assessing different versions of the phenomenon under study. In his view, complementary triangulation takes into account both that subjective knowledge and social interactions should be understood as parts of social, local and institutional contexts and in the historical backgrounds of these contexts.

## 11.3.2 Snapshot methodologies and their limitations

The use of triangulation, particularly with regard to the combination of qualitative and quantative approaches, enables the researcher to avoid one of the major pitfalls of modern research methods. In a discussion of organisational modelling, Hayes (2003) pointed out that many, if not most, of the models adopted and developed by organisational researchers are severely limited in their ability to deal with the real world of the organisation, owing to (among other things) the use of 'snapshot methodologies'.

Organisations are social worlds, in which both social identification and social representations are of primary importance (Hayes, 1998a, 1998b). These social processes have emerged during the life of the organisation and are shaped primarily by its history and the real-world experiences of those working in it. Organisational modelling, however, is often derived from large-scale questionnaire studies, taken only on one single occasion, and reflecting the organisation at one particular point in time – hence the term 'snapshot'. Longitudinal research within a single organisation is uncommon, as is the use of qualitative methods for collecting data. This results in a simplistic, ahistorical image of the organisation, which in turn leads to simplistic modelling (often in the use of typologies, e.g. Harrison, 1972; Pheysey, 1993).

As we have already seen, while this type of approach to data collection may highlight areas of concern at the time that it is carried out, it is insufficient to enable the researcher to comprehend the subtleties underlying those concerns, or how such concerns change over time. Yet this is at the core of people's everyday experience at work. The understanding of current events is shaped by the social representations shared by those working in the organisation (Hayes, 1998a); and these in turn have developed with the organisation's history and result from the cognitive restructurings which have arisen during the interaction between workers, management and other participants over the course of time (Cinnirella, 1998; Hayes, 2003). If that history is not taken account of in some way during the course of the research process, it is unlikely that a valid model of the communicative or cultural processes occurring between people in that particular context can be obtained.

### 11.3.3 The participant as social agent

Snapshot methodologies also limit recognition of another key factor in the development and transmission of social representations: the recognition of the participant as an active agent in social processes. Individuals, as we have shown, do not simply receive and reproduce social representations passively: they adapt, adjust and modify them in consonance with their personal understandings and experience as well as with the wide range of information available from external sources. Costalat-Founeau (1999), in an exploration of the relationship between representations and action, found the two concepts to be closely interlinked and impossible to prioritise or sequence. Each interacts with, and reacts to, the other. The picture which emerges is of the person as an actor within their environment, concretising and activating social representations through actions, which are directed in their own right by those representations. The methodological implications of perceiving the person as a dynamic agent in the social process, are profound. It challenges many of the assumptions of formal scientific research – most specifically, the idea of the inert 'subject' simply responding passively to experimental manipulation. This may be a useful model in physics, but cannot give other than misleading answers when applied to real human beings in real social situations, whose own actions are contributory to the representations they apply in those settings.

Seeing the participant as a social agent also places the emphasis on the need for insight into what the person believes they are doing at the time that they are being studied. As a result, many researchers into social representations have found benefit from discursive methodologies. Laszlo (1998) argued for the recognition of the narrative character of social knowledge or social thought, showing how narrative accounts are a common feature of groups expressing social representations; while Harré (1999) pointed out that what we are studying when we are 'doing psychology' are discursive practices of various kinds, some of which could exist only in actual or potential interpersonal interactions. Potter and Wetherell (1998) argue that the combination of discourse analysis and social representation theory presents the researcher with an enriched methodology which enables investigation of communication and social construction, as well as content, in the exploration of real-world social action.

The close interlinking between social representation and everyday social experience argues for an approach to analysis which places social experience in a primary rather than a secondary role. M. Bauer and Gaskell (1998) propose that the basis unit of analysis in such research should be the triangle of mediation: subject 1, object, project, and subject 2. This, they argued, is the basic social unit which produces, circulates and receives representation; which in turn may be embodied in habitual behaviour, individual cognition and informal and formal communication, and may therefore be examined using words, visual images or non-linguistic sounds. For many researchers investigating social representations, it is the combination of qualitative and quantitative methods which has become the preferred approach. Combining the two approaches enables comparisons to be made between groups (e.g. Gracio, 1998) and facilitates the exploration of the epidemiology of social representations (Farr, 1987; Markovà, Moodie, Farr et al., 1998), as well as enabling interpretation of the deeper content of the representation itself.

Some reseachers, too, have found benefit in combining insights gained at a different level of theoretical analysis with social representation theory, as part of a wider interpretation of outcomes. Moscovici and Hewstone (1983) used attribution theory to examine modifications to the 'split-brain' theory as it developed from a limited scientific theory into a full-scale social representation. Hewstone and Agoustinos (1998) discussed how the two theories: attribution theory and social representation theory, can be used in a complementary fashion at different levels of analysis; while much of this text has examined the relationship between social identification and the social representation process. The diverse manifestations of social representations illustrate the multi-level nature of the representation process, and suggest that without such 'theory-knitting', many of the subtleties and refinements of social representations could easily pass unremarked.

In his discussion of the epistemology of social representation, Harré (1999) pointed out that what we ascribe to people, on the basis of our studies of their practices, are the skills necessary to perform them. We therefore need to bear in mind that it may often be the case that more than one persona is needed to bring a skilled activity to fruition. In short, we need to deal with reality: that social practice is a co-operative, not an individual, affair; that the people participating in it are active agents who transform as they participate; and that investigations of social practice which fail to take its multi-level relevance and the social dynamic into account are unlikely to achieve a true impression of what is going on. It is a message which is easily forgotten.

# Notes

## Chapter 1 Introduction

1. The 'Secrets of History' became the 'History of Secrets'.
2. However, there are definitely differences to be expected between social and natural scientific knowledge, the truth of which is, among others, proved by technical application.

## Chapter 2 Everyday life, knowledge and rationality

1. Here is not the place to go into the psychology of personality or the psychological dynamics of the researcher of psychology. We will just refer to the already classic work by Devereux (1973) which deals with the relationship between individual psychological dynamics and the topics and methods of research.
2. Burton's (1986) criticism that Heider's analyses of naive psychology are already contained in linguistic usage therefore leads us nowhere. Heider was obviously aware that this is the case.
3. By using informants as ethnographers do, for example.
4. On the problem of everyday life in sociology cf. e.g. Hammerich and Klein (1978) and Remy, Voye and Servais (1991).
5. The microsociology of Alfred Schütz and his students provides a valuable store of theoretical ideas precisely for a 'socialised' social psychology. Closer knowledge of the phenomenological philosophies of Bergson, Husserl and James could deal with it more accurately, however, so that a more general depiction would be out of place.
6. At the same time the possibility of constant transitions between the two poles is not disputed.
7. For more reasoning and discussion of the 'modal' explanation used here, see Chapter 10.
8. Since this research only serves as an illustration, we do not intend to go into later developments and experiments on this theory (e.g. Cooper and Fazio, 1984; Steele and Liu, 1983).

9. Of course, more or fewer levels of abstraction can also be defined for other purposes. The argumentation pursued here reveals the most familiar that have been selected.
10. Schooling varied between one and 15 years, age between 7 and 35.
11. Or formulated differently: is anthropological research psychological, or psychology anthropological? (Bock, 1988; Bril and Lehalle, 1988).
12. More or less arbitrary contents are frequently construed in cover stories of experiments, certain laboratory situations and the conditions and groups of test subjects that the researcher selects for fieldwork.
13. The Wason Selection Task is a typical experiment which can help to measure cognitive context effects. This experiment involves an inference test in which the test subject must ascertain whether a conditional statement 'If $p$ then $q$' is infringed by one of four presented statements. Four detailed cards are placed in front of the test subject upon one side of which $p$ or $NOTp$ or $q$ or $NOTq$ are represented as correct. The other, hidden side of the card shows the logically correct complement. The task of the test subject is to either declare or turn over those cards which will allow verification of the correctness of the condition statement.

    For example, the test subject is to imagine being employed in a school and having to check the documents of the students. The Wason task is this:

    'If a student has a "good" mark (condition $p$), then the letter "D" (implication $q$) must be on the document.'
    Four student documents, or cards, are presented with the following markings:
    'GOOD' ($p$),
    'SATISFACTORY' ($NOTp$),
    'D' ($q$) and
    'A' ($NOTq$)

    The card(s) are to be chosen from these and must be checked as to whether they fulfil the logical demand given above. It would be logically correct of the test subjects to check the logical statement by picking out cards $p$ and $NOTq$.

    The same logical structure in a different situation but still portraying a familiar social challenge might be, e.g.: the test person is to imagine being an attendant in an American bar, in which the law states:

    'If a person drinks beer (condition $p$), then they must be older than 20 years (implication $q$).'

Which of the following people must the attendant therefore inspect:
'a person drinking beer' ($p$),
'a person drinking Coca-Cola' ($NOTp$),
'a 25-year-old person' ($q$) or
'a 16-year-old person' ($NOTq$)?

As in the previous case, the logically correct answer would be $p$ and $NOTq$. Surprisingly, however, in the first, rather abstract problem only 4 per cent to 25 per cent of the test subjects choose these two cards, whilst in the second case, around 75 per cent of the test subjects make the logically correct decision.

14. *Modus tollens:* '*If a is a b, then c is a d*', '*c is not a d*', therefore '*a is not a b.*' Or: '*a* → *b, NOTb* → *NOTa.*'

15. The quotation by Murdock should not remain completely unchallenged. Of course the mental constructs mentioned do not really exist; yet this is only the case to the extent that the underlying criteria of scientific rigour, its criteria of truth and effectiveness, its methodology and so forth, are recognised. In this way, however, scientists become part of a belief system (putting it 'rationally'), the basis of which is no more certainly determined by collective consensus of the scientific community nor perhaps by its pragmatic-technological effectiveness according to effectiveness criteria that remains to be determined. This itself cannot substantiate the basis of this rationality, but is part of a non-rational decision as above (cf. also Howard, 1985; Kukla, 1982).

16. The concept of belief as a precept and requirement of religious belonging, as used in Christian churches above all, then, entirely takes on the character of knowledge. Such belief is not (only) based on the factual, but actually on the evidence of insight which, in principle, is accessible to every truly interested person. All the same, this is not the place to go into the highly specialised theological discussion about this topic. For the social psychology of orthodox belief systems, cf. Deconchy (1989b).

17. For everyday 'knowledge' this text generally uses the term 'knowledge' and not 'opinion' or 'belief'. Should contents of everyday knowledge be distinguished from scientific knowledge systems, then this will be indicated by the appropriate adjectives 'scientific' or 'everyday'.

18. The relativity of content and process (touched upon in the previous section) is explicitly recognised here in the form of subjective logics.

19. It should be mentioned that cognitive theories of consistency, balance and dissonance can also be embedded within the approach presented here, and especially illuminate the motivational aspects of epistemological process (Kruglanski and Klar, 1987).

20. This is not to say that possession of alphabet and written record automatically leads to these 'Western' process systematics in knowledge acquisition (cf. the excellent collection of essays by Goody, 1981), nor is it to be implied this form of knowledge acquisition is the best of all possible ones.

21. Not being an anthropologist it is certainly risky to write about Lévi-Strauss (even if it is just a paragraph) if one has no detailled knowledge of the great number and complexity of the relevant debates about his theory. Insofar as it is accessible to the psychologist, only his basic idea is essential in this context.

22. 'Schematisation' is not to be equated with the term 'schema' in cognitive psychology.

23. The original reads: 'L'Ame et le Corps s'endorment ensemble. A mesure que le mouvement du sang se calme un doux sentiment de paix et de tranquillité se répand dans toute la Machine; L'Âme se sent mollement s'appesantir, avec les fibres du cerveaux; elle devient ainsi peu à peu paralytique, avec tous les muscles du corps.'

24. For the relationship touched on here between the development and origin of abstract forms of thinking, cf. Demele (1988).

25. The writings of attribution theoreticians largely do not make clear whether they wish to understand the variance-analytical model, e.g., as either a functional, explicative or descriptive one. A functional model would view the actual subject matter, attributive thought, as a 'black box' and look at its own structure and effects as a copy of the actual function elements. It depends entirely on the model of transformation from 'input' to 'output', independent of actual phenomena. In contrast to this, a descriptive model makes the additional claim of also naming the function elements in their actual context. Even if we accept the 'softer' case of the functional model in this context, we believe that the following criticism remains valid.

26. The polythetical approach is presented in Chapter 7.2.

27. This is a form of mnemonics still taught today.

28. Despite a number of attempts over the years, one of us (Wagner) has not been successful in consistently confirming this result in his seminars, with the result that maybe a culture-specific result is hiding here as well.

29. Viewed superficially it seems as though all the parameters which accompany such a decision could also become established in a rational, multidimensional decision-making model with evaluated dimensions. If one refrains from the necessity of taking into account the fuzzyness of the dimensions, which is complicated but can still be modelled (see W. Wagner, 1980), such a model presupposes that the relevant dimensions can already be hypothetically established

before any decision-making situation. But the problem with this *a priori* realisation is that such dimensions relevant in everyday life only themselves appear to become 'salient' in the act of decision making and might go by the board in a decision that is introduced. But, unfortunately, we do not know of any empirical works that concentrate on the theory of decision making pertaining to this problem.

## Chapter 3 Universes of everyday knowledge

1. The specific rational reasoning schema required by a highly specialised world of work are applied by the people concerned only in their jobs. Their use is abandoned when people leave the narrow problem field of their specific work, i.e., more or less at the limit of their desks. Many readers will surely be aware of numerous examples illustrating the difficulties which rationally working specialists have with their colleagues or families when it comes to solving everyday problems, i.e., in a sphere which countermands the validity of the strict rationality of science.

2. In all countries, the daily newspapers and magazines that have the most readers are those that contain an above average proportion of local news. Local reports are in general news about concrete events from the immediate world in which people live. They possess a high degree of concreteness, are comprehensible to the readers, comparable with their own experiences, and are frequently used to draw generalised conclusions about the state of society. It is not far-fetched for one to suspect that the reason for the popularity of these blocks of reports lies in the need for concreteness, and as such it is taken here as the basis for everyday-pragmatic thought.

3. Also compare the remarks on the illiterate mind (Chapter 2.3).

4. As is known, the logotherapy by Viktor Frankl builds on this principle.

5. The concept of the 'sensible' has taken on such a comprehensive and specialised character in the philosophical, sociological and anthropological discussions of this century that we have refrained from making systematic reference to it in this context (cf. Elster, 1983; Hollis and Lukes, 1982; Schnädelbach, 1984; Wilson, 1970, and others). If reference is made here to everyday reason, then the remarks are to be taken with a pinch of salt as research-pragmatic reflections referring to the social-psychological object.

6. One can point to real phenomena not only in a physical sense. Imagined objects also have their geographical co-ordinates in everyday understanding. One can refer to the soul by pointing out the

stomach, heart or brain regions of people, to God by, e.g., either pointing upwards – to heaven – or expanding one's arms to refer to the entire world, in order to express pantheistic views.

7. A walking bird that lives on the ground, of the *casuarii* order.

8. An evidence experience understood in this way here probably has great affinity to the concept of evidence experience of phenomenologists from Brentano to the therapeutist Rogers. Their view is that internal perception, the feeling of consistency, is the ultimately single criterion for personal evidence experience (cf. Noack, 1976, p. 182 onwards). The idea of social evidence expressed here, however, additionally inquires about the roots of this subjective evidence experience in the unexamined sharedness.

9. Riedl (1980) and other evolutionary epistemologists offer an evolutionary theoretical interpretation of biology for the restricted human freedom of classification. This would have us understand the cognitive abilities of organisms and ultimately of humans too as a structural analogy between the conditions of the world in which they live and the perception mechanisms evolved in it; it was, after all, Goethe, and the Greek philosopher Plotinus before him, who said: 'If the eye were not sunlike, it would not be able to see the sun' (p. 25).

10. Unfortunately a large part of work in the tradition of social comparison theory was carried out on the basis of the dependent variable 'ability' and not by opinions, although conformity research very often refers to Festinger's theory (cf. Witte, 1987). Performance is of course much less likely to be part of collective knowledge, and even when it is, it is of a fundamentally different character than opinions about social facts.

11. The immanent primacy that Festinger in his second postulation awards to physical over social validation could make one assume that the original theory of social comparison processes reproduces the cultural ideology of industrial society from the prevalence of scientific or natural scientific cognitive methods. This would expose it to the suspicion of everyday-logical analysis, an ethnocentric analysis at least, however (see Chapter 10.1).

# Chapter 4  Introducing social representations

1. Durkheim was obviously following a scientific trend of his time by having a material understanding of the term 'individual representation' and embodying it in the biological substratum of the brain. He does not distinguish between a psychological concept which demands no statements about material localisations and a physio-

logical concept which refers to the anatomical-physiological material substrata of psychic phenomena. The two concepts each touch on different fields of explanation and are distinguished in this text. By individual representations we understand a scientific construct to describe psychic, but not material phenomena.

2. The word for perception in German is 'Wahrnehmung'. To perceive something means literally to 'take something as being true'.

3. If this way of defining is to be used as a demarcation against 'natural objects', then Fiske and Taylor are admittedly shortening the current research paradigms of the natural sciences in an improper, if not naive way. They overlook the fact that the features of natural objects: physical, chemical, etc., can also only be ascertained by measurement. They are ultimately therefore constructs and epistemic things and cannot be directly observed, as elucidated by Rheinberger (1997).

4. We are aware that the concept of 'thinking' in the context of society or other macro-entities must meet with a spontaneous and violent contradiction by psychologists. 'Thinking' here is certainly not to be understood as the cognitive problem-solving and decision-making processes, as can be studied in the individual, but a social process to be concretised later.

5. For a more detailed discussion cf. Cummins (1989) and Putnam (1988).

6. For example by political exertions of influence and financing measures.

# Chapter 5 The topography of modern mentality

1. Oral communication by Geneviève Coudin.

2. The theoretical reasoning of the Nazis regarding race constitutes another prominent example of the use of pseudo-scientific statements as a system of justification.

3. Historical background: this period takes on a central position in the conception that Austria and the Austrian population officially have of themselves because it is associated with great ambivalence. Strengthened by the views of politically relevant people (e.g. Karl Renner, Otto Bauer, etc.) who believed years before actual union with the German Reich that such a link would be advantageous, the Austrians did not show much opposition when the Nazis marched in. A union with powerful and economically potent Germany promised a prompt improvement in the economic situation. In addition, many Austrians occupied important positions in Nazi Germany's machine of war and repression later.

When it became important for the Austrians to demonstrate a non-Nazi past after the war and the end of the German Reich, they had experienced three different state systems within only ten years (corporative state, Austrian fascism, National Socialism), three different state ideologies and three different systems of law and sanction. When the *Ostmark* period with Austria – a part of the German Reich – collapsed, along with the end of the war, the National Socialist system took on a vital and therefore highly affectively charged meaning for the personal life stories of those affected. This great meaning can be recognised by the fact that the issues of fascism, Hitler, anti-Semitism, Jews and national identity still regularly crop up even today in everyday discourse, whether it be within the family in the course of intergenerational friction, whilst talking with locals in the pub, or as a spontaneous comment of annoyance in public.

4. If this statement means 'being able to make large transactions', then it was certainly not true during the Nazi regime. A glaring contradiction.

5. The term 'imagination' has an odd effect in a social-psychological text. It has the aura of being an inexact and unscientific conceptualisation. We, too, find it hard to fend off, yet we see no other term which could express in a comparably exact way what must be described here.

6. There are, however, also cultural symbols which refer to nothing other than themselves. Such self-referential systems may be more widespread than they would appear. They may arise on occasions when someone presenting a hetero-referential symbol gets lost in the course of historic changes and cataclysms in a society, and the symbolic structure remains intact exclusively due to its formal, and perhaps also aesthetic, features and functions (R. Wagner, 1986).

# Chapter 6 The organisation and structure of social representations

1. It seems questionable, however, whether one should actually speak of physical characteristics when judging taste as Asch does. Rather one ought to speak of synaesthesias, i.e., 'a conscious experience in which qualities normally associated with one sensory modality are or seem to be sensed in another' (Graham, 1995, p. 783).

2. With the exception of the term 'complex', which comes from C. G. Jung (but compare Laplanche and Pontalis, 1972, p. 252 onwards).

3. To gain a picture of the mutual dependence of self-image, social belonging and cognitive as well as emotional mental contents, Zavalloni (1986) suggests the model of an 'affective-representa-

tional circuit'. By this she understands an 'internal ecology' which as a result of life-long experiences is subjected to lasting change and controls the individual psychic processes in the service of personal identity (cf. also Zavalloni, 1989).

# Chapter 7 Dynamics of social representations

1. Augoustinos and Innes (1990) give a comprehensive account of the relationship between 'classical' schemata and social representations. Arnault and Montmollin (1985), on the other hand, stress the reducibility of social representations to the classical concept of schema.
2. Which at the same time also has consequences for the epistemological position of social representations as a macro-reduction (cf. Chapter 10).
3. Social marking reminds us in a way of the structuralist interpretation of totemistic practices. According to this, the fictitious relations between the totem animals and them and their environment reproduce certain relevant family or social relations between people or clans (Lévi-Strauss, 1972).
4. Osherson and Smith (1981) criticise this approach for only superficial similarity having a part to play in classification using the prototype, whilst the intensional characteristics of a concept are lost. Their opinion is that prototypical classification characterises only a heuristic identification process, without taking into account the core defining elements of the concept or class (cf. Eysenck, 1984, p. 318ff.).
5. This way of grouping also proves its worth in biological classifications, such as numerical taxonomy (Sokal and Sneath, 1963).
6. Polythetical classes have a certain affinity to the statistical method of correspondence analysis, which is frequently used in social representations research. Some options in this method also yield subclasses in sets of items with overlapping attributes. See Chapter 11 on this issue.
7. Some authors (e.g. Doise, Clémence and Lorenzi-Cioldi, 1993, p. 110–11) use the term 'anchoring' in social representation literature in the sense of a representation being anchored to a particular group, in addition to the sense treated in this chapter.
8. For the present purpose we distinguish between these two aspects of objectification that can be studied on the level of the representation itself, i.e., its internal dynamics and individual use (Chapter 7), and on the level of the collective, where, for example, discursive construction, institutions and institutionalising practices are prime

examples of the objectifying power of social representations (Chapter 9). The order implied by the chapters does not indicate a priority of any of the two aspects, but only the order in which they are covered in the text. This distinction is of course a bit artificial, because of the integral nature of representations embracing both the social and the individual levels, which we must keep in mind.

9. Carmen Huici, personal communication.

## Chapter 8 Discourse, transmission and the shared universe

1. See Shiffrin (1994) for a more extended discussion of the term 'discourse'.
2. More often this kind of analysis is called discourse analysis. We avoid this term in the present context as explained in the preceding paragraph.
3. The term would actually be 'orthodox', but nowadays this is too strongly linked to religious and certain political systems.
4. It is not to be forgotten, however, that the temporary rulers of democratic societies are also frequently subject to the temptation of controlling the wrong sort of public discourse, albeit with different means and much more stealthily.
5. In some of the literature, therefore, the term 'consensus' is replaced by the more neutral term 'widespread beliefs' (Fraser and Gaskell, 1990).
6. This is a reassuring result if one thinks of the frequent use of association tests in the context of social representations research.
7. Note that speaking of consensual representation misses the point in the same way as if we spoke of 'consensual cognition' instead of shared cognition in social psychology. Representation is not only content, but also an – epistemological or metacognitive – process, which may be shared but not 'consented' to.
8. For those readers who are unaware of the historical 'institution' of the bassena in the Vienna of yesteryear: All storeys of town houses built up to the turn of the twentieth century in Vienna had a watering place next to the shared toilets common to all flats on that floor. This was called the bassena and was where the inhabitants fetched their water. The bassena was therefore often the focal point for housewives peddling the latest gossip, the rumours of the neighbourhood, and their own experiences.

# Chapter 9 Action, objectification and social reality

1. This is an important clue for the problem of validly measuring intelligence and creativity if the tasks of the tests are not presented against the backdrop of the usual lives lived by those taking the tests.

2. The works by Kempton are cited more as an illustration of theory-like knowledge than as an example of social representations although this knowledge falls broadly in the category of 'subjective theories', since their appearance is not bound to specific social entities.

3. In view of the common foreknowledge, a decidedly unsuitable attribute in this context!

4. It is comforting to know that Sugiman (1997), based on the philosophy of Japanese philosopher Wataru Hiromatsu, came to very similar conclusions in his perspective of group dynamics. This can be seen as a kind of 'cultural triangulation' of theoretical ideas.

5. This is not far off the definition of natural kinds in science (Quine, 1969).

6. In the original sense hysteresis means 'lagging of the magnetization of a ferromagnetic material, such as iron, behind variations of the magnetizing field' (Encyclopaedia Britannica, DVD 2000).

7. For a critique of habitus theory, see Caille (1988), Mary (1988), M. Miller (1989).

   The conceptions of so-called chaos theory provide us with new conceptual images which can be applied to the habitus as a principle of creating social practice. Within the apparently 'chaotic' interaction phenomena of social protagonists, one can identify in the 'longue durée' recurring patterns which are called 'strange attractors' in chaos theory. These attractors, as seemingly teleological fixed points of phenomena, correspond to the idea of the habitus as a principle of structuring long-lasting and *en masse* interactions which, taken on their own, do not have any aim, but collectively appear very regular indeed (verbal communication by Rainer Born).

8. For a discussion on subjectivist and objectivist research orientation, cf. Bourdieu (1983, ch. 1; 1987, pp. 7–46).

9. An example of a detailed conceptual analysis of socially directed actions can be found in Schütz and Luckman (1984, p. 95ff.), Shotter (1993) and others.

10. The technology of holographic photography may serve to illustrate the relation between an individual and the social whole described as holomorphism. If a conventional print is cut into pieces, then every piece – as will be instantly clear – contains only a small part of the information of the whole photograph. If, on the other hand, one were to cut up a hologram, then each of the resulting pieces con-

tains all the information and the whole picture can be reproduced. While the reproduced image will be more blurred the smaller the individual piece this does not alter the fact that each piece carries all the information of the original (Pribram, Nuwer and Baron, 1974). The technology of holography gives a very clear illustration of the way in which social representations function as a crossing-over point between the part and the whole.

11.  Although irrational actions by individual group members can be consensually categorised as 'irrational' and may also be emphatically understood, it is very unlikely that they are based on shared representations of the social reality. Actions which can be categorised and understood as being 'irrational' (cf. Chapter 3.3), or are similarly incompatible are not part of this discussion.

12.  In minerology 'idiomorphic' minerals are those that have their own crystal form.

13.  On these pages the term 'explanation' is used in the sense of a 'weak' explanation, that is to say, a description of the type of rational behaviour discussed in Chapter 10.1.

# Chapter 10  Epistemological aspects of social representation theory

1.  Contrary to what the person carrying out the experiment had assumed, however, the distraction task prevented the enlightenment effect.

2.  The years 1989 and 1990 of all occasions were the ones to deliver an object lesson about the consequences of a falsely understood social technology. The revolutions in the countries of Eastern Europe can be viewed as examples of enlightenment effects which bore witness to how social-technologically understood theories – of Marxism interpreted in a social-technological manner – are historically transitory.

3.  The adjective 'modal' in the term 'modal explanation' has nothing to do with modal logic, but refers to the great frequency with which this simple form of explanation can be observed.

4.  In making this inference we do not in any way harbour the intention of denying every possibility of truly causal explanations in social-psychological theory. However, every theory of such nature with a causal claim will have to prove that it satisfies the criteria.

5.  This view triggered an extensive discussion (Coudin, 1994; Duveen, 1994; Echebarría Echabe, 1994; Horenczyk and Bekerman, 1995; von Cranach, 1995; W. Wagner, 1994, 1995).

6. A similar view, though with a different angle, is expressed in cognitive science (Horgan and Woodward, 1991; Margolis, 1991).

7. The physicalism debate is still in progress, the extent of which cannot be presented here. An interesting development in the debate is Kim's (1993) theory of supervenience.

8. As the appropriate observations by Riedl refer to ontologically understood levels of complexity in support of Hartmann (1964) and in opposition to the idea of levels of analysis, only his structural arguments are relevant here.

9. In mathematical terms this would be a homomorphic bottom-up mapping.

10. At least, this was the case at the time when the idea of the lever was formulated.

11. Of course, the four dimensions cannot ensure an exact, let alone exhaustive description of the sciences mentioned. Their attributes and research traditions are far more complex than could be treated here. What is of importance here are the global and abstract attributes which, in our opinion, characterise these sciences in the wider field of social psychology. In particular, this refers to the formation of an essential difference, i.e., the population criterion.

12. This is also the reason why some experimentalists are so desperately trying to 'clean' their stimulus material of any meaning.

## Chapter 11 Methods in social representation research

1. The presentation of some of the following research (Duveen, Jovchelovitch, Lorenzi-Cioldi, Marková, Rose) reported in this and the following subsections is based on these researcher's own summary in a collaborative text with one of the authors (W. Wagner).

2. Before interpreting a correspondence analysis graph, the relevant statistical literature should be consulted. Not all proximity in the graphs, particularly if they are biplots, can be interpreted in terms of similarity of meaning.

3. Five major Brazilian quality dailies and the two most influential weekly magazines: *Folha de São Paulo, Estado de São Paulo, Jornal do Brasil, Zero Hora, Correio Brasiliense*; magazines *Veja* and *Isto É*.

4. Professionals, manual workers, students, taxi drivers, policeman and street children.

5. Members of the Brazilian Parliament at the federal level.

# References

Abrams, D. (1990). How do group members regulate their behaviour? An integration of social identity and self-awareness theories. In: D. Abrams and M. A. Hogg (Eds), *Social Identity Theory*. New York: Harvester-Wheatsheaf.

Abric, J.-C. (1971). Experimental study of group creativity: Task representation, group structure, and performance. *European Journal of Social Psychology*, 1, 311–26.

Abric, J.-C. (1976). Jeux, conflits et représentations sociales. Thèse d'Etat, Université de Provence.

Abric, J.-C. (1982). Cognitive processes underlying cooperation: The theory of social representation. In: V. J. Derlega and J. Grzelak (Eds), *Cooperation and Helping Behavior: Theories and Research*. New York: Academic Press.

Abric, J.-C. (1984). A theoretical and experimental approach to the study of social representations in a situation of interaction. In: R. Farr and S. Moscovici (Eds), *Social Reperesentations*. Cambridge: Cambridge University Press.

Abric, J.-C. (1987). *Coopération, compétition et représentations sociales*. Fribourg: DelVal.

Abric, J.-C. (1989). L'étude expérimentale des représentations sociales. In: D. Jodelet (Ed), *Les représentations sociales*. Paris: Presses Universitaires de France.

Abric, J.-C. (2001). A structural approach to social representations. In: K. Deaux and G. Philogène (Eds), *Representations of the Social*. Oxford: Blackwell.

Abric, J.-C., and Kahan, J. (1972). The effects of representations on behavior in experimental games. *European Journal of Social Psychology*, 2, 129–44.

Abric, J.-C., and Mardellat, R. (1973–4). Etude experimentale des représentations dans une situation conflictuelle: Rôle du contexte de la tâche, de la place et de la pratique des sujets dans la formation sociale. *Bulletin de Psychologie*, 27, 146–52.

Abric, J.-C., and Vacherot, G. (1975–6). Méthodologie et étude expérimentale des représentations sociales: Tâche, partenaire et comportements en situation de jeu. *Bulletin de Psychologie*, 29, 735–46.

Abric, J.-C., Faucheux, C., Moscovici, S., and Plon, M. (1967). Rôle de l'image du partenaire sur la coopération en situation de jeu. *Psychologie Française*, 12, 267–75.

Adler, T. (1990). Researchers agree data sharing is good, but specifics elude them. *APA-Monitor*, July 1990.

Aebischer, V. (1985). *Les femmes et le language – Représentations sociales d'une différence*. Paris: Presses Universitaires de France.

Aebischer, V., Deconchy, J.-P., and Lipiansky, E. M. (Eds) (1991). *Idéologies et représentations sociales*. Fribourg: DelVal.

Ajzen, I., and Fishbein, M. (1980). *Understanding Attitudes and Predicting Social Behaviour*. Englewood Cliffs, NJ: Prentice-Hall.

Alexander, J. C. (1995). *Fin de Siécle Social Theory*. London: Verso.

Alexander, P. (1981). The case of the lonely corpuscle: Reductive explanation and primitive expressions. In: R. Healey (Ed), *Reduction, Time and Reality*. Cambridge: Cambridge University Press.

Allen, R. (1992). *Channels of Discourse, Reassembled*. Chapel Hill: University of North Carolina.

Allport, F. H. (1924). *Social Psychology*. New York: Johnson Reprint.

Amir, Y., and Sharon, I. (1988). Are social-psychological laws cross-culturally valid? *Journal of Cross-Cultural Psychology*, 18, 383–470.

Anderson, N. H. (1974). Information integration theory: A brief survey. In: D. H. Krantz, R. C. Atkinson, R. D. Luce and P. Suppes (Eds), *Contemporary Developments in Mathematical Psychology, Vol. 2*. San Francisco: Freeman.

Angermeyer, M. C. (1991). 'Zuviel Streß!' Vorstellungen von Patienten mit funktionellen Psychosen über die Ursachen ihrer Krankheit. In: U. Flick (Hg.), *Alltagswissen über Gesundheit und Krankheit*. Heidelberg: Asanger.

Antaki, C. (1985). Ordinary explanation in conversation: Causal structures and their defence. *European Journal of Social Psychology*, 15, 213–30.

Antaki, C., and Fielding, G. (1981). Research on ordinary explanations. In: C. Antaki (Ed), *The Psychology of Ordinary Explanations of Social Behavior*. London: Academic Press.

Apostolidis, T. (2001). *Penser le rapport au sexuel à 'époque du SIDA*. Lille: Presse Universitaires du Septentrion.

Ardelt, E., Wagner, W., and Wieser, P. (1991). Morality of upperclass managers and lower class criminals. Paper presented at the Annual Colloquium of the International Association for Research in Economic Psychology, Stockholm, June 1991.

Argyle, M., Furnham, A., and Graham, J. A. (1981). *Social Situations*. Cambridge: Cambridge University Press.

Ariés, P. (1975). *Geschichte der Kindheit*. München: Hanser.

Ariés, P., and Duby, G. (Eds) (1987). *Histoire de la vie privée (5 tomes)*. Paris: Seuil.

Arnault, M., and de Montmollin, G. (1985). La représentation comme structure cognitive en psychologie sociale. *Psychologie Française*, 30, 239–44.

Aronson, E. (1980a). *The Social Animal*. San Francisco: Freeman.

Aronson, E. (1980b). Persuasion via self-justification: Large commitments for small rewards. In: L. Festinger (Ed), *Retrospections on Social Psychology*. New York: Oxford University Press.

Arruda, A. (2003). Living is dangerous: Research challenges in social representations. *Culture and Psychology*, 9, 339–59.

Asch, S. E. (1956). Studies on independence and conformity: A minority of one against a unaninomous majority. *Psychological Monographs*, 70, 416–23.

Asch, S. E. (1958). The metaphor: A psychological inquiry. In: R. Tagiuri and L. Petrullo (Eds), *Person Perception and Interpersonal Behavior*. Stanford, CA: Stanford University Press.

Augé, M. (1982). *The Anthropological Circle*. Cambridge: Cambridge University Press.

Augé, M., and Herzlich, C. (1984). *Le sens du mal. Anthropologie, histoire, sociologie de la maladie*. Paris: Éditions des Archives contemporaines.

Augoustinos, M. (1990). The mediating role of representations on causal attributions. *Social Behaviour*, 5, 49–62.

Augoustinos, M. (1991). Consensual representations of social structure in different age groups. *British Journal of Social Psychology*, 30, 193–205.

Augoustinos, M. (1998). Social representations and ideology: Towards the study of ideological representations. In U. Flick (Ed), *The Psychology of the Social*. Cambridge: Cambridge University Press.

Augoustinos, M., and Innes, J. M. (1990). Towards an integration of social representations and social schema theory. *British Journal of Social Psychology*, 29, 213–31.

Augoustinos, M., and Penny, S. L. (2001). Reconciliation: The genesis of a new social representation. *Papers on Social Representations*, 10, 4.1–4.18. [http://www.psr.jku.at/]

Augoustinos, M., and Walker, I. (1995). *Social Cognition: An Integrated Introduction*. London: Sage.

Axelrod, R. (1984). *The Evolution of Cooperation*. New York: Basic Books.

Backman, C. W. (1979). Soziale Norman. In: A. Heigl-Evers (Hg.), *Psychologie des 20. Jahrhunderts, Bd. VIII*. München: Kindler.

Bäckström, A., Pirttilä-Backman, A. M., and Tuorila, H. (2003). Dimensions of novelty: A social representation approach to new foods. *Appetite*, 40, 299–307.

Baldwin, J. M. (1911). *The Individual and the Society*. London: Rebman.

Banchs, M. A. (2000). Aproximaciones procesuales y estructurales al estudio de las representaciones sociales. *Papers on Social Representations*, 9, 3.1–3.15. [http://www.psr.jku.at/]

Bandura, A. (1977). Self-efficacy: Towards a unifying theory of behavioral change. *Psychological Review*, 84, 191–215.

Bangerter, A. (2000). Transformation between scientific and social representations of conception: The method of serial reproduction. *British Journal of Social Psychology*, 39, 521–36.

Bangerter, A., and Heath, C. (2004). The Mozart effect: Tracking the evolution of a scientific legend. *British Journal of Social Psychology*, 43(4), 605–23.

Barker, R. G. (1968). *Ecological Psychology*. Stanford: Stanford University Press.

Barkow, J. H., Cosmides, L., and Tooby, J. E. (Eds) (1992). *The Adapted Mind – Evolutionary Psychology and the Generation of Culture*. New York: Oxford University Press.

Bar-Tal, D. (1990). Israeli-Palestinian conflict: A cognitive analysis. *International Journal of Intercultural Relations*, 14, 7–29.

Bar-Tal, D., and Antebi, D. (1992). Siege mentality in Israel. Ongoing Production on Social Representations/*Papers on Social Representations*, 1, 49–68. [http://www.psr.jku.at/]

Barthes, R. (1964). *Mythen des Alltags*. Frankfurt: Suhrkamp.

Barthes, R. (1988). Introduction to the structural analysis of narratives, *The Semiotic Challenge*. Oxford: Basil Blackwell.

Bartlett, F. C. (1932). *Remembering*. Cambridge: Cambridge University Press.

Bauer, I. (1988). '*Tschikweiber haum's uns g'nennt . . .' Frauenleben und Frauenarbeit an der 'Peripherie': Die Halleiner Zigarrenfabriksarbeiterinnen 1869 bis 1940*. Wien: Europaverlag.

Bauer, M. (1996). *The Narrative Interview: Comments on a Technique for Qualitative Data Collection, Vol. 1*. London: London School of Economics.

Bauer, M. (2001). Ethical framing in the elite press. *Notizie di Politeia*, 17, 51–66.

Bauer, M., and Gaskell, G. (1999). Towards a paradigm for research on social representations. *Journal for the Theory of Social Behaviour*, 29, 136–86.

Bauer, M., and Gaskell, G. (Eds). (2000). *Qualitative Researching with Text, Image and Sound*. Londonn: Sage.

Bauer, M., and Gaskell, G. (Eds). (2002). *Biotechnology – the Making of a Global Controversy*. Cambridge: Cambridge University Press.

Bauer, M., Kohring, M., Allansdottir, A., and Gutteling, J. (2001). The dramatisation of biotechnology in elite mass media. In G. Gaskell and M. Bauer (Eds), *Biotechnology 1996–2000, the Years of Controversy*. London: The National Museum of Science and Industry.

Beals, R. L., Hoijer, H., and Beals, A. R. (1977). *An Introduction to Anthropology*. New York: Macmillan.

Beattie, J. (1964). *Other Cultures*. New York: The Free Press.

Beaudouin, V., and Lahlou, S. (1993). L'analyse lexicale: Outil d'exploration des représentations. *Cahier de Recherche CREDOC*, 48 (September 1993.).

Beauvois, J.-L. (1984). *La psychologie quotidienne*. Paris: Presses Universitaires de France.

Beauvois, J.-L., and Joule, R. (1981). *Soumission et ideologie. Psychosociologie de la rationalisation*. Paris: Presses Universitaires de France.

Beck, U. (1992). *Risk Society: Towards a New Modernity*. London: Sage.

Behar, J. (1988). Dimensión social de la pubertad. In: T. Ibañez Gracia (Ed), *Ideologías de la vida cotidiana*. Barcelona: Sendai.

Benjamin, W. (1974). Über den Begriff der Geschichte. In: *Gesammelte Schriften, Band I.2*. Frankfurt: Suhrkamp.

Berelson, B. (1952). *Content Analysis in Communication Research*. Illinois: Glencoe Free Press.

Berger, P., and Kellner, H. (1964). Marriage and the construction of reality. *Diogenes*, 46, 1–25.

Berger, P., and Luckmann, T. (1979). *The Social Construction of Reality*. Harmondsworth: Peregrine.

Bergmann, M. M. (1999). Would the real social representation please stand up? Three levels of analysis of social representations of European American and Mexican American identity. *Papers on Social Representations*, 8, 4.1–4.17. [http://www.psr.jku.at/]

Berlyne, D. E. (1960). *Conflict, Arousal and Curiosity*. London: McGraw-Hill.

Bevan, W. (1991). Contemporary psychology – a tour inside the onion. *American Psychologist*, 46, 475–83.

Billig, M. (1982). *Ideology and Social Psychology*. Oxford: Basil Blackwell.

Billig, M. (1987). *Arguing and Thinking – A Rhetorical Approach to Social Psychology*. Cambridge: Cambridge University Press.

Billig, M. (1988). Social representation, objectification and anchoring: A rhetorical analysis. *Social Behavior*, 3, 1–16.

Billig, M. (1993). Studying the thinking society: social representations, rhetoric, and attitudes. In: G. M. Breakwell and G. V. Canter (Eds). *Empirical Approaches to Social Representations*. Oxford: Clarendon Press.

Billig, M., Condor, S., Edwards, D., Gane, M., Middleton, D., and Radley, A. (1988). *Ideological Dilemmas*. London: Sage.

Black, M. B. (1973). Belief systems. In: J. J. Honigman (Ed), *Handbook of Social and Cultural Anthropology*. Chicago: Rand McNally.

Bock, P. K. (1988). *Rethinking Psychological Anthropology*. New York: Freeman.

Boesch, E. E. (1971). *Zwischen zwei Wirklichkeiten*. Bern: Huber.

Boesch, E. E. (1991). *Symbolic Action Theory and Cultural Psychology*. Berlin: Springer.

Bohn, C. (1991). y. Opladen: Westdeutscher Vlg.

Boltanski, L. (1971). Les usages sociaux du corps. *Annales: Economies – sociétés – civilisations*, 26, 205–33.

Boltanski, L., and Thévenot, L. (1991). *De la Justification. Les Économies de la Grandeur*. Paris: Gallimard.

Bond, M. H. (1983). A proposal for cross-cultural studies of attribution. In: M. Hewstone (Ed), *Attribution Theory – Social and Functional Extensions*. Oxford: Blackwell.

Born, R. (1983). Schizo-Semantik: Provokationen zum Thema Bedeutungstheorien und Wissenschaftsphilosophie im Allgemeinen. *Conceptus*, 40/1, 101–16.

Born, R. (1991). Untersuchungen über wissenschaftliche und alltägliche Erfahrungen. Unveröffentlichtes Manuskript, Universität Linz.

Boster, J. S. (1987). Introduction. *American Behavioral Scientist*, 31, 150–62.

Bourdieu, P. (1976). *Entwurf einer Theorie der Praxis*. Frankfurt: Suhrkamp.

Bourdieu, P. (1980). *Le sens pratique*. Paris: Les Editions de Minuit.

Bourdieu, P. (1983). *Zur Soziologie der symbolischen Formen*. Frankfurt: Suhrkamp.

Bourdieu, P. (1984a). *Die feinen Unterschiede. Kritik der gesellschaftlichen Urteilskraft*. Frankfurt: Suhrkamp.

Bourdieu, P. (1984b). *Questions de sociologie*. Paris: Les Editions de Minuit.

Bourdieu, P. (1985). *Sozialer Raum und 'Klassen' – Leçon sur la leçon*. Frankfurt: Suhrkamp.

Bourdieu, P. (1987). *Sozialer Sinn. Kritik der theoretischen Vernunft*. Frankfurt: Suhrkamp.

Bourdieu, P. (1988). Vive la crise! For heterodoxy in social science. *Theory and Society*, 17, 773–87.

Bourdieu, P., and Passeron, J.-C. (1971). *Die Illusion der Chancengleichheit*. Stuttgart: Klett.

Boyd, R. (1979). Metaphor and theory change. In: A. Ortony (Ed), *Metaphor and Thought*. Cambridge: Cambridge University Press.

Brandstätter, H. (1981). Time sampling of subjective well-being. In: H. Hartmann, W. Molt and H. Stringer (Eds), *Advances in Economic Psychology*. Heidelberg: Meyn.

Brandstätter, H. (1983). *Sozialpsychologie*. Stuttgart: Kohlhammer.

Brandstätter, H. (1989). Stabilität und Veränderbarkeit von Persönlichkeitsmerkmalen. *Zeitschrift für Arbeits- und Organisationspsychologie*, 33, 12–20.

Brandstätter, H. (1990). Emotions in everyday life situations. Time sampling of subjective Experience. In: F. Strack and N. Schwarz (Hg.), *Subjective Well-Being*. Oxford: Pergamon Press.

Brandstätter, H., and Wagner, W. (1989). *Alltagserfahrung berufstätiger Ehepaare*. Forschungsbericht, Universität Linz.

Brandstätter, H., Barthel, E., and Fünfgelt, V. (1984). Beruf 'Hausfrau': Eine psychologische Studie mit dem Zeitstichproben-Tagebuch. In: R. Blum and M. Steiner (Hg.), *Aktuelle Probleme der Marktwirtschaft aus Einzel- und gesamtwirtschaftlicher Sicht*. Berlin: Duncker & Humblot.

Brandtstädter, J. (1982). Apriorische Elemente in psychologischen Forschungs-programmen. *Zeitschrift für Sozialpsychologie*, 13, 267–77.

Breakwell, G. M., and Canter, D. V. E. (1993). *Empirical Approaches to Social Representations*. Oxford: Oxford University Press.

Breakwell, G. M., and Lyons, E. (Eds) (1996). *Changing European Identities: Social Psychological Analyses of Social Change*. Oxford: Buttenworth-Heinemann.

Breakwell, G. M., Hammond, S., and Fife-Schaw, C. (1995). *Research Methods in Psychology*. London: Sage.

Brehm, J. W., and Cohen, A. R. (1959). Re-evaluation of choice alternatives as a function of their number and qualitative similarity. *Journal of Abnormal and Social Psychology*, 58, 373–8.

Brewer, M. (2001). Social identities and social representations: A question of priority. In: K. Deaux and G. Philogène (Eds), *Representations of the Social: Bridging Theoretical Traditions*. Oxford: Blackwell.

Brewer, W. F., and Nakamura, G. V. (1984). The nature and functions of schemata. In: R. S. Wyer and T. K. Srull (Hg.), *Handbook of Social Cognition, Vol. 1*. Hillsdale, NJ: Lawrence Erlbaum.

Bril, B., and Lehalle, H. (1988). *Le développement psychologique est-il universel?* Paris: Presses Universitaires de France.

Bruner, J. S., and Postman, L. (1947). Emotional selectivity in perception and reaction. *Journal of Personality*, 16, 69–77.

Budd, R., and Spencer, C. (1986). Lay theories of behavioral intentions: A source of response bias in the theory of reasoned action? *British Journal of Social Psychology*, 25, 109–17.

Bulman, R. J., and Wortman, C. B. (1977). Attributions of blame and coping in the 'real world': Severe accident victims react to their lot. *Journal of Personality and Social Psychology*, 35, 351–63.

Bulmer, R. (1967). Why is the Cassowary not a bird? A problem of zoological taxonomy among the Karam of the New Guinea Highlands. *Man*, 2, 5–25.

Burton, A. (1986). Programming common sense: Analytic consequences of Heider's naïve analysis of action. *Human Relations*, 39, 725–44.

Buss, A. H. (1989). Personality as traits. *American Psychologist*, 44, 1378–88.

Buss, D. M. (1991). Evolutionary personality psychology. *Annual Review of Psychology*, 42, 459–91.

Byford, J. (2002). Anchoring and objectifying 'neocortical warfare': Representation of a biological metaphor in Serbian conspiracy

literature. *Papers on Social Representations*, 11, 3.1–3.14. [http://www.
psr.jku.at/]

Caille, A. (1988). Esquisse d'une critique de l'économie generale de la pratique. *Cahiers du L.A.S.A*, 89, 103–214.

Campbell, A., Muncer, S. (1994). Sex differences in aggression: Social representation and social roles. *British Journal of Social Psychology*, 33,
233–45.

Campbell, D. T., and Jovchelovitch, S. (2000). Health, community and
development: Towards a social psychology of participation. *Journal of
Community and Applied Social Psychology*, 10, 255–70.

Cantor, N., and Mischel, W. (1979). Prototypes in person perception. In:
L. Berkowitz (Ed), *Advances in Experimental Social Psychology, Vol. 12*.
New York: Academic Press.

Capozza, D., Falvo, R., Robusto, E., and Orlando, A. (2003). Beliefs about
the internet: Methods of elicitation and measurement. *Papers on Social
Representations*, 12, 1.1–1.14. [http://www.psr.jku.at/]

Capozza, D., Robusto, E., Squarza, R., and De Carlo, N. A. (1995). La
représentation sociale de l'argent. *Papers on Social Representations*, 4,
p. 85–104. [http://www.psr.jku.at/]

Caron, J. (1983). L'idée de 'pensée naturelle': quelques réflexions. In:
*Publications de l'Université de Rouen, La pensée naturelle*. Paris:
Presses Universitaires de France.

Carugati, F., Emiliani, F., and Molinari, L. (1990). Being a mother is not
enough. Theories and images in the social representations of childhood.
*Revue Internationale de Psychologie Sociale*, 3, 289–306.

Casti, J. L. (1990). *Verlust der Wahrheit – Streitfragen der Naturwissenschaften*. München: Droemer Knaur.

Castro, P., and Lima, M. L. (2001). Old and new ideas about the environment and science: An exploratory study. *Environment and Behaviour*, 33(3), 400–23.

Chafe, W. L. (1977). The recall and verbalization of past experience. In:
R. W. Cole (Ed), *Current Issues in Linguistic Theory*. Bloomington:
Indiana University Press.

Chapman, L. J. (1967). Illusory correlation in observational report.
*Journal of Verbal Learning and Verbal Behavior*, 6, 151–5.

Chapman, L. J., and Chapman, J. P. (1967). Genesis of popular but erroneous diagnostic observations. *Journal of Abnormal Psychology*, 72,
193–204.

Cheal, D. (1980). Rule-governed behavior. *Philosophy of the Social
Sciences*, 10, 39–49.

Cheng, P., and Holyoak, K. J. (1985). Pragmatic reasoning schemas.
*Cognitive Psychology*, 17, 391–416.

Cheng, P., Holyoak, K. J., Nisbett, R. E., and Oliver, L. M. (1986).
Pragmatic versus syntactic approaches to training deductive reasoning.
*Cognitive Psychology*, 18, 293–328.

Chombart de Lauwe, M.-J. (1971). *Un monde autre: l'enfance. De ses représentations à son mythe*. Paris: Payot.

Chombart de Lauwe, M.-J. (1984). Changes in the representation of the child in the course of social transmission. In: R. Farr and S. Moscovici (Eds), *Social Representations*. Cambridge: Cambridge University Press.

Chryssochoou, X. (2000a). How superordinate identity is formed? The case of the European. *European Psychologist*, 5, 269–77.

Chryssochoou, X. (2000b). Memberships in a superordinate level: Rethinking European Union as a multinational society. *Journal of Community and Applied Social Psychology*, 10, 403–20.

Chryssochoou, X. (2004). *Cultural Diversity: It's Social Psychology*. Oxford: Blackwell.

Cialdini, R. B. (1984). *Influence*. New York: Quill.

Cialdini, R. B., and Petty, R. E. (1981). Anticipatory opinion effects. In: R. E. Petty, T. M. Ostrom and T. C. Brock (Eds), *Cognitive Responses in Persuasion*. Hillsdale, NJ: Lawrence Erlbaum.

Cialdini, R. B., Herman, C. P., Levy, A., Kozlowski, L. T., and Petty, R. E. (1976). Elastic shifts of opinion: Determinants of direction and durability. *Journal of Personality and Social Psychology*, 34, 663–72.

Cinnirella, M. (1998) Exploring temporal aspects of social identity: The concept of possible social identities. *European Journal of Social Psychology* 28(2), 227–48.

Clark, M. S., and Isen, A. M. (1982). Toward understanding the relationship between feeling states and social behavior. In: A. Hastorf and A. Isen (Eds), *Cognitive Social Psychology*. Amsterdam: Elsevier.

Clark, M. S., and Waddell, B. A. (1983). Effects of moods on thoughts about helping, attraction and information acquisition. *Social Psychology Quarterly*, 46, 31–5.

Clémence, A. (2001). Social positions and social representations. In: K. Deaux and G. Philogène (Eds), *Representations of the Social*. Malden, MA: Blackwell.

Clémence, A., Devos, T., and Doise, W. (2001). Social representations of human rights violations: Further evidence. *Swiss Journal of Psychology*, 60, 89–98.

Codol, J.-P. (1972). Représentations et comportements dans les groupes restreints. Manuscrit inédit, Université de Provence, Aix-en-Provence.

Codol, J.-P. (1974). On the system of representations in a group situation. *European Journal of Social Psychology*, 4, 343–65.

Codol, J.-P. (1984). On the system of representations in an artificial social situation. In: Farr and Moscovici (Eds), *Social Reperesentations*.

Cohen, Y.-A. (Ed) (1968). *Man in Adaptation: The Cultural Present*. Chicago: Chicago University Press.

Cole, M., and Scribner, S. (1975). Theorizing about socialization of cognition. *Ethos*, 3, 249–68.

Collins, A. W. (1979). Could beliefs be representations in our brains? *The Journal of Philosophy*, 76, 225–43.

Conde Rodriguez, E. G. (1985). Privatización del espacio urbano en el barrio de Tepito y repercusión psicosocial en la vida colectiva del mismo. Tesis de Licenciatura, Universidad Nacional Autónoma de México.

Cooper, J., and Fazio, R. H. (1984). A new look at dissonance theory. In: L. Berkowitz (Ed), *Advances in Experimental Social Psychology, Vol. 17*. New York: Academic Press.

Corsaro, W. A. (1990). The underlife of the nursery school: Young children's social representations of adult rules. In: G. Duveen and B. Lloyd (Eds), *Social Representations and the Development of Knowledge*. Cambridge: Cambridge University Press.

Cosmides, L. (1989). The logic of social exchange: Has natural selection shaped how humans reason? Studies with the Wason selection task. *Cognition*, 31, 187–276.

Costalat-Founeau, A. M. (1999) Identity dynamics, action, and context. *Journal for the Theory of Social Behaviour* 29(3), 289–300.

Costalat-Founeau, A.-M., Picot, M.-C., Hauchard, D., Klimekova, M., and Favier, F. (2002). Représentation du corps et de l'alimentation chez une population de femmes de plus de 75 ans. *Papers on Social Representations*, 11, 4.1–4.20. [http://www.psr.jku.at/]

Coudin, G. (1994). Commentaire de 'The Fallacy of Misplaced Intentionality . . .' by W. Wagner. *Papers on Social Representations*, 3, 210–11. [http://www.psr.jku.at/]

Coulter, J. (1983). *Rethinking Cognitive Theory*. New York: St. Martins Press.

Coulter, J. (1985). Two concepts of the mental. In: K. J. Gergen and K. E. Davis (Eds), *The Social Construction of the Person*. New York: Springer.

Courtial, J. P. (1999). Analyse dynamique des représentations sociales des chercheurs: le cas de l'autisme. *Papers on Social Representations*, 8, 3.1–3.22. [http://www.psr.jku.at/]

Cox, J. R., and Griggs, R. A. (1982). The effects of experience on performance in Wason's selection task. *Memory and Cognition*, 10, 496–502.

Cronbach, L. J. (1975). Beyond the two disciplines of scientific psychology. *American Psychologist*, 30, 116–27.

Cummins, R. (1989). *Meaning and Mental Representation*. Cambridge, MA: MIT Press.

D'Alessio, M. (1990). Social representations of childhood: An implicit theory. In: Duveen and Lloyd (Eds), *Social Representations and the Development of Knowledge*.

D'Andrade, R. G. (1976). A propositional analysis of US-American beliefs about illness. In: K. H. Basso and H. A. Selby (Eds), *Meaning in Anthropology*. Albuquerque: University of New Mexico Press.

D'Andrade, R. G. (1981). The cultural part of cognition. *Cognitive Science*, 5, 179–95.

D'Andrade, R. G. (1986). Three scientific world views and the covering law model. In: D. W. Fiske and R. A. Shweder (Eds), *Metatheory in Social Science*. Chicago: Chicago University Press.

D'Andrade, R. G. (1987). Modal responses and cultural expertise. *American Behavioral Scientist*, 31, 194–202.

D'Andrade, R. G. (1989). Culturally based reasoning. In: A. Gellatly, D. Rogers and J. A. Sloboda (Hg.), *Cognition and Social Worlds*. Oxford: Clarendon Press.

Dann, H.-D. (1992). Subjective theories and their foundation in education. In: M. von Cranach, W. Doise and G. Mugny (Eds), *Social Representations and the Social Bases of Knowledge*. Lewiston, NJ: Hogrefe & Huber.

Danziger, K. (1997). *Naming the Mind – How Psychology Found its Language*. London: Sage.

Darley, J. M., and Fazio, R. H. (1980). Expectancy confirmation processes arising in the social interaction sequence. *American Psychologist*, 35, 867–81.

Darley, J. M., and Gross, P. H. (1983). A hypothesis-confirming bias in labeling effect. *Journal of Personality and Social Psychology*, 44, 20–33.

Darmon, P. (1977). *Le mythe de la procreation à l'âge baroque*. Paris: J.-J. Pauvert.

Davidson, D. (1978). What metaphors mean. *Critical Inquiry*, 5, 31–47.

Davidson, D. (1980). *Essays on Actions and Events*. Oxford: Clarendon Press.

de Abreu, G. (1995). Understanding how children experience the relationship between home and school mathematics. *Mind, Culture, and Activity*, 2, 119–42.

de Abreu, G., and Cline, T. (1998). Studying social representations of mathematics learning in multi-ethnic primary schools – work in progress. *Papers on Social Representations*, 7, 1–20. [http://www.psr.jku.at/]

de Paolis, P. (1982). Marquage social et developpement cognitif. Paper presented at Colloquium on New Perspectives in the Experimental Study of the Social Development of Intelligence, Geneva.

de Paolis, P. (1990). Prototypes of the psychologist and professionalisation: Diverging social representations of a developmental process. In: Duveen and Lloyd (Eds), *Social Representations and the Development of Knowledge*.

de Paolis, P., Doise, W., and Mugny, G. (1987). Social markings in cognitive operations. In: Doise and Moscovici (Eds), *Current Issues in European Social Psychology, Vol. 2*. Cambridge: Cambridge University Press.

de Rosa, A. S. (1987). The social representation of mental illness in children and adults. In: Doise and Moscovici (Eds), *Current Issues in European Social Psychology*, Vol. 2.

de Rosa, A. S. (1994). From theory to metatheory in social representations: The lines of argument of a theoretical-methodological debate. *Social Science Information*, 33, 255–72.

de Rosa, A. S. (1996). Reality changes faster than research: National identity in social representations of the European Community in the context of changes in international relations. In: Breakwell and Lyons (Eds), *Changing European Identities* (pp. 381–402).

de Sa, C. P., Bello, R., and Jodelet, D. (1997). Representaciones sociales y practicas religiosas afro-brasilenas en Rio de Janeiro. In: L. d. Hetier and L. Pargas (Eds), *Fermentum: Representaciones Sociales Complejidad diversidad de las voces de la social* (pp. 65–74). Merida, Venezuela: GISAC.

Deconchy, J.-P. (1987). Conduites sociales, comparaison sociale et représentation du patrimoine comportemental commun à l'homme et à l'animal. In: J.-L. Beauvois, R.-V. Joule and J.-M. Monteil (Eds), *Perspectives cognitives et conduites sociales*, Vol. 1. Fribourg: DelVal.

Deconchy, J.-P. (1989). *Psychologie sociale. Croyances et idéologies*. Paris: Klincksieck.

Deconchy, J.-P. (1990). La représentation sociale de la causalité biologique. In: X. Seron (Ed), *Psychologie et cerveau*. Paris: Presse Universitaires de France.

Dee-Lucas, D., and Larkin, J. H. (1986). 'Novices' strategies for processing scientific texts'. *Discourse Processes*, 9, 329–54.

Degen, R. (1991). Der Fall Freud. *Bild der Wissenschaft*, Heft 2, Februar 1991, 42–5.

Demele, I. (1988). *Abstraktes Denken und Entwicklung – Der unvermeidliche Bruch mit der Tradition*. Frankfurt: Brandes & Apsel.

Dennett, D. C. (1987). *The Intentional Stance*. Cambridge, MA: MIT Press.

Denzin, N. K., and Lincoln, Y. S. (Eds). (1994). *Handbook of Qualitative Research*. Thousand Oaks, CA: Sage.

Desautels, J., and Larochelle, M. (1987). Connaisance, représentation et aprentissage. Qu'est-ce qu'une connaissance dite scientifique? Les modèles spontanés d'adolescents. *Prospectives*, 23, 163–71.

Deschamps, J.-C. (1983). Social attribution. In: J. Jaspars, F. D. Fincham and M. Hewstone (Eds), *Attribution Theory and Research*. London: Academic Press.

Deutscher, I. (1984). Choosing ancestors: Some consequences of the selection from intellectual traditions. In: Farr and Moscovici (Eds), *Social Representations*.

Devereux, G. (1973). *Angst und Methode in den Verhaltenswissenschaften*. München: Hanser.

Dewsbury, D. A. (1991). 'Psychobiology'. *American Psychologist*, 46, 198–205.

DiGiacomo, J.-P. (1980). Intergroup alliances and rejections within a protest movement (Analysis of social representations). *European Journal of Social Psychology*, 10, 329–44.

DiGiacomo, J.-P. (1985). *Rappresentazioni sociali e movimenti collettivi*. Napoli: Liguori Editore.

Doise, W. (1976). Structural homologies, sociology and experimental social psychology. *Social Science Information*, 15, 929–42.

Doise, W. (1978a). *Groups and Individuals*. Cambridge: Cambridge University Press.

Doise, W. (1978b). Images, représentations, idéologies et expérimentation psychosociologique. *Social Science Information*, 17, 41–69.

Doise, W. (1980). Levels of explanation in the *European Journal of Social Psychology*. *European Journal of Social Psychology*, 10, 213–31.

Doise, W. (1985). Social regulations in cognitive development. In: R. A. Hinde, A.-N. Perret-Clermont and J. Stevenson-Hinde (Eds), *Social Relationships and Cognitive Development*. Oxford: Clarendon Press.

Doise, W. (1986a). Les représentations sociales: définition d'un concept. In: W. Doise and A. Palmonari (Eds), *L'étude des représentations sociales*. Neuchâtel: Delachaux & Niestlé.

Doise, W. (1986b). *Levels of Explanation in Social Psychology*. Cambridge: Cambridge University Press.

Doise, W. (1986c). Décrire et éxpliquer ou comment gérer penurie et abondance? *Psychologie et Education*, 10, 3–19.

Doise, W. (1987a). Pratiques scientifiques et représentations sociales – Que faire de la psychologie de Piaget? *Cahiers du Centre de Rechérche interdisciplinaire de Vaucresson*, 3, 89–108.

Doise, W. (1987b). Le social et l'individuel: théories générales et recherches intergroup. *Psychologie et Education*, 11, 57–74.

Doise, W. (1989). Attitudes et représentations sociales. In: D. Jodelet (Ed), *Les représentations sociales*. Paris: Presses Universitaires de France.

Doise, W. (1990). Les représentations sociales. In: R. Ghiglione, C. Bonnet and J. F. Richard (Eds), *Traité de psychologie cognitive, Vol. 3*. Paris: Dunod.

Doise, W. (1992). L'ancrage dans les études sur les représentations sociales. *Bulletin de Psychologie*, 45, 189–95.

Doise, W. (1993). Debating social representations. In: Breakwell and Canter (Eds), *Empirical Approaches to Social Representations*.

Doise, W., and Palmonari, A. (Eds) (1986). *L'étude des Représentations Sociales*. Neuchâtel: Delachaux & Niestlé.

Doise, W., and Papastamou, S. (1987). Représentationes sociales des causes de la délinquance: Coryances générales et cas concrets. *Déviance et Société*, 11, 153–62.

Doise, W., Clémence, A., and Lorenzi-Cioldi, F. (1992). *Représentations sociales et analyses de donneés*. Grenoble: Presses Universitaires de Grenoble.

Doise, W., Clémence, A., and Lorenzi-Cioldi, F. (1993). *The Quantitative Analysis of Social Representations*. London: Harvester-Wheatsheaf.

Doise, W., Deschamps, J.-C., and Mugny, Y. G. (1980). *Psicología social experimental*. Barcelona: Editorial Hispano Europea.

Doise, W., Dionnet, S., and Mugny, G. (1978). Conflit sociocognitif, marquage social et developpement cognitif. *Cahiers de Psychologie*, 21, 231–43.

Doise, W., Spini, D., and Clémence, A. (1999). Human rights studied as social representations in a cross-national context. *European Journal of Social Psychology*, 29, 1–30.

Domo, J. (1984). Identité culturelle et représentation socile: la culture du riz au Cameroun. Thése de Doctorat, Université de Provence.

Douglas, M. (1966). *Purity and Danger: An Analysis of Concepts of Pollution and Taboo*. London: Routledge & Kegan Paul.

Douglas, M. (1982a). *In the Active Voice*. London: Routledge & Kegan Paul.

Douglas, M. (1982b). Introduction to grid/group analysis. In: M. Douglas (Ed), *Essays in the Sociology of Perception*. London: Routledge & Kegan Paul.

Douglas, M. (1986). *How Institutions Think*. New York: Syracuse University Press.

Douglas, M., and Wildavsky, A. (1982). *Risk and Culture: An Essay on the Selection of Technological and Environmental Dangers*. Berkeley: University of California Press.

Driver, H. E. (1975). *Indians of North America*. Chicago: University of Chicago Press.

Dross, M. (1991). 'Warum bin ich trotz allem gesund geblieben?' Subjektive Theorien von Gesundheit am Beispiel von psychisch gesunden Frauen. In: U. Flick (Hg.), *Alltagswissen über Gesundheit und Krankheit*. Heidelberg: Asanger.

Durant, J., Gaskell, G., and Bauer, M. (Eds). (1998). *Biotechnology in the Public Sphere: a European Sourcebook*. London: Museum of Science and Industry.

Durkheim, E. (1967/1898). Individuelle und kollektive Vorstellungen. In: E. Durkheim, *Soziologie und Philosophie*. Frankfurt/M: Suhrkamp.

Durkheim, E. (1981/1968). *Die elementaren Formen des religiösen Lebens*. Frankfurt: Suhrkamp.

Durkheim, E. (1984/1895). *Die Regeln der soziologischen Methode*. Frankfurt: Suhrkamp.

Duveen, G. (1993). The development of social representations of gender, *Papers on Social Representations*, 2, 171–7. [http://www.psr.jku.at/]

Duveen, G. (1994). Unanalysed Residues: Representations and behaviours – a comment on W. Wagner. *Papers on Social Representations*, 3, 204–9. [http://www.psr.jku.at/]

Duveen, G. (1997). Psychological development as a social process. In: L. Smith, P. Tomlinson and J. Dockerell (Eds), *Piaget, Vygotsky and Beyond*. London: Routledge.

Duveen, G. (2002). Construction, belief, doubt. *Psychologie et Societé*, 5, 139–56.

Duveen, G., and Lloyd, B. (1986). The significance of social identities. *British Journal of Social Psychology*, 25, 219–30.

Duveen, G., and Lloyd, B. (1993). An ethnographic approach to social representations. In Breakwell and Canter (Eds), *Empirical Approaches to Social Representations*.

Duveen, G., and Shields, M. (1985). Children's ideas about work, wages and social rank. *Cahiers de psychologie cognitif*, 5, 411–12.

Eagle, M. (1967). The effect of learning strategies upon free recall. *American Journal of Psychology*, 80, 421–5.

Echebarría Echabe, A. (1994). Social representations, social practices, and causality – A reply to W. Wagner. *Papers on Social Representations*, 3, 195–200. [http://www.psr.jku.at/]

Echebarría Echabe, A., Guede, E. F., and Castro, J. L. G. (1994). Social representations and intergroup conflicts: who's smoking here? *European Journal of Social Psychology*, 24, 339–56.

Eder, K. (1989). Klassentheorie als Gesellschaftstheorie. In: K. Eder (Hg.), *Lebensstil und kulturelle Praxis*. Frankfurt: Suhrkamp.

Edwards, D., and Potter, J. (1992). *Discursive Psychology*. London: Sage.

Eigen, M. (1971). Selforganization of matter and the evolution of biological macromolecules. *Die Naturwissenschaften*, 58, 465–528.

Einsiedel, E. (2001). Citizen voices: Public participation on biotechnology. *Notizie di Politeia*, 17, 94–104.

Einsiedel, E., Allansdottir, A., Allum, N., Bauer, M., Berthomier, A., Chatjouli, A., De Cheiveigné, S., Downey, R., Gutteling, J., Kohring, M., Leonarz, M., Manzoli, F., Olofsson, A., Prztestalski, A., Rusanen, T., Seifert, F., Stathopoulou, A., and Wagner, W. (2002). Brave new sheep – the clone named Dolly. In Bauer and Gaskell (Eds), *Biotechnology – the Making of a Global Controversy*.

Elejabarrieta, F. (1994). Social positioning: A way to link social identity and social representations. *Social Science Information*, 33, 241–53.

Elias, N. (1977). *Über den Prozeß der Zivilisation*. Frankfurt: Suhrkamp.

Elias, N. (1978a). Zum Begriff des Alltags. In: K. Hammerich and M. Klein (Hg.), *Materialien zur Soziologie des Alltags*. Opladen: Westdeutscher Vlg.

Elias, N. (1978b). *Was ist Soziologie?* München: Juventa.

Elster, J. (1979). *Ullysses and the Sirens*. Cambridge: Cambridge University Press.

Elster, J. (1983). *Sour Grapes: Studies in the Subversion of Rationality.* Cambridge: Cambridge University Press.

Emler, N., and Dickinson, J. (1985). Children's representations of economic inequalities: The effects of social class. *British Journal of Developmental Psychology,* 3, 191–8.

Emler, N., Ohana, J., and Moscovici, S. (1987). Children's beliefs about institutional roles: A cross-national study of representations of the teacher's role. *British Journal of Educational Psychology,* 57, 26–37.

Enzensberger, H. M. (1972). Über die Geschichte als kollektive Fiktion. In: *Der kurze Sommer der Anarchie.* Frankfurt: Suhrkamp.

Evans, J. (1983). Selective processes in reasoning. In: J. Evans (Ed), *Thinking and Reasoning: Psychological Approaches.* London: Routledge & Kegan Paul.

Evans, J. (1991). Theories of human reasoning: The fragmented state of the art. *Theory and Psychology,* 1, 83–105.

Evans-Pritchard, E. E. (1976). *Witchcraft, Oracles, and Magic among the Azande.* Oxford: Clarendon Press.

Eysenck, M. W. (1984). *A Handbook of Cognitive Psychology.* London: Erlbaum.

Faina, A. M. (1984). Stili di comportamento minoritario: Alcuni elementi di una rappresentazione sociale. *Giornale Italiano di Psicologia,* 11, 335–55.

Fajans, J. (1985). The person in social context: The social character in Baining "psychology". In: G. M. White and J. Kirkpatrick (Eds), *Person, Self and Experience.* Berkeley: University of California Press.

Farina, A., Fisher, J. D., Getter, H., and Fischer, E. H. (1978). Some consequences of changing people's views regarding the nature of mental illness. *Journal of Abnormal Psychology,* 87, 272–9.

Farr, R. (1976). Experimentation: a social psychological perspective. *British Journal of Social and Clinical Psychology,* 15, 225–38.

Farr, R. M. (1984). Social representations: Their role in the design and execution of laboratory experiments. In: Farr and Moscovici (Eds), *Social Representations.*

Farr, R. M. (1986). Las representaciones sociales. In: S. Moscovici (Ed), *Psicología social,* Vol. 2. Barcelona: Paidós.

Farr, R. M. (1987). Social representations: A French tradition of research. *Journal for the Theory of Social Behaviour* 17, 343–69.

Farr, R. M., and Moscovici, S. (Eds) (1984). *Social Representations.* Cambridge: Cambridge University Press.

Faucheux, C. (1975). Des représentations sociales de la réalité sociale. *Études psychotherapeutiques,* 20, 103–8.

Faucheux, C. (1976). Cross-cultural research in experimental social psychology. *European Journal of Social Psychology,* 6, 269–322.

Faucheux, C., and Moscovici, S. (1968). Self-esteem and exploitative behavior in a game against chance and nature. *Journal of Personality and Social Psychology,* 8, 83–8.

Feldman, C., and Toulmin, S. (1975). Logic and the theory of mind. *Proceedings of the Nebraska Symposium on Motivation.*

Fernandez, J. (1974). The mission of metaphor in expressive culture. *Current Anthropology*, 15, 119–33.

Festinger, L. (1954). A theory of social comparison processes. *Human Relations*, 40, 427–48.

Festinger, L. (1957). *A Theory of Cognitive Dissonance.* Stanford, CA: Stanford University Press.

Festinger, L., and Carlsmith, J. M. (1959). Cognitive consequences of forced compliance. *Journal of Abnormal and Social Psychology*, 58, 203–10.

Feuerhahn, N. (1980). La représentation de l'enfant et sa manipulation par la publicité. *Bulletin de Psychologie*, 33, 949–55.

Feyerabend, P. K. (1962). Explanation, reduction, and empiricism. In: H. Feigl and G. Maxwell (Eds), *Minnesota Studies in the Philosophy of Science, Vol. 3.* Minneapolis: University of Minnesota Press.

Feyerabend, P. K. (1963). How to be a good empiricist: A plea for tolerance in matters epistemological. In: D. Baumrin (Ed), *Delaware Seminar 1962–1963, Vol. 2.* New York: Wiley.

Feyerabend, P. K. (1978). *Against Method.* London: Verso.

Fincham, F. D., and Jaspars, J. M. (1980). Attribution of responsibility: From man the scientist to man the lawyer. In: L. Berkowitz (Ed), *Advances in Experimental Social Psychology, Vol. 13.* New York: Academic Press.

Fishbein, M., and Ajzen, I. (1975). *Belief, Attitude, Intention and Behavior.* Reading, Mass.: Addison-Wesley.

Fisher, J. D., and Farina, A. (1979). Consequences of beliefs about the nature of mental disorders. *Journal of Abnormal Psychology*, 88, 320–7.

Fiske, D. W. (1979). Two worlds of psychological phenomena. *American Psychologist*, 34, 733–9.

Fiske, J. (1987). *Television Culture.* London: Methuen.

Fiske, S. T. (1982). Schema-triggered affect: Applications to social perception. In: M. S. Clark and S. T. Fiske (Eds), *Affect and Cognition.* Hillsdale, NJ: Erlbaum.

Fiske, S. T., and Taylor, S. E. (1984). *Social Cognition.* Reading, MA: Addison-Wesley.

Fiske, T. S., and Taylor, S. E. (1991). *Social Cognition.* New York: McGraw-Hill.

Flament, C. (1981). Sur le pluralisme methodologique dans l'étude des représentations sociales. *Cahiers de psychologie cognitive*, 1, 423–7.

Flament, C. (1982). Du bias d'équilibre structural à la représentation du groupe. In: J.-P. Codol and J.-P. Leyens (Eds), *Cognitive Analysis of Social Behavior.* Den Haag: Martinus Nijhoff.

Flament, C. (1987). Pratiques et représentations sociales. In: J.-L. Beauvois, R.-V. Joule and J.-M. Monteil (Eds), *Perspectives cognitives et conduites sociales*. Cousset: Delval.

Flament, C., and Moliner, P. (1989). Contribution expérimentale à la théorie du noyeau central d'une représentation. In: J.-L. Beauvois, R.-V. Joule and J.-M. Monteil (Eds), *Perspective cognitives et conduites sociales*, Vol. 2. Fribourg: DelVal.

Fletcher, G. J. O. (1984). Psychology and common sense. *American Psychologist*, 39, 203–13.

Flick, U. (1991). Alltagswissen über Gesundheit und Krankheit – Überblick und Einleitung. In: U. Flick (Hg.), *Alltagswissen über Gesundheit und Krankheit*. Heidelberg: Asanger.

Flick, U. (1992a). Combining methods – lack of methodology: Discussion of Sotitakopoulou and Breakwell. *Ongoing Production on Social Representations*, 1, 43–8.

Flick, U. (1992b). Triangulation revisited: Strategy of validation or alternative. *Journal for the Theory of Social Behavior*, 22, 175–98.

Flick, U. (Hg.) (1991). *Alltagswissen über Gesundheit und Krankheit*. Heidelberg: Asanger.

Flick, U., Fischer, C., Neuber, A., Schwartz, F. W., and Walter, U. (2003). Health in the context of growing old: Social representations of health. *Journal of Health Psychology*, 8, 539–56.

Flick, U., von Kardoff, E., and Steinke, I. (Eds). (2004). *A Companion to Qualitative Research*. London: Sage.

Flores Palacios, F. (1997). Representación social de la feminidad y masculinidad en un grupo de profesionales de la salud mental: Discusión en torno a la categoría de género. *Papers on Social Representations*, 6, p. 95–108. [http://www.psr.jku.at/]

Foon, A. E. (1986). Social psychology as science or history: An experimental approach. *The Journal of Social Psychology*, 126, 431–5.

Forgas, J. P. (1983). What is social about social cognition? *British Journal of Social Psychology*, 22, 129–44.

Forgas, J. P. (1985). Person prototypes and cultural salience: The role of cognitive and cultural factors in impression formation. *British Journal of Social Psychology*, 24, 3–17.

Forgas, J. P., and Bond, M. H. (1985). Cultural influences on the perception of interaction episodes. *Personality and Social Psychology Bulletin*, 11, 75–88.

Foster, J. (2001). Unification and differentiation: a study of the social representations of mental illness. *Papers on Social Representations*, 10, p. 3.1–3.18. [http://www.psr.jku.at/]

Foster, J. (2003). Representational projects and interacting forms of knowledge. *Journal for the Theory of Social Behavior*, 33, 231–44.

Foucault, M. (1969). *Wahnsinn und Gesellschaft*. Frankfurt: Suhrkamp.

Fournier, M., Schurmans, M.-N., and Dasen, P. R. (1994). Utilisation de langues differentes dans l'étude des représentations sociales. *Papers on Social Representations*, 3, 152–65.

Fraisse, C., and Stewart, I. (2002). Basic cognitive schemes: An application concerning the social representation of alternative medicine. *European Review of Applied Psychology*, 52, 281–92.

Frake, C. O. (1964). A structural description of Subanum 'religious behavior'. In: W. H. Goodenough (Ed), *Explorations in Cultural Anthropology*. New York.

Fransella, F. (1984). The relationship between Kelly's constructs and Durkheim's representations. In: Farr and Moscovici (Eds), *Social Representations*.

Fraser, C., and Gaskell, G. (Eds) (1990). *The Social Psychological Study of Widespread Beliefs*. Oxford: Clarendon Press.

Freeman, L. C., and Romney, A. K. (1987). Words, deeds and social structure: A preliminary study of the reliability of informants. *Human Organization*, 46, 330–4.

Friedman, M. (1981). Theoretical explanation. In: R. Healey (Ed), *Reduction, Time, and Reality*. Cambridge: Cambridge University Press.

Funder, D. C. (1987). Errors and mistakes: Evaluating the accuracy of social judgment. *Psychological Bulletin*, 101, 75–91.

Furnham, A. (1986). Children's understanding of the economic world. *Australian Journal of Education*, 30, 219–40.

Furnham, A. (1988). *Lay Theories: Everyday Understanding of Problems in the Social Sciences*. Oxford: Pergamon Press.

Furnham, A., and Taylor, L. (1990). Lay theories of homosexuality: Aetiology, behaviours and 'cures'. *British Journal of Social Psychology*, 29, 135–47.

Furnham, A., and Wardley, Z. (1990). Laytheories of psychotherapy I: Attitudes toward, and beliefs about psychotherapy and therapists. *Journal of Clinical Psychology*, 46, 878–90.

Furnham, A., and Wardley, Z. (1991). Laytheories of psychotherapy II: The efficacy of different therapies and prognosis for different problems. *Human Relations*, 44, 1197–211.

Furth, H. G. (1996). *Desire for Society*. New York: Plenum Press.

Galam, S., and Moscovici, S. (1991). Towards a theory of collective phenomena: Consensus and attitude changes in groups. *European Journal of Social Psychology*, 21, 49–74.

Galeano, E. (1985). *Memoria del fuego, I. Los nacimientos*. Madrid: Siglo Veintiuno de españa.

Garfinkel, H. (1967). *Studies in Ethnomethodology*. Englewood Cliffs, NJ: Prentice Hall.

Gaskell, G. (1997). Europe ambivalent on biotechnology. *Nature*, 387, 26 June 1997, 845–8.

Gaskell, G. (2001). Attitudes, social representations and beyond. In K. Deaux and G. Philogène (Eds), *Representations of the Social*. Oxford: Blackwell.

Gaskell, G., and Allum, N. (2001). Sound science, problematic publics? Contrasting representations of risk and uncertainty. *Notizie di Politeia*, 17, 13–25.

Gaskell, G., and M. Bauer (Eds) (2001). *Biotechnology 1996–2000: The Years of Controversy*. London: The National Museum of Science and Industry.

Gaskell, G., Allum, N., Wagner, W., Nielsen, T. H., Jelsø, E., Kohring, M., and Bauer, M. (2001). In the public eye: Representations of biotechnology in Europe. In Gaskell and Bauer (Eds), *Biotechnology 1996–2000*.

Gaskell, G., Allum, N. C., Wagner, W., Kronberger, N., Torgersen, H., Hampel, J., and Bardes, J. (2004). GM foods and the misperception of risk perception. *Risk Analysis*, 24, 185–94.

Geertz, C. (1973). *The Interpretation of Cultures*. New York: Basic Books.

Geertz, C. (1983). *Dichte Beschreibung. Beiträge zum Verstehen kultureller Systeme*. Frankfurt: Suhrkamp.

Geertz, C. (1984). 'From the native's point of view': On the nature of anthropological understanding. In R. A. Shweder and R. A. LeVine (Eds), *Culture Theory: Essays on Mind, Self and Emotion* (pp. 123–36). Cambridge: Cambridge University Press.

Geertz, C. (1988). *Works and Lives: The Anthropologist as Author*. Stanford, CA: Stanford University Press.

Gehring, R. E., Toglia, M. P., and Kimble, G. A. (1976). Recognition memory for words and pictures at short and long intervals. *Memory and Cognition*, 4, 256–60.

Genneret, C. (1990). Pratiques des usagers et stratégies institutionelles: représentations de l'exclusion. In: D. Martin and P. Royer-Rastoll (Eds), *Représentations sociales et pratiques quotidiennes*. Paris: L'Harmattan.

Gerard, H. B., and Wagner, W. (1981). Opinion importance, coorientation and social comparison. Unpublished manuscript, University of California, Los Angeles.

Gergen, K. J. (1973). Social psychology as history. *Journal of Personality and Social Psychology*, 26, 309–20.

Gergen, K. J. (1982). From self to science: What is there to know? In: J. Suls (Ed), *Psychological Perspectives on the Self, Vol. 1*. Hillsdale, NJ: Erlbaum.

Gergen, K. J. (1985). The social constructionist movement in modern psychology. *American Psychologist*, 40, 266–75.

Gergen, K. J. (1986). Correspondence versus autonomy in the language of understanding human action. In: D. W. Fiske and R. A. Shweder (Eds), *Metatheory in Social Science*. Chicago: Cambridge University Press.

Gergen, K. J. (1988). Toward a post-modern psychology. Invited Address, International Congress of Psychology, Sidney.

Gergen, K. J. (1991). Emerging challenges for theory and psychology. *Theory and Psychology*, 1, 13–36.

Gergen, K. J., and Gergen, M. M. (Eds) (1984). *Historical Social Psychology*. Hillsdale, NJ: Erlbaum.

Gergen, K. J., and Gergen, M. M. (1986). *Social Psychology*. New York: Springer.

Gergen, K. J., Gloger-Tippelt, G., and Berkowitz, P. (1990). The cultural construction of the developing child. In: G. R. Semin and K. J. Gergen (Eds), *Everyday Understanding*. London: Sage.

Gergen, M. M. (1987). Toward a diachronic social psychology: Pointing with more than one finger. In: H. J. Stam, T. B. Rogers and K. J. Gergen (Eds), *The Analysis of Psychological Theory*. London: Hemisphere.

Gervais, M.-C. (1997). *Social Representations of Nature: The Case of the Braer Oil Spill in Shetland*. PhD thesis, London School of Economics.

Gervais, M.-C., Morant, N., and Penn, G. (1999). Making sense of 'absence': Towards a typology of absence in social representations theory and research. *Journal for the Theory of Social Behaviour*, 29, 419–44.

Giami, A. (1989). La représentation: à l'articulation du sujt et de l'objet. *Technologies, Idéologies et Pratiques*, 8, 379–87.

Giami, A. (1991). De Kinsey au sida : l'évolution de la construction du comportement sexuel dans les enquêtes quantitatives. *Sciences Sociales et Santé*, 9, 23–56.

Giami, A., Assouly-Piquet, C., and Berthier, F. (1988). La figure fondamentale du handicap: Représentations et figures fantasmatiques. *Rapport de Recherche*, Paris: MIRE-GERAL.

Giami, A., Humbert-Viveret, C., and Laval, D. (2001). *L'ange et la bête: Représentations de la sexualité des handicapés mentaux par les parents et les éducateurs*. Paris: Éditions du CTNERHI.

Gibson, J. J. (1979). *The Ecological Approach to Visual Perception*. Boston, MA: Houghton Mifflin.

Gigerenzer, G. (1987). Probabilistic thinking and the fight against subjectivity. In: L. Krüger, G. Gigerenzer and M. S. Morgan (Eds), *The Probabilistic Revolution, Vol. 2, Ideas in the Sciences*. London: Bradford/MIT.

Gigerenzer, G. (1988). Woher kommen Theorien über kognitive Prozesse? *Psychologische Rundschau*, 39, 91–100.

Gigerenzer, G., and Murray, D. J. (1987). *Cognition as Intuitive Statistics*. Hillsdale, NJ: Lawrence Erlbaum.

Gigling, M, Guimelli, C., and Penochet, J.-C. (1996). Les représentations sociales de la dépression chez des médicins: Entre pratiques et normes. *Papers on Social Representations*, 5, 27–40. [http://www.psr.jku.at/]

Giorgi, A. (1990). Phenomenology, psychological science, and common sense. In: G. R. Semin and K. J. Gergen (Eds), *Everyday Understanding*. London: Sage.

Girotto, V. (1985a). Connotazione sociale e fattori funzionali in prove de trasformazione spaziale. Unpublished Research Report, Universitá di Padova.

Girotto, V. (1985b). Effeti della connotazione sociale del materiale in compiti di trasformazione spaziale. Paper presented at 2. Convegno Nazionale SIPS, Urbino.

Girotto, V., Light, P., and Colbourn, C. (1988). Pragmatic schemas and conditional reasoning in children. *The Quarterly Journal of Experimental Psychology*, 40A, 469–82.

Gonzales, M. H., Davis, J. M., Loney, G. L., LuKens, C. K., and Junghans, C. M. (1983). Interactional approach to interpersonal attraction. *Journal of Personality and Social Psychology*, 44, 1192–7.

Goodenough, W. (1963). *Cooperation in Change*. New York: Russel Sage.

Goodnow, J. J. (1989). Expanding accounts of cognition: Adding everyday content and links to action. In: J. P. Forgas and J. M. Innes (Eds), *Recent Advances in Social Psychology: An International Perspective*. Amsterdam: Elsevier.

Goodwin, R. B., Kozlova, A., Kwiatkowska, A., Nguyen Luu, L. A., Nizharadze, G., Realo, A., et al. (2003). Social representations of HIV/AIDS in Central and Eastern Europe. *Social Science and Medicine*, 56, 1373–84.

Goody, J. (1977). *The Domestication of the Savage Mind*. Cambridge: Cambridge University Press.

Goody, J. (Ed.) (1981). *Literalität in traditionellen Gesellschaften*. Frankfurt: Suhrkamp.

Goody, J., Cole, M., and Scribner, S. (1977). Writing and formal operations: A case study among the Vai. *Africa*, 47, 289–304.

Gracio, M.-L. (1998) Representação social da crianca em educadores de infancia e professores do 1. deg. Ciclo do Ensino Basico portugueses / Social representation of children among Portuguese kindergarten and primary school teachers. *Analise Psicologica*, 16(2), 285–300 (English abstract).

Graham, G. A. (1995). Synaesthesia. In R. Audi (Ed), *The Cambridge Dictionary of Philosophy*. Cambridge: Cambridge University Press.

Graumann, C. F. (1979). Die Scheu des Psychologen vor der Interaktion. Ein Schisma und seine Geschichte. *Zeitschrift für Sozialpsychologie*, 10, 284–304.

Graumann, C. F. (Ed) (1978). *Ökologische Perspektiven in der Psychologie*. Bern: Huber.

Green, D. W., Muncer, S. J., Heffernan, T., and McManus, I. C. (2003). Eliciting and representing the causal understanding of a social concept:

A methodological and statistical comparison of two methods. *Papers on Social Representations*, 12, 2.1–2.23.

Greenacre, M. J. (1993). *Correspondence Analysis in Practice*. London: Academic Press.

Greenfield, P. M. (1972). Oral or written language: The consequences for cognitive development in Africa, the United States and England. *Language and Speach*, 15, 169–78.

Greenwald, A. G. (1980). The totalitarian ego: Fabrication and revision of personal history. *American Psychologist*, 35, 603–18.

Greenwald, A. G., and Pratkanis, A. R. (1984). The self. In: R. S. Wyer and T. K. Srull (Eds), *Handbook of Social Cognition, Vol. 3*. Hillsdale, NJ: Erlbaum.

Greve, W. (2001). Traps and gaps in action explanation: Theoretical problems of a psychology of human action. *Psychological Review*, 108, 435–51.

Griffitt, W., and Veitch, R. (1974). Preacquaintance attitude similarity and attraction revisited: Ten days in a fallout shelter. *Sociometry*, 37, 163–73.

Grice, H. P. (1989). *Studies in the Way of Words*. Cambridge, MA: Harvard University Press.

Griggs, R. A., and Cox, J. R. (1982). The elusive thematic-materials effect in Wason's selection task. *British Journal of Psychology*, 73, 407–20.

Griséz, J. (1975). *Méthodes de la psychologie sociale*. Paris: Presses Universitaires de France.

Grize, J.-B. (1989). Logique naturelle et représentations sociales. In: D. Jodelet (Ed), *Les représentations sociales*. Paris: Presses Universitaires de France.

Grize, J.-B., Vergès, P., and Silem, A. (1988). *Les salariés face aux nouvelles technologies. Vers une approche socio-logique des représentations sociales*. Paris: CNRS.

Groh, D. (1987). The temptation of conspiracy theory, or: Why do bad things happen to good people? Part 1: Preliminary draft of a theory of conspiracy theories. In: C. F. Graumann and S. Moscovici (Eds), *Changing Conceptions of Conspiracy*. New York: Springer.

Gruman, J., and Sloan, R. (1983). Disease as justice: Perceptions of the victims of physical illness. *Basic and Applied Social Psychology*, 4, 49–56.

Guerin, B. (2001). Replacing catharsis and uncertainty reduction theories with descriptions of historical and social context. *Review of General Psychology*, 5, 44–61.

Guimelli, C. (1989). Pratiques nouvelles et transformation sans rupture d'une représentation sociale: la représentation de la chasse et de la nature. In: J.-L. Beauvois, R.-V. Joule and J.-M. Monteil (Eds), *Perspectives cognitives et conduites sociales, Vol. 2*. Cousset: DelVal.

Guimelli, C. (1991). Contribution du modele associatif des schemes cognitifs de base à la validation de la theorie du noyau central des représentations sociales. Unpublished Manuskript, Université Montpellier III.

Guimelli, C., and Jacobi, D. (1990). Pratiques nouvelles et transformation des représentations sociales. *Revue Internationale de Psychologie Sociale*, 3, 307–34.

Gustavsson, A. (1996). Reforms and everyday meanings of intellectual disability. In J. Tøssebro, A. Gustavsson and G. Dyrendahl (Eds), *Intellectual Disabilities in the Nordic Welfare States*. Kristiansand: Høyskole Forlaget.

Gustavsson, A. (1997). Integration, stigma and autonomy: Bright and dark sides of the subculture of integration. In A. Gustavsson and E. Zakrzewska-Manterys (Eds), *Social Definitions of Disability*. Warsaw: Zak.

Gutteling, J., Olofsson, A., Fjaestad, B., Kohring, M., Goerke, A., Bauer, M., Rusanen, T., Allansdottir, A., Berthomier, A., de Cheveigné, S., Frederiksen, H., Gaskell, G., Leonarz, M., Liakopulos, M., Mortensen, A. T., Przestalski, A., Ruhrmann, G., Rusanen, M., Schanne, M., Seifert, F., Stathopoulou, A., and Wagner, W. (2002). Media coverage 1973–1996: Trends and dynamics. In Bauer and Gaskell (Eds), *Biotechnology – the Making of a Global Controversy*.

Guttmann, G. (1972). *Einführung in die Neuropsychologie*. Bern: Huber.

Habermas, J. (1968). *Technik und Wissenschaft als Ideologie*. Frankfurt: Suhrkamp.

Habermas, J. (1985). *Theorie des kommunikativen Handelns Band 1: Handlungsrationalität und gesellschaftliche Rationalisierung*. Frankfurt: Suhrkamp.

Habermas, J. (1989). *The Structural Transformation of the Public Sphere: An Inquiry into a Category of Bourgeois Society*. Cambridge: Polity Press.

Hacking, I. (1995). The looping effects of human kinds. In D. Sperber, D. Premack and A. J. Premack (Eds), *Causal Cognition*. Oxford: Clarendon Press.

Halbwachs, M. (1985/1952). *Das Gedächtnis und seine sozialen Bedingungen*. Frankfurt: Suhrkamp.

Hamilton, D. L., and Gifford, R. K. (1976). Illusory correlation in interpersonal perception: A cognitive basis of stereotypic judgments. *Journal of Experimental Social Psychology*, 12, 392–407.

Hammerich, K., and Klein, M. (Hg.) (1978). Materialien zur Soziologie des Alltags. *Sonderband der Kölner Zeitschrift für Soziologie und Sozialpsychologie*.

Hansen, R. D. (1985). Cognitive economy and commonsense attribution processing. In: *Attribution: Basic Issues and Applications*. New York: Academic Press.

Harbridge, J., and Furnham, A. (1991). Lay theories of rape. *Counselling Psychology Quarterly*, 4, 3–25.

Haroche, C., and Pécheux, M. (1971). Etude expérimentale de l'effet des représentations sociales sur la résolution d'une épreuve logique à présentation variable. *Bulletin du CERP*, 20, 115–29.

Harré, R. (1979). *Social Being*. Totowa, NJ: Rowman & Littlefield.

Harré, R. (1980). Making social psychology scientific. In: R. Gilmour and S. Duck (Eds), *The Development of Social Psychology*. London: Academic Press.

Harré, R. (1981a). Expressive aspects of descriptions of others. In: C. Antaki (Ed), *The Psychology of Ordinary Explanations of Social Behavior*. London: Academic Press.

Harré, R. (1981b). Rituals, rhetoric and social cognition. In: J. P. Forgas (Ed), *Social Cognition*. London: Academic Press.

Harré, R. (1984). Some reflections on the concept of 'social representations'. *Social Research*, 51, 927–38.

Harré, R. (1985). Review: Social representations. *British Journal of Social Psychology*, 76, 138–40.

Harré, R. (1989). Metaphysics and methodology: Some prescriptions for social psychology. *European Journal of Social Psychology*, 19, 439–53.

Harré, R. (1990). Explanation in psychology. *Annals of Theoretical Psychology*, 6, 105–24.

Harré, R. (1998). The epistemology of social representations, In: U. Flick (Ed), *The Psychology of the Social*. New York: Cambridge University Press.

Harré, R., and Gillett, G. (1994). *The Discursive Mind*. London: Sage.

Harré, R., and Secord, P. F. (1972). *The Explanation of Social Behaviour*. Oxford: Blackwell.

Harré, R., and van Langenhove, L. (1999). *Positioning Theory*. Oxford: Blackwell.

Harris, L. M., and Sadeghi, A. R. (1987). Realizing: How facts are created in human interaction. *Journal of Social and Personal Relationships*, 4, 481–95.

Harrison, R. (1972). Understanding your organisation's character. *Harvard Business Review*, May–June 1972.

Hartmann, N. (1964). *Der Aufbau der realen Welt*. Berlin: DeGruyter.

Harwood, F. (1976). Myth, memory, and the oral tradition. *American Anthropologist*, 78, 783–96.

Haste, H. (1993). *The Sexual Metaphor*. New York: Harvester Wheatsheaf.

Hastie, R. (1983). Social inference. *Annual Review of Psychology*, 34, 511–42.

Hastie, R., Park, B., and Weber, R. (1984). Social memory. In: R. S. Wyer and T. K. Srull (Eds), *Handbook of Social Cognition*, Vol. 2. Hillsdale, NJ: Erlbaum.

Hawking, S. W. (1988). *A Brief History of Time*. New York: Bantham.

Hayes, N. (1997). *Doing Qualitative Analysis in Psychology*. Hove: Psychology Press.

Hayes, N. (1998a). Psychological processes in organisational cultures I: Social representations and organisational semiotics. *Human Systems: The Journal of Systemic Consultation and Management*, 9(1), 59–65.

Hayes, N. (1998b). Psychological processes in organisational cultures II: Social identification and organisational groups. *Human Systems: The Journal of Systemic Consultation and Management*, 9(3/4), 231–7.

Hayes, N. (1999). Some cognitive implications of human social evolution. *Cognitive Systems*, 5, 123–35.

Hayes, N. (2000). *Doing Psychological Research* Buckingham: Open University Press.

Hayes, N. (2002). *Psychology in Perspective*. Basingstoke: Palgrave Macmillan.

Hayes, N. (2003). Description, prescription and ideal forms: The nature of modelling in organisational theory. *Human Systems: The Journal of Systemic Consultation and Management*, 14, 27–34.

Heelas, P., and Lock, A. (Eds) (1981). *Indigenous Psychologies: The Anthropology of the Self*. London: Academic Press.

Heider, F. (1977/1958). *Psychologie der interpersonellen Beziehungen*. Stuttgart: Klett.

Heller, A. (1981). *Das Alltagsleben. Versuch einer Erklärung der individuellen Reproduktion*. Frankfurt: Suhrkamp.

Hempel, C. G. (1962). Explanation in science and history. In: R. Colodny (Ed), *Frontiers of Science and Philosophy*. Pittsburgh: University of Pittburgh Press.

Hempel, C. G. (1977). *Aspekte wissenschaftlicher Erklärung* (Aspects of scientific explanation, German). Berlin: deGruyter.

Henley, N. M. (1977). *Body Politics*. Englewood Cliffs, NJ: Prentice Hall.

Herkner, W. (1981). *Einführung in die Sozialpsychologie*. Bern: Huber.

Herzlich, C. (Ed.) (1973). *Health and Illness: A Social Psychological Analysis*. London: Academic Press.

Herzlich, C. (1975). Die soziale Vorstellung. In: S. Moscovici (Hg.), *Forschungsgebiete der Sozialpsychologie, Bd. 1*. Frankfurt: Athenäum.

Herzlich, C., and Pierret, J. (1984). *Malades d'hier, malades d'aujourd'hui*. Paris: Payot.

Hewstone, M., and Augoustinos, M. (1998) Social attributions and social representations. In: U. Flick (Ed.), *The Psychology of the Social*. New York: Cambridge University Press.

Hewstone, M., and Jaspars, J. (1982). Intergroup relations and attribution processes. In: H. Tajfel (Ed), *Social Identity and Intergroup Relations*. Cambridge: Cambridge University Press.

Hewstone, M., Jaspars, J., and Lalljee, M. (1982). Social representation, social attribution and social identity: The intergroup images of 'public' and 'comprehensive' schoolboys. *European Journal of Social Psychology*, 12, 241–69.

Higgins, E. T., King, G. A., and Mavin, G. H. (1982). Individual construct accessibility and subjective impressions and recall. *Journal of Personality and Social Psychology*, 43, 35–47.

Himmelweit, H. T. (1990). Societal psychology: Implications and scope. In H. T. Himmelweit and G. Gaskell (Eds), *Societal Psychology*. London: Sage.

Hintikka, J. (1961). *Knowledge and Belief*. Ithaka, NY: Cornell University Press.

Hofstätter, P. R. (1966). *Einführung in die Sozialpsychologie*. Stuttgart: Kröner.

Hogg, M. A., and McGarty, C. (1990). Self-categorization and social identity. In: D. Abrams and M. A. Hogg (Eds), *Social Identity Theory*. New York: Harvester-Wheatsheaf.

Holland, D. (1987). Culture sharing across gender lines: An interactionist corrective to the status-centered model. *American Behavioral Scientist*, 31, 234–49.

Holland, D., and Quinn, N. (Eds) (1987). *Cultural Models in Language and Thought*. Cambridge: Cambridge University Press.

Hollis, M., and Lukes, S. (Eds) (1982). *Rationality and Relativism*. Oxford: Basil Blackwell.

Holtz, R., and Miller, N. (1985). Assumed similarity and opinion certainty. *Journal of Personality and Social Psychology*, 48, 890–8.

Holzkamp, K. (1977). Die Überwindung der wissenschaftlichen Beliebigkeit psychologischer Theorien durch die Kritische Psychologie, Teil 1 und 2. *Zeitschrift für Sozialpsychologie*, 8, 1–22, 78–97.

Holzkamp, K. (1986). Wie weit können sozialpsychologische Theorien experimentell geprüft werden? *Zeitschrift für Sozialpsychologie*, 17, 216–38.

Honneth, A. (1986). The fragmented world of symbolic forms: Reflections on Pierre Bourdieu's sociology of culture. *Theory, Culture and Society*, 3, 55–66.

Horenczyk, G., and Bekerman, Z. (1995). The pervasiveness of the beliefs in causality and cognitive consistency: Some comments on a paper by W. Wagner. *Papers on Social Representations*, 4, 105–8. [http://www.psr.jku.at/]

Horgan, T., and Woodward, J. (1991). Folk psychology is here to stay. In: J. D. Greenwood (Ed), *The Future of Folk Psychology – Intentionality and Cognitive Science*. Cambridge: Cambridge University Press.

Howard, G. S. (1985). The role of values in the science of psychology. *American Psychologist*, 40, 255–65.

Howard, G. S., and Conway, C. G. (1986). Can there be an empirical science of volitional action? *American Psychologist*, 41, 1214–51.

Howarth, C. S. (2001). Towards a social psychology of community: A social representations perspective. *Journal for the Theory of Social Behaviour*, 31, 223–38.

Hraba, J., Hagendoorn, L., and Hagendoorn, R. (1989). The ethnic hierarchy in The Netherlands: Social distance and social representation.
*British Journal of Social Psychology*, 28, 57–69.

Hubert, H., and Mauss, M. (1974/02). Entwurf einer allgemeinen Theorie
der Magie. In: M. Mauss, *Soziologie und Anthropologie, Bd. 1.*
München: Hanser.

Hyman, H. H. (1942). The psychology of status. *Archives of Psychology*,
No. 269, New York: Columbia University.

Ibañez, T. G. (1991). Social psychology and the rhetoric of truth. *Theory
and Psychology*, 1, 187–201.

Iser, M. (1983). Der Habitus als illegitimer Normalfall gesellschaftlicher
Reproduktion. Univeröffentlichte Dissertation, Wirtschaftsuniversität Wien.

Ivinson, G. M. (1998). The child's construction of the curriculum. *Papers
on Social Representations*, 7, 21–40. [http://www.psr.jku.at/]

Jahoda, G. (1970). A cross-cultural perspective in psychology. *The
Advancement of Science*, 27, 57–70.

Jahoda, G. (1980). *Psychology and Anthropology*. London: Academic Press.

Jahoda, G. (1986). Nature, culture and social psychology. *European
Journal of Social Psychology*, 16, 17–30.

Jahoda, G. (1988a). J'accuse. In: M. H. Bond (Ed), *The Cross-Cultural
Challenge to Social Psychology*. Newbury Park: Sage.

Jahoda, G. (1988b). Critical notes and reflections on 'social representations'. *European Journal of Social Psychology*, 18, 195–209.

Jahoda, M. (1986). In defence of a non-reductionist social psychology.
*Social Behaviour*, 1, 25–9.

Jahoda, M. (1989). Why a non-reductionist social psychology is almost
too difficult to be tackled but too fascinating to be left alone. *British
Journal of Social Psychology*, 28, 71–8.

James, W. (1890). *Principles of Psychology*. New York: Holt.

Janoff-Bulman, R. (1979). Characterological versus behavioral self-blame:
Inquiries into depression and rape. *Journal of Personality and Social
Psychology*, 37, 1789–809.

Jaspars, J. (1983). The process of causal attribution in common sense. In:
M. Hewstone (Ed), *Attribution Theory*. Oxford: Blackwell.

Jaspars, J., and Fraser, C. (1984). Attitudes and social representations. In:
Farr and Moscovici (Eds), *Social Representations*.

Jennings, D., Amabile, T. M., and Ross, L. (1982). Informal covariation
assessment: Databased versus theory-based judgments. In: D.
Kahneman, P. Slovic and A. Tversky (Eds), *Judgment under Uncertainty:
Heuristics and Biases*. New York: Cambridge University Press.

Jodelet, D. (1984a). The representation of the body and its transformations. In: Farr and Moscovici (Eds), *Social Representations*.

Jodelet, D. (1984b). Réflexions sur le traitement de la notion de représentation sociale en psychologie sociale. *Communication – Information*,
6(2/3), 15–42.

Jodelet, D. (1985). Civils et bredins. Manuscrit inédit, EHESS, Paris.

Jodelet, D. (1989a). Représentations sociales: un domaine en expansion. In: Jodelet (Ed), *Les représentations sociales*.

Jodelet, D. (1989b). *Folies et représentations sociales*. Paris: Presses Universitaires de France.

Jodelet, D. (Ed.) (1989c). *Les Représentations Sociales*. Paris: Presses Universitaires de France.

Jodelet, D. (1991a). L'idéologie dans l'étude des représentations sociales. In: V. Aebischer, J.-P. Deconchy and E. M. Lipiansky (Eds), *Idéologies et représentations sociales*. Fribourg: DelVal.

Jodelet, D. (1991b). *Madness and Social Representations*. London: Harvester Wheatsheaf.

Jodelet, D. (1992). Mémoire de masses: le côté moral et affectif de l'histoire. *Bulletin de Psychologie*, 45, 239–56.

Jodelet, D., and Moscovici, S. (1976). La représentation sociale du corps. Rapport scientifique, Ecole des Hautes Etudes en Sciences Sociales, Paris.

Jodelet, D., Ohana, J., Bessis-Monino, C., and Dannenmüller, E. (1982). Systèmes de représentation du corps et groupes sociaux. Rapport scientifique, Ecole des Hautes Etudes en Sciences Sociales, Paris.

Joffe, H. (1995). Social representations of AIDS: Towards encompassing issues of power. *Papers on Social Representations*, 4, 29–40. [http://www.psr.jku.at/]

Joffe, H. (2003). Risk: From perception to social representation. *British Journal of Social Psychology*, 42, 55–74.

Joffe, H., and Farr, R. (1996). Self-proclaimed ignorance about public affairs. *Social Science Information*, 35, 69–92.

Joffe, H., and Haarhof, G. (2002). Representations of far-flung illnesses: The case of Ebola in Britain. *Social Science and Medicine*, 54, 955–69.

Johnson, J. E. (1975). Stress reduction through sensation information. In: I. G. Sarason and C. D. Spielberger (Eds), *Stress and Anxiety*. Washington, DC: Hemisphere.

Johnson, M. (1987). *The Body in the Mind*. Chicago, IL: University of Chicago Press.

Johnson-Laird, P. N. (1982). Thinking as a skill. *Quarterly Journal of Experimental Psychology*, 34, 1–29.

Johnson-Laird, P. N. (1983). *Mental Models*. Harvard, MA: Harvard University Press.

Jones, E. E., and Davis, K. E. (1965). From acts to dispositions: The attribution process in person perception. In: L. Berkowitz (Ed), *Advances in Experimental Social Psychology, Vol. 2*. New York: Academic Press.

Jones, E. E., and Gerard, H. B. (1967). *Foundations of Social Psychology*. New York: Wiley.

Jost, J. T. (1992). Social representations and the philosophy of science: Belief in ontological realism as objectification. *Ongoing Production on Social Representations*, 1, 116–24.

Jovchelovitch, S. (1995a). Vivendo a vida com os outros: Intersubjetivi-dade, Espaco Publico e Representacoes Sociais. In P. Guareschi and S. Jovchelovitch (Eds), *Textos em Representacoes Sociais* (pp. 63–85). Petropolis: Editora Vozes.

Jovchelovitch, S. (1995b). Social representations in and of the public sphere: Towards a theoretical articulation. *Journal for the Theory of Social Behaviour*, 25, 81–102.

Jovchelovitch, S. (2001). Social representations, public life and social con-struction. In: K. Deaux and G. Philogène (Eds), *Representations of the Social*. Oxford: Blackwell.

Jovchelovitch, S. (2002). Narratives and social representations: Stories of public life in Brazil. In: J. Laszlo and W. Stainton-Rogers (Eds), *Narra-tive Approaches in Social Psychology*. Budapest: New Mandate.

Jovchelovitch, S., and Bauer, M. (2000). Narrative interviewing. In: Bauer and Gaskell (Eds), *Qualitative Researching with Text, Image and Sound*.

Jovchelovitch, S., and Gervais, M.-C. (1999). Social representations of health and illness: The case of the Chinese community in England. *Journal of Community and Applied Social Psychology*, 9, 247–60.

Kagan, J. (1998). *Three Seductive Ideas*. Cambridge, MA: Harvard Uni-versity Press.

Kahneman, D., and Tversky, A. (1982a). The simulation heuristic. In: Kahneman, Slovic and Tversky (Eds). *Judgment under Uncertainty: Heuristics and Biases*.

Kahneman, D., Slovic, P., and Tversky, A. (Eds) (1982b). *Judgment under Uncertainty: Heuristics and Biases*. New York: Cambridge University Press.

Kalampalikis, N. (2002). Représentations et mythes contemporains. *Psy-chologie et Societé*, 5, 61–86.

Kalampalikis, N., and Buschini, F. (2002). The Prospero software program: An alternative tool for the study of social representations. *European Review of Applied Psychology*, 52, 241–52.

Kaminski, G. (Hg.) (1986). *Ordnung und Variabilität im Alltagsgeschehen*. Göttingen: Hogrefe.

Kantor, D., and Lehr, W. (1975). *Inside the Family*. San Francisco: Jossey-Bass.

Kashima, Y. (2000). Recovering Bartlett's social psychology of cultural dynamics. *European Journal of Social Psychology*, 30, 383–404.

Keesing, R. M. (1987). Models, 'folk' and 'cultural': Paradigms regained. In: D. Holland and N. Quinn (Eds), *Cultural Models in Language and Thought*. Cambridge: Cambridge University Press.

Kelle, U. (1995). *Computer-Aided Qualitative Data Analysis: Theory, Methods and Practice*. London: Sage.

Kelley, H. H. (1967). Attribution theory in social psychology. In: D. Levine (Ed), *Nebraska Symposium on Motivation, Vol. 15*. Lincoln: University of Nebraska Press.

Kelley, H. H. (1972). Attribution in social interaction. In: E. E. Jones, D. E. Kanouse, H. H. Kelley, R. E. Nisbett, S. Valins and B. Weiner (Eds), *Attribution: Perceiving the Causes of Behavior*. Morristown, NJ: General Learning Press.

Kempton, W. (1986). Two theories for home heat control. *Cognitive Science*, 10, 75–90.

Kempton, W. (1987). Variation in folk models and consequent behavior. *American Behavioral Scientist*, 31, 203–18.

Kette, G. (1991). *Haft. Eine sozialpsychologische Analyse*. Göttingen: Hogrefe.

Kim, J. (1993). *Supervenience and Mind*. Cambridge: Cambridge University Press.

Kim, J. (1998). *Mind in a Physical World: An Essay on the Mind-Body problem and Mental Causation*. 'Representation and Mind Series'. Cambridge, MA: MIT Press.

Kimble, G. A. (1984). Psychology's two cultures. *American Psychologist*, 39, 833–9.

Kimmel, M. (2002). Metaphor, imagery, and culture: Spatialized ontologies, mental tools, and multimedia in the making. Unpublished PhD Thesis, Department of Philosophy, University of Vienna.

Kirchler, E. (1984). *Arbeitslosigkeit und Alltagsbefinden*. Linz: Trauner.

Kirchler, E. (1989a). *Kaufentscheidungen im privaten Haushalt*. Göttingen: Hogrefe.

Kirchler, E. (1989b). Everyday life experiences at home: An interaction diary approach to assess marital relationships. *Journal of Family Psychology*, 2, 311–36.

Kirchler, E. (1991). Resigniert erstarren oder erfolgreich sein Schicksal schmieden? Determinanten der Wiederbeschäftigung von Arbeitslosen. *Veröffentlichungen des österreichischen Instituts für Arbeitsmarktpolitik*, Heft 36, Linz.

Kirk, J. L., and Miller, M. (1986). *Reliability and Validity in Qualitative Research*. Beverly Hills: Sage.

Klaus, G. (1973). *Moderne Logik*. Berlin: Deutscher Verlag der Wissenschaften.

Klix, F. (1980). *Erwachendes Denken*. Berlin: Deutscher Verlag der Wissenschaften.

Kornblit, A. L., and Petracci, M. (1996). Représentations sociales du harcelement sexuel dans les milieux du travail. *Papers on Social Representations*, 5, 51–66. [http://www.psr.jku.at/]

Krause, M. (2002). Social representations of psychological problems: Contents and transformations. *Social Science Information*, 41, 603–24.

Krause, M. (2003). The transformation of social representations of chronic disease in a self-help group. *Journal of Health Psychology*, 8, 599–615.

Kripke, S. A. (1972). Naming and necessity. In: D. Davidson and G. Harman (Eds), *The Semantics of Natural Language*. Dordrecht: Reidel.

Kronberger, N. (1999). Schwarzes Loch, geistige Lähmung und Dornröschenschlaf: Ein metaphernanalytischer Beitrag zur Erfassung von Alltagsvorstellungen von Depression. *Psychotherapie und Sozialwissenschaft*, 1, 85–104.

Kronberger, N., and Wagner, W. (2000). Keywords in context: Statistical analysis of text features. In: Bauer and Gaskell (Eds), *Qualitative Researching with Text, Image and Sound*.

Kronberger, N., Dahinden, U., Allansdottir, A., Seger, N., Pfenning, U., Gaskell, G., Allum, N., Rusanen, T., Montali, L., Wagner, W., Cheveigné, S., Diego, C., and Mortensen, A. (2001). 'The train departed without us' – Public perceptions of biotechnology in ten European countries. *Notizie di Politeia*, 17, 26–36.

Kruglanski, A. W. (1979). Causal explanation, teleological explanation: On radical particularism in attribution theory. *Journal of Personality and Social Psychology*, 37, 1447–57.

Kruglanski, A. W. (1980). Lay epistemo-logic – process and contents: Another look at attribution theory. *Psychological Review*, 87, 70–87.

Kruglanski, A. W. (1989). The psychology of being 'right': The problem of accuracy in social perception and cognition. *Psychological Bulletin*, 106, 395–409.

Kruglanski, A. W., and Ajzen, I. (1983). Bias and error in human judgment. *European Journal of Social Psychology*, 13, 1–44.

Kruglanski, A. W., and Klar, Y. (1987). A view from a bridge: Synthesizing the consistency and attribution paradigms from a lay epistemic perspective. *European Journal of Social Psychology*, 17, 211–42.

Kruglanski, A. W., Hamel, I. A., Maides, S. A., and Schwartz, J. M. (1978). Attribution theory as a special case of lay epistemology. In: J. H. Harvey, W. J. Ickes and R. F. Kidd (Eds), *New Directions in Attribution Research, Vol. 2*. Hillsdale, NJ: Erlbaum.

Kruse, L. (1986). Drehbücher für Verhaltensschauplätze oder: Scripts for settings. In: Kaminski (Hg.), *Ordnung und Variabilität im Alltagsgeschehen*.

Kruse, L., Graumann, C. F., and Lantermann, E.-D. (Hg.) (1990). *Ökologische Psychologie*. München: Psychologie Verlags Union.

Kruse, L., Weimer, E., and Wagner, F. (1988). What women and men are said to be: Social representation and language. *Journal of Language and Social Psychology*, 7, 243–62.

Kuhn, T. S. (1970). *The Structure of Scientific Revolutions*. Chicago: University of Chicago Press.

Kuhn, T. S. (1979). Metaphor in science. In: A. Ortony (Ed), *Metaphor and Thought*. Cambridge: Cambridge University Press.

Kukla, A. (1982). Logical incoherence of value-free science. *Journal of Personality and Social Psychology*, 43, 1014–17.

Laboratory of Comparative Human Cognition (1979). What's cultural about cross-cultural cognitive psychology? *Annual Review of Psychology*, 30, 145–72.

LaFrance, M. (1981). Gender gestures: Sex, sex-role, and nonverbal communication. In: C. Mayo and N. M. Henley (Eds), *Gender and Nonverbal Behavior*. New York: Springer.

Lahlou, S. (1996). A method to extract social representations from linguistic corpora. *Japanese Journal of Experimental Social Psychology*, 35, 278–91.

Lahlou, S. (1998). *Penser manger: Alimentation et représentations sociales*. Paris: Presses Universitaires de France.

Lakatos, I. (1974). Falsifikation und die Methodologie wissenschaftlicher Forschungsprogramme. In: I. Lakatos and A. Musgrave (Hg.), *Kritik und Erkenntnisfortschritt*. Braunschweig: Vieweg.

Lakoff, G. (1987). *Women, Fire and Dangerous Things*. Chicago: University of Chicago Press.

Lakoff, G., and Johnson, M. (1980). *Metaphors We Live by*. Chicago: University of Chicago Press.

Lakoff, G., and Johnson, M. (1999). *Philosophy in the Flesh*. New York: Basic Books.

Lalljee, M., Watson, M., and White, P. (1982). Explanations, attributions and the social context of unexpected behavior. *European Journal of Social Psychology*, 12, 17–29.

Langdridge, D. (2004). *Research Methods and Data Analysis in Psychology*. Essex: Pearson.

Laplanche, J., and Pontalis, J. B. (1972). *Das Vokabular der Psychoanalyse*. Frankfurt: Suhrkamp.

Laszlo, J. (1997). Narrative organisation of social representations. *Papers on Social Representations*, 6, 155–72. [http://www.psr.jku.at/]

Laszlo, J. (1998) *Szocialis reprezent acio es narrativitas II: A tarsas tudas narrativ svervezoedese* (Social representations and narratives II: A theory of social knowledge, Hunagrian). *Pszichologia: Az Mta Pszichologiai Intezetenek folyoirata*, 18, 239–60.

Laszlo, J., and Stainton-Rogers, W. (Eds) (2002). *Narrative Approaches in Social Psychology*. Budapest: New Mandate.

Laucken, U. (1974). *Naive Verhaltenstheorie*. Stuttgart: Klett.

Lave, J. (1988). *Cognition in Practice: Mind, Mathematics, and Practice in Everyday Life*. New York: Cambridge University Press.

Le Goff, J. (1989). Eine mehrdeutige Geschichte. In: Raulff (Hg.), *Mentalitäten-Geschichte*.

Le Goff, J. (1990). Neue Geschichtswissenschaft. In: J. Le Goff, R. Chartier and J. Revel (Hg.), *Die Rückeroberung des historischen Denkens*. Frankfurt: Fischer.

Leach, E. R. (1966). *Rethinking Cultural Anthropology*. London: Athlone Press.

Lefebvre, H. (1977). *Kritik des Alltagslebens*. Kronberg/Ts: Athenäum.

Lem, S. (1972). *Solaris*. München: DTV.

León Zermeño, M. de Jesús (2003). *La representación social del trabajo doméstico – Un problema de la construcción de la identidad feminina*. Puebla, México: BUAP.

Lerner, M. J. (1971). Justice, guilt, and veridical perception. *Journal of Personality and Social Psychology*, 20, 127–35.

Levine, J. M., and Moreland, R. L. (1991). Culture and socialization in work groups. In: L. B. Resnick, J. M. Levine and S. D. Teasley (Eds), *Perspectives on Socially Shared Cognition*. Washington, DC: American Psychological Association.

LeVine, R. A. (1982). *Culture, Behavior and Personality*. New York: Aldine.

LeVine, R. A. (1984). Properties of culture. In: R. A. Shweder and R. A. LeVine (Eds), *Culture Theory*. Cambridge: Cambridge University Press.

Levine, R., Chein, J., and Murphy, G. (1942). The relation of the intensity of a need to the amount of perceptual distortion. *Journal of Psychology*, 13, 283–93.

Levin-Rozalis, M. (2000). Social representations as emerging from social structure: the case of the Ethiopian immigrants to Israel. *Papers on Social Representations*, 9, p. 1.1–1.22. [http://www.psr.jku.at/]

Lévi-Strauss, C. (1967). *Strukturale Anthropologie*. Frankfurt: Suhrkamp.

Lévi-Strauss, C. (1968). *Das wilde Denken*. Frankfurt: Suhrkamp.

Lévi-Strauss, C. (1972). *Das Ende des Totemismus*. Frankfurt: Suhrkamp.

Lévy-Brühl, L. (1921). *Das Denken der Naturvölker*. Wien: Braumüller.

Lewis, A. (1990). Shared economic beliefs. In: Fraser and Gaskell (Eds), *The Social Psychological Study of Widespread Beliefs*.

Licata, L. (2003). Representing the future of the European Union: Consequences on national and European identifications. *Papers on Social Representations*, 12, 5.1–5.22. [http://www.psr.jku.at/]

Lilli, W. (1978). Die Hypothesentheorie der sozialen Wahrnehmung. In: D. Frey (Hg.), *Kognitive Theorien der Sozialpsychologie*. Bern: Huber.

Lilli, W., and Rehm, J. (1983). Theoretische und empirische Untersuchungen zum Phänomen der 'illusorischen Korrelation'. I. Ableitung von Randbedingungen für das Auftreten von Effekten der illusorischen Korrelation aus dem Konzept der Verfügbarkeits-Heuristik. *Zeitschrift für Sozialpsychologie*, 14, 251–61.

Lilli, W., and Rehm, J. (1984). Theoretische und empirische Untersuchungen zum Phänomen der Zusammenhangstäuschung. II. Entwicklung eines Modells zum quantitativen Urteil und Diskussion seiner Implikationen für die soziale Urteilsbildung. *Zeitschrift für Sozialpsychologie*, 15, 60–73.

Lindblom, C. E. (1979). Still muddling, not yet through. *Public Administration Review*, 39, 517–26.

Lindeman, M., Pyysiäinen, I., and Saariluoma, P. (2002). Representing God. *Papers on Social Representations*, 11, 1.1–1.13. [http://www.psr.jku.at/]

Lingle, J. H., Altom, M. W., and Medin, D. L. (1984). Of cabbages and kings: Assessing the extendability of natural concept models to social things. In: R. S. Wyer, Jr., and T. K. Srull (Eds), *Handbook of Social Cognition, Vol. 1.* Hillsdale, N. J.: Lawrence Erlbaum.

Liu, J. H. (1999). Social representations of history: Preliminary notes on content and consequences around the Pacific rim. *International Journal of Intercultural Relations*, 23, 215–36.

Liu, J. H., and Hilton, D. J. (forthcoming). How the past weighs on the present: Social representations of history and their role in identity politics. *British Journal of Social Psychology.*

Liu, J. H., Wilson, M. S., McClure, J., and Higgins, T. R. (1999). Social identity and the perception of history: cultural representations of Aotearoa/New Zealand. *European Journal of Social Psychology*, 29, 1021–48.

Liu, J. H., Ng, S. H., Loong, C., Gee, S., and Weatherall, A. (2003). Cultural stereotypes and social representations of elders from Chinese and European perspectives. *Journal of Cross-Cultural Gerontology*, 18, 149–68.

Livingstone, S. (1991). Audience reception: The role of the viewer in retelling romantic drama. In: J. Curran and M. Gurevitch (Eds), *Mass Media and Society.* London: Edward Arnold.

Lloyd, B., and Duveen, G. (1989). The reconstruction of social knowledge in the transition from sensorimotor to conceptual activity: The gender system. In: A. Gellatly, D. Rogers and J. Sloboda (Eds), *Cognition and Social Worlds.* Oxford: Oxford University Press.

Lloyd, B., and Duveen, G. (1990). A semiotic analysis of social representations of gender. In: G. Duveen and B. Lloyd (Eds), *Social Representations and the Development of Knowledge.* Cambridge: Cambridge University Press.

Lloyd, B., and Duveen, G. (1992). *Gender Identities and Education – The Impact of Starting School.* New York: Harvester-Wheatsheaf.

Lonner, W. J. (1980). The search for psychological universals. In: H. C. Triandis and W. W. Lambert (Eds), *Handbook of Cross-Cultural Psychology, Vol. 1.* Boston: Allyn & Bacon.

Lopes, L. L. (1991). The rhetoric of irrationality. *Theory and Psychology*, 1, 65–82.

Lorenz, K. (1973a). *Die Rückseite des Spiegels.* München: Piper.

Lorenz, K. (1973b). Analogy as a source of knowledge. *Nobel Lecture*, December 12, 1973.

Lorenzi-Cioldi, F. (1988). *Individus dominantes, groupes dominés. Images masculines et feminines.* Grenoble: Presses Universitaires de Grenoble.

Lorenzi-Cioldi, F. (1994). *Les androgynes*. Paris: Presses Universitaires de France.

Lorenzi-Cioldi, F. (1997). *Questions de méthodologie en sciences sociales*. Paris: Delachaux and Niestlé.

Lorenzi-Cioldi, F., and Clémence, A. (2004). Group processes and the construction of social representations. In: M. B. Brewer and M. Hewstone (Eds), *Social Cognition*. Oxford: Blackwell.

Lucchetti, S. (1991). Zwischen Herausforderung und Bedrohung. Subjektive Krankheitstheorien bei HIV-Infektion und AIDS. In: U. Flick (Hg.), *Alltagswissen über Gesundheit und Krankheit*. Heidelberg: Asanger.

Lugg, A. (1975). Putnam on reductionism. *Cognition*, 3, 289–93.

Lukes, S. (1973). *Individualism*. Oxford: Basil Blackwell.

Luria, A. R. (1981). *Language and Cognition*. New York: Wiley.

Lyman, S. M., and Scott, M. B. (1970). *A Sociology of the Absurd*. New York: Appleton-Century-Crofts.

Lyotard, J.-F. (1986). *Das postmoderne Wissen*. Wien: Böhlau.

Lyotard, J.-F. (1987). *Der Widerstreit*. München: Fink.

Major, B., Cozzorelli, C., Testa, M., and McFarlin, D. (1988). Self-verification versus expectancy confirmation in social interaction: The impact of self-focus. *Personality and Social Psychology Bulletin*, 14, 346–59.

Malinowski, B. (1975). *Eine wissenschaftliche Theorie der Kultur*. Frankfurt: Suhrkamp.

Mandelblit, N., and Zachar, O. (1998). The notion of dynamic unit: Conceptual developments in cognitive science. *Cognitive Science*, 22, 229–68.

Mandl, H., and Spada, H. (1988). *Wissenspsychologie*. München: Psychologische Verlagsunion.

Mandler, G. (1982). The structure of value: Accounting for taste. In: M. S. Clark and S. T. Fiske (Eds), *Affect and Cognition*. Hillsdale, NJ: Erlbaum.

Mandler, J. M. (1984). *Stories, Scripts, and Scenes: Aspects of Schema Theory*. Hillsdale, NJ: Erlbaum.

Manicas, P. T., and Secord, P. F. (1983). Implications for psychology of the new philosophy of science. *American Psychologist*, 38, 399–413.

Mannetti, L., and Tanucci, G. (1993). The meaning of work for young people: The role of parents in the transmission of a social representation. In: Breakwell and Canter (Eds), *Empirical Approaches to Social Representations*.

March, J. G., and Olson, J. P. (1986). Garbage can models of decision making in organizations. In: J. G. March and R. Weissinger-Baylon (Eds), *Ambiguity and Command: Organizational Persepctives on Military Decision Making*. Cambridge: Ballinger.

Margolis, J. (1991). The autonomy of folk psychology. In: J. D. Greenwood (Ed), *The Future of Folk Psychology – Intentionality and Cognitive Science*. Cambridge: Cambridge University Press.

Markovà, I. (1996). Towards an epistemology of social representations. *Journal for the Theory of Social Behaviour*, 26, 177–96.

Markovà, I. (2000). Amedee or how to get rid of it: Social representations from a dialogical perspective. *Culture and Psychology*, 6, 419–60.

Markovà, I. (2003). *Dialogicality and Social Representations – the Dynamics of Mind*. Cambridge: Cambridge University Press.

Markovà, I., and Wilkie, P. (1987). Representations, concepts and social change: The phenomenon of AIDS. *Journal for the Theory of Social Behaviour*, 17, 389–410.

Markovà, I., Moodie, E., and Plichtova, J. (1998). The social representations of democracy: Stability and change. In: A. V. Rigas (Ed), *Social Representations and Contemporary Social Problems* (pp. 155–77). Athens: Ellinika Grammata.

Markovà, I., Moodie, E., and Plichtova, J. (2000). Democracy as a social representation. In: M. Chaib and B. Orfali (Eds), *Social Representations and Communicative Processes*. Jönköping: Jönköping University Press.

Markovà, I., Moodie, E., Farr, R., Drozda-Senkowska, E., Erös, F., Plichtova, J., Gervais, M.-C., Hoffmannova, J., and Mullerova, O. (1998). Social representations of the individual: A post-communist perspective. *European Journal of Social Psychology*, 28, 797–830.

Marks, G., and Miller, N. (1985). The effect of certainty on consensus judgments. *Personality and Social Psychology Bulletin*, 11, 165–77.

Marks, G., and Miller, N. (1987). Ten years of research on the false-consensus effect. *Psychological Bulletin*, 102, 72–90.

Martin, D. (1990). Représentations du possible et pratiques de l'impossible. In: D. Martin and P. Royer-Rastoll (Eds), *Représentations sociales et pratiques quotidiennes*. Paris: L'Harmattan.

Martin, D., and Royer-Rastoll, P. (1990). Postface: Représentations sociales et pratiques quotidiennes. In: D. Martin and P. Royer-Rastoll (Eds), *Représentations sociales et pratiques quotidiennes*. Paris: L'Harmattan.

Mary, A. (1988). Le corps, la maison, le marché et les jeux. *Cahiers du LASA*, 8/9, 9–102.

Matlin, M., and Stang, D. (1978). *The Polyanna Principle*. Cambridge, MA: Schenkman.

Matthes, J., and Schütze, F. (1981). Alltagswissen, Interaktion und gesellschaftliche Wirklichkeit. In: Arbeitsgruppe Bielefelder Soziologen (Hg.), *Alltagswissen, Interaktion und gesllschaftliche Wirklichkeit*. Opladen: Westdeutscher Verlag.

Maze, J. R. (1991). Representationism, realism and the redundancy of 'mentalese'. *Theory and Psychology*, 1, 163–86.

McArthur, L. Z. (1972). The how and what of why: Some determinants and consequences of causal attribution. *Journal of Personality and Social Psychology*, 22, 171–93.

McArthur, L. Z. (1981). What grabs you? The role of attention in impression formation and causal attribution. In: E. T. Higgins, P. Herman and

M. P. Zanna (Eds), *The Ontario Symposium on Personality and Social Psychology, Vol. 1.* Hillsdale, NJ: Erlbaum.

McArthur, L. Z., and Baron, R. M. (1983). Toward an ecological theory of social perception. *Psychological Review*, 90, 215–38.

McGuire, W. J. (1960). Cognitive consistency and attitude change. *Journal of Abnormal and Social Psychology*, 60, 345–53.

McGuire, W. J. (1983). A contextualist theory of knowledge: Its implications for innovation and reform in psychological research. In: L. Berkowitz (Ed), *Advances in Experimental Social Psychology, Vol. 16.* New York: Academic Press.

McKinlay, A., Potter, J., and Wetherell, M. (1993). Discourse analysis and social representations. In: Breakwell and Canter (Eds), *Empirical Approaches to Social Representations.*

Mehan, H. (1996). Benath the skin and between the ears: A case study in the politics of representation. In: S. Chaiklin and J. Lave (Eds), *Understanding Practice: Perspectives on Activity and Context.* Cambridge: Cambridge University Press.

Mehrabian, A. (1976). *Public Places and Private Spaces.* New York: Basic Books.

Meier, K., and Kirchler, E. (1998). Social representations of the euro in Austria. *Journal of Economic Psychology*, 19, 755–74.

Merton, R. K. (1957a). The role-set: Problems in sociological theory. *British Journal of Sociology*, 8, 110–20.

Merton, R. K. (1957b). *Social Theory and Social Structure.* Glencoe, IL: The Free Press.

Michael, M. (1991). Some postmodern reflections on social psychology. *Theory and Psychology*, 1, 203–21.

Miles, M. B., and Huberman, A. M. (1994). *Qualitative Data Analysis.* Thousand Oaks, CA: Sage.

Milgram, S. (1984). Cities as social representations. In: Farr and Moscovici (Eds), *Social Representations.*

Miller, G. A. (1969). Psychology as a means of promoting human welfare. *American Psychologist*, 24, 1063–75.

Miller, J. G. (1984). Culture and the development of everyday social explanation. *Journal of Personality and Social Psychology*, 46, 961–78.

Miller, M. (1989). Systematisch verzerrte Legitimitätsdiskurse. Einige kritische Überlegungen zu Bourdieus Habitustheorie. In: K. Eder (Hg.), *Klassenlage, Lebensstil und kulturelle Praxis.* Frankfurt: Suhrkamp.

Minsky, M. (1975). A framework for representing knowledge. In: P. H. Winston (Ed), *The Psychology of Computer Vision.* New York: McGraw-Hill.

Mixon, D. (1990). Getting the science right is the problem, not the solution: A matter of priority. *Journal for the Theory of Social Behaviour*, 20, 97–110.

Molinari, L. (2001). Social representations of children's rights: The point of view of adolescents. *Swiss Journal of Psychology*, 60, 231–43.

Molinari, L., and Emiliani, F. (1990). What is an image? The structure of mothers' images of the child and their influence on conversational styles. In: G. Duveen and B. Lloyd (Eds), *Social Representations and the Development of Knowledge*. Cambridge: Cambridge University Press.

Molinari, L., and Emiliani, F. (1993). Structures and functions of social representations: Theories of development, images of child and pupil. *Papers on Social Representations*, 2, 95–106. [http://www.psr.jku.at/]

Molinari, L., Emiliani, F., and Carugati, F. (1992). Development according to mothers: A case of social representations. In: von Cranach, Doise and Mugny (Eds) *Social Representations and the Social Bases of Knowledge*.

Moliner, P. (1992). Représentations sociales, schèmes conditionelles et schèmes normatifs. *Bulletin de Psychologie*, 45, 325–9.

Moliner, P. (1995). A two-dimensional model of social representations. *European Journal of Social Psychology*, 25, 27–40.

Moliner, P. (2002). Ambiguous-scenario and attribute challenge techniques: Social representations of 'The Firm' and 'The Nurse'. *European Review of Applied Psychology*, 52, 273–80.

Moloney, G., and Walker, I. (2000). Messiahs, pariahs, and donors: The development of social representations of organ transplants. *Journal for the Theory of Social Behaviour*, 30, 203–28.

Moloney, G., and Walker, I. (2002). Talking about transplants: Social representations and the dialectical, dilemmatic nature of organ donation and transplantation. *British Journal of Social Psychology*, 41, 299–320.

Monteil, J. M., and Mailhot, L. (1988). Eléments d'une représentation sociale de la formation: analyse d'une enquête auprès d'une population de formateurs. *Connexions*, 51, 9–26.

Moodie, E., Markova, I., and Plichtova, J. (1995). Lay representations of democracy: A study in two cultures. *Culture and Psychology*, 1, 423–53.

Morant, N. (1995). What is mental illness? Social representations of mental illness. *Papers on Social Representations*, 4, 41–52. [http://www.psr.jku.at/]

Moscovici, S. (1961/1976). *La psychoanalyse son image et son public*. Paris: Presses Universitaires de France.

Moscovici, S. (1963). Attitudes and opinions. *Annual Review of Psychology*, 14, 231–60.

Moscovici, S. (1972). Society and theory in social psychology. In: J. Israel and H. Tajfel (Eds), *The Context of Social Psychology*. London: Academic Press.

Moscovici, S. (1973). Introduction. In: Herzlich (Ed), *Health and Illness*.

Moscovici, S. (1979). *Sozialer Wandel durch Minoritäten.* Wien: Urban & Schwarzenberg.

Moscovici, S. (1981). On social representations. In: J. P. Forgas (Ed), *Social Cognition: Perspectives on Everyday Knowledge.* London: Academic Press.

Moscovici, S. (1982). The coming era of social representations. In: J. P. Codol and J. P. Leyens (Eds), *Cognitive Approaches to Social Behaviour.* The Hague: Nijhoff.

Moscovici, S. (1984). The phenomenon of social representations. In: Farr and Moscovici (Eds), *Social Representations.*

Moscovici, S. (1987a). Answers and questions. *Journal for the Theory of Social Behaviour,* 17, 513–29.

Moscovici, S. (1987b). The conspiracy mentality. In: C. F. Graumann and S. Moscovici (Eds), *Changing Conceptions of Conspiracy.* New York: Springer.

Moscovici, S. (1988). Notes towards a description of social representations. *European Journal of Social Psychology,* 18, 211–50.

Moscovici, S. (1989a). Des représentations collectives aux représentations sociales: Éléments pour une histoire. In: Jodelet (Ed), *Les Représentations Sociales.*

Moscovici, S. (1989b). Preconditions for explanations in social psychology. *European Journal of Social Psychology,* 19, 407–30.

Moscovici, S. (1992a). The psychology of scientific myths. In: von Cranach, Doise and Mugny (Eds), *Social Representations and the Social Bases of Knowledge.*

Moscovici, S. (1992b). La nouvelle pensée magique. *Bulletin de Psychologie,* 45, 301–23.

Moscovici, S. (2000). The concept of themata. In: G. Duveen (Ed.), *Social Representations – Explorations in Social Psychology.* Cambridge: Polity.

Moscovici, S. (Ed) (1985–6). *Psicología social, 2 Vols.* Barcelona: Paídos.

Moscovici, S., and Hewstone, M. (1983). Social representations and social explanations: From the 'naive' to the 'amateur' scientist. In: M. Hewstone (Ed), *Attribution Theory. Social and Functional Extensions.* Oxford: Blackwell.

Moscovici, S., and Hewstone, M. (1986). De la ciencia al sentido común. In: Moscovici (Ed), *Psicología Social, Vol. 2.* Barcelona: Paidós.

Moscovici, S., and Markovà, I. (1998). Social representations in retrospect and prospect: A dialogue with Serge Moscovici. *Culture and Psychology,* 4, 371–410.

Mugny, G., and Carugati, F. (1985). *L'intelligence au pluriel.* Cousset: DelVal.

Mugny, G., and Pérez, J. A. (1988). Las representaciones sociales de la inteligencia: de la observación a la experimentación. In: T. Ibañez Gracia (Ed), *Ideologías de la vida cotidiana.* Barcelona: Sendai.

Mummendey, A. (Ed) (1984). *Social Psychology of Aggression.* Berlin: Springer.

Munné, F. (1980). *Psicología social.* Barcelona: CEAC.

Munro, D. (1992). Process vs structure and levels of analysis in psychology. *Theory and Psychology,* 2, 109–27.

Murdock, G. P. (1980). *Theories of Illness: A World Survey.* Pittsburgh: University of Pittsburgh Press.

Murray, M. (2002). Connecting narrative and social representation theory in health research. *Social Science Information,* 41, 653–74.

Nadler, A. (1992). 'Siege mentality in Israel': Fact, fiction or what? Discussion of Bar-Tal and Antebi. *Ongoing Production on Social Representations,* 1, 73–8.

Namer, G. (1987). *Mémoire et société.* Paris: Méridiens Klincksieck.

Nascimento-Schulze, C. M. (1999). Social representation of the universe – a study with doctors in human and natural sciences. *Papers on Social Representations,* 8, 5.1–5.13. [http://www.psr.jku.at/]

Nascimento-Schulze, C. M., Fontes Garcia, Y., and Costa Arruda, D. (1995). Health paradigms, social representations of health and illness and their central nucleus. *Papers on Social Representations,* 4, 187–198. [http://www.psr.jku.at/]

Nau, J.-Y. (1994). 'Le viol de l'ovule' (The rape of the ovum). *Le Monde,* Paris, Sunday 26 and Monday 27 June 1994, 1 and 10f.

Needham, R. (1972). *Belief, Language and Experience.* Oxford: Blackwell.

Needham, R. (1973). *Right and Left-Essays on Dual Symbolic Classification.* Chicago, IL: University of Chicago Press.

Needham, R. (1975). Polythetic classification: Convergence and consequences. *Man,* 10, 349–69.

Neisser, U. (1974). *Kognitive Psychologie.* Stuttgart: Klett.

Neisser, U. (1981). John Dean's memory: A case study. *Cognition,* 9, 1–22.

Newcomb, T. M. (1943). *Personality and Social Change.* New York: Dryden.

Nida, E. (1964). *Towards a Science of Translating.* Leiden: Brill.

Nielsen, T. H., and Berg, S. F. (2001). Goethe's homunculus and Shelley's monster: On the romantic prototypes of modern biotechnology. *Notizie di Politeia,* 17, 37–50.

Nisbett, R. E., and Borgida, E. (1975). Attribution and the psychology of prediction. *Journal of Personality and Social Psychology,* 32, 932–43.

Nisbett, R. E., and Ross, L. (1980). *Human Inference: Strategies and Shortcomings of Social Judgment.* Englewood Cliffs, NJ: Prentice-Hall.

Nisbett, R. E., and Wilson, T. D. (1977). Telling more than we can know: Verbal reports on mental processes. *Psychological Review,* 84, 231–59.

Nisbett, R. E., Peng, K., Choi, I., and Norenzayan, A. (2001). Culture and systems of thought: Holistic versus analytic cognition. *Psychological Review,* 108, 291–310.

Noack, H. (1976). *Die Philosophie Westeuropas.* Darmstadt: Wissenschaftliche Buchgesellschaft.

Oberlechner, T., Slunecko, T., and Kronberger, N. (2004). Surfing the money tides: Understanding the foreign exchange market through metaphors. *British Journal of Social Psychology*, 43, 133–56.

Offe, C. (1970). *Leistungsprinzip und industrielle Arbeit.* Frankfurt: Europäische Verlagsanstalt.

O'Leary, V. E., and Hansen, R. D. (1984). Sex as an attributional fact. *Nebraska Symposium on Motivation.*

Opler, M. E. (1946). Themes as dynamic forces in culture. *American Journal of Sociology*, 51, 198–206.

Oppitz, M. (1975). *Notwendige Beziehungen.* Frankfurt: Suhrkamp.

Orfali, B. (1990). *L'Adhesion au Front National.* Paris: Éditions Kime.

Orr, E., Assor, A., and Cairns, D. (1996). Social representations and group membership: Shared and diffused parental ideas in three Israeli settings. *European Journal of Social Psychology*, 26, 703–26.

Orr, E., Sagi, S., and Bar-On, D. (2000). Social representations in use: Israeli and Palestinian high school students' collective coping and defense. *Papers on Social Representations*, 9, 2.1–2.20. [http://www.psr.jku.at/]

Ortiz, R. (1986). *Cultura Brasileira e Identidade Nacional.* São Paulo: Brasiliense.

Osherson, D. N., and Smith, E. E. (1981). On the adequacy of prototype theory as a theory of concepts. *Cognition*, 9, 35–58.

Ostrom, T. M. (1984). The souvereignty of social cognition. In: R. S. Wyer and T. K. Srull (Eds), *Handbook of Social Cognition, Vol. 1.* Hillsdale, NJ: Erlbaum.

Páez, D. (Ed) (1987). *Pensamiento, individuo y sociedad. Cognición y representación social.* Madrid: Fundamentos.

Páez, D., Echebarria, A., Valencia, J., Romo, I., San Juan, C., and Vergara, A. (1991). AIDS social representations: Contents and processes. *Journal of Community and Applied Social Psychology*, 1, 29–32.

Paicheler, H. (1985–1986). La epistemología del sentido común. In: Moscovici (Ed), *Psicología Social, Vol. 2.*

Paivio, A. (1971). *Imagery and Verbal Processes.* New York: Holt, Rinehart & Winston.

Papineau, D. (1978). *For Science in the Social Sciences.* New York: St. Martin's Press.

Parales Quenza, C. J. (1999). *Social Representations of Healthy Eating: An Empirical Study in Colombia.* Unpublished PhD thesis, London School of Economics, London.

Parsons, T. (1977). *The Evolution of Societies.* Englewood Cliffs, NJ: Prentice-Hall.

Pelto, P. J., and Pelto, G. H. (1975). Intra-cultural diversity: Some theoretical issues. *American Ethnologist*, 2, 1–18.

Penz, E., and Sinkovics, R. R. (2001). Money matters – a social representations approach for the investigation of consumer attitudes towards electronic payment systems. In: E. Breivik, A. W. Falkenberg and K. Grønhaug (Eds). 30th EMAC Conference, Bergen, Norway: Norwegian School of Economics and Business Administration, CD-Rom.

Pepitone, A., and Triandis, H. C. (1988). On the universality of social psychological theories. *Journal of Cross-Cultural Psychology*, 18, 471–98.

Perlman, D., and Cozby, P. C. (Eds) (1983). *Social Psychology*. New York: Holt, Rinehart & Winston.

Petrillo G. (1996). Changes in social representations of mental illness: The last twenty-five years on the Italian press. *Papers on Social Representations*, 5, 99–112. [http://www.psr.jku.at/]

Pheysey, D. C. (1993) *Organisational Cultures: Types and Transformations* London: Routledge.

Philo, G. (1996). *Media and Mental Distress*. London: Methuen.

Philogène, G. (1994). 'African American' as a new social representation. *Journal for the Theory of Social Behaviour*, 24, 89–110.

Philogène, G. (1999). *From Black to African American – A New Social Representation*. Westport, CT: Greenwood-Praeger.

Piattelli-Palmarini, M. (Ed) (1980). *Language and Learning: The Debate between Jean Piaget and Noam Chomsky*. Cambridge: Harvard University Press.

Pirttilä-Backman, A.-M. (2000). Notes on democracy and the citicens's free choice. In: M. Chaib and B. Orfali (Eds), *Social Representations and Communicative Processes*. Jönköping: Jönköping University Press.

Poeschl, G. (2001). Social comparison and differentiation strategies in social representations of intelligence. *Swiss Journal of Psychology*, 60, 15–26.

Pollner, M. (1974). 'Mundane reasoning'. *Philosophy of the Social Sciences*. 5, 411–30.

Popper, K. R. (1935/1976/1994). *Logik der Forschung*. Tübingen: Mohr-Siebeck.

Popper, K. R. (1972). *Objective Knowledge*. Oxford: Clarendon Press.

Posner, M. I. (1969). Abstraction and the process of recognition. In: G. H. Bower and J. T. Spence (Eds), *The Psychology of Learning and Motivation, Vol. 3*. New York: Academic Press.

Posner, M. I., and Keele, S. W. (1968). On the genesis of abstract ideas. *Journal of Experimental Psychology*, 77, 353–63.

Posner, M. I., and Keele, S. W. (1970). Retention of abstract ideas. *Journal of Experimental Psychology*, 83, 304–8.

Postman, L. (1951). Toward a general theory of cognition. In: J. H. Rohrer and M. Sheriff (Eds), *Social Psychology at the Crossroads*. New York: Harper.

Potter, J. (1996). *Representing Reality: Discourse, Rhetoric and Social Construction*. London: Sage.

Potter, J., and Litton, I. (1985). Some problems underlying the theory of social representations. *British Journal of Social Psychology*, 24, 81–90.

Potter, J., and Wetherell, M. (1987). *Discourse and Social Psychology – Beyond Attitudes and Behaviour*. London: Sage.

Potter, J., and Wetherell, M. (1998). Social representations, discourse analysis, and racism. In: U. Flick et al. (Eds) *The Psychology of the Social*. New York: Cambridge University Press.

Pribram, K., Nuwer, M., and Baron, R. (1974). The holographic hypothesis of memory structure in brain function and perception. In: D. H. Krantz, R. D. Luce, R. C. Atkinson and P. Suppes (Eds), *Contemporary Developments in Mathematical Psychology, Vol. 2*. San Francisco: Freeman.

Propp, V. (1969). *The Morphology of the Folktale*. Austin: University of Texas Press.

Purkhardt, S. C. (1993). *Transforming Social Representations – A Social Psychology of Common Sense and Science*. London: Routledge.

Purkhardt, S. C., and Stockdale, J. E. (1993). Multidimesnional scaling as a technique for the exploration and description of a social representation. In: Breakwell and Canter (Eds), *Empirical Approaches to Social Representations*.

Putnam, H. (1974). Reductionism and the nature of psychology. *Cognition*, 2, 131–46.

Putnam, H. (1975). Reply to Lugg. *Cognition*, 3, 295–98.

Putnam, H. (1981). *Reason, Truth, and History*. Cambridge: Cambridge University Press.

Putnam, H. (1988). *Representation and Reality*. Cambridge, MA: MIT Press.

Putnam, H. (1990). *Realism with a Human Face*. Cambridge, MA: Harvard University Press.

Quijano, A. (1993). Modernity, identity and utopia in Latin America. *Boundary*, 2(20), 140–55.

Quine, W. V. (1961). *From a Logical Point of View*. Cambridge, MA: Harvard University Press.

Quine, W. V. (1969). *Ontological Relativity and Other Essays*. New York: Columbia University Press.

Quine, W. V. (1980). *Wort und Gegenstand*. Stuttgart: Kröner.

Quinn, A. (1982). 'Commitment' in American marriage: A cultural analysis. *American Ethnologist*, 9, 775–98.

Quinn, N., and Holland, D. (1987). Culture and cognition. In: Holland and Quinn (Eds), *Cultural Models in Language and Thought*.

Radley, A. (1990). Artefacts, memory, and a sense of the past. In: D. Middleton and D. Edwards (Eds), *Collective Remembering*. London: Sage.

Ragin, C. C. (1987). *The Comparative Method: Moving beyond Qualitative and Quantitative Strategies.* Berkeley: The University of California Press.

Rangel, M. (1997). The representations of the students, as a means of practical knowledge, and the learning of scientific knowledge at school. *Papers on Social Representations,* 6, 51–8. [http://www.psr.jku.at/]

Räty, H., and Snellman, L. (1992). Making the unfamiliar familiar – some notes on the criticism of the theory of social representations. *Ongoing Production on Social Representations,* 1, 3–14.

Räty, H., and Snellman, L. (1995). On the social fabric of intelligence. *Papers on Social Representations,* 4, 177–86. [http://www.psr.jku.at/]

Raulff, U. (1989). Mentalitäten-Geschichte. In: U. Raulff (Hg.), *Mentalitäten-Geschichte.* Berlin: Wagenbach.

Rauscher, F. H., Shaw, G, L., and Ky, K. N. (1993). Music and spatial task performance. *Nature,* 365, 611.

Read, S. J. (1983). Once is enough: Causal reasoning from a single instance. *Journal of Personality and Social Psychology,* 45, 323–34.

Reicher, S., and Potter, J. (1985). Psychological theory as intergroup perspective: A comparative analysis of "scientific" and "lay" accounts of crowd events. *Human Relations,* 38, 167–89.

Reinert, M. (1990). ALCESTE – Une methodologie d'analyse des donnees textuelles et une application: AURELIA de Gerard de Nerval. *Bulletin de Methodologie Sociologique,* 26, 24–54.

Reiss, D. (1981). *The Family's Construction of Reality.* Cambridg, MA: Harvard University Press.

Remy, J., Voye, L., and Servais, E. (1991). *Produire ou reproduire. Une sociologie de la vie quotidienne, 2 Vols.* Bruxelles: De Boeck-Wesmael.

Rexilius, G., and Grubitzsch, S. (Hg.) (1986). *Psychologie.* Reinbek: Rowohlt.

Rheinberger, H.-J. (1997). *Toward a History of Epistemic Things – Synthesizing Proteins in the Test Tube.* Stanford, CA: Stanford University Press.

Rice, G. E. (1980). On cultural schemata. *American Ethnologist,* 7, 152–71.

Riedl, R. (1976). *Die Strategie der Genesis.* München: Piper.

Riedl, R. (1980). *Biologie der Erkenntnis.* Berlin: Parey.

Riessman, C. K. (1993). *Narrative Analysis.* London: Sage.

Rijsman, J. (1983). The dynamics of social competition in personal and categorical comparison-situations. In: W. Doise and S. Moscovici (Eds), *Current Issues in European Social Psychology, Vol. 1.* Cambridge: Cambridge University Press.

Rijsman, J., and Stroebe, W. (1989). The two social psychologies or whatever happened to the crisis. *European Journal of Social Psychology,* 19, 339–44.

Robson, C. (1993). *Real World Research: A Resource for Social Scientists and Practitioner-Researchers.* Oxford: Blackwell.

Rohracher, H. (1966). *Einführung in die Psychologie.* Wien: Urban & Schwarzenberg.

Roiser, M. (1987). Commonsense, science and public opinion. *Journal for the Theory of Social Behaviour,* 17, 411–32.

Rollins, B. C., and Bahr, S. J. (1976). A theory of power relationships in marriage. *Journal of Marriage and the Family,* 38, 619–27.

Romney, A. K., Batchelder, W. H., and Weller, S. C. (1987). Recent applications of cultural consensus theory. *American Behavioral Scientist,* 31, 163–77.

Romney, A. K., Weller, S. C., and Batchelder, W. H. (1986). Culture as consensus: A theory of culture and informant accuracy. *American Anthropologist,* 88, 313–38.

Rosch, E. H. (1975). Cognitive representative of semantic categories. *Journal of Experimental Psychology (General),* 104, 192–233.

Rosch, E. H., and Mervis, C. B. (1976). Family resemblances – studies in the internal structure of categories. *Cognitive Psychology,* 7, 382–439.

Rose, D. (1996). *Representations of Madness on British Television.* Unpublished PhD Thesis, London University, London.

Rose, D. (1998). Television and community care. *Journal of Community and Applied Social Psychology,* 8, 213–28.

Rose, D., Efraim, D., Gervais, M.-C., Joffe, H., Jovchelovitch, S., and Morant, N. (1995). Questioning consensus in social representation theory. *Papers on Social Representations,* 4, 150–76. [http://www.psr.jku.at/]

Rose, D., Ford, R., Lindley, P., Gawith, G., and KCW-Users'-Group. (1998). *In Our Experience: User-Focused Monitoring in Mental Health Services.* London: The Sainsbury Centre for Mental Health.

Ross, L. D., and Anderson, C. (1980). Shortcomings in the attribution process: On the origins and maintenance of erroneous social assessments. In: A. Tversky, D. Kahneman and P. Slovic (Eds), *Judgment under Uncertainty: Heuristics and Biases.* New York: Cambridge University Press.

Ross, L. D., and Lepper, M. R. (1980). The perseverance of beliefs: Empirical and normative considerations. In: R. A. Shweder and D. Fiske (Eds), *New Directions for Methodology of Behavioral Science: Fallible Judgment in Behavioral Resarch.* San Francisco: Jossey Bass.

Ross, L. D., Amabile, T. M., and Steinmetz, J. L. (1977a). Social roles, social control, and biases in social-perception process. *Journal of Personality and Social Psychology,* 35, 485–94.

Ross, L. D., Green, D., and House, P. (1977b). The "false consensus effect": An egocentric bias in social perception and attribution processes. *Journal of Experimental Social Psychology,* 13, 279–301.

Roth, G. (1981). Biological systems theory and the problem of reductionism. In: G. Roth and H. Schwegler (Eds), *Self-Organizing Systems.* Frankfurt: Campus.

Rothbaum, F., Weisz, J. R., and Snyder, S. S. (1982). Changing the world and changing the self: A two-process model of perceived control. *Journal of Personality and Social Psychology*, 42, 5–37.

Rouquette, M.-L. (1996). Social representations and mass communication research. *Journal for the Theory of Social Behaviour*, 26, 221–31.

Roussiau, N. (2002). Similitude analysis: A methodology for studying the structure of social representations. *European Review of Applied Psychology*, 52, 293–304.

Roux, J.-P., and Gilly, M. (1984). Aide apportée par le marquage social dans un procedure de resolution chez des enfants de 12–13 ans: données et refléxion sur les mecanismes. *Bulletin de Psychologie*, 38, 145–55.

Rozin, P., and Nemeroff, C. (1990). The laws of sympathetic magic: A psychological analysis of similarity and contagion. In: J. W. Stigler, R. A. Shweder and G. Herdt (Eds), *Cultural Psychology – Essays on Comparative Human Development*. Cambridge: Cambridge University Press.

Rubin, J. Z., Provenzano, F. J. and Luria, Z. (1974). The eye of the beholder: Parents' views on the sex of new borns. *American Journal of Orthopsychiatry*, 44, 512–19.

Rumelhart, D. E. (1980). Schemata: The building blocks of cognition. In: R. J. Spiro, B. C. Bruce and W. F. Brewer (Eds), *Theoretical Issues in Reading Comprehension*. Hillsdale, NJ: Erlbaum.

Rumelhart, D. E. (1984). Schemata and the cognitive system. In: R. S. Wyer and Th. K. Srull (Eds), *Handbook of Social Cognition, Vol. 1.* Hillsdale, NJ: Lawrence Erlbaum.

Rumelhart, D. E., and Ortony, A. (1977). The representation of knowledge in memory. In: R. C. Anderson, R. J. Spiro and W. E. Montague (Eds), *Schooling and the Acquisition of Knowledge*. Hillsdale, NJ: Erlbaum.

Rutland, A. (1998). Social representations of Europe among 10–16 year old British children. *Papers on Social Representations*, 7, 61–76. [http://www.psr.jku.at/]

Saito, A. (1996). 'Bartlett's Way' and social representations: The case of Zen transmitted across cultures. *The Japanese Journal of Experimental Social Psychology*, 35, 263–77.

Salmaso, P., and Pombeni, L. (1986). Le concept de travail. In: Doise and Palmonari (Eds), *L'Etude des Représentations Sociales*.

Salmon, M. H. (1989). Explanation in the social sciences. In: P. Kitcher and W. C. Salmon (Eds), *Scientific Explanation*. Minnesota Studies in the Philosophy of Science. Minneapolis: University of Minnesota Press.

Sampson, E. E. (1977). Psychology and the American ideal. *Journal of Personality and Social Psychology*, 35, 767–82.

Sampson, E. E. (1991). The democraticization of psychology. *Theory and Psychology*, 1, 275–98.

Scanzoni, J., and Fox, G. L. (1980). Sex roles, family and society: The seventies and beyond. *Journal of Marriage and the Family*, 42, 743–56.

Scheele, B., and Groeben, N. (1988). *Dialog-Konsensus-Methoden zur Rekonstruktion subjektiver Theorien*. Tübingen: Francke.

Schiele, B. (1984). Note pour une analyse de la notion de coupure épistémologique. *Communication – Information*, 6, 43–100.

Schmidt, H. (1969). *Philosophisches Wörterbuch*. Stuttgart: Kröner.

Schmitz, M. F., Fillipone, P., and Edelman, E. M. (2003). Social representations of attention deficit/hyperactivity disorder. *Culture and Psychology*, 9, 383–406.

Schnädelbach, H. (Hg.) (1984). *Rationalität – philosophische Beiträge*. Frankfurt: Suhrkamp.

Schneider, D. M. (1976). Notes toward a theory of culture. In: K. H. Basso and H. A. Selby (Eds), *Meaning in Anthropology*. Albuquerque: University of New Mexico Press.

Schurmans, M.-N. (1984). Le fou pollueur. *Revue Européennes des Sciences Sociales*, 22, 187–201.

Schurz, G. (Ed) (1988). *Erklären und Verstehen in der Wissenschaft*. München: Oldenburg.

Schütz, A. (1981/1932). *Der sinnhafte Aufbau der sozialen Welt*. Frankfurt: Suhrkamp.

Schütz, A., and Luckmann, T. (1979). *Strukturen der Lebenswelt, Band 1*. Frankfurt: Suhrkamp.

Schütz, A., and Luckmann, T. (1984). *Strukturen der Lebenswelt, Band 2*. Frankfurt: Suhrkamp.

Scott, M. B., and Lyman, S. M. (1968). Accounts. *American Sociological Review*, 33.

Scott, W. A. (1962). Cognitive structure and social structure: Some concepts and relationships. In: N. F. Washburn (Ed), *Decisions, Values, and Groups*. New York: Pergamon Press.

Scribner, S., and Cole, M. (1978). Unpackaging literacy. *Social Science Information*, 17, 19–40.

Searle, J. R. (1995). *The Construction of Social Reality*. London: Penguin.

Sears, D. O. (1986). College sophomors in the laboratory: Influences of a narrow data base on social psychology's view of human nature. *Journal of Personality and Social Psychology*, 51, 515–30.

Semin, G. R. (1986). The individual, the social, and the social individual. *British Journal of Social Psychology*, 25, 177–80.

Semin, G. R. (1987). On the relationship between representation of theories in psychology and ordinary language. In: W. Doise and S. Moscovici (Eds), *Current Issues in European Social Psychology, Vol. 2*. Cambridge: Cambridge University Press.

Semin, G. R. (1989). Prototypes et représentations sociales. In: D. Jodelet (Ed), *Les Représentations Sociales*. Paris: Presses Universitaires de France.

Semin, G. R., and Manstead, A. S. R. (1983). *The Accountability of Conduct*. London: Academic Press.

Semin, G. R., and Rubini, M. (1992). Examining the cultural constitution of the category of person. In: von Cranach, Doise and Mugny (Eds), *Social Representations and the Social Bases of Knowledge*.

Sen, R., and Wagner, W. (2004). Representations of history as a symbolic ressource for propaganda and mass action: The Hindu-Muslim conflict in India. Paper presented at the EAESP small group meeting "Collective Remembering, Collective Emotions and Shared Representations of History: Functions and Dynamic", Aix-en-Provence, June 2004.

Shepard, R. M. (1967). Recognition memory for words, sentences and pictures. *Journal of Verbal Learning and Verbal Behavior*, 6, 156–63.

Sherif, M. (1936). *The Psychology of Social Norms*. New York: Harper & Row.

Sherif, M. and Sherif, C. W. (1969). Interdisciplinary coordination as a validity check: Retrospect and prospect. In: M. Sherif and C. W. Sherif (Eds), *Interdisciplinary Relationships in the Social Sciences*. Chicago: Aldine.

Shiffrin, D. (1994). *Approaches to Discourse*. Oxford: Blackwell.

Shore, B. (1982). *Sala'ilua: A Samoan Mystery*. New York: Columbia University Press.

Shotter, J. (1978). Towards a psychology of everyday life: A standpoint 'in action'. In: M. Brenner, P. Marsh and M. Brenner (Eds), *The Social Context of Methods*. London: Croom Helm.

Shotter, J. (1981). Are Fincham and Schultz's findings empirical findings? *British Journal of Social Psychology*, 20, 121–3.

Shotter, J. (1984). *Social Accountability and Self-Hood*. Oxford: Blackwell.

Shotter, J. (1990). The social construction of remembering and forgetting. In: D. Middleton and D. Edwards (Eds), *Collective Remembering*. London: Sage.

Shotter, J. (1993). *Conversational Realities*. London: Sage.

Shweder, R. A. (1977). Likeness and likelihood in everyday thought: Magical thinking in judgments about personality. *Current Anthropology*, 18, 637–48.

Shweder, R. A. (1980). Scientific thought and social cognition. In: W. A. Collins (Ed), *Development of Cognition, Affect and Social Relations: The Minnesota Symposia in Child Psychology*, Vol. 13. Hillsdale, NJ: Erlbaum.

Shweder, R. A. (1986). Divergent rationalities. In: D. W. Fiske and R. A. Shweder (Eds), *Metatheory in Social Science*. Chicago: University of Chicago Press.

Shweder, R. A. (1990). Cultural psychology – what is it? In: J. W. Stigler, R. A. Shweder and G. Herdt (Eds), *Cultural Psychology – Essays on*

*Comparative Human Development*. Cambridge: Cambridge University Press.

Shweder, R. A., and Bourne, E. J. (1984). Does the concept of the person vary cross-culturally? In: R. A. Shweder and R. A. Levine (Eds), *Culture Theory*. Cambridge: Cambridge University Press.

Signorelli, N. (1989). The stigma of mental illness on television. *Journal of Broadcasting and Electronic Media*, 33, 325–31.

Singer, J. E. (1980). Social comparison: The process of self-evaluation. In: L. Festinger (Ed), *Retrospections on Social Psychology*. New York: Oxford University Press.

Sinowjew, A., and Wessel, H. (1975). *Logische Sprachregeln*. Berlin: Deutscher Verlag der Wissenschaften.

Slovik, P., Fischhoff, B., and Lichtenstein, S. (1976). Congitive processes and societal risk taking. In: J. S. Carroll and J. W. Payne (Eds), *Cognition and Social Behavior*. Hillsdale, NJ: Erlbaum.

Smedslund, J. (1978a). Bandura's theory of self-efficacy: A set of commonsense theorems. *Scandinavian Journal of Psychology*, 19, 1–14.

Smedslund, J. (1978b). Some psychological theories are not empirical: Reply to Bandura. *Scandinavian Journal of Psychology*, 19, 101–2.

Smedslund, J. (1979). Between the analytic and the arbitrary: A case study of psychological research. *Scandinavian Journal of Psychology*, 20, 129–40.

Smedslund, J. (1985). Necessarily true cultural psychologies. In: K. J. Gergen and K. E. Davis (Eds), *The Social Construction of the Person*. New York: Springer.

Smedslund, J. (1988). *Psycho-Logic*. Berlin: Springer.

Sneed, J. D. (1979). *The Logical Stucture of Mathematical Physics*. Dordrecht: Reidel.

Snellman, L., and Räty, H. (1995). Conceptions of intelligence as social representations. *European Journal of Psychology of Education*, 10, 273–81.

Snyder, M. (1981a). Seek and ya shall find: Testing hypotheses about other people. In: E. T. Higgins, C. P. Herman and M. P. Zanna (Eds), *Social Cognition: The Ontario Symposium, Vol. 1*. Hillsdale, NJ: Erlbaum.

Snyder, M. (1981b). On the influence of individuals on situations. In: N. Cantor and J. F. Kihlstrom (Eds), *Personality, Cognition, and Social Interaction*. Hillsdale, NJ: Erlbaum.

Snyder, M. (1983). The influence of individuals on situations: Implications for understanding the links between personality and social behavior. *Journal of Personality*, 51, 497–516.

Snyder, M. (1984). When belief creates reality. In: L. Berkowitz (Ed), *Advances in Experimental Social Psychology, Vol. 18*. New York: Academic Press.

Snyder, M., and Campbell, B. H. (1980). Testing hypotheses about other people: The role of the hypothesis. *Personality and Social Psychology Bulletin*, 6, 421–6.

Snyder, M., and Cantor, N. (1979). Testing hypotheses about other people: The use of historical knowledge. *Journal of Experimental Social Psychology*, 15, 330–42.

Snyder, M., and Swann, W. B. (1978). Behavioral confirmation in social interaction: From social perception to social reality. *Journal of Experimental Social Psychology*, 14, 148–62.

Snyder, M. L., and Wicklund, R. A. (1981). Attribution ambiguity. In: J. H. Harvey, W. Ickes and R. F. Kidd (Eds), *New Directions in Attribution Research, Vol. 3*. Hillsdale, NJ: Lawrence Erlbaum.

Snyder, M., Campbell, B., and Preston, E. (1982). Self-monitoring the self in action. In: J. Suls (Ed), *Psychological Perspectives on the Self, Vol. 1*. Hillsdale, NJ: Erlbaum.

Sokal, R. R., and Sneath, P. H. A. (1963). *Principles of Numeric Classification*. Cambridge: Cambridge University Press.

Solso, R. L., and McCarthy, J. E. (1981). Prototype formation of faces: A case of pseudo memory. *British Journal of Psychology*, 72, 499–503.

Sperber, D. (1982). Apparently irrational beliefs. In: M. Hollis and S. Lukes (Eds), *Rationality and Relativism*. Oxford: Basil Blackwell.

Sperber, D. (1985). Anthropology and psychology: Towards an epidemiology of representations. *Man (N.S.)*, 20, 73–89.

Sperber, D. (1989). L'étude anthropologique des représentations: problèms et perspectives. In: D. Jodelet (Ed), *Les Représentations Sociales*. Paris: Presses Universitaires de France.

Sperber, D. (1990). The epidemiology of beliefs. In: Fraser and Gaskell (Eds), *The Social Psychological Study of Widespread Beliefs*.

Sperber, D., and Wilson, D. (1986). *Relevance – Communication and Cognition*. Oxford: Blackwell.

Spini, D. (2002). Multidimensional Scaling: A technique for the quantitative analysis of the common field of social representations. *European Review of Applied Psychology*, 52, 231–40.

Spini, D., and Doise, W. (1998). Organizing principles of involvement in human rights and their social anchoring in value priorities. *European Journal of Social Psychology*, 28, 603–22.

Spinner, H. F. (1973). Science without reduction. *Inquiry*, 16, 16–94.

Spiro, M. E. (1990). On the strange and the familiar in recent anthropological thought. In: J. W. Stigler, R. A. Shweder and G. Herdt (Eds), *Cultural Psychology: Essays on Comparative Human Development*. Cambridge: Cambridge University Press.

Sprondel, W. M. (1979). "Experte" und "Laie": Zur Entwicklung von Typenbegriffen in der Wissenssoziologie. In: W. M. Sprondel and R. Grathoff (Hg.), *Alfred Schütz und die Idee des Alltags in den Sozialwissenschaften*. Stuttgart: Enke.

Srivastava, A. K., and Misra, G. (1999). Social representation of intelligence in the Indian folk tradition: An analysis of Hindi proverbs. *Journal of Indian Psychology*, 17, 23–38.

Staerklé, C., Clémence, A., and Doise, W. (1998). Representation of human rights across different national contexts: The role of democratic and non-democratic populations and governments. *European Journal of Social Psychology*, 28, 207–26.

Stähelin, N. (1991). Agent des Geistes. Der Standard – Album, 19. April, 1991.

Staub, E., and Kellet, D. S. (1972). Increasing pain tolerance by information about aversive stimuli. *Journal of Personality and Social Psychology*, 21, 198–203.

Steele, C. M., and Liu, T. J. (1983). Dissonance processes as self-affirmation. *Journal of Personality and Social Psychology*, 45, 5–19.

Stegmüller, W. (1973). *Theorie und Erfahrung: Theorienstrukturen und Theoriendynamik*. Berlin: Springer.

Stegmüller, W. (1974). *Wissenschaftliche Erklärung und Begründung*. Berlin: Springer.

Stegmüller, W. (1986). *Theorie und Erfahrung: Die Entwicklung des neuen Strukturalismus seit 1973*. Berlin: Springer.

Stegmüller, W. (1987a). *Hauptströmungen der Gegenwartsphilosophie, Band 2*. Stuttgart: Kröner.

Stegmüller, W. (1987b). *Hauptströmungen der Gegenwartsphilosophie, Band 3*. Stuttgart: Kröner.

Steward, J. H. (1955). *Theory of Culture Change*. Urbana: University of Illinois Press.

Storms, M. D. (1973). Videotape and the attribution process: Reversing actors' and observers' point of view. *Journal of Personality and Social Psychology*, 27, 165–75.

Strauss, A. L. (1987). *Qualitative Analysis for Social Scientists*. Cambridge: Cambridge University Press.

Strodtbeck, F. L. (1958). Family interaction, values and achievement. In: D. C. McClelland, A. L. Baldwon and U. Bronfenbrenner (Eds), *Talent and Society*. Princeton, NJ: Van Nostrand.

Sturgis, P., and Allum, N. (2004). Science in society: Re-evaluating the deficit model of public attitudes. *Public Understanding of Science*, 13, 55–74.

Sugiman, T. (1997). A new theoretical perspective of group dynamics. In: K. Leung et al. (Eds), *Progress in Asian Social Psychology, Vol. 1*. Singapore: J. Wiley.

Swann, W. B. (1983). Self-verification: Bringing social reality into harmony with the self. In: J. Suls and A. G. Greenwald (Eds), *Psychological Perspectives on the Self, Vol. 2*. Hillsdale, NJ: Erlbaum.

Swann, W. B. (1984). Quest for accuracy in person perception: A matter of pragmatics. *Psychological Review*, 91, 457–76.

Swann, W. B., and Ely, R. J. (1984). A battle of wills: Self-verification versus behavioral confirmation. *Journal of Personality and Social Psychology*, 46, 1287–302.

Swann, W. B., and Read, S. J. (1981a). Acquiring self-knowledge: The search for feedback that fits. *Journal of Personality and Social Psychology*, 41, 1119–28.

Swann, W. B., and Read, S. J. (1981b). Self-verification processes: How we sustain our self-conceptions. *Journal of Experimental Social Psychology*, 17, 351–72.

Swanson, J. W., Holzer, E., Ganju, V. K., and Jono, R. T. (1990). Violence and psychiatric disorder in the community: Evidence from the epidemiological studies. *Hospital and Community Psychiatry*, 41, 761–70.

Sykes, J. B. (1976). *The Concise Oxford Dictionary of Current English*, 6th Edn. Oxford: Clarendon Press.

Tajfel, H. (1972). Experiments in a vacuum. In: J. Israel and H. Tajfel (Eds), *The Context of Social Psychology*. London: Academic Press.

Tajfel, H. (1975). Soziales Kategorisieren. In: S. Moscovici (Hg.), *Forschungsgebiete der Sozialpsychologie, Band 1*. Frankfurt: Fischer-Athenäum.

Tajfel, H. (1978). Social categorization, social identity and social comparison. In: H. Tajfel (Ed), *Differentiation between Social Groups*. London: Academic Press.

Tajfel, H. (1981). *Human Groups and Social Categories*. Cambridge: Cambridge University Press.

Tajfel, H., and Forgas, J. P. (1981). Social categorization: Cognitions, values and groups. In: J. P. Forgas, (Ed), *Social Cognition*. London: Academic Press.

Tajfel, H., and Fraser, C. (Eds) (1978). *Introducing Social Psychology*. Harmondsworth: Penguin.

Talbot, S. (1981). *Roots of Oppression: The American Indian Question*. New York: International Publishers.

Tapper, K., and Boulton, M. (2000). Social representations of physical, verbal, and indirect aggression in children: Sex and age differences. *Aggressive Behaviour*, 26, 442–54.

Taylor, S. E. (1979). Hospital patient behavior: Reactance, helplessness, or control? *Journal of Social Issues*, 35, 156–84.

Taylor, S. E., and Fiske, S. T. (1975). Point of view and perceptions of causality. *Journal of Personality and Social Psychology*, 32, 439–45.

Taylor, S. E., and Fiske, S. T. (1978). Salience, attention and attribution: To of the head phenomena. In: L. Berkowitz (Ed), *Advances in Experimental Social Psychology, Vol. 11*. New York: Academic Press.

Taylor, S. E., and Thompson, S. C. (1982). Stalking the elusive 'vividness' effect. *Psychological Review*, 89, 155–81.

Tedeschi, J. T. (1988). How does one describe a Platypus? An outsider's questions for cross-cultural psychology. In: M. H. Bond (Ed), *The Cross-Cultural Challenge to Social Psychology*. Newbury Park: Sage.

Tedeschi, J. T., and Lindskold, S. (1976). *Social Psychology*. New York: J. Wiley.

Thomas, W. I., and Znaniecki, F. (1918–20). *The Polish Peasant in Europe and America, 5 Vols*. Boston, MA: Badger.

Thommen, B., Ammann, R., and von Cranach, M. (1988). *Handlungsorganisation durch soziale Repräsentationen – Welchen Einfluß haben therapeutische Schulen auf das Handeln ihrer Mitglieder*. Bern: Huber.

Thompson, M. (1982). A three-dimensional model. In: M. Douglas (Ed), *Essays in the Sociology of Perception*. London: Routledge & Kegan Paul.

Thorngate, W., and Plouffe, L. (1987). The consumption of psychological knowledge. In: H. J. Stam, T. B. Rogers and K. J. Gergen (Eds), *The Analysis of Psychological Theory*. Cambridge: Hemisphere.

Tischner, H. (1959). *Völkerkunde*. Frankfurt: Fischer.

Torgersen, H., and Hampel, J. (2001). *The Gate Resonance Model: The Interface of Policy, Media and the Public in Technology Conflicts*. Vienna: Austrian Academy of Sciences.

Triandis, H. C. (1974). Major theoretical and methodological issues in cross-cultural psychology. In: J. L. M. Dawson and W. J. Lonner (Eds), *Readings in Cross-Cultural Psychology*. Hong Kong: The University Press.

Turner, J. C. (1987). *Rediscovering the Social Group: A Self-Categorization Approach*. Oxford: Blackwell.

Turner, J. C., and Oakes, P. J. (1986). The significance of the social identity concept for social psychology with reference to individualism, interactionism and social influence. *British Journal of Social Psychology*, 25, 237–52.

Turner, V. (1974). *Dramas, Fields, and Metaphors*. Ithaca, NY: Cornell University Press.

Turner, V. (1985). *The Ritual Process*. Ithaka, NY: Cornell University Press.

Tversky, A., and Kahneman, D. (1973). Availability: A heuristic for judging frequency and probability. *Cognitive Psychology*, 5, 207–32.

Tversky, A., and Kahneman, D. (1974). Judgment under uncertainty: Heuristics and biases. *Science*, 185, 1124–31.

Tversky, A., and Kahneman, D. (1982). Judgments of and by representativeness. In: Kahneman, Slovic and Tversky (Eds), *Judgment under Uncertainty*.

Tyler, S. A. (1978). *The Said and the Unsaid*. New York: Academic Press.

Vala, J., García-Marques, L., Gouveia-Pereira, M., and Lopes, D. (1998). Validation of polemical social representations: Introducing the intergroup differentiation of heterogeneity. *Social Science Information*, 37, 469–92.

Valencia, J. F., Elejabarrieta, F., Páez, D., Villareal, M., and Wagner, W. (2003). Génération, polémique publique, climat social et mémoire collective des événements politiques. *Connexions*, 80, 151–5.

Vallone, R. P., Ross, L., and Lepper, M. R. (1985). The hostile media phenomenon: Biased perception and perceptions of media bias in coverage of the Beirut massacre. *Journal of Personality and Social Psychology*, 49, 577–85.

Valsiner, J. (2003). Beyond social representations: A theory of enablement. *Papers on Social Representations*, 12, 6.1–6.16. [http://www.psr.jku.at/]

Valsiner, J., and Capezza, N. (2002, 23 August). *Creating Arenas for Action: Videogames and Violence*. Paper presented at the Fifth International Baltic Psychology Conference, Tartu, Estonia.

Van de Geer, J. P. (1993a). *Multivariate Analysis of Categorical Data: Applications*. London: Sage.

Van de Geer, J. P. (1993b). *Multivariate Analysis of Categorical Data: Theory*. London: Sage.

van Dijk, T. A. (1980). *Macrostructures*. Hillsdale, NJ: Erlbaum.

van Dijk, T. A. (1997). *Discourse as Social Interaction*. London: Sage.

van Dijk, T. A. (1998). *Ideology – a Multidisciplinary Approach*. London: Sage.

van Dijk, T. A., and Kintsch, W. (1983). *Strategies of Discourse Comprehension*. New York: Academic Press.

van Gennep, A. (1960). *The Rites of Passage*. London: Routledge & Kegan Paul.

van Ginneken, J. (1989). Die Theorie sozialer Repräsentationen als das Ergebnis einer fünfundachtzig Jahre alten Debatte. *Psychologische Rundschau*, 40, 85–6.

Van Langenhove, L., and Harré, R. (1999). Introducing positioning theory. In: Harré and van Langenhove (Eds), *Positioning Theory*.

Varenne, H. (1984). Collective representation in American anthropological conversations about culture: Individual and culture. *Current Anthropology*, 25, 281–99.

Vergès, P. (1987). A social and cognitive approach to economic representations. In: W. Doise and S. Moscovici (Eds), *Current Issues in European Social Psychology*. Cambridge: Cambridge University Press.

Vergès, P. (1989). Représentations sociales de l'économie: une forme de connaisance. In: D. Jodelet (Ed), *Les Représentations Sociales*. Paris: Presses Universitaires de France.

Verheggen, T., and Baerveldt, C. (2001). From shared representations to consensually coordinated actions: Towards an intrinsically social psychology. In: J. R. Morss, N. Stephenson and H. von Rappard (Eds), *Theoretical Issues in Psychology: Proceedings of the International Society for Theoretical Psychology 1999 Conference*. Boston, MA: Kluwer Academic.

Viaud, J. (2002). Multidimensional analysis of textual data using Alceste and the social representation of unemployment. *European Review of Applied Psychology*, 52, 201–12.

Vincent, G. (1987). Secrets de l'histoire et histoire du secret. In: P. Ariés and G. Duby (Eds), *Histore de la vie privée, Tome 5*. Paris: Seuil.

Vivelo, F. R. (1981). *Handbuch der Kulturanthropologie*. Stuttgart: Klett-Cotta.

von Cranach, M. (1992). The multi-level organisation of knowledge and action – an integration of complexity. In: von Cranach, Doise and Mugny (Eds), *Social Representations and the Social Bases of Knowledge*.

von Cranach, M. (1995). Social representations and individual actions. *Journal for the Theory of Social Behaviour*, 25, 285–94.

von Cranach, M., Doise, W., and Mugny, G. (Eds) (1992). *Social Representations and the Social Bases of Knowledge*. Lewiston, NY: Hogrefe and Huber.

von Cranach, M., Kalbermatten, U., Indermühle, K., and Gugler, B. (1980). *Zielgerichtetes Handeln*. Bern: Huber.

von Gadenne, V. (2004). *Philosophie der Psychologie*. Bern: Huber.

von Kutschera, F. (1982). *Grundfragen der Erkenntnistheorie*. Berlin: de Gruyter.

Wagner, D. A. (1974). The development of short-term and incidental memory: A cross-cultural study. *Child Development*, 45, 389–96.

Wagner, D. A. (1978). Memories of Morocco: The influence of age, schooling, and environment on memory. *Cognitive Psychology*, 10, 1–28.

Wagner, R. (1981). *The Invention of Culture*. Chicago: The University of Chicago Press.

Wagner, R. (1986). *Symbols that Stand for Themselves*. Chicago: University of Chicago Press.

Wagner, W. (1980). "Fuzzy Sets" als formales Modell kognitiver Strukturen – Ein Überblick. *Archiv für Psychologie*, 133, 85–115.

Wagner, W. (1981). A fuzzy model of concept representation in memory. *Fuzzy Sets and Systems*, 6, 11–26.

Wagner, W. (1984). Glaubensfestigung durch Wissenschaft am Beispiel von Anhängern Transzendentaler Meditation. Unveröffentlichetes Manuskript, Universität Linz.

Wagner, W. (1989a). Wenn geschichtliche Erfahrung zur Alltagstheorie wird: Zur sozialen Repräsentation von Nationalsozialismus und Weltkrieg. Unveröffentlichtes Manuskript, Universität Linz.

Wagner, W. (1989b). Social representation and habitus – Some problems in relating psychological with sociological concepts. Paper presented at the First European Congress of Psychology, Amsterdam.

Wagner, W. (1990). Der Sozialpsychologe, sein Objekt und die Distanz: Alltagswissen und systemisches Denken. In: E. Witte (Hg.), *Sozialpsy-*

*chologie und Systemtheorie.* Braunschweig: Braunschweiger Studien zur Erziehungswissenschaft.

Wagner, W. (1994a). The fallacy of misplaced intentionality in social representation research. *Journal for the Theory of Social Behaviour,* 24, 243–66.

Wagner, W. (1994b). Speaking is acting is representation – Comments on the reply by A. Echebarría. *Papers on Social Representations,* 3, 201–6. [http://www.psr.jku.at/]

Wagner, W. (1995a). Représentations sociales en situation – commentaires à propos de politique quotidienne et théorie (Situated social representations – a comment on folk-politics and theory). *Cahiers Internationaux de Psychologie Sociale,* 28, 56–66.

Wagner, W. (1995b). Social representations, group affiliation and projection: Knowing the limits of validity. *European Journal of Social Psychology,* 25, 125–39.

Wagner, W. (1995c). Everyday folk-politics, sensibleness and the explanation of action – an answer to Cranach. *Journal for the Theory of Social Behaviour,* 25, 295–302.

Wagner, W. (1996). Queries about social representation and construction. *Journal for the Theory of Social Behaviour,* 26, 95–120.

Wagner, W. (1997). Local knowledge, social representations and psychological theory. In K. Leung, U. Kim, S. Yamaguchi, and Y. Kashima (Eds), *Progress in Asian Social Psychology, Vol. 1.* Singapore: J. Wiley.

Wagner, W. (1998). Social representations and beyond – Brute facts, symbolic coping and domesticated worlds. *Culture and Psychology,* 4, 297–329.

Wagner, W., and Ardelt, E. (1990). Bounded morality: Accounting for immoral acts in private and business contexts. Paper presented at the Annual Colloquium of the Association for Research in Economic Psychology, Exeter, England.

Wagner, W., and Elejabarrieta, F. (1992). El nivel de las teorías en psicología social. In: D. Páez (Ed), *Teoría y método en psicología social.* Barcelona: Anthropos.

Wagner, W., and Gerard, H. B. (1982). Impliziter sozialer Vergleich und Einstellungs-extremisierung. Vortrag auf der 24. Tagung experimentell arbeitender Psychologen, Trier/BRD.

Wagner, W., and Gerard, H. B. (1983a). Action imperative and attitude shifts. Vortrag auf der 25. Tagung experimentell arbeitender Psychologen.

Wagner, W., and Gerard, H. B. (1983b). Similarity of comparison group, opinions about facts and values ans social projection. *Archives of Psychology,* 135, 313–24.

Wagner, W., and Kronberger, N. (2001). Killer Tomatoes! Collective symbolic coping with biotechnology. In K. Deaux and G. Philogène (Eds),

*Representations of the Social – Bridging Theoretical Traditions.* Oxford: Blackwell.

Wagner, W., and Kronberger, N. (2002). Mémoires des mythes vecus – Représentations de la technologie génétique. In: S. Laurens and N. Roussiau (Eds), *La mémoire sociale: représentations et identité sociales. Didact, psychologie sociale.* Rennes: Presses Universitaires de Rennes.

Wagner, W., and Mecha, A. (2003). On discursive construction, representation and institutions: A meta-empirical study. In: J. Laszlo and W. Wagner (Eds), *Theories and Controversies in Societal Psychology.* Budapest: New Mandate.

Wagner, W., and Ploner, M. (1993). Die Erinnerung der Österreicher an 1492 – Wissen und kollektives Gedächtnis. In: Österreichische Nationalbibliothek (Hg.), *Österreich und die Neue Welt.* Wien: Biblos.

Wagner, W., and Szabo, E. (1991). *Sex Bias in Managerial Job Advertisements: Were There Changes from 1968 through 1988?* Unpublished Manuscript, Universität Linz.

Wagner, W., and Wagner, G. P. (2003). Examining the modularity concept in evolutionary psychology: The level of genes, mind and culture. *Journal of Cultural and Evolutionary Psychology,* 1, 135–66.

Wagner, W., and Yamori, K. (1999). Can culture be a variable? Dispositional explanation and cultural metrics. In: T. Sugiman, M. Karasawa, J. H. Liu and C. Ward (Eds), *Progress in Asian Social Psychology, Vol.* 2. Seoul: Kyoyook-Kwahak-Sa.

Wagner, W., Elejabarrieta, F., and Lahnsteiner, I. (1995). How the sperm dominates the ovum – Objectification by metaphor in the social representation of conception. *European Journal of Social Psychology,* 25, 671–88.

Wagner, W., Glatz, W., and Brandstätter, H. (1982). Zur Wirkung verbaler Aggression in Diskussionen. *Archiv für Psychologie,* 134, 237–56.

Wagner, W., Kronberger, N., and Seifert, F. (2002). Collective symbolic coping with new technology: Knowledge, images and public discourse. *British Journal of Social Psychology,* 41, 323–43.

Wagner, W., Valencia, J., and Elejabarrieta, F. (1996). Relevance, discourse and the "hot" stable core of social representations – A structural analysis of word associations. *British Journal of Social Psychology,* 35, 331–52.

Wagner, W., Duveen, G., Themel, M., and Verma, J. (1999). The modernisation of tradition: Thinking about madness in Patna, India. *Culture and Psychology,* 5, 413–46.

Wagner, W., Duveen, G., Verma, J., and Themel, M. (2000). "I have some faith and at the same time I don't believe in it" – Cognitive polyphasia and culture change. *Journal of Community and Applied Social Psychology,* 10, 102–314.

Wagner, W., Kronberger, N., Berg, S., and Torgersen, H. (forthcoming). The monster and the difference: Cultural imaginations of monstrosity in responses to biotechnology. In: G. Gaskell and M. Bauer (Eds), *Genomics: Ethical, Legal and Social Dimensions*. London: Earthscan.

Wagner, W., Kirchler, E., Clack, F., Tekarslan, E., and Verma, J. (1990). Male dominance, role segregation and spouses' interdependence in conflict. *Journal of Cross-Cultural Psychology*, 21, 48–70.

Wagner, W., Kronberger, N., Gaskell, G., Allum, N., Allansdottir, A., Cheveigné, S., Dahinden, U., Diego, C., Montali, L., Mortensen, A., Pfenning, U., Rusanen, T., and Seger, N. (2001). Nature in disorder: The troubled public of biotechnology. In: Gaskell and Bauer (Eds), *Biotechnology 1996–2000*.

Wagner, W., Kronberger, N., Allum, N., De Cheveigné, S., Diego, C., Gaskell, G., Heinßen, M., Midden, C., Ødegaard, M., Öhman, S., Rizzo, B., Rusanen, T., and Stathopoulou, A. (2002). Pandora's genes – images of genes and nature. In: Bauer and Gaskell (Eds), *Biotechnology – the Making of a Global Controversy*.

Wahl, O. (1992). Mass media images of mental illness: A review of the literature. *Journal of Community Psychology*, 20, 343–52.

Wason, P. C. (1968). Reasoning about a rule. *Quarterly Journal of Experimental Psychology*, 20, 273–81.

Wason, P. C. (1980). The verification task and beyond. In: D. R. Olson (Ed), *The Social Foundations of Language and Thought*. New York: Norton.

Wason, P. C. (1983). Realism and rationality in the selection task. In: J. S. T. Evans (Ed), *Thinking and Reasoning: Psychological Approaches*. London: Routledge & Kegan Paul.

Wearing, M. (1989). Professional discourse and sensational journalism: Media constructions of violent insanity. *Australian Journal of Communication*, 20, 84–98.

Weber, M. (1972). *Die protestantische Ethik und der Geist des Kapitalismus*. Tübingen: Mohr.

Weimer, W. B. (1976). *Psychology and the Conceptual Foundations of Science*. Hillsdale, NJ: Erlbaum.

Weiner, B. (1985). An attributional theory of achievement motivation and emotion. *Psychological Review*, 92, 548–73.

Weiss, G. (1973). A scientific concept of culture. *American Anthropologist*, 75, 1376–413.

Weisz, J. R., Rothbaum, F. M., and Blackburn, T. C. (1984). Standing out and standing in: The psychology of control in America and Japan. *American Psychologist*, 955–69.

Weitzman, E. A., and Miles, M. B. (1995). *Computer Programs for Qualitative Data Analysis – A Software Sourcebook*. Thousand Oaks, CA: Sage.

Weizenbaum, J. (1990). Artifical Intelligence as Ideology. Vortrag an der Universität Linz, 26 November 1990.

Weller, S. C. (1984). Consistency and consensus among informants: Disease concept in a rural Mexican town. *American Anthropologist*, 86, 966–75.

Weller, S. C. (1987). Shared knowledge, intracultural variation, and knowledge aggregation. *American Behavioral Scientist*, 31, 179–93.

Weller, S. C., and Romney, A. K. (1990). *Metric Scaling-Correspondence Analysis*. London: Sage.

Wells, G. L., and Harvey, J. H. (1977). Do people use consensus information in making causal attributions? *Journal of Personality and Social Psychology*, 35, 279–93.

White, P. (1984). A model of the layperson as pragmatist. *Personality and Social Psychology Bulletin*, 10, 333–348.

Wicklund, R. A. (1975). Objective self-awareness. In: L. Berkowitz (Ed), *Advances in Experimental Social Psychology, Vol. 8*. New York: Academic Press.

Wilson, B. R. (Ed) (1970). *Rationality*. Oxford: Basil Blackwell.

Windisch, U. (1982). *Pensée sociale, langage en usage et logiques autres*. Lausanne: L'Age d'Homme.

Windisch, U. (1990). *Speech and Reasoning in Everyday Life*. Cambridge: Cambridge University Press.

Winograd, E., and Neisser, U. (Eds) (1992). *Affect and Accuracy in Recall: Studies of 'Flashbulb' Memories*. New York: Cambridge University Press.

Witte, E. (1987). Konformität. In: D. Frey and S. Greif (Hg.), *Sozialpsychologie*. Wien: Urban & Schwarzenberg.

Witte, E. (1989). *Sozialpsychologie*. München: PVU.

Witte, E. (1990). Consequences of the critique of existing social psychology: Paradigm enrichment. Unpublished manuscript, Universität Hamburg.

Wittgenstein, L. (1969/45). *Philosophische Untersuchungen. In: Schriften Bd. 1*. Frankfurt/Main: Suhrkamp.

Wittgenstein, L. (1984). *Über Gewiß heit* (On certainty, German). Frankfurt: Suhrkamp.

Wittgenstein, L. (1997). *Philosophical Investigations-Philosophische Untersuchungen*. Oxford: Blackwell.

Wolin, S. J., Bennett, L. A., and Noonan, D. L. (1979). Family rituals and the recurrence of alcoholism over generations. *American Journal of Psychiatry*, 136, 589–93.

Wong, P., and Weiner, B. (1981). When people ask "why" questions, and the heuristics of attributional search. *Journal of Personality and Social Psychology*, 40, 650–63.

Wortman, C. B. (1976). Causal attribution and personal control. In: J. H. Harvey and R. F. Kidd (Eds), *New Directions in Attribution Research, Vol. 1*. Hillsdale, NJ: Erlbaum.

Wright, J., and Mischel, W. (1982). Influence of affect on cognitive social learning person variables. *Journal of Personality and Social Psychology*, 43, 901–14.

Wundt, □ (1900–1920). *Völkerpsychologie*, 10 Bände. Leipzig: Kröner.

Wygotski, L. S. (1971/1934). *Denken und Sprechen*. Frankfurt: Fischer.

Yamori, K. (2001). Active faults as social representations. *Japanese Journal of Experimental Social Psychology*, 41, 1–15.

Yamori, K. (2001). Social representation theory and social constructionism: critical comments on Wagner's view. *Japanese Journal of Experimental Social Psychology*, 40, 95–114.

Yang, K.-S. (1988). Will societal modernization eventually eliminate cross-cultural psychological differences? M. H. Bond (Ed), *The Cross-Cultural Challenge to Social Psychology*. Newbury Park: Sage.

Zadeh, L. A. (1965). Fuzzy sets. *Information and Control*, 8, 338–53.

Zajonc, R. B. (1989). Styles of explanation in social psychology. *European Journal of Social Psychology*, 19, 345–68.

Zani, B. (1993). Social representations of mental illness: Naive and professional perspectives. In: Breakwell and Canter (Eds), *Empirical Approaches to the Study of Social Representations*.

Zavalloni, M. (1986). The affective-representational circuit as the foundation of identity. *New Ideas in Psychology*, 4, 333–49.

Zavalloni, M. (1989). L'effet de résonance dans la création de l'identité et des représentations sociales. *Revue Internationale de Psychologie Sociale*, 3, 407–28.

Zebrowitz, L. A. (1990). *Social Perception*. Buckingham: Open University Press.

Zilsel, E. (1976). *Die sozialen Ursprünge der neuzeitlichen Wissenschaft*. Frankfurt: Suhrkamp.

Zimbardo, P. G. (1983). *Psychologie*. Berlin: Springer.

Zittoun, T., Duveen, G., Gillespie, A., Ivinson, G. M., and Psaltis, C. (2003). The use of symbolic resources in developmental transitions. *Culture and Psychology*, 9, 415–48.

# Name Index

# Subject Index